C000004614

HOWARD BARKER

HOWARD BARKER

COLLECTED PLAYS

VOLUME FOUR

THE BITE OF THE NIGHT
SEVEN LEARS
THE GAOLER'S ACHE
HE STUMBLED
THE HOUSE OF CORRECTION

CALDER PUBLICATIONS · RIVERRUN PRESS
Paris London New York

First published in Great Britain in 1998 by
John Calder Publisher
126 Cornwall Road, London SE1 8TQ.

and in the United States of America in 1988 by
Riverrun Press Inc
100 Newfield Ave, Edison N.J.

Copyright © Howard Barker 1998

ALL RIGHTS RESERVED

ISBN 0 7145 4279 2

The right of Howard Barker to be identified as author of this work
has been asserted by him in accordance with the Copyright Design
and Patents act 1988.

Applications for a licence to perform these plays should be made to:
Judith Daish associations, 2 St Charles Place, London W10 6EG.

British Library cataloguing in Publication Data
A catalogue record of this title is available from the British Library.

Library of Congress cataloguing in Publication Data
A catalogue record of this title is available from the library of
congress.

Apart from any fair dealing for the purposes of research or private
study, or criticism or review, as permitted under the Copyright
Designs and Patents act, 1988, this publication may not be
reproduced, stored or transmitted in any form or by any means,
without the prior consent of the publishers, or in the case of
reprographic reproduction in accordance with the terms of licences
issued by the Copyright Licensing Agency, London. Inquiries
concerning reproduction outside these terms should be sent to the
publishers.

Any paperback edition of this book is sold subject to the condition
that it shall not, by way of trade, be lent, resold, hired out, or
otherwise disposed of, without the consent, of the publishers, in any
form of binding or covers other than that in which it is published.

Set in 9/10 pt Times by Pure Tech India Ltd, Pondicherry
Printed and bound in Great Britain by Redwood Books, Trowbridge, Wiltshire

CONTENTS

'All is True'

(Title of play ascribed to Shakespeare)

'Beauty is not truth, but the best available lie on the subject of truth...'

(Act 3, *The Bite of the Night*)

'Every man's evil expresses me.'

(Poem 13, *The Breath of the Crowd*)

THE BITE OF THE NIGHT
An Education

CHARACTERS

MACLUBY	a soap boiler
CREUSA	a woman of Troy
SAVAGE	a scholar
BOY	his son
OLD MAN	his parent
HOGBIN	his pupil
HELEN	a defector
FLADDER	her husband, King of the Greeks
GUMMERY	a soldier
EPSOM	a soldier
SHADE	a soldier
A BOY	of Troy
GAY	a daughter of Helen
HOMER	a poet
BOY	son of Savage (adult)
ASAFIR	a Truce official
YORAKIM	a Truce official
JOHN	their servant
CHARITY	daughter of Gay
SCHLIEMANN	an archaeologist
YORAKIM	a labourer
ASAFIR	a labourer
OFFICERS	
YOUTHS	
PUBLIC	

First Prologue

MACLUBY: They brought a woman from the street
And made her sit in the stalls
By threats
By bribes
By flattery
Obliging her to share a little of her life with actors

But I don't understand art

Sit still, they said

But I don't want to see sad things

Sit still, they said

And she listened to everything
Understanding some things
But not others
Laughing rarely, and always without knowing why
Sometimes suffering disgust
Sometimes thoroughly amazed
And in the light again said

If that's art I think it is hard work
It was beyond me
So much of it beyond my actual life

But something troubled her
Something gnawed her peace
And she came a second time, armoured with friends

Sit still, she said

And again, she listened to everything
This time understanding different things
This time untroubled that some things
Could not be understood
Laughing rarely but now without shame
Sometimes suffering disgust
Sometimes thoroughly amazed
And in the light again said

That is art, it is hard work

And one friend said, too hard for me
And the other said if you will
I will come again

Because I found it hard I felt honoured

Second Prologue

It is not true that everyone wants to be
Entertained
Some want the pain of unknowing
Shh
Shh
Shh
The ecstasy of not knowing for once
The sheer suspension of not knowing
Shh
Shh
Shh
Three students in a smoke-filled room
Three girls on holiday
A pregnancy on a Saturday night
I knew that
I knew that
I already knew that

The marriage which was hardly
The socialist who wasn't
The American with the plague
I knew that
I knew that

I already knew that

We can go home now
Oh, car seat kiss my arse
We can go home now
Oh, underground upholstery
Caress my buttock
I loved that play it was so true
Take your skirt off
I loved that play it was so
Take your skirt off
What are theatres for
Take your skirt off

This has to be the age for more musicals
Declares the manager
The people are depressed

This has to be the age for more musicals
Declares the careerist
Who thinks the tilted face is power
Who believes humming is believing

No
The problems are different
They are
They really are
I say this with all the circumspection
A brute can muster

I ask you
Hatred apart
Abuse apart
Boredom in abeyance
Politics in the cupboard
Anger in the drawer
Should we not

I know it's impossible but you still try

Not reach down beyond the known for once

I'll take you

I'll hold your throat
I will
And vomit I will tolerate
Over my shirt
Over my wrists
Your bile
Your juices
I'll be your guide
And whistler in the dark
Cougher over filthy words
And all known sentiments recycled for this house

Clarity
Meaning
Logic
And Consistency

None of it
None

I honour you too much
To paste you with what you already know so

Beyond the slums of England
Tower blocks floating on ponds of urine
Like the lighthouse on its bed of mercury

Beyond the screams of women fouled
Who have lost sight and sense of all desire

And grinning classes of male satirists
Beyond
The witty deconstruction of the literary myth
And individuals in the web of class

No ideology on the cheap
No ideology on the cheap

You think a thing repeated three times is a truth
You think to sing along is solidarity

No ideology on the cheap

Apologies
Old spasms
Apologies
Old temper
Apologies
Apologies

I charm you
Like the Viennese professor in the desert
Of America
My smile is a crack of pain
Like the exiled pianist in the tart's embrace
My worn fingers reach for your place
Efficiently

It's an obligation ... !

ACT ONE

Scene One

The Ruins of a University

CREAUSA: Lost in Troy. (*Pause.*) Listen, getting lost. (*Pause.*)
   That also is an infidelity (*Pause.*) I walked behind. Wife bear-
   ing the food. The flask. The diapers. Wife under the bundle.
   The clock. The colander. The old man's vests. Through flaming
   alleys by clots of rapists whose glistening arses caught the light.
   The chess set and the fruit cake. Wives under the soldiers. The
   flannel and the toothbrushes (*Pause.*)
   Turks in Smyrna
   Romans in Carthage
   Scots in Calais
   Swedes in Dresden
   Goths in Buda
   Japs in Nanking
   Russians in Brandenburg

   Unbelted and unbuttoned they thrust their arms into the well
   of skirt

   I did prefer
   I did
   To continuing this marriage in another place
   Prefer to get lost
   The gutters bubbling with semen notwithstanding
   The spontaneous stabbings of intoxicated looters
   Notwithstanding
   I slipped down Trader's Avenue and hid

And he came back
I will say this
I will give credit where it's
He did
He did come back
A dozen paces boy in hand and dad on back
His eyes shouted
His mouth hung speechless as a ripped sheet
I could have
I wanted to
That grey and never happy face

Creu — sa!

Once my name heaved out his gob and stuck to
Falling arches
Once
His last call
Only once
It drifted down with burning papers
It sailed on draughts like embers of old frocks

And turned away
Triangle of males
The three degrees of man

I vomited my shame into the shop
On all smashed things I added pounds of self disgust
And wiping on a dead man's curtain stood up frail
But light

Widowhood is grief but also chance
And falls of cities both finishes and starts

Scene Two

A MAN *and* A CHILD

SAVAGE: **I will end up killing you.**
BOY: Yes.

SAVAGE: I think we know that, don't we? I will end up killing
   you?

BOY: Yes.

SAVAGE: And burying you in the coke. Under the power
   station floor. Or sling you in a rusty truck...

BOY: Yes.

SAVAGE: One eye hanging from some almighty blow. **We do
   know that, don't we?**

BOY: Yes.

SAVAGE (*sits*):   Through no fault of your own...

BOY: Not really, no...

SAVAGE: My character being what it is. And the times being
   what they are. The state of the world and my temper. I think
   murdering you is inevitable. Kiss me. (THE BOY *kisses him*.)

BOY: You have to have freedom.

SAVAGE: I must have it. I am forty and I must have it.

BOY: Everything's against you.

SAVAGE: Every fucking thing.

BOY: And I'm a constant irritation.

SAVAGE: Not constant.

BOY: Not constant, but an irritation.

SAVAGE: Children are.

BOY: We are, and then there's grandad. We're both an irritation and we are obviously holding up freedom.

SAVAGE: Yes...

BOY: You're forty and freedom's like a muscle, if it isn't used it
   at — it at —

SAVAGE: Shut up.

BOY: It atrophies—

SAVAGE: **Shut up.** (*Pause*.) Kiss me. Kiss me! (THE BOY
   kisses him. AN OLD MAN *enters with a pot*.)

OLD MAN: Done the potatoes.

BOY: What does atrophy mean?

OLD MAN: Done the potatoes.

SAVAGE: Oh, the gnawed bone of my mind...the bloody,
   gnawed bone of my mind... (*Pause. They look at him*.) Dirty
   butcher's bone in the gutter no dog would stoop to lick...
   (*Pause*.)

BOY: You always say that.

SAVAGE: I do. I do say that

BOY: You put your hands to your head and you say the
   gnawed bone of my mind...

SAVAGE: Yes...

BOY: What's the matter with it?

OLD MAN: Lucky to find potatoes... (*He goes off.*)

SAVAGE: I woke in the night. I woke in the night and the sky was purple with the bruise of cities. I thought of avenues where they sleep the sleep of family love, the pillowcase, the nightdress, the twitching of the poodle. **You call that life?**

BOY: Call that life?

SAVAGE: The dozing daughter in the dormitory town has tossed off the eiderdown. Down it goes, hiss to the nylon carpet and piles like warm shit from the sphincter of the dog. **You call that life?**

BOY: Call that life?

SAVAGE: Every dead clerk is a slab on the causeway to liberty.

BOY: Down with clerks! Down with documents!

SAVAGE: I taught Homer here... (HOGBIN *enters.*)

HOGBIN: Sorry I'm late. (*Pause.*) Am I late? (*Pause.*) Am I sorry? (*He sits.*) I had an excuse, and then I thought, he does not care if I have an excuse or not. I thought in fact, if I do not appear he will not notice, so I would only demean myself by inventing an excuse in the first place. Why appear at all, in fact? **Homeric fucking Greece, what does that say to me?** Sitting on the bus this was, at the back eye-deep in soup of fags and women's underwear. **Homeric fucking Greece?**

SAVAGE: You barren filth.

HOGBIN: Now, then...

SAVAGE: You ephemeral spewing of suburban couplings.

HOGBIN: Of course I am ephemeral. So are we all.

SAVAGE: Abuse and more abuse.

HOGBIN: *Merci.* I didn't do the essay. But here's the notes.

SAVAGE: The notes?

BOY: He doesn't want your notes!

HOGBIN: I heard the reggae through the wall. The beat bored into me. I looked at Homer. Dead letters swum before my eyes. Old Europe struggling with the beat. The beat! The fucking beat! **Give us knowledge, Doctor Savage!** (*Pause.*)

SAVAGE: The Trojan War. (*Pause.*) The Trojan War occurred because a married woman lent her body to a stranger. (*Pause.*) That's all for today. (*Pause.*)

HOGBIN: I knew that.

SAVAGE: Excellent.

HOGBIN: **I knew that, git.**

SAVAGE: You read it. You did not know it. Knowledge is belief. (*He gets up to go.*)

HOGBIN: **Don't get up.** (*Pause.*) The seduction of Helen. The seduction of Helen is a metaphor for the commercial success of the tribes of Asia Minor and the subsequent collapse of the Peloponnesian carrying trade. Only a military alliance of the Greek states restored the monopoly. In classical fashion the outcome of trade wars is the enslavement of populations in the interests of cost-free labour and the eradication of the infrastructure of the rival enterprise, namely the razing of cities. (*Pause.*)

SAVAGE: No. It was cunt.

HOGBIN: Cunt's the metaphor, trade's the —

SAVAGE: **Helen's cunt.** (*Pause.*)

BOY: That's it for today, Mr Hogbin. (*Pause.*)

HOGBIN: I hate my father. He is a big-bollocked snob who walks the streets in shorts and stares at women. Intellectuals he calls bums. Bums, he calls them. He has foreign holidays and speaks American. What does bums mean? Bums means arses but I think he means tramps. **Give us your intuitions and stuff the facts.** (*Pause. He gets up.*) Cunt, was it... (*He goes out. MACLUBY enters, looks at SAVAGE, describes:*)

MACLUBY: Been crouching here since the final tutorial. The door shut and they left. Down slid the timetable with the rust. The tinkling of drawing pins, the descent of postcards. Then the lampshade crashed. The splintering of fluorescent lances in cracked corridors. The mole's disdain of plastic tiles. And then the landscape yawned, and chalk breathed out, undoing the keystone of the library arch. **We all heard the Library crash.**

SAVAGE: I heard it.

BOY: I heard it! Books blew everywhere!

MACLUBY: And you stayed put. While demolition cowboys ripped the wiring out.

SAVAGE: **Knowledge!**

MACLUBY: While they smashed the basins kept your seat.

SAVAGE: **Knowledge!**

MACLUBY: Their curses, their pornographic sentiments.

SAVAGE: **Knowledge!**

MACLUBY: The clatter of their arid minds and mundane politics.

SAVAGE (*pause*): It was a paper overcoat against their spit... (THE BOY *holds* SAVAGE.) I lost his mother. She could not stomach me. My whine and bite. My sitting on the edge of the

chair. **Put your arse back in the chair!** I could not. My whine
and bite...

MACLUBY: Give us the kid. (*Pause.*)

SAVAGE: Give you the —

MACLUBY: Give us him, why don't you? (*Pause.*)

SAVAGE: Who are —

MACLUBY: Harry MacLuby. Soap boiler.

SAVAGE: Soap boiler?

MACLUBY: Well, do you want him or not? (*Pause.*) On your
sick bed, writhing like a worm on baking bricks, shouting the
whole length of the ward, **I did nothing with my life, because of
them, they weighed on me**. Your cry of misery would lift the
gutters off the hospital... (*Pause.*)

SAVAGE: **Soap boiler**...?

MACLUBY: Ashes of Roses. (*Pause.*)

SAVAGE: My mother ditched me also...

MACLUBY: There you go...

SAVAGE: A poor boy will find his benefactress...

MACLUBY: Inevitably, and what use are you?

SAVAGE: No use...

MACLUBY: All your kisses papered over hate...

SAVAGE: **I drink his fondness and resent his life**.

MACLUBY: You know, you see, you do know...

SAVAGE: Love of children, what is it? Self-love. The clinging
of a desperate mortality. You have to understand the feeling.
Not just feel the feeling or you are a mollusc. What are you, a
murderer?

MACLUBY: Silly.

SAVAGE: And in five years he will not lend me one stale
breath...

MACLUBY: It's so, it is...

SAVAGE (*to* THE BOY):   **This man wants you**.

BOY: Wants me?

SAVAGE: He says.

BOY: What for?

SAVAGE: Apprentice in the soap trade.

BOY: Soap?

SAVAGE: **Soap, Yes, Soap!** (*Pause.*) Get your things. (*Pause.*)

BOY: I think, in spite of everything, although you will probably
murder me, I would prefer to stay with —

SAVAGE: Toothbrush. Flannel. And clean pants.

BOY: Rather die from you bashing me in one of your fits
than —

SAVAGE: Pyjamas if you've got some —

BOY: **Live with anybody else.** (*Pause.* SAVAGE *refuses to look at him.*) **I love you.**

SAVAGE: Love, he says. That word. Emaciated syllable. (*He looks at him.*) Replace the word love with another. And you will see how thin it is.

BOY: There is no other.

SAVAGE: **Mollusc!**

BOY: You are always calling me a mollusc...

SAVAGE: Yes... (*Pause.*)

BOY: You are so unhappy. And I can't help... (*Pause, then* THE BOY *goes off.*)

SAVAGE: You see, how I have become his child, and he is burdened with me. I make him suffer for me. (*He looks at* MACLUBY.) Teach him Ashes of Roses. The man who can smother mortality in scent, or wash blood off the hands of killers will not lack for friends. (THE OLD MAN *enters with a plate of dinner. He looks at* SAVAGE, *pitying him.*)

OLD MAN (*to* MACLUBY): I said to him, travel. Travel the world, go on.

MACLUBY: He hates the world...

OLD MAN: The merchant navy, for example. See things while you have the power.

MACLUBY: The Taj Mahal. The pyramids...

OLD MAN: The Taj Mahal. The pyramids...

SAVAGE: The truth is not in all that junk, you —

MACLUBY: Old Moscow's onion domes... (THE BOY *returns, with a small bag. He stands waiting.* SAVAGE *looks at him, suddenly weeps.* THE BOY *goes to touch him.*)

SAVAGE: No...! (*Pause, then* MACLUBY *leads the way and* THE BOY *follows. Pause.*)

OLD MAN: Football, is it? (*He puts the plate down, starts to go.*)

SAVAGE: I owe you nothing, do I? (*He stops.*) Because you grated on my mother, what's the debt?

OLD MAN: No debt, son.

SAVAGE: And because one not-so-very-mad night I squirmed against his mother, to the ticking of the wedding present and the clatter of the drunkards in the sick-swamped street, so setting in motion the torture of paternity, **I owe no debt, me neither, do I?** (*Pause.*) Argue. Argue for your rights to me.

OLD MAN: No rights.

SAVAGE: No rights... (THE OLD MAN *turns to leave again.*) And what is intimacy anyway?

OLD MAN: Search me...

SAVAGE: I clung to her and it was two pebbles clashing. (THE OLD MAN *looks*). When I was in her, hard against her womb, some razor slashed my head, some miniature blade designed to kill conception **you don't expect to find knives in there of all places.** Anyway, it failed, and he was born...

OLD MAN (*nodding after* THE BOY): Football today, is it? (*A hiatus of pity.*) Did I ever thank you for the books?

SAVAGE: Books?

OLD MAN: On Homeric Metre. By Dr Savage of the University. To My Father on that great big empty page.

SAVAGE: Christ knows why I —

OLD MAN: An Introduction to the Iliad. In Memory of My Mother.

SAVAGE: Barmy reflex of a clever son —

OLD MAN: No, I —

SAVAGE: **Don't lick feeling off that line of arid print.** (*Pause.*)

OLD MAN: Wha'? (*Pause.*)

SAVAGE: The binding was so poor the leaves fell out. As if they were ashamed to hang with such a dedication —

OLD MAN: Wha'?

SAVAGE: **The sentimental liar I have been.**

OLD MAN: Kind thought I thought...

SAVAGE: Kind thought? I hated you. Your mundane opinions. Your repetition of half-truths. Straddling my back. You burden. You dead weight. **He's gone so why don't you.** (THE OLD MAN *turns.*) No one is here for long. Who knows, some death might be already on me. Some growth in the dark, deep wet. Give us some time for my own needs. Old bones. Old pelt. (THE OLD MAN *withdraws some yards behind* SAVAGE, *and sits.*) We can have knowledge, but not in passivity. Knowledge exists, but the path is strewn with obstacles. (THE OLD MAN *breaks the plate.*) These obstacles we ourselves erect. (*He takes a shard.*) The conspiracy of the ignorant against the visionary can be broken only by the ruthless intellect. (*He undoes his vest.*) Pity also is a regime. (*He attempts to cut his throat.*) And consideration a manacle.

OLD MAN: Trying...

SAVAGE: Manners —

OLD MAN: Trying...

SAVAGE: Loyalty —

OLD MAN: Trying, fuck it —

SAVAGE: Responsibility, **iron bands on the brain**. (HOGBIN *enters with a book*.)

HOGBIN: Helen was a whore in any case, it says — (*He sees* THE OLD MAN.) Oi.

SAVAGE: **Knowledge is beyond kindness you know —**

HOGBIN: **Oi!**

SAVAGE: Shut up... (THE OLD MAN *succeeds, gurgles*.)

HOGBIN: Hey! Fucking hey!

SAVAGE: I know. I know he is. (HOGBIN *stares at him*. THE OLD MAN *dies*. SAVAGE *suddenly seizes* HOGBIN, *in a horrified embrace*.) **Kiss me, then! My triumph! Kiss me, then!**

HOGBIN: Oh, fucking —

SAVAGE: **Kiss me!**

HOGBIN: Oh, bloody 'ell —

SAVAGE: **My liberty! My appalling liberty!**

HOGBIN (*tearing from his embrace*): Oh, shit and shit —

SAVAGE: Don't leave me.

HOGBIN: **He — lp**

SAVAGE (*grasping him tightly*): Did it... did it... did it. (*They rock to and fro. Pause*.)

HOGBIN: Blood's tickling my toes... warm tickle... old man's contents... old man's drain... (*He shudders*.)

OLD MAN: We left the lorry on the road, looking for crashed bombers on the scarp, sun in, sun out, behind these towering clouds and dark drenches of rain, I was alone and saw the tailplane in a smudge of trees, or wing was it, with roundels of the R.A.F., and my boots went swish towards it, swish through downland flowers while the wind creaked faintly in the breached boughs of the thorny trees, alone and hot, smell of tunic, smell of blanco, swish went the poppy heads, alone and hot **up shot like rabbits from a dip two naked arses** brown as polish, gipsies fucking to the rhythm of that wing in scattered tracer belts and navigation clocks, swish the pelting of their feet, leaving her arse print in the turf, her shoulder blades were printed in the turf until with little jerks the grass stood up again. (*Pause*.)

SAVAGE: The death of my father necessitates the cancellation of our next tutorial.

HOGBIN: For grief, is that?

SAVAGE: Grief, yes.

HOGBIN: The socialized consequence of death is naturally bereavement but under grief the individual might conceal some inexplicable delight. (*Pause*.) I pose the question only —

SAVAGE: **I said you hungry adolescent no tutorial**.

HOGBIN: Not a tutorial, no, but —

SAVAGE: My old man's dead, whose dry hand was the only proof of goodness I knew yet, I carried him through Troy! (*Pause.*) 'To think my boy taught brilliance here,' he said, to reprimand the red-backed bastards ripping off the roof. He never read books but still he hated televisions, he chucked them out the windows of the flats, some instinct he had for shattering mendacity, the incorruptible old sod...

HOGBIN: The spontaneity of violence is surely the formal resistance of the proletariat to —

SAVAGE: **Won't teach.** (*He goes to arrange* THE OLD MAN.)

HOGBIN: Give us yer handkerchief... (SAVAGE *gives him a rag. He wipes the blood from his feet.*)

SAVAGE: I'm sorry I was born, and sorry I was cured, sorry I fell in love, and sorry I was married, sorry and sorry again for every choice I —

HOGBIN (*wiping himself*): Yeah, but was it choice? You presuppose the possibility of refusals —

SAVAGE: Oh, you arid youth, I think the young are barren as a shaft of concrete in Sahara sun.

HOGBIN: Bollocks, you rhetorical shitter —

SAVAGE: **Wisdom**, not cleverness, **Knowledge,** not retorts, **Truth,** not wit. One bit of truth felt in the veins!

HOGBIN: You are a pile of metred drivel, why I sit here fuck knows, when —

SAVAGE: One truth! One truth! **Not a lot to ask is it!**

HOGBIN: Read Buka on the nature of hyperbole, it's 'ere somewhere — (*He pulls filthy pages from a pocket.* SAVAGE *kicks it across the floor.*)

SAVAGE: **Got to suffer!**

HOGBIN (*gathering the precious pages*): You are a plastic bag of urine —

SAVAGE: **Suffer, youth!**

HOGBIN: Tossed against a corrugated fence — there, now I'm doin' it. (MACLUBY *appears. Pause.*)

MACLUBY: I gave the boy a ball. His eyes went big. He's nine and he can't catch.

SAVAGE: I hate balls. The ball returns the idea after every revolution. No effort, no struggle of the intellect. Give him a polygon to kick. (MACLUBY *turns to go.*) **A father also loves but through a grating.** Tell him that...

Scene Three

HELEN *with* A HUSBAND, *seated.*

HELEN: I'm back. (*Pause.*) My arse in the marital chair. (*Pause.*) My piss in the marital pan. (*Pause.*) **Well, be delighted.** (*Pause.*) You ache to touch me, but you won't. And silence is your knife. Twist away! (*Pause.*) Troy was full of intellectuals. I saw their corpses. Their corpses hung on wires. **Do hit me if you want to, others did.** (*Pause.*) And all of them kept diaries, always their diaries in a miniature hand like lice had crept through inkwells **Any paltry thought they deemed immortal.** Fevered note-takers and every scrap was burned by troops, every leaf! (*Pause.*) The comedy of history. (*Pause.*) **Burst my face or I shall go on talking.** (*Pause.*) I saw one on his knees to drunken squaddies who said not **Spare my life,** not like the shopkeeper who offered to reveal his hidden loot, not like the civil servant who offered them his wife to whip to pulp, but **I beg you smuggle out this book.** I saw the thing kicked down a gutter, the pages bound in fat and sweat, the banality, the futility! **I am philistine and loveless** . . . (*Pause.*)

FLADDER: Helen fucks the wounded in the wards, they said. (*Pause.*) Which aroused me. **Shamefully.** (*Pause.*) Or dogs, some ventured to suggest. Which aroused me. **Shamefully.** (*Pause.*) The filthy infantry. The long lick of their dreams. (*Pause.*) I crept to the canvas in the dew, sodden and erect, to eavesdrop what malpractice their knotted maleness would inflict on you. (*Pause.*) Our suffering. Our ecstasy. (SOLDIERS *enter, with* CREUSA)

GUMMERY: Every light bulb. Every cage bird.

SHADE/EPSOM: **Pulver!**

GUMMERY: Pity was our banner, as you wrote in final orders. So the tarts we spared . . .

EPSOM: And infants, if they did not cry too loud.

GUMMERY: Troy's gone. Nothing to block the wind off Asia now. **Arseholes to this bitch.** I must say that. (*He bows to* HELEN.) Your servant, etcetera.

SHADE: Ten years goes by in a flash . . .

EPSOM: That final bugle made my heart sink. I never smelled depression like it, even in defeat. It hung over the trenches like a fog, and the champagne corks were miserable squibs. No one could work up any speeches, we drifted past old weapon pits and put our lips against the hinges of burnt tanks. Go home? My wife is fucking with the priest, I had it from my brother. What did he think, I'd put a pistol in my gob and make him heir to seven dirty acres? Not that I blame him. Nor the priest, him neither. I blame no one. **Arseholes to this bitch however.** (*He bows to* HELEN.) I must say that. (*He sits on the floor.*)

CREUSA (*looking at her*): Helen...!

FLADDER (*pause*): The word. (*Pause.*) **Helen**. (*Pause.*) The idea. (*Pause.*) **Helen**. (*Pause.*)

CREUSA: Alive...!

FLADDER: She stinks like a horse. I say this, I announce this, I announce this because the idea has got round she is ethereal. No, I assure you it is not the case. I know she stood naked on the battlements in the seventh year —

GUMMERY: The eighth —

FLADDER: The eighth year, was it, stood naked and the wind sneaked round her parts, the cool wind out the Caucasus, fresh with snow and hibiscus, but still she had the odour of the mare, why did you do that? The army laughed, seeing you less than perfect. Seeing your body rather flawed. Of course they knew the sex is not in the proportions, but still they laughed, calling the cooks out of their tents, staring and jabbering, why did she do that? (*Pause.*)

CREUSA: I've been passed round a bit myself... not bad... not the worst thing in the world, to have no choice. (*Pause.*) Not the worst thing.

EPSOM (*nudging his neighbour*): Oi...

CREUSA: The worst thing is —

GUMMERY (*indicating* FLADDER, *who weeps*): Oi...

CREUSA: To imagine choice exists... (*Two of the soldiers go to* FLADDER *placing their hands on his shoulders.*)

HELEN: Oh, the solidarity of weeping men... (HOGBIN *enters, stops.*)

HOGBIN: Europe's a mess... (*They look at him.*) I say the only ideology is total scepticism... That's not an ideology, he says. (*He looks them over.*) What's this...? (*They examine him.*) This is a university, so point yer firearms downwards, there's a love... (*They make no move.*) What's this...? (*Pause. He is undeterred.*) Ruins or not, it's still a seat of learning, and so is any place where questions are still asked. Balls to chancellors, and piss on economics, **The Trojans did not scatter,** why should we? Some remained, he says so, fat guts says they fucked their conquerors, **Message for the oppressed!** (SAVAGE *enters.*

HOGBIN *bows mockingly*.) The wobbling residue of culture! (*He rises*.) He imitates the amoeba, which cannot be squashed by jeeps.

HELEN: I know him.

HOGBIN: She knows you...!

HELEN: Staggering through courtyards under books. Boiled in your sweat. A stew of anger and unhealthy fat...

HOGBIN: She knows you...!

HELEN: And looking along the wires of dangling intellects I thought, the fat one has escaped my husband's spite...

SAVAGE: Eventually the camps will shut, and rusty execution sheds fall down in gales, and guards retire to plant begonias, **All forgotten!** (*Pause*.) But one still excavates the files, plucks memoirs out of bonfires, and keeps testimony safe in his archival head... (EPSOM *moves to threaten* SAVAGE, *who shrinks to the ground*.) Don't spill the head! (EPSOM *stops, bemused*.) It contains the agony of others, like a cup... (*He looks up*.) You are Helen of Troy... (*She weeps suddenly, cradling him in her arms*.)

HELEN: Yes...and now...obscurity...! (*Pause*. SHADE *picks up his kit*.)

SHADE: Home, James...!

FLADDER: Home?

SHADE: Bands playing on the quay. And similar shit. Flags in babies' gobs. And similar shit. (*To* CREUSA.) Carry my loot, you!

FLADDER: This is home.

SHADE: Wha'?

FLADDER: Where so much hate has concentrated, that must be home also.

SHADE (*to* CREUSA): Mind my mirror!

GUMMERY: **It's home he says.** (SHADE *stops*).

SHADE: Wha'? (*Pause*.)

GUMMERY: I never knew a Trojan, nor heard of Troy. And yet, no sooner had my boot touched Trojan pebble but —

FLADDER: You hated.

GUMMERY: Just like that. Peculiar.

SAVAGE: Not peculiar. (*Pause. They look at him*.)

HOGBIN: Careful, clever...

SAVAGE: May I speak?

HOGBIN: **Care — ful**...! (*Pause*.)

SAVAGE: The war was already in you. Do you think hatred has no life? It's born with you. It howls in your first howl.

Impatient loathing coiled behind your tongue which on the pretext **rolled out like a python**, a hundred feet of scales... (*Pause.*) The kind man racks his mind how thousands might grapple in the mud for a single woman. The disbelief! Or the lout stab the pensioner's eyes! The kind man should stare down his own throat... (*Pause.*)

SHADE (*in realisation*): Whad' yer mean, this is home?

FLADDER (*leaping up*): Nobody goes!

SHADE: Fuck that —

FLADDER: **Gendarmes!** (GUMMERY *goes to grab the mirror from* CREUSA.)

SHADE: **My mirror!**

FLADDER: Home the lie, home the sentiment!

SHADE (*grabbing one end of the mirror*): My mirror!

FLADDER: The knife under the pillow, the long, cold marital stare...

EPSOM (*wading in*): **Stuff it, Barry!** (*Gendarmes rush in, pin back* SHADE'S *arms. A breathless pause.*)

FLADDER: Home? What's that? The dead eye of the widow who finds she is no widow? The child's sullen resignation of its place? **Home what's that**. (*Pause.*) Go, if you wish. (*The Gendarmes release him.* SHADE *goes to take the mirror from* GUMMERY.) No Mirror (*He stops.*)

SHADE: No mirror? (*He looks about him.*) **I suffered for that mirror. It's my prize!** (*Pause.*)

FLADDER: The ship goes hoooooooooo... (*Pause.*) The ship goes hoooooooooo... (*Pause, then* SHADE *dumps to the ground.* GUMMERY *returns the mirror.*)

HELEN: First Troy is under the ashes. Second Troy now. (*She goes to leave.*)

GUMMERY: Second Troy? Of what, lady? Paper?

FLADDER: Paper, yes. Paper Troy now! No more weapons! No more walls! Write everywhere our shame! (HELEN *goes out and* FLADDER *rises.*) **Constitution writers!** (*To* SAVAGE.) How's your spelling?

SAVAGE: Adequate.

FLADDER: Spell agony.

SAVAGE: H — E — L — E

FLADDER: You'll do! (*He sweeps out, followed by* GUMMERY *and* EPSOM. CREUSA *remains, staring at* SAVAGE. *Pause.*)

CREUSA: So there you are...

SAVAGE: Don't start —

CREUSA: There you fucking are —

SAVAGE: **Don't start I said** —

CREUSA: **The Imagination, The Intellect** —

SAVAGE: The rattle of your mundane prejudice and —

CREUSA: **Barmy notions** —

SAVAGE: **Domestic triviality you** —

CREUSA: **Posturing as visions you** —

SAVAGE: **Microscopic obsessionist!**

CREUSA: **Snob!** (*A pause of exhaustion.*)

SHADE: It's mine, now. (*He indicates* CREUSA *with a nod.*)

SAVAGE: Yes.

SHADE: The arse. The cry. The dream. Mine. (*Pause.*)

SAVAGE: Yes. (CREUSA *looks at* SAVAGE, *pitifully.*)

CREUSA: Oh, you mad and forlorn bastard...I couldn't take
any more of you! (*Wearily, she takes the mirror and bundle
from* SHADE *and goes off.* SHADE *looks a long time into*
SAVAGE.)

SHADE: I also have a mind. (SAVAGE *turns to look at him.*)

SAVAGE: You —

SHADE: I also have a mind. (*Pause.*) I don't exhibit it, like a
balloon. **The mind**. (*Pause.*) I don't **wag** it.

SAVAGE: No...

SHADE: But it exists. And it has archways, upon archways.
And cisterns, and reservoirs also. Fuckall books and fuckall
songs but. And anyway, what are those things? They are daggers, also. **Song in the eyes!** (*He feints at* SAVAGE, *and goes
off, watched by* HOGBIN.)

HOGBIN (*fearfully*): Get out of 'ere...

SAVAGE: Why?

HOGBIN: This crew. This regiment. 'alf off their 'inges, gates
swinging in the 'urricane, **mind yer gob!**

SAVAGE: Why?

HOGBIN: **Mad gates banging!**

SAVAGE: **Go where anyway?** (*Pause.*) Go, he says...the spontaneous retort if things degenerate...nomadic instinct of the
urban boy...what are you, a sparrow, off at the first pin drop?
A rabbit, pelting at the shadow of the cloud? Nomads have no
written culture, you know that...

HOGBIN: Fuck your comprehensiveness...

SAVAGE: **No knowledge on the hoof**.

HOGBIN: Yes, but this — (*Pause.*)

SAVAGE: To go beyond. That's our hunger, that's our thirst.
To go beyond, you must stand still. **First paradox of all great**

journeys. (*He opens his arms.*) Kiss me, I have told you something.

HOGBIN:　You always wanna be kissed —

SAVAGE:　**Do it out of gratitude!** (HOGBIN *pecks him.*)

HOGBIN:　Who was that, your Mrs who got lost? I think you
shoved your cold chisel in 'er cracks and drove a decent woman
barmy. Did you? But I think she's kind, as all blasphemers
are . . .

Scene Four

A tumult of paper. Men folding. HOGBIN *on his knees, copying.*
HELEN *enters with* A DAUGHTER.

HELEN:　**Will whoever brings dead men's ribs and things into my
bedroom stop!**

FLADDER (*entering*):　Second Troy has paper walls because
they offer no defence, and having no defence invite no enemies.
All the energies of the inhabitants will be directed towards the
examination of our errors. Write reconciliation everywhere,
and artists, if there are any, stick pictures on it!

HELEN:　It is an offence to tamper with war graves in any case,
who is doing it, do you know?

HOGBIN:　Not the foggiest . . .

HELEN:　Someone is, I'm not imagining it.

FLADDER:　**Where's Savage? Has he made the loving constitution yet?**

HELEN:　A bit of thigh, or skull with weird red hair on it?
Perhaps the dogs do it?

HOGBIN:　Maybe dogs . . .

HELEN:　No shortage of dogs in Second Troy.

HOGBIN:　Dogs all over the shop . . .

HELEN:　No, it isn't dogs, it's men. **A corpse in the bed will be
next**. (SAVAGE *enters.*)

SAVAGE:　The Seven Principles of New Troy.

FLADDER:　Seven is it . . . good . . .

SAVAGE:　The poor will apologize. The rich will forgive. The
thief will be compensated. The victim accused.

FLADDER: Of what?

SAVAGE: Tempting the thief.

FLADDER: Good.

SAVAGE: All governors will swim rivers at seventy.

FLADDER: Why?

SAVAGE: To prove their minds are still good.

FLADDER: Yes...

SAVAGE: The sick will dictate morality. The healthy will never be paid.

FLADDER: They have health.

SAVAGE: They have health, yes. The intellectual will be revered until he speaks. The passionate will be in receipt of pension books. (*Pause.*)

FLADDER: That's eight, surely? (SAVAGE *bows.*)

HELEN: When I was fourteen I could tell jokes. And men said, you tell jokes better than a man!

GUMMERY: I don't call that a constitution...

HELEN: But for all their laughing, not one of them would lay a hand on me. Not one!

GUMMERY: Do you, Les?

HELEN: So I stopped telling jokes. And they were all over me! Breaking one another's jaws, and scrapping in the gutter.

GUMMERY (*to* SAVAGE): **I don't call that a constitution**.

HELEN: There is a time for jokes, but it's not now.

SAVAGE (*to* GUMMERY): Nail it to the doors, and all the citizens of Paper Troy will be outraged and stamp their feet, and go around shouting 'Never!' (*Pause.*) Which is good, and the proper condition for a populace to be in.

FLADDER: **Paint it. The seven principles of Paper Troy**.

EPSOM (*to* WORKERS *off*): **Paints!**

GUMMERY (*confused*): Seven? You said eight...

FLADDER: Seven, yes! (*To* SAVAGE.) You see, they gawp at your magnificence... (GUMMERY *stares at the paper*.)

SAVAGE (*patiently, to* GUMMERY): This gives you freedom...

GUMMERY: Freedom?

SAVAGE: To break the stranglehold of the consecutive. You can write seven twice. Or not number them at all.

GUMMERY (*shaking his head*): Confusing...

SAVAGE: Yes!

GAY: My mother called me Gay. Do you know why? I don't know why, I'm sure. And I had a sister called FELICITY. What was that about? Felicity died, naturally, and of such a painful illness! But I am going to be gay. I am. (HELEN *leans fondly over her daughter*.) **Don't touch me with those gnawed and kneaded tits**. (*Pause. She smiles, kissing her mother fondly*.)

SAVAGE: Knowledge is a suite of rooms. Dirty rooms, unswept as museums in the provinces. And to enter each room you must leave with the woman at the door some priceless thing, which feels part of yourself and your identity, so that it feels like ripping skin. And the keepers sit in piles of discarded treasures, like the pelts of love or children's pity, and at each successive door the piles are less because few stagger such long distances, until there comes a door at which there lies a small, white rag stained as a dishcloth, which may be sanity. **And if you think that is the end you are mistaken, it is the beginning**. (*Pause*.) And people say, 'I know myself.' Have you heard that? Never! they know the contents of one room. (*Pause*.)

FLADDER: But who'd want knowledge if knowledge meant I could simply look at her, and looking see only a hundred pounds of flesh, which by virtue of its shape defines her beautiful? If knowledge is to be so cool I'd say stuff knowledge **what do you find Helen, Dr Savage? She made me think appalling thought**. (*Pause*.) Lay down for my inspection every inch of your infatuation. (*Pause*.) What, no words, and you a teacher? (*Pause*.) You see, if she is not impossible to see without she wrecks our peace, what did we suffer for? **Imagine the temper in the war cemeteries!** (*Pause*.)

SAVAGE: All my life I have searched out Helen of Troy. And if you stuck a bin of offal there and called it Helen, I should have to stoop to it. (*The fraction of a pause*.)

FLADDER: Bin! (*He goes out*.)

SHADE (*calling off*): **A bin!**

HELEN: Oh, doctor, they will chain you to it and you will suffocate on stench for uttering one solid truth upon another... (*A bin is manoeuvered on*.)

CREUSA (*entering*): Oh God, what has he done?

HOGBIN: Been a silly bugger all over again — (THE SOLDIERS *chain him to the bin by his wrists*. GAY *sits down on the floor*.)

GAY: The amount of killing I have seen! My father, for example, on the floor and skinned. Paris! Yes, it's true! They skinned him. And my grandfather was **inside out**. I have seen the lot, I can assure you, and I thought to myself, Gay, they want you to go **insane**. So I decided there and then I would not. **I declined to**

be insane. (*Pause.*) I think Paper Troy won't last. And then what? Another pile of murders and a skinning or two! (*Pause.*) My mother gave birth to me with my father's thing in her gob **I just know it**. He took his clothes off while she contracted and lay beside her. **I just know he did they were like that**. So I've seen the lot, really, and am I insane? **Quite the contrary**. (*She skips out.*)

HOGBIN (*a crablike move to* SAVAGE):   Too fucking clever —

SAVAGE: Away you skinny newt —

HOGBIN: Night's coming in and storm clouds full of freezing rain —

SAVAGE: You book-snapping terrier —

HOGBIN: You will perish of exposure you unhealthy sod of fat —

SAVAGE: You whimpering abortion of a greyhound's toss —

HOGBIN: **Now, then, truth-teller!** (*He rolls about the floor.*) No chains! (*He somersaults.*) No bin! (*He goes towards* CREUSA, *who has drawn a paper over herself. A storm rumbles.* HOGBIN *gets under with her. He pokes out his head.*) Adopt the nature of the chameleon. (*He withdraws. A ragged book flies out. Then* HOGBIN'S *head.*) Borkman and Salberstein. (*He goes back in.*)

SAVAGE: Oh, rain on, oh, dark on, and gales roar up the beach like bombers levelling the streets. I know what Helen is, I know what Helen is! Another shell in the boiling breech! Oh, to be at sieges, at every siege that ever was, and throw in death from hills, the breakfast goes, the kitchen goes, the crockery went up a hundred feet, the horse stood at the traffic lights and then down came its parted hooves, one in the garden of the spinster, one in the orphanage. I trawl, I dig, I excavate! Under your half-truths! The lecturer's voice is a whip, the vicar's lectern is a rack for thrashing youth! Who trusts the smiles on the library steps? Razor blades in the dictionary! I know! I know what Helen is! She's all that's unforgivable! (FLADDER *enters in an overcoat. He sits.*)

FLADDER: I like the night. I feel what in the day I must deny has every right to full consideration. Say you understand me. (*He looks at the paper tent.*) What is going on in the paper house?

SAVAGE: My student is struck dumb by the body of my wife and theoryless for once, explores her with his tongue. And she's another man's thing, by which he risks castration at the least. A real cocktail of pleasures, but you'd appreciate it, what's love without the risk of death?

FLADDER (*implacably*): I wish to be tried, and if necessary, executed. (*Pause.*)

SAVAGE (*astutely*): On no charge, presumably?

FLADDER: No charges.

SAVAGE: And the verdict?

FLADDER: Guilty. And I prosecute myself.

SAVAGE: So new Troy opens with the execution of the governor?

FLADDER: I'll demand the ultimate penalty.

SAVAGE: And I'll grant it. I take it I'm the magistrate?

FLADDER: Who else? Are you not the only criminal? (*He goes out.*)

SAVAGE: If every man is ashamed, and you are not ashamed. If every man is guilty, and you refuse guilt... **What then!**

CREUSA (*emerging, adjusting her clothing*): He says... (*A small, dry laugh.*) He says... I drive all anger from his mind... he says... listen to this... to see me naked kills ambition... the peace, the peace, he says...

SAVAGE: Listen, I have —

CREUSA: **No, you listen.** (*Pause.*) He says incredible things no man ever said of me. But he's impotent as yet. **Understandable!** If you put such store by one woman, to come erect at once would be no compliment, would it? I'm honoured by his crisis. (*She looks at herself, bemused.*) I've been through hell, but you were hell as well... what happened to our son? (*Pause.*) Oh, look, I ask as casually as one might for a book or newspaper! I had all the instincts but I learned to suffocate them in a bag, I don't threaten you with maternal rages, so where did he, you can tell... (*Pause.*)

SAVAGE: He. (*Pause.*)

CREUSA: It's me who broke the bond, and watched the three of you stagger out of my life, no claims and no reproaches, what's a child in any case, we stepped across whole ditchfuls, I remember... (*Pause.*)

SAVAGE: He. (*Pause.*)

CREUSA: The product of a joyless copulation, no I have no temper, boot the sentiment, boot the mother stuff, **He what**. (*Pause.*)

SAVAGE: Whatever you imagine is as likely as the truth. As painful, or as painless.

CREUSA: Still, I want to know, however futile —

SAVAGE: Dream it instead —

CREUSA: I do, I dream it often but —

SAVAGE: **What difference does it make**.

CREUSA: **It makes a difference!** (*Pause.*) Tell me, and I'll swallow it. Down, like a single pill, gollop, and gone! Life continues, under Hogbin's fascinated stare or beaten by the Greeks, today it's rheumatism, tomorrow, plague, the sticky belt of crisis but first what happened to my son? (*Pause.*) The mundane bit of life I mundanely delivered... (*Pause.*)

SAVAGE: I don't know. I lost him. (*Pause.*)

CREUSA: Lost him...

SAVAGE: Lost him, yes...

CREUSA: Mislaid him...

SAVAGE: Mislaid him, yes, no, I lost him.

CREUSA: Lost him?

SAVAGE: **Lost, you know the word, it happened all over Europe**. Drifting infants, in dead men's uniforms...

CREUSA: You —

SAVAGE: **Lost my child and helped my father die!**

CREUSA: Oh, you —

SAVAGE: And not guilty!

CREUSA: You —

SAVAGE: **Not guilty, no!** (*She stares at him. Pause.*)

CREUSA: Hold my hand, you terrible mouth, biting the concrete, your gums all shredded and your lips all torn... terrible mouth on you... (*She holds his hands. HOGBIN emerges and looks. To HOGBIN, not turning.*) It's all right... these are old bruises we have to bruise again... (*She gets up, goes out.*)

HOGBIN: Funny, ain't it, any bastard can serve a woman properly but me. Any phlegm-stained criminal to do a violation of a child is rigid as a tree branch. Any dancing mannikin dribbling on a deb gets seven inches on request. **What about me!**

SAVAGE: Patience...

HOGBIN: **Patience**...!

SAVAGE: She is. (*Pause.*) It's only a space.

HOGBIN: A space?

SAVAGE: A mobile space.

HOGBIN: **A mobile space?**

SAVAGE: You think by parroting you diminish truth you hate to entertain —

HOGBIN: **It's oblivion!** (*Pause.*)

SAVAGE: So's a grave. A space enclosing oblivion. (*Pause.*)

HOGBIN: Want it anyway. So did you, once... (HELEN *enters, holding a fragment.*)

HELEN: Neck bone. (*She lifts the lid of* SAVAGE'S *bin, drops it in, replacing the lid.*) I think they do this because they desire me. I may be wrong. It could be hatred, but then, what's hatred? I think it's desire also, what do you say? (*She looks at* HOGBIN.)

HOGBIN (*cautiously*):   I wouldn't disagree with you —

HELEN: Oh listen, I am sad tonight, so stuff your tact. I want a conversation.

HOGBIN: Stuff it, yes...

HELEN: I get no sleep. I go to my room, and even as I go towards the door I think to myself, oh, the futility of this...

HOGBIN: Know the feeling...

HELEN: I fling the sheet aside and there — **Why do you always agree with me?** (*Pause.* HOGBIN *shrugs.*) I fling the sheet back and — (*Pause.*) Of course I suffer all the consequences. More lined. And more bad tempered. The face becomes a landscape of insomnia and yet the overall effect is I am **more desirable**. Yes! It's true! Do you think I am insane? Do you think, poor thing, she is deluded? There is no point in the conversation if you hold that opinion, none at all, no, I tell you the truth because you are unhappy, I ditched modesty decades ago and so would you, I have had nine children, my belly's a pit, or as the poetically-inclined say when they're lapping me, a sandy strand from which the tide receded leaving feathered frontiers. Ugly, but who's deterred? You see, for compliments I have a perfect memory... (*Pause.*) This is not a conversation, is it? I am doing all the talking. (EPSOM *and* GUMMERY *rush in with* FLADDER *between them, stripped and beaten.*)

FLADDER: I am the murderer! I am the victim!

HELEN (*horrified*):   **What have you done to him!**

FLADDER: I am the killer! **Hangman in attendance, please!**

HELEN: **What have you done to his face!**

GUMMERY: He told me to!

FLADDER (*to* SAVAGE):   **Sentence me, then!**

HELEN: His face, look...

GUMMERY: **He told me to...!**

FLADDER: Innocent squaddies! (*She goes to wipe away the blood.*) **Don't touch the assassin's face!** (*She stands back.*) I asked them to hurt me, and all they could think of was their fists, what other tortures do they know about? Love? **No chair for the accused**, I kneel, no, that's too comfortable, I squat, what was the sentence, death?

SAVAGE: Yes...

FLADDER: Didn't hear it.

SAVAGE: It goes without saying...

FLADDER: **Cacophony in court!** Listen, the destruction of cities, the wrecking of fleets, the burning of crops, infanticide by numbers, all this is so much **trivia**. War crimes, rubbish, no. In Paper Troy the only crimes are crimes against the self.

HELEN: I think you are the most insatiable exhibitionist.

FLADDER (*glaring at her*): Exhibitionism you would know about, who hung your cunt out to all youth, **I've seen her do it like the butcher showing meat**.

HELEN: Get up and wash your face, will you...?

FLADDER: What we do to others is no sin, it's self-murder I prosecute, the only crimes are crimes against the self, that's the source of cruelty!

HELEN: Wash your face, please...

FLADDER: Wash it, why? Wash yours, it's black with terror. **You think to show your arse is revelation?** (*She slaps him. Pause.*)

HELEN: You see, you bring out the worst in everyone. (*Pause. FLADDER hangs his head.*)

GUMMERY: He was such a bugger once, a proper head-hacker, I saw him swallow blood hot from the severed arteries, the head still rolling in the fosse...

HELEN: Terrible decline...It comes from having Helen back...

SAVAGE (*briskly*): No executioner. Pity. Paper gaol, then, until such time as paper death sets in.

FLADDER (*seeing SHADE enter*): **Here's the man to do it**. (*They look at SHADE.*)

EPSOM: Go 'ome now, Barry, if yer wish. And take the mirror. (*Pause.*)

SHADE: Home? What's that?

FLADDER: In him, even, whose mouth is a brass purse of pain, some rotted quality of personal perfection must persist, all gnawed and spoiled by terror and abuse, **deep though!** (*Suddenly*, SHADE *flies at him.*)

HOGBIN (*horrified*): Hey...!

SAVAGE (*looking*): Not looking...

HOGBIN: Oi, you're the —

SAVAGE: **Not looking** —

HOGBIN: **Magistrate!**

HELEN (*as SHADE works on FLADDER*).
    His little sob at coming
    His great shout at coming

His little spilling
His great splash of fluid
His snivelling at betrayal
His great cataclysms of despair
His skittering with infants
His flinging of the baby at the wall
What could you make of that brute and boy (*Pause.*)
No man made me more eager to betray him or more willing to
come back ... (*Pause.*)

HOGBIN: He ain't dead ... (*Pause.*)

HELEN: Not dead? (*She laughs, as* SHADE *walks away from
the kneeling* FLADDER.)

SHADE: The worst thing that can happen to a compulsive
apologist I think, is to lose his tongue ...

HELEN: Lose his ...

SHADE: Finish Paper Troy.

HELEN: His tongue ...

SHADE (*tossing it away*): And paper knives —

HELEN: **No tongue** —

SHADE (*holding a vile thing*): I had to rip it by its roots. **No
private life in New Troy! No clamour of apology!** (*Pause.*)

HELEN: Put it back ...

SHADE (*turning to her*): Put it back? Why, did it please you
very much, lapping your sour flavours? (EPSOM *laughs.*) **No
more of that either**. He only watches now, his eyeballs do the
talking.

HELEN: Put it back ...

SHADE (*thrusting it at her*): You.

HELEN: The voice. The words. Are what desire is. The message is arousal. Or we're cattle. You have castrated him.

SHADE: No, I left those shrivelled things intact.

HELEN: **You have castrated him**. (*Pause.*) He could mutter me
into upheavals no shoving hip could copy, earthquakes by his
bawdy —

EPSOM: **Lend us the tongue, then!**

HELEN: Oh, you sham male, dog on its hind legs dancing —

EPSOM: **Lend us it!**

HELEN: Parody of masculinity —

SHADE (*flinging the tongue to* EPSOM): Bury it, with honours, since it commanded us at epic slaughters, or pickle it for
youth to gawp at. And this fat one, let him record its wit from
recollections, in eight volumes. As for this bitch, new queen
now, for new Troy. Where's my looted woman?

CREUSA: No thank you.

SHADE: **New Queen I said**. (*To* HELEN.) And you, her slut. (*He goes to the kneeling figure of* FLADDER, *puts his hands on* FLADDER'S *shoulders, embraces him*.) Don't think cruel men have not also suffered, or victims spluttered terrible savagery in tears... (*Pause*.) I'm looking for a god. (*Pause He turns to* SAVAGE.) Could it be you?

Scene Five

A Beach. GAY, *with a stick*. A BOY, *seated*.

GAY: Reasons for the fall of Paper Troy. One! (THE BOY *hesitates*.) Come on, oh, do come on, or I will beat you!

BOY: Erm...

GAY: One! The degeneracy of the aristocracy and their flirtation with the arts. Two! The martial ardour of the warriors could find no satisfaction in origami! Three! Are you listening, I don't think you try at all, this is **History** I'm teaching you! And stop fidgetting, or I will beat you! (*Exasperated pause*.) I sometimes think, people are such swine, such inveterate swine. And then I think, no, you can make them better.

BOY: By beating them?

GAY: By beating them, yes! How else? (*She sees a figure, off*.) Oh, no, here comes that horrid old man again! Don't encourage him. Because he's blind we all go silly, he knows that, he uses that to exploit us. (HOMER *enters, blind*.) **You are not to put your hand into my dress again**. (*He stops*.) I think the beach should be a place for children to be children and not poked about by peculiar old men.

HOMER: You are not a child.

GAY: I am a child. I am thirteen. Obviously I am a child.

HOMER: You are not a child, and I am not an old man.

GAY: Conundrum.

BOY: What?

GAY: Conundrum. He says all these things, these conundrums and things, and the next thing you know —

HOMER: Stop —

GAY: Hand up your —

HOMER: **Stop**. (*She concedes.*) I am not an old man because I know nothing. And you are not a child because you know it all. Now give me your hand. (*She extends it.* HOMER *draws it quickly to his crutch.*)

GAY: There! I knew that would happen!

HOMER: **A god lives there**.

HELEN (*entering*):   The author of the Iliad.

GAY: He is trying to make me insane...

HELEN: The author of the Odyssey.

GAY: **He is trying to make me insane!** (*She pulls away, runs off.*)

HOMER: The young...! No charity! So cruel, which is their fascination...

BOY: She beats me with a twig!

HOMER: Lucky fellow...

BOY: Right round the face sometimes, whip! Because I don't know ten reasons for the fall of Paper Troy.

HOMER: There are not ten reasons.

BOY: That's what I say! (*He hurries off.*)

HELEN: I hate your songs. Do you mind this? The ripping livers and the splash of brains. The prosody is marvellous but. I must say this and fuck the consequences. The torrents of intestine and the ravens picking skulls **I also am so violent**, were you always blind? When their attacks were beaten off we maimed the wounded. With kitchen knives, me and the Trojan women, hacked them in the ditch, trimming the features off their heads like turnips for the market and their cocks we cropped **Don't say you never heard of this** were you born blind or was it horror spread some merciful film across your retina, and what's pity, I do think pity is no substitute for truth —

HOMER: Helen —

HELEN: **I refuse to clap your songs**. (*Pause.*) I loved Troy, because Troy was to sin. Why did you never say that? But him who took me there was not a sinner, only an exhibitionist, and not my equal. **Don't you know the hell it is to find no man your equal?** Say that, in your next book. That was the agony of Troy, not slippery swords or old men massacred, but Helen's awful loneliness in dream...

HOMER: Helen...

HELEN: Do what you like with my daughter — when history gets to a child no mother can be of the least relief.

HOMER (*holding out his arms*):   Helen! (*He encloses her. She weeps.* SAVAGE *appears with* HOGBIN *pushing the bin.*)

SAVAGE: I said, if I am the god, why do I have to drag the bin? Put wheels on it, he said...

HELEN (*pulling free of* HOMER):   What are you?

SAVAGE: What am I?

HELEN: You come here, first a clerk and now a god — it's obvious you want to destroy me —

SAVAGE: Me —

HELEN: **What else are you here for!**

HOGBIN (*demonstratively*):   The Interlude of the Bin! Within the bin — (*He removes the lid.*) The fruits of the hospital! I construct — I demonstrate — the vital elements of the Suffering Biped — **One!** (*He reaches into the offal.*) It's a — (*He looks at a shapeless thing.*) Call it a foot — (*He places it on the ground.*) This transports the lie around — the biped is manoeuverable, it is not still, no, it stamps in unison, the foot being also for **dancing**, a futile repetition aimed at creating social unity, **Another lie** and also, **kicking**, the ecstasy experienced by the biped in inflicting pain, **Two!** (*He dips in again.*) The knee! (*He looks at a shapeless thing.*) Call it a knee —

SAVAGE (*staring at* HOMER):   Listen —

HOGBIN: Why not a knee —

SAVAGE: Listen, will you?

HOGBIN (*laying the piece down*):   I'm talking —

SAVAGE: This is him who —

HOGBIN: **I'm talking, aren't I?** (*Pause.*) Knee. For kneeling with. To imaginary forces such as God, or actual forces such as the party, the murderer, etcetera, a complex joint enabling the biped to grovel most convincingly —

SAVAGE: **Ho — mer!** (*He throws himself at* HOMER'S *feet and kisses the hem of his garment.*)

HOGBIN: Also, for driving into softer organs such as the stomach or the genitals, to render ineffective the thing I number **Three** — (*He dips in again at random.*) The organ of increase! (*He pulls out a shapeless thing.*) Call it a dick — why not a dick — and with the other bit — two elements with which... (*he stares at the thing*) the biped...in an extravaganza of futility...pretends to...shake off consciousness...or fails to...**Ribs!** (*He reaches in, stops in mid-movement. To* SAVAGE.) You mustn't do that...he may be the very wickedest of bastards...

SAVAGE: **The great man lends us hope...**

HOGBIN: You say that because you sense you are a great man yourself, but undiscovered...

SAVAGE (*to* HOMER):   We squabble, my student and I, my
    desperate and sadistic student, we — but you would know, you
    with your flocks of followers —
HOGBIN: Creeping...
SAVAGE: Clustering around you for the least perception
    which —
HOGBIN: Creeping...
SAVAGE: **Let me worship somebody!** (*Pause.*) So barren, isn't
    it, a life without prostration? (*To* HOGBIN.) **And that goes for
    all juvenile iconoclasts!** (*Pause. To* HOMER.) Savage, PhD,
    lecturer in classics, theses on metre and the first six books...
    (*Pause.*) Beloved genius...I call you genius... though he
    would say there's no such thing...**There is and this is it**...
    (*Pause.*) Speak to me...a little philosophical deduction...no,
    that's a lot to ask, a real impertinence, forgive me...anything
    would do... (*Pause.*) Not anything, that's silly, not anything,
    not the time of day, no, but a little distillation? Or is distillation
    now impossible? (*Pause.*) **Come on, I wrote two books about
    you!**
HOGBIN: Ribs! (*He pulls a shapeless thing from the bin.*) Call it
    ribs, all right? (*He places it down.*) In the shelter of which the
    biped hides his **heart,** formerly conceived as organ of feeling,
    passion, etcetera, but now exposed as leathery and boring
    pump.
HOMER: I hate the young. When I was young even, I hated the
    young... (*Pause.*)
SAVAGE (*to* HOMER):   You are the greatest poet in the world.
    Of any time. Of any culture. (*Pause.*) I wonder if you heard? I
    said —
HOMER: You imagine you compliment me.
SAVAGE: Don't I?
HOMER: And having complimented me, you expect the com-
    pliment to give me pleasure.
SAVAGE: Doesn't it? (*Pause. Suddenly, shockingly,* HELEN
    leaps on HOGBIN *and wrestles him.*)
HOGBIN: Oi! (HELEN *and* HOGBIN *roll about. She bears him
    down.*) Oi! (*She laughs with delight.*) Oi! (*They roll over the
    floor.*)
HOMER: The great artist drifts beyond the common con-
    sciousness, like a child carried to sea by a raft. The beach
    gets further, the paddlers get further, the weak swimmers,
    then the strong swimmers, all out of reach, until — **You are
    writing it down!**

SAVAGE: No, I —

HOMER: **Liar. Heard the pen.**

SAVAGE (*innocently*): Was I?

HELEN (*to* HOGBIN, *climbing off him*): Be my lover.

HOGBIN: No!

HELEN: They say no now! Listen! No, he says. Look, I plead...!

HOGBIN: Don't wanna...

HELEN: We will have a child and call it — (*To* HOMER.) **Don't look at me like that I am not infertile.** (HOGBIN *scrambles to his feet.*)

HELEN: Listen...! (*She cups her ear.*) The daily chant of Laughing Troy...

SHADE (*entering*): The word. (*He looks at them.*)
The word today is Us.
All say it.
Us.
It soothes the soul, it calms the temper, can't hear you.
Us. (HOMER *starts to leave.*)
I thought you were blind, not dumb. (*He stops.*) I also have a mind.

HOMER: Us.

SHADE: Excellent. I think with vast and bloated genius, to stoop is healthy. (*He turns to the others.*) Everybody!

ALL: Us. (*Pause. He turns to leave.*)

SAVAGE: Excuse me, am I still a god?

SHADE: Why not? Aren't you still ugly? (*He goes to leave again.*)

SAVAGE: Tomorrow's word then! (SHADE *stops.*) If you're looking for suggestions... (*Pause.*) **Must.**

SHADE: Must...?

SAVAGE: **Us** and **Must.** The twin pillars of history... (SHADE *goes out. Pause. They look at* SAVAGE *critically.*) I did not come here to sit on a beach... (*They stare at him.*) Where's knowledge? Where does it lie? In meditation? The lillies and the rhyming couplets? The whispering sandal in the aromatic garden? **No poet ever told us anything.** (HOGBIN *looks at* HOMER.) And why? **Because he never governed.** That's why he's blind, he only looks inside. **All right Mr Homer you can abuse me now.** (*Pause.*) I'm waiting, in a lather of submission... (*Pause.*)

HELEN: You are not a very great man, Dr Savage...

SAVAGE: His lashing, please...

HELEN: Or even very dignified...

SAVAGE: His lashing, not yours...! (*Pause, then* HOMER
goes off.) I am beneath contempt...
HELEN: Yes, but he's looking for my daughter. (*She turns to
go, stops, looks at* HOGBIN, *who is replacing the offal in the
bin.*) What's the matter, do you love another woman?
(HOGBIN *shrugs.*) I hope I shan't hate you. I'm such a
hater. It's the burden of my life.
HOGBIN: I'm sorry, I —
HELEN: Don't! (*Pause. To* SAVAGE.) He was going to apologize! Or is that right? Perhaps he knows, if he really tried, he
could love me? (*She goes out.* MACLUBY *appears.*)
MACLUBY: The Pruning of Helen. (SAVAGE *and* HOGBIN
fill the bin, replace the lid.) The pruning of Helen may have
been — this is the nature of political decisions — spontaneous.
A flash of intuition or a stab of malice, **What do you think
History is, deliberation?** On the other hand it may have been the
outcome of long and acrimonious debate within the ruling
circle, **What do you think History is, spasms?** (*To* SAVAGE,
who is going out.) Oi! (SAVAGE *stops.*) He also sins who only
writes the words. But you know that. (MACLUBY *goes out.*
CREUSA *enters.*)
CREUSA: Slave one day. Queen the next. Would you believe?
The transformations! But happy by order, and to be illiterate.
Difficult, when I was not illiterate in the first place. This Troy to
be in single syllables. Difficult. Or hard, should say. (*She exerts
her imagination.*) My — plain — face — to — be — the — badge
— of — Troy. Done it! (*She tries again.*) And — in — my — life
— the — crowd — will — see — and — love — its — self — not
— stoop — to — snobs — nor — lick — the — arse — of —
beauty — Beauty's two... (*Pause.*) Shade's Troy. (*She parrots.*)
I also have a mind...! (*Pause. She looks at* HOGBIN.) Will you
talk to me, I have given up all hope of a quiet life, and a quiet
life when I had it I despised, it was not quiet, it was clay, it was
not quiet, it was mud, quiet is something else, not dense but
light I think. I left notes for you in so many places, my scrambling love, my rodent, I was burrowed, I was tunnelled, all my
dark exposed to daylight, a tent uptipped, a parcel with your
fingers at the strings, the haste, the impatience, the breathless
hunt, and your great wail of desperation, did you get my notes,
every tree trunk I left letters in and every litterbin, no, I exaggerate, some I did pass by, do I embarrass you at all, you look
so, I am so rarely this enthusiastic and you look, **oh, fuck I have
offended him,** calm down, calm down, there I'm calm now, I am

so glad to see you, there, statement of extreme reserve, **don't you want to fuck now,** shh! I could, almost, I could, yes, I could almost **beat you, I also have a mind,** please speak or don't I leave you room, I don't, do I, here's room. (*She stops. Pause.*)

HOGBIN: Cold today... (*Pause.*)

CREUSA: Cold today. You? Ah. Shh! Could let out such a torrent. Could let out such a volley but no, shh. I have done everything. I have been everythinged, and you, a balding and precocious youth can **Who's impotent at that** for which no criticism can make me who has done everything and been everythinged — (*Pause.*) If I believed in gods I'd say some godlike bugger had sprinkled me with what — delirium — to entertain himself — cold, is it? All right, just sit, to sit with you would be enough, and say a few words, or nothing if you — (*He sits.*) Thank you. (*Pause.*) I thank him. (*Pause.*)

HOGBIN: Cold today...

CREUSA: We are like that. We are! We are so inconsistent. We are liars without meaning it. And now I'm cold as well. Excellently cold. Excellently off the idea. Excellent. I could no more have you than. I am to speak in words of single syllables I must remind you. It is the function of my majesty. (*Pause.*) Arse is one syllable. Cunt obviously. It is a miracle when two moods coincide. It is a sacrament. **Three syllables!** (*A long pause, then she lets out a cry.*) Oh, God... (*Pause.*) Oh, God, you have met someone else... (*Pause.*)

Scene Six

The Government. EPSOM *carries on the mirror.*

SHADE: Gather round me. Come on, gather round me, comrades in arms, etcetera, treaders of the bowel carpet and the brain mat — (*He opens his arms to them. He clutches them round the shoulders. They stare into the mirror.*) Oh, we are ageing! Oh, we are shedding! Look, the ploughed up skins, we are hanging off our cheek bones and our eyes are dim. Look deep, look deep, we slew arbitrarily and we pitied arbitrarily. Look deep. Speech, Les.

EPSOM: Speech?

SHADE: Speech! Yes! This is the frame of greatness, did you think battle was your forte? Never, battle's for the bullock this is where proper violence belongs. **Words!** Les!

EPSOM: Can't —

SHADE: He can't, he can't, Brian, you —

GUMMERY: Must I?

SHADE: You must, old friend.

GUMMERY: Look at yourself then, Barry —

SHADE: Brian, I do —

GUMMERY: Look 'ard and tell us, is it a healthy face is looking back at you?

SHADE: Not healthy, no —

GUMMERY: Or noble?

SHADE: Noble, no —

GUMMERY: Regard the beak, the way the eyes protrude —

SHADE: They do, and I forgive your rudeness —

EPSOM: Yellow skin —

SHADE: Thank you —

EPSOM: And puffy round yer lids —

SHADE: Oh, Les, you have discovered speech —

GUMMERY: Is there pity in the eyeball?

SHADE: Pity? None —

GUMMERY: Mercy?

SHADE: Mercy? **Keep the mirror still** we're looking for my — what —

GUMMERY: Mercy —

SHADE: No, can't see it, Brian, unless that bloodshot vein is it... I think sometimes, they want me to be cruel. They bay at cruelty, but still I think they want me to be cruel. I think even the beaten man wants to be beaten. Why is that?

SAVAGE (*entering*): The governor is the nightmare of the populace... (*Pause.*)

SHADE: Leave me with the doctor. We must define new life, the gutters and the ceilings of New Troy. How laughter might be made as sharp as wire, and dancing a new drill... (GUMMERY *and* EPSOM *leave.* SHADE *looks into* SAVAGE. *Pause.*) **Supposing we trusted one another!** (*Silence.*) Supposing. (*Pause.*) Just supposing. (*Pause.*) I use the word trust loosely. Because I imagine there is trust and trust. Trust I think I fathom, but **Trust**...! What's that? (*Pause.* GUMMERY *comes back in.* SHADE *detects him in the mirror*

with alarm.) **Don't return without warning me!** (GUMMERY
freezes.) What is it, Brian, you made me jump.

GUMMERY: Old Helen of Old Troy

SHADE: What about her?

GUMMERY: Is carrying 'er 'usband round the 'ouse on 'er
back. 'e croaks on 'er like a sun-burned frog. Down alleys and
through the estates. And 'is saliva everywhere, buckets of, the
tongueless dribble, it appears, in excess, and it's making pud-
dles where women exercise their dogs...

SHADE: All right...

GUMMERY: This was the cause of ten years' bleeding and
now look at 'er, bare legs and filthy black — It makes a pig
of everyone who raged for ten years at the gates if she's to be a
slut with unwashed legs —

SHADE: I can see you're anxious —

GUMMERY: History, Barry!

SHADE: History, yes, but even Helen ages —

GUMMERY: Quicker than most, but dignity would help. (*He
goes out.*)

SHADE: I take his point. And once they sold her piss in little
bottles. Well, so it was said by servants who crossed to our
lines with buckets of the stuff. Could have been the cat's for all
we knew. One piss is just like any other. (*Pause.*) Or isn't it?

SAVAGE: No.

SHADE: Some smeared their wounds with it. Some swallowed
it with cordials. The very depth of barminess. Or was it?

SAVAGE: No. (*Pause.*)

SHADE: What do you want, Doctor Savage?

SAVAGE: Knowledge.

SHADE: How?

SAVAGE: Through you.

SHADE: Through me? But aren't I coarse and stupid?

SAVAGE: Yes. But stupidity's my instrument.

SHADE (*smiles*):   It's night, I let all insults fly, like vermin
coming through the floorboards **rat on the gob!**

SAVAGE: You hate all kisses which aren't quick —

SHADE: Yes, I admit it.

SAVAGE: And whispers of impossible intentions —

SHADE: I admit that too! Night's the time for filth and for
confessions! **Loathsome insect in the sink!** You think I will
like you if you abuse me. Intellectual's privilege? (*He goes
to* SAVAGE, *close.*) I think my whim, my unrestrained
and brutal impulse, spewed from the depths of my defective

character and made by you into the monosyllables of late Trojan law, would in their essence be no worse than all the caring calculations of fifty trembling humanists, do you agree or not? (*Pause.*)

SAVAGE: Reserve my judgement.

SHADE: Reserve your judgement — (*He sees* EPSOM *in the mirror.*) **What is it Les yer made me jump!** (EPSOM *enters.*) Still up, old son? What is it, indigestion?

EPSOM: She's placed these adverts. (*He holds out some post-cards.*)

SHADE: Must I look?

EPSOM: In corner shops.

SHADE: Must I? You read. (*He goes to the window.*) Look, the very paring of a moon, a nail of moon, against the plague pit of the sky, the word tonight is **Hack.** You could hack pods of pregnancy with the moon's hook...

EPSOM (*reading*): Helen, formerly of Troy —

SHADE: Don't you love moons, doctor? They teach us all is shit, by shining on the good and bad alike...

EPSOM: Model, seeks interesting work part-time —

SHADE: **Stop that!**

EPSOM (*stops reading*): I mean, if she's no better than a whore — then what did we — ten years of — (*Pause.*)

SHADE: She was a whore! Why else did we go there? I think the sex thing is such a punishment to us. I think you cattle. Don't you? Copulating cattle? Seeing the rear of a cow I think, its hips are not unlike a stooping tart, and us likewise no doubt, our bits droop like a dog's. **Human dignity what's that.**

SAVAGE: I don't know.

SHADE: Don't you?

SAVAGE: I think it's love.

SHADE: What love? You chuck words up like a dead man's ashes, what love? The love of criminals in cars or bankrupt marriages. **What?**

SAVAGE: I don't know! I'm frightened to know!

SHADE: The love of old men for their benches, what!

SAVAGE: **I'm frightened to know!**

SHADE: Stare in the glass! (*He fetches the mirror.*) Stare in the glass.

SAVAGE (*on his knees still*): I don't like mirrors...

SHADE: No one does. (*He places it close to* SAVAGE.)

SAVAGE: Avoided mirrors all my life —

SHADE: Because you're ugly —

SAVAGE: Am I? Yes I —

SHADE: Ugly, yes, go on —

SAVAGE: Shaved without one, you can see —

SHADE: Go on —

SAVAGE: Lots of hairs get missed, my wife, she used to say you are the most ungroomed and unprepossessing man I ever — do you think it honours you to be dishevelled — I shun fashion like a —

SHADE: Digressing, doctor —

SAVAGE: As if for some reason there was sin in elegance.

SHADE: Digression on digression —

SAVAGE: I do find speaking to a mirror very —

SHADE: Now your eyes are shut —

SAVAGE: Are they — my eyes —

SHADE: Shut, yes —

SAVAGE: **I think if love lies anywhere it's on the other side of shame.** (*Pause.*)

CREUSA (*who has entered*):   Don't believe him, will you? His confessions? The routine torrent of his preposterous sins... (SAVAGE *looks at her, very long.*)

SAVAGE (*pause*):   This — vilifying hag — obsessed me with her fundament. The breath turned lead, went solid in my lung, to see her knicker on the stair... I have to say this, she moved me to oaths and superlatives, so I won't speak. Knowledge compels stillness.

SHADE: This private life! I do shudder. This stew of knotted flesh! I do writhe. (*Pause. He turns to* SAVAGE.) How can we make the new man? (*Pause.*) I think he must live in the street. In public always, where nothing uncommon can be done. Can you do this?

SAVAGE: Yes...

SHADE: Laughing. Dancing. I think he should move and think in crowds. Can you write this?

SAVAGE: Yes...

SHADE: Once, when I saw men with miserable faces, staring at the ground, I nutted them. In streets in Attica where I ran yobbish prior to the war I said cheer up you cunt and if they did not grin to order rammed my forehead through their gristle. This was instinct but now I see it also must be politics. (*Pause.*) New Troy. The land of laughter... (*Pause. He looks to* SAVAGE.) Write it, then...

CREUSA: And Helen? (*They look at her.*) Helen who is all clandestine fuck? (*Pause.*)

SHADE: I see no place for Helen, do you, Dr Savage? No place for her in Laughing Troy? Her ego and her filthy legs? Her mouth and acts of endless privacy? She is all I and this is the age of we...

SAVAGE: I has no arms. (*Pause. He looks up, half-curious.*) Does it? The letter? (*Pause.*) I is a single stem? (*Pause.*)

CREUSA (*with rising horror*): Oh, God, he's —

SHADE (*to* SAVAGE): Go on. More cogitation. Further elaboration of the infant thought...

CREUSA: Listen —

SHADE: **I think because I have to.**

SHADE: Oh, yes, you do, you do.

SAVAGE: **And having thought it — out thought! Vile object, out for scrutiny!** (*Pause.*) Helen, who has grown so wild, Helen might be — (*He struggles.*)

CREUSA: Listen, I said —

SHADE: **Shut up, you.** (*Pause. He goes to* SAVAGE.) Won't help the thought to birth. You birth it, you conceived...

SAVAGE: Yes...

SHADE: **Terrible labour of the thought!**

SAVAGE: Pruned... (*Pause.*)

SHADE: Pruned? (*Pause. He walks up and down. Suddenly* SAVAGE *lets out a terrible cry.*)

SAVAGE: **Knowledge!** (SHADE *hurries out, bundling* CREUSA *with him.* SAVAGE *rocks on his knees.* MACLUBY *appears.*)

MACLUBY: Knowledge... (SAVAGE *turns, sees him. He scrambles to his feet.*)

SAVAGE: Helen — got to — Helen — Where's she?

MACLUBY: Wrong way.

SAVAGE: Is it? (*He turns to go the other way.*) Can't move with this —

MACLUBY: Solidarity Street.

SAVAGE: Where's that?

MACLUBY: Near the Us Museum.

SAVAGE: Which way's —

MACLUBY: Quick!

SAVAGE (*tugging at the bin*): How can I, with this thing! (*Pause.* SHADE *enters again, with the key to the manacles. He unlocks them.*)

SHADE: Genius can't be encumbered, can it? Genius? (*He goes out again.* SAVAGE *rubs his wrists.*)

MACLUBY: Moon's gone again... (*Pause.*) Never find yer way...

SAVAGE: Free concerts block the avenues...
MACLUBY (*gazing into him*): Unfortunately... (*Pause.
  Suddenly* SAVAGE *confronts the horror.*)
SAVAGE: All right! (*Pause. He crawls to the mirror* SHADE
  has left, and looks in it.) All right...! (MACLUBY *goes out.*)

Scene Seven

The Street. Sounds of A CONGA. HOGBIN *rushes in.*

HOGBIN: Oi! (THE CONGA *appears, the dancers in sacks.*)
  Somebody! (*They chant.*)
THE CONGA: Got — to — be — so — glad — now —
            Got — to — be — so — glad — now —
            Oh — so — glad —
            Oh — so — glad —
HOGBIN: Listen, will yer! (*They pass by.*) I must stop doin'
  that. I shout oi! And no one shifts. Why should they? The
  Redundant Oi, by Kevin Hogbin. (*He sees* HOMER.) Oi!
  (*He runs up to him.*) I saw three geezers drag a woman off!
HOMER: The first duty of the poet is to survive. (*Pause.*)
HOGBIN: Is it...? (THE CONGA *returns.*)
THE CONGA: Got — to — be — so — glad — now —
            Got — to — be — so — glad — now —
            Oh — so — glad —
HOGBIN (*in despair*):   Can't think, can yer? **Can't fuckin' think!**
  (THE CONGA *departs.*)
HOMER: Testament... Not participation... testament!
HOGBIN: An' 'alf of me says 'dance, Kevin! the beat!' An' 'alf
  says 'put wax in yer ears! Tie down yer feet!'
HOMER: How hard that is! (*He grabs him.*) Listen, my third
  book.
HOGBIN: **Third** book?
HOMER: I sing you my third book.
HOGBIN: Third book...?
HOMER: Listen, I give it to you! Listen! (*Pause.*) The Heroic
  Life of the Citizens of Sacked Cities.
HOGBIN: Long title for you.

HOMER (*pause*):   The Ruinad. (*Pause.*) I sang it once before.
   And they left, singly or in groups, like men who had forgotten
   to post letters, until at the end, I was singing to myself... (*He
   suddenly sobs.*)

HOGBIN: All right...all right...so what...if it's true —
   (THE CONGA *reappears.*) **Oh, fuck them...!** (HOMER *begins
   to sing, but is drowned by* THE CONGA.)

THE CONGA: Got — to — be — so — glad — now —
   Got — to — be — so — glad — now —
   Oh — so — glad —
   Oh — so — glad — (THE CONGA *leaves,
   except for its last member,* GAY, *who listens.*)

HOMER (*audible now*):   You ask me to believe,
   You ask me to believe,
   In the mercy of the gods,
   I say their mercy is only
   A refreshment to their malice... (*He fades, falters.*)

HOGBIN: What? (*Pause.* HOMER *is peering blindly, off.*)
   'omer? (*Pause.*) I'm still 'ere. (*Pause.*) As long as one child is
   'alf attentive, you 'ave an audience. (*Pause.*) 'omer. (*Pause.*) **I
   command the power of your genius!** The people's right to your
   imagination...Give us it! (*Pause, then* EPSOM *passes
   through.*)

EPSOM: Old times...Suddenly, what seemed like always and
   forever, is old times...

HELEN (*entering, supported by* FLADDER, *and bandaged*):
   Murder me. (*She looks round.*) **Murder me**.

HOMER (*who sees nothing*):   Murder Helen? Why?

HELEN: **Murder!** (*Pause.*)

HOMER: You don't mean that.

HELEN: I do. I do mean it.

HOMER: Then why ask? There are cliffs. And ponds. Railway
   tracks, and dynamos —

HELEN: I want to die —

HOMER: Liar —

HELEN: **Look at me**.

HOMER: **Liar**. (*Pause.*)

HOGBIN (*who has been transfixed by the sight of her
   wounds*):   Giggle...! Want to giggle...! Try to be grown up
   but want to giggle...! (*He throws himself at* HELEN'S *feet,
   clasping her ankles.*)

GAY: Has anybody got a doctor?

HELEN: It was a doctor did it.

GAY: Oh, good. Oh, good, because... Let's face it, we have seen some awful things and the presence of trained specialists is comforting... it is! I hate bad hangmen, for example. Ask the hanged, they will tell you, *merci, merci,* for a trained professional...! (*She goes to* FLADDER *and puts her arms round him affectionately.*) She can always grip with her thighs, and her tongue, which they say is of such great versatility, that could become as tensile as a cable... (THE BOY *enters, staring.*)

BOY: Woman got no arms... (*They ignore him. He addresses* HOMER.) Why did you cut her arms off?

GAY: No, it wasn't him...

BOY: Must have been, he —

GAY: No, he only —

BOY: **Yes he did.** (*Pause.*)

HOMER: If I had not made Helen, Helen would not have been disfigured... (*Pause.*) But Helen had to be made...

GAY: **She did not have to be made!** (*She claps her hand to her mouth.*) Oh, I —

Oh, I — Now that was — Really, that was so — Outburst in defiance of all — All right now — (*She is straight, still.*) Still as, and level as, the strand of sand when tides have all receded... there... (*She smiles, cooly.*) Euphoric Gay. (*She goes out.*)

HOGBIN (*going to* HELEN): Be arms for you. Brush teeth. Rub eyes. And scratch you where you itch. Anticipate every move your invisible limbs would make... (*He encloses her.*)

Interlude

TWO MUSLIMS *enter, with a hamper carried by* A EUROPEAN SERVANT. *They gaze over the country.*

ASAFIR: John, flag please.

YORAKIM: Or someone will take a shot.

ASAFIR: Will pot away.

YORAKIM: And make a shambles of the lunch. (THE SERVANT *erects a white flag.*)

ASAFIR: Thank you, now dish away, I famish, I absolutely famish, oh, look, a skull.

YORAKIM: Trojan.

ASAFIR: Greek.

YORAKIM: The unmistakable long jaw of all —

ASAFIR: The instantly recognizable short forehead of the —

TOGETHER: **We joke like this to keep the horror down.**

YORAKIM: Another flag there, John —

ASAFIR: He's serving lunch —

YORAKIM: Yes —

ASAFIR: He's only got two —

YORAKIM: So he has. Two only. I was thinking, however, is it visible from all the promontories?

ASAFIR: Get a flag yourself. (YORAKIM *stares at* ASAFIR.) All right, I will —

YORAKIM: No, John will. (*Pause.*) I do not think myself better than the servant. That is not the issue. The issue is that in showing myself willing to perform his functions, we —

ASAFIR: I can perfectly well —

YORAKIM: **Erode the basis of service.** (*Pause.*) It would. Erode it.

ASAFIR: Yes, but if, in this instance, a flag of truce would make the crucial difference between life and death —

YORAKIM: **It's false! It's false!**

TOGETHER: **We get like this when drawing lines across the world.**

JOHN (*pointing*): **Terrorists!**

YORAKIM (*spilling his tray*): Fuck...!

JOHN: Hundreds of —

YORAKIM: Oh, fuck...!

ASAFIR (*to* JOHN): The pilchards, please...! (*They sit rigidly on the stools.* THE SERVANT *serves.*) Ah, pilchards...!

YORAKIM: Oh, Allah —

ASAFIR: Pilchards, I remark —

YORAKIM (*in control*): Yes

ASAFIR: Pilchards, etcetera.

YORAKIM (*seeing* THE TERRORISTS): With knives...!

ASAFIR: The pilchards have knives...?

YORAKIM: **We are in mortal —**

ASAFIR (*to* THE SERVANT): Show them the maps. Shake out the maps. (THE SERVANT *indicates maps. They fall into sheets. He exhibits them.*) Good. Tell them we are of the neutral powers. Tell them we are mappers of the frontier, accredited by the armistice commission, cartographers with no axe to grind. Show them the seals and *laissez passers* of all parties —

YORAKIM: Fuck and fuck —

ASAFIR: We have no weapons but — (THE SERVANT *is demonstrating certificates*.) **Should hands be raised against us we will call down strikes** —

JOHN (*demonstrating*): Crops — **WOOF!**

ASAFIR: And terrible vengeance will be —

JOHN (*miming*): Huts — **WOOF!**

ASAFIR (*to* YORAKIM): Pilchard?

YORAKIM: I think we are going to be killed.

ASAFIR: Not for the first time.

YORAKIM: Not killed for the first time...?

ASAFIR: Not the first time you have —

YORAKIM: I dreamed this.

ASAFIR: I know.

YORAKIM: When I was a child I dreamed this moment —

ASAFIR: We should have asked for guards. In retrospect we obviously should have asked for guards. I thought the flag would speak but clearly it does not. At least not adequately. I do apologize.

YORAKIM (*describing the dream*): I fall to the ground —

ASAFIR: I don't think John is getting anywhere —

YORAKIM: My head is separated from my body by a single blow —

ASAFIR: Are you, John? Getting anywhere?

YORAKIM: Bounce it goes, and bounce —

ASAFIR (*standing now*): Thank you, anyway —

YORAKIM (*as* GAY *and* OTHERS *enter, armed*): The unusual perspective of a severed head... (*Pause*.)

GAY: I am going to cut your throats. (*Pause*.)

ASAFIR: Why, for goodness' sake?

GAY (*to* JOHN): And you, collaborator, you will be burned in a dust-bin.

ASAFIR: Make the following points, please —

JOHN (*to* GAY): **I wanted a job, mate.**

ASAFIR: One.

YORAKIM: Get a move on, she —

ASAFIR: One. (*He pauses, wearily*.)

YORAKIM: **Go on, then...!** (*Pause*.)

ASAFIR: No, I don't think there is any point...

GAY: You arrogant and half-dead mannikins.

YORAKIM: You have offended her, and now we shall be most cruelly used.

GAY: In your imperialist silks and turbans spun of slavery...

ASAFIR: I have no political opinions, I am a simple adminis- trator of a frontier line but I will not stoop to plead to a European bitch. There! I have given away my feelings and please do it quickly.

JOHN (*desperately*): **I wanted a job for my Mum whose spine has turned to biscuit — all day she cries in bed —**

GAY: Extenuating gibberish. Many of us suffer but how few of us betray.

JOHN: Many of us don't love our mothers —

GAY: **Oh, burn him quick!** (*They drag him away.*) I think, if we heard all the excuses in the world, no action could occur, and justice would attenuate, an incomprehensible word.

ASAFIR: Not a bad thing, surely?

GAY: **You would say that because you are on top.**

ASAFIR: Admittedly. Such is the yawning gulf between our cultures nothing I say can possibly affect you —

YORAKIM: No —

ASAFIR: Were I possessed of all the wisdom of my race it could not —

YORAKIM (*in despair*): No, no, **wrong argument!**

ASAFIR (*to* YORAKIM): I am not concerned with survival, I am concerned with truth.

GAY: Excellent! Because I shall cut your throats whatever you say. You could be utterly persuasive, logically coherent and morally supreme, and I would still act. **Knife!** (*She holds out a hand to* A FOLLOWER.) Does that fill you with despair?

YORAKIM: Yes...

ASAFIR: No...

YORAKIM: **It fills me with despair.**

ASAFIR: I regard it as the essence of the human condition.

GAY (*triumphantly*): In which case it would be a disappoint- ment if you were spared!

ASAFIR (*conceding*): I am hoist with my own philosophy.

GAY: You are! Now take your funny clothes off, you are dying naked.

ASAFIR: Are we not sufficiently within your power but you —

GAY: **Never sufficiently.** (*Pause.*) Do you think I'll let you die with dignity? Your dignity affronts me. **Strip them if they —** (*They let fall their clothes.*) (*of* YORAKIM.) Take this one away and cut his throat.

ASAFIR: Don't kill my colleague. He is terribly in love with life and —

GAY: **That's why I want to rob him of it.** (*They take him out.*) You really do not understand the nature of revenge. Its satisfactions. Do you?

ASAFIR: No. I just draw maps.

GAY: Your false neutrality.

ASAFIR: I make lines on cartridge paper.

GAY: Your spurious privilege.

ASAFIR: And even as I draw the line I think, this line can't last. Sometimes we draw the line down the middle of a church, and sometimes through a mosque. A dozing drunkard with a reed could mark the frontiers just as well.

GAY: Then why —

ASAFIR: It brings me near the essence of all life. (*Pause. She looks at him for a long time. Then extends the knife to another.*)

GAY: Execute him. Because what he tells me I don't wish to know. (*They lead ASAFIR out.*)

ACT TWO

Prologue

MACLUBY: In the ribbon of green a man is hoeing
Refugees

This one tried wit on thieves
This one tried pity on the police
This one wasted irony on the fanatic

In the ribbon of fertility rich horticulturalists
Dispute the skills of sportsmen

The hours are dying like wasps in the jam
Even blood
Would creep out of an artery
With the stray cat's indolence

And the murdered mistress makes no special noise
She does not beat
She does not hammer with her heels
The hanging gong of the afternoon

The silence of the valley is held breath
The outbreak
Lives in the contingency
The effect of the day's taste in the mouth
Not just the act
But the choice the act induced

Sarajevo did not cause the death of fifteen
Million

The theft of Helen did not cause the Siege of Troy

Or Japan's atrocity Hiroshima

No more causes of wars will do
Not just the act
But the choice the act induced

Shh
All peace is stopped breath
Shh
All love's suspension of returning solitude

At night the temple trembles
And the park is tense

Its false orders
Its unearthly symmetry

It knows its chance is brief

We inscribed the fountain as if we believed
This dispensation was eternal
The empire was unshakable
And at the spectacle of culture
Dirty tribesmen would not
                    could not
                    but kneel

Oh, the tomb's false request for exemption
                    This at least
                    This surely must
                    This cannot but command
Your temperance
You yet unborn
You yet to conquer

The cynicism of the generations
Is no less atomizing than the swipe of weapons
Wielded by the hour's enemy

                    That was my only
                    What is that trivial thing to you
                    Your passion for destruction might at
                    Least

The litter of unavailing arguments
A cloud of disbelief in every tongue

Drifts out of cities
Giving earth her rings
More terrible than Saturn

We enter after the siege
We do a little killing

We are not old fashioned
We do not spare the women

We string up the resisters
As we are permitted

We tickle the infant's chin
And watch its sister spitted

And with the draining out of this joyful
Malevolence experience depression such as the
Act of an unequal love induces

We played cards with the survivors
Whose grins were false
I was sorry to detect...

Scene One

SAVAGE *is seated and with authority.*

SAVAGE: My great peace. **Who could like me now?** My restoration. **Who could see me without hatred?** I no longer sit on the edge of the chair. My arse spreads. My arse occupies! **Dr Savage supremely vile, enter all suppliants!** (*He leaps up as a crowd surrounds him.*) Not there! Don't come any nearer! Not there, there! **Silence!** Speak when I indicate you thus — a finger pointed — no shoving — **My wisdom is available to all** — I said no shoving — thus far and no further — **Shut up and still as gargoyles** — (*He points.*) You! (*He feigns attention.*) Mm. (*Pause.*) Mm. (*Pause.*) Mm. (*Pause.*) Enough. The details are — you go on — like an old woman who has the doctor's ear — **Stop.** (*Pause.*) I meditate. (*Pause.*) I pass judgement. Of course the verdict's the source of future quarrel! **Next!** You! Not you! The one with the bulbous nose — **Have you got a bulbous nose?** You have? The physiognomy of Trojan archetypes! The wall-eyed, then. (*Pause.*) Mm. (*Pause.*) Mm. (*Pause.*) Mm. (*As he performs this,* HELEN *enters, watches unseen.*) Mm. (*Pause.*) **Stop!** I meditate. (*Pause.*) I pass judgement. Of course the wrong man suffers! **Next!** You! Not you! The one with jug ears — not you — **Have you got jug ears?** You have? The classic feature of the Trojan race! The hare-lipped, then. (*Pause.*) Mm. (*Pause.*) Mm. (*Pause.*) Mm. (*Pause.*) I tire of — the plethora of ramification — **Precis is the key to justice, stop!** (*He rolls on his knees, laughing, sees* HELEN, *is still. He holds up his hands.*) No bin. (*He stares at her. He claps his hands.* THE SUPPLIANTS *depart.*) The political arrangements of Laughing Troy leave much to be desired but — (*Pause.*) Always we talk of making a new man but the old man will insist — (*Pause.*) His servile habits — his melancholy aspect — (*Pause.*) And the tendency of poets to crop up like weeds and spread dissent but only for dissension's sake, why? Why? (*Pause.*) Someone is chalking walls with very long words, who? (*Pause.*) And laughter...! You would think sometimes they were pissing milk crates, judging by their rictus jaws. (*Pause.*) There is a medical disorder called Iron Cheek, have you heard? The oiling of the jawbone with whalefat offers some relief but laughter seems to hurt the face as I imagine endless weeping would, it's epidemic and some have died, no one predicted this but — (*He stares at her.*) When you were whole I did not feel for you what — (HOGBIN *appears, skips behind* HELEN.) **Who said he could come in...!** This retinue, this circus of the maimed and callow — it spoils your —

HOGBIN: 'ho says I'm callow? I say you're 'ollow.

SAVAGE: Dignity in suffering!

HOGBIN: You say callow, I say hollow, you say shallow, and I say —

SAVAGE: **Does he have to accompany you at all times of —**

HELEN: Yes. (*Pause.*)

HOGBIN: I say you could 'ave more limbs than an octopus and still not grasp a simple truth, such as —

SAVAGE: **Shut up you —**

HOGBIN: Pity makes your cock big, so pity's only power — **Oi!**

SAVAGE: **I do not see you**. (*Pause.*)

HOGBIN: 'e doesn't see me ...

SAVAGE: He does not exist, however present he may be.

HOGBIN: I don't exist ...

SAVAGE: Like the butler in the bedroom, or the skivvy at the hearth, to the master you're invisible.

HOGBIN (*screwing himself into a combination of the three monkeys*): I'm invisible ... (*Pause.* SAVAGE *grapples with speech.*)

SAVAGE: I have followed you down streets ... and where I saw you once ... returned ... at the same hour ... fruitlessly, of course ... what is your itinerary ... you do presumably go ... I **will persist with this** ... you have your places but I obviously (*Pause.*) My lungs, my stomach have all gone void and howling with — (*In desperation he extends a hand to her.*) Helen — (*Suddenly* HOGBIN *slaps his face.*)

HOGBIN: There!

SAVAGE (*reeling*): What —

HOGBIN (*darting behind* HELEN): Her arms, not mine! (SAVAGE *makes to grab him.*) **Her arms ...!** (*He pretends to scratch* HELEN'S *neck.*)

HELEN: What?

SAVAGE: How can I when —

HELEN: What? (*Pause.*)

SAVAGE: I have to be your lover. I who invented your condition **Must**. (*Pause.*)

HELEN: To be my lover? And what is that? (*Pause.*)

SAVAGE: What is it ...?

HELEN: **What is it, yes!**

HOGBIN (*to* SAVAGE): Are you deaf or something? You talk about the beginning and she wants to know the end. (SAVAGE *reaches out. Again* HOGBIN *beats his hand away.* SAVAGE *reels.*) Thinks to finger me. Thinks to touch specific parts will weaken all resistance. He's read a book on the erogenous zones which says the touch kills argument.

SAVAGE: Help me.

HOGBIN: **Help you? Help you?**

SAVAGE: I twist. I writhe. I'm poisoned. Mind a slab of concrete and the minutes hang off me like crankshafts, I could snap the hands off clocks they move so sullenly, **The length of a**

night, do you know **the impossible duration of a single night,** I lick the clouds for dawn, and cats, I know their tracks and habits, the wriggle of the tomcat's arse and all the lashing of dawn choruses, **It hurts to look at you,** I would chuck imagination in the ditch and bury it for one moment of your sad mouth against my sad mouth — (*He sees* HOGBIN'S *expression.*) **What's he to you, the grinning bastard?** (*He bites his lip. Pause.*)

HELEN: Nothing new. (*Pause.*)

SAVAGE: No...

HELEN: In your message. (*Pause.*)

SAVAGE: Well, no...

HELEN: Is there?

SAVAGE: I suppose there wouldn't be —

HELEN: Nothing new in that. (*Pause.*) Why maim me? (*Pause.*) **I was already a spectacle of pain, why else did they want me?** (SAVAGE *stares at her.*) Beauty did you say? No, it's pain they loved... (HOGBIN'S *hands reach up to* SAVAGE'S *face, and hold him.*) My kiss is stiff as brick, and my womb full of straw...but he won't mind... (*He draws* SAVAGE *to* HELEN'S *breast.*) Arid Helen...But he won't mind... (SAVAGE *shudders.*) Listen, his male murmur, his male thirst... (CREUSA *enters, looks.*)

CREUSA: Who needs arms to fasten in their buttocks? (*Pause.*)

HOGBIN: I can't see you today...

CREUSA: **I'll thrust my arms in a reaping machine, will that make me popular?** (*Pause.*)

HOGBIN: I can't see you today...

CREUSA: Well, no, you've got work to do. **Should I stuff my arse in a shredder?**

SAVAGE (*catching a sound*): Shh! (*Pause.*)

CREUSA: Mums' Troy.

SAVAGE: Shh!

CREUSA: I plant it like a seed. Mums' Troy. It sprouts. It blooms. It sends out runners.

SAVAGE (*getting to his feet*): Listen! (*Pause. He cups his ear.*) No laughter...

HOGBIN (*straining his ear*): No drums.

SAVAGE: Or rattles. **The tambourine has ceased, hey!**

SHADE (*running in*): **Silence...! Where's it coming from?**

HOGBIN (*pointing arbitrarily*): There... (EPSOM *and* GUMMERY *hurry in.*)

SHADE (*indicating*): There! (EPSOM *rushes in the direction.*)

HOGBIN: No, there! (GUMMERY *looks in bewilderment, and* EPSOM *returns, blankly.*)

EPSOM: Hold it ...

SHADE: Noises are starting in my head. The whispering of shared and subtle sacraments. Start a carnival! (*No one moves. Pause.*) I hear the little stirring of the private act. Make the bands play! (*Still no one moves. Realisation dawns on* SHADE. *He walks slowly across the stage, stops.*) The word today is — (*Suddenly, as if impulsively,* GUMMERY *seizes* SHADE *in his arms, pinioning him and lifting him off the ground.*)

GUMMERY: No word!

SHADE: Oh, Brian, you — Oh, Brian, you magnificent specimen, I twitch in your embrace as the helpless hamster in the infant's fingers. **But to what effect!** (*Pause.*) All right, I'll have a tantrum. (*He kicks his legs like a baby.*) Tantrum, all right? Now, can we get back to politics, we have a state to govern. (*Pause.*)

GUMMERY: What shall I do? (*He turns to anyone who will listen.*) What shall I do? (*Pause.*)

SHADE: Come on, Brian, they will be missing you in the gymnasium. Put me down, will you. (*Pause.*)

GUMMERY: I can't put you down.

SHADE: You can't? Why not?

GUMMERY: Because I picked you up.

SHADE: What? Logic! Logic! Can't put me down because you — logic! Logic!

GUMMERY: I picked you up to stop you, and if I put you down you'll start again. So I can't put you down. (*Pause.*)

SHADE: Well, Brian, you have a problem. It comes of making gestures that you can't complete.

EPSOM: Put him down if he promises to —

SHADE: **No deals**.

EPSOM: Barry, you ain't in much of a position to —

SHADE: **I am in the best position. I have the brain**. (*Pause.*) Really, who would credit this? People don't know how they're governed.

GUMMERY (*to* EPSOM): I don't know what to do ...

SHADE: You don't, do you? You really don't.

GUMMERY: Les? (EPSOM *shrugs.*)

SHADE: No luck with Les.

GUMMERY: **Shuddup will yer!** (*Pause.*)

SHADE: I won't ask if your arms are aching because you are in such wonderful condition no doubt you could keep this up for weeks, I only ask you, in all humbleness, do you know what you're doing? (*Pause*.)

GUMMERY: No.

SHADE: Excellent. Point of departure. Now, put me on the ground and we —

CREUSA: No —

SHADE: What?

CREUSA: No —

SHADE: Come again —

CREUSA: Don't —

SHADE: Brian, this is a Trojan bitch —

CREUSA: Put him down and they'll hate you in every bar between the dockyards and the allotments —

SHADE: Brian —

CREUSA: Women will knit your shape in wool and men throw darts at it —

SHADE: Listen, we fought ten years for one whore, don't let another —

CREUSA: **Keep him up, I said.**

SHADE: **Come on, Doctor, it's your government!** (*Pause*.) Oh doctor...I think you wear silence like a tart wears frocks, half off the shoulder...to make more appetizing the hagflesh underneath... **Anything underneath?** (*Pause*.)

SAVAGE: I must betray you, do you mind? (*Pause*.) I am a traitor by instinct, because to doubt is treason, and I doubt commitment even as I utter it, whether to women or the state. Have you not noticed, I write constitutions as boys make planes from glue and balsa? (*Pause*.) And now you ache to punish me. I do understand that, the thirst for punishment, I do know disloyalty burns the stomach to a cinder. (*Pause*.) Don't put him down, he'll only ram sharp things in our eyes...

Scene Two

FLADDER, *seated, weaves a massive basket.*

HELEN: When you lost your tongue, did you stop thinking? (*He looks at her.*) The contrary, of course. (*Pause*.) And so with

me. (*Pause.*) **Armless I still reach out, why?** (*Pause. He works.*) I
tell you this because you are my husband. Come what may, this
fuck or that, this famine or this riot, you are my husband.
(*Pause.*) Funny word. I think it means, like old domestic dog,
or cat, **had teeth once. Was wild in certain states.** (*He stops.*) Oh,
don't weep. **Don't weep I honour you.** (*Pause.*) All right, not
honour, I don't honour you. I retail my life. (*Pause.*) **Who else
should I tell?** I am carrying the doctor's child. (*Pause.*) I think.
(*Pause.*) Do do the raffia. Weave on. (*Pause. She spontaneously
goes to him, nuzzles his head.*) Oh, you must have developed so
much in your silence, I think if your late wisdom was inscribed
I'd say, **Brilliant but utterly incomprehensible!** So remote you
are, so distant from our — (CREUSA *appears.* HELEN *turns
to face her.*) Don't pester me, I can still kick.

CREUSA: Answer —
HELEN: You bother like a barmy wasp — you cling —
CREUSA: Answer —
HELEN: **What is it, jam on my lip?**
CREUSA: **Why aren't you ashamed of your life? I insist you're
ashamed of your life.** (*Pause.*) I think my cunt drips acid and if
he were to enter me I'd scald the seven skins off him, **Whose
child is it,** I make a fool of myself, obviously, an utter fool, they
say the ex-queen's cracked, half her head's turned biscuit, and
then I think, a fool, so what, a fool to who? I won't stuff hatred
down, a little wire sawing away inside my gut and grin all
rights, I won't! (*Pause.*)
HELEN: He stands behind me.
CREUSA: Yes.
HELEN: And close.
CREUSA: Go on.
HELEN: His belly — you want to know this, do you —
CREUSA: Yes —
HELEN: To my arse and so — (*Pause.*)
CREUSA: Go on — please — (*Pause.*)
HELEN: No more.
CREUSA: **More. Yes!**
HELEN: You want the pain. You want it…how you want…
(*Pause.*)
CREUSA: The hate grows on my gums at night. Thick paste of
loathing. I spit it in the sink. (HOGBIN *enters gaily.*)
HOGBIN (*holding them out*): Washed our hands! (*He sees*
CREUSA, *stops. She goes out.*)

HELEN: Twelve Troys! (*He goes to feed her from a bowl.*)
Twelve Troys and then —
HOGBIN: Egg mayonnaise!
HELEN: Twelve Troys and then what?
HOGBIN: Twelve?
HELEN: Twelve, yes. And me to suffer under every one!
(*Pause. He stares at her.*)
HOGBIN (*thrusting it to her lips*):   Brown bread —
HELEN: **No bread!**
HOGBIN: Egg, then —
HELEN: **No egg!**
HOGBIN: Must eat —
HELEN: Why eat? To live? For what? For love? Whose love?
HOGBIN: Yer going on —
HELEN: Your love? **I have no arms! I watch, I listen, Helen has
nine Troys to suffer, all right, I eat, all right, the bread, the egg, I
persevere, shh!** (*He feeds her.*)
GAY (*entering*).**Mums' Troy**:   The first lesson. (*Pause.*) I am not
a mum. But I did write the lesson. (*Pause.*) In the first place
was the **Aristocracy,** and they were so idle they gave away their
infants to others to suckle, so the infants grew up most confused regarding love, not distinguishing their mothers from
their nurses or their arses from their lips, and consequently
plundered the world with icy hardness. And after them came the
Democrats, who believed life was too short for privilege, so
they sent their infants into **schools** to learn the way of the
world, and they emerged from schools like tigers, intent on
butchering the **weak**. And finally there came the **Loving
Mothers,** who kept their infants close, breathing the breath of
the child and sleeping its sleep, so each single child grew up full
of certainty the world loved her, which it did, to some extent.
But so did all the others, **Love's a drug, you see,** and they tore
each other to ribbons in their jealousy! (*Pause.*) Unofficial
version. (*A thunderous noise.*)

Scene Three

SHADE, *imprisoned in the woven basket, is raised by pulleys drawn by* EPSOM *and* GUMMERY. SAVAGE *watches.*

SHADE: Oh, dear, I shall get wet...! The piss of Zeus will shrink me like a garment, sodden one minute and bleached the next **I like it here incidentally** I'll shrivel until this little floor is vast as plains which take me days to scuttle over **I always wanted this, didn't you know?** My longing to be stopped — (*He touches the sides.*) Edge! Edge! **Oh, lovely limit to my dream!** Goodbye, Brian, and goodbye, Les, I shrink, you great empire builders, *au revoir*, I have my provinces as well, **What's Rome to a galaxy? What's Russia in the sun? Speck, Brian, Speck!** (*He is still.* GUMMERY *and* EPSOM *leave.* SAVAGE *watches the basket.*)

SAVAGE: Because I was an intellectual I chose to follow thought, thought to the finish, that is the duty of one, isn't it? The finger of thought beckoned me past the frontier post where others who had been my equals stood or waved me through, **Yes, you stay behind and court your admirers,** oh, the teachers with their followings, the gifted with their cliques, they carve their names in wet cement to the sound of the acolyte's giggles, **Dance on the skin of knowledge** but don't fall through, you'll drop forever. (*Pause.*) **Helen!** (*Pause.*) It howls here and no cunning girls of seventeen think I am fascinating, no youths can be seduced in my dim study or learn the trivial habits of depravity over set texts, **Knickers and Kafka, Saliva and The Greeks! Helen!** (*She enters, with* HOGBIN, *looks at him.*)

HELEN: Oh, my ugly lover...

SAVAGE: Yes...

HELEN: Oh, my shapeless adorer, would you hack my legs off also? Legless, would you desire me more?

SAVAGE: I don't...

HELEN: You do know, yes, you do...

SAVAGE: I don't...

HELEN: **What part, then...!** (*He hides his face.*) What joint or knuckle, what pared-down, shredded, particle would serve to be the point at which your love would say stop, **Essential Helen?** Slithering over rocks, some sliver of cheek or gum, there! Saw her! Flap of appendix in the rock pool! (*He goes to reach for her.*) Don't come near me. The greater the space between us, the more I suffer. It conducts my heat. She tells me I must be ashamed. I'm unashamed. And so are you. Twice the dead of Troy and I would not apologize. I have your child or maybe not, all this and unashamed. (*He goes to reach for her.*) Don't come nearer...! You will kill my ecstasy! (*He stops.*) They hate me in Mums' Troy, they hate me worse than ever Shade or Fladder did, can it be true that every life is precious, can it? Mums' Troy is babies, all the kerbs are padded and the rivers hung with nets, breasts out in the market and the endless music of their gurgles, the **preposterous claim of life** —

SAVAGE: Kiss me —

HELEN: Your squirt, my fluid, look out, **Claims from the muddy water!** They all want their ninety years and I brought whole regiments to earth like flies on wallpaper...

SAVAGE: Kiss me —

HELEN: **The Snail's insistence on its rights!** (*She halts him.*) If I saw a baby drift by on a raft of rushes I would not lift a finger for it, though the river bubbled it to sharks or iceflows, pity, the great unending ribbon of pity, it has no end except exhaustion, I have a child in me and yet I hacked the features off dying boys, and I have watched priests visit the starving whilst eating sandwiches, but listen, the doctor must be fed! The doctor must eat even if the patient starves, that's logical! All this logic! All this pity! Kiss me, now. Kiss me...! (*He kisses her.*) Your mouth would draw me in and make me vanish, a sweet in your jaw, sucked to oblivion... (*They kiss.*)

HOGBIN (*withdrawing from their embrace*): Nine Troys to go...!

GAY (*off*): Psst!

HOGBIN: Wha'?

GAY: Psst!

HOGBIN: Where! (*He stares in the dark.*) Can't see yer, here —

GAY (*emerging*): Got to have a baby.

HOGBIN: Got to 'ave a —

GAY: You'll do.

HOGBIN: Me? What 'ave you —

GAY (*jerking her skirt up*): Like this —

HOGBIN: Hold on —

GAY. **What for**. (*She glares at him.*) New Troy's for babies. So. (*Pause.*)

HOGBIN: Look I —

GAY: **What!** (*Pause.*)

HOGBIN: No will. And no desire. Sorry.

GAY: Look, pregnant women get three ration books. That's will. I got my legs open. That's desire. Now do it.

HOGBIN: I can't just —

GAY: **You are interfering with my happiness.** (*Pause.*) The happiness I'm entitled to, you are frustrating it.

HOGBIN: Ask someone else.

GAY: I have done. I just asked Homer. Homer can't.

HOGBIN: He can't!

GAY: Apparently he can't. He wept. Absurd. And he's been pestering me for years. (*Pause. He looks away.*) Really, if you were a dog, you would. Have you seen dogs? (*He shakes his head.*) If you don't, I'm down the harbour. (*Pause. She turns swiftly.*)

HOGBIN: Don't do that.

GAY: Why not? Lots of dogs down there, in sailors' outfits, woof! (*She laughs. Then she puts her arms round his neck. Sound of infantile wailing.*)

Scene Four

GUMMERY, EPSOM *enter with babies under each arm, which they place on the ground.* MACLUBY *enters, passing* HOGBIN, OTHERS, *also carrying babies. The stage rapidly fills with babies, as the carriers come and go.*

MACLUBY: The land restocked. (*They gurgle.* CREUSA *brings two further armfuls.*) The terrible regime of innocence. (*And others.*) Its jurisprudence.

CREUSA: **Why fucking not**.

MACLUBY (*shrugs*): No reason.

CREUSA: No reason. And who wants it? Reason brought us to extinction's edge. **No reason in Mums' Troy**. (*Babies are filling the stage.*) We found a scientist and made him sweep the street. He swept the street but chalked formulae on kerbs. So we gave him lavatories to swab. He swabbed the lavatories but made secret drawings on the underside of seats. So we executed him. It is a sickness, curiosity.

EPSOM (*putting down* A BABY):   'oo's a little baby, then, 'oo's a little —

CREUSA: You are mocking that child.

EPSOM: Am I? Sorry.

CREUSA: The child is your superior.

EPSOM: Yup.

CREUSA: A moral genius compared to you.

EPSOM: Yup.

CREUSA (*to* GAY):   Gay, please.

GAY: The Second Lesson of Mums' Troy.

CREUSA: Louder. They will be silent if you interest them. They will be attentive if you win their respect.

GAY: Yes... (*She clears her throat.*) **The Second Lesson of Mums' Troy**.

CREUSA: A baby is not a baby.

GAY: No.

CREUSA: It is an adult in a state of moral excitement.

GAY: Yes.

CREUSA: Go on.

GAY: Innocence is not without authority! Nor does purity go unarmed! The meaningless violence of Old Troys is replaced by the liberating force of pre-articulacy — (*To* CREUSA.) They aren't listening —

CREUSA: Oh, yes, they are —

GAY: Are they?

CREUSA: Go on —

GAY (*louder*):   Spared language but also spared — (*She turns to* CREUSA *in despair.*) I can't seem to make them —

CREUSA: You are imposing oppressive notions of silence and discipline on them. They are engrossed —

GAY (*puzzled*):   They're —

CREUSA. **Engrossed**. (*She stamps her foot on the ground.*) **Shhh**. (*Silence. Pause.*) Where's Helen? (EPSOM *looks at* GUMMERY.) Fetch Helen, please. (*They go out. Gurgles of contentment fill the stage.* CREUSA *walks up and down between* THE BABIES. HELEN *appears, with* SAVAGE. *Pause.*) Helen, where's your baby? (*Pause.*) Ask you again. (*Pause.*) Where's your baby? (*Pause.* THE BABIES *begin to fret.*) Oh, God, they sense catastrophe... (*She stamps her foot. Silence.*) Helen, is your baby still alive? (*Pause.* THE BABIES *start to cry.*) Oh, they cry with horrible anticipation...!

SAVAGE: She —

CREUSA: **Shut up, you.** Helen, have you...terrible to speak this but...have you...awful but we must endure...

SAVAGE: She is the —

CREUSA: **Shut up, you!** (*Pause.*) Betrayed the sacred trust of motherhood...? (*Pause.*) Have you, my dear? (*She stamps her foot.* THE BABIES *are still.*)

HELEN: It died.

CREUSA: Of what?

HELEN: Insignificance. (THE BABIES *screech.*)

GUMMERY: **Mur — der!**

HELEN: You should know.

CREUSA: You stifled innocence. You hung a cloth over its face.

HELEN: Innocence? No, it was guilty. They all are.

CREUSA: Of what?

HELEN: Aborting love.

CREUSA (*to a rage of* BABIES): They accuse! They prosecute!

GAY (*ignoring* THE COURT, *to* HOGBIN): Love you.

HOGBIN: What?

GAY: Love you!

HELEN: The more you sin yourselves, the more you must insist on innocence, you impose it on your infants.

CREUSA: **To kill your own child...**

HELEN: It would have been a killer, too, of the love I suffer for its father. I never let a child come in the way of love. You know the appetite of babies. And this one was voracious. (THE BABIES *strike new notes.*) Half my sons slew men they never knew, and half my daughters slept with murderers...!

CREUSA: You stuffed a pillow on its face!

HELEN: I was more charitable than that.

CREUSA: How, then?

HELEN: I did it with my breast. (THE BABIES *are stunned with horror.*) A breast is milk, but also, pillow...

EPSOM: Brian, I think I will be sick...

GUMMERY: A mother kills her — I can't say it — with 'er — I can't say it —

GAY (*to* HOGBIN): We'll grow old together! I'll be an old apple, and you'll be an old pear...!

EPSOM: We should 'ave murdered 'er! (*He comforts a nearby* BABY.*) Oochie, coochie, coochie...When she stood in the ruins of Old Troy — oochie, coochie! Murdered her!

CREUSA (*walking among* THE BABIES): Some want revenge ...but others...call for clemency...

HELEN: They hate...

CREUSA: Not hate...

HELEN: Hate, wordlessly. What they would not give for a word! And we, who have words, **scream...**

CREUSA: Call for clemency, from there... (*She indicates* A BABY.) He argues...

EPSOM: It's a she.

CREUSA: She persuades. She is most effective. And they (*she indicates all* THE OTHERS.) agree! Your plea —

HELEN: I made no plea —

CREUSA: Your plea finds sympathy! I am so happy for you! (*Pause.*) But at the same time — our disapproval must be registered. The act may be forgiven, but it must be marked... (*Pause. She walks among* THE BABIES.) How quiet they are, not vindictive, but melancholy, philosophical...

HELEN: Oh, listen...the prelude to my pain...

SAVAGE: Helen!

HELEN: The gulf of imagination yawns...

SAVAGE: Helen! (*Pause.* CREUSA *moves silently among* THE BABIES. *Stops. Pause.*)

CREUSA: They ask...in all humility...for him who suffers most...to choose... (*She looks at* SAVAGE. HELEN *lets out a terrible laugh. Pause.*)

HOGBIN: Hold it...

CREUSA: Shut up...

HOGBIN: Not 'im, not 'im, 'e's —

HELEN (*to* HOGBIN): **You stifle him. His mind. Its dream. You trample him**. (*Pause.*)

SAVAGE: They say... (*Pause.*) If I interpret them... (*Pause.*) You have failed to be a mother, and therefore should not look like one... (THE BABIES *screech.*) **I said it! I said it!**

CREUSA (*to* EPSOM, GUMMERY): Out — quick — and do it!

HELEN: Oh, I'll be good! Oh, this time, promise! I'll be good!

HOGBIN (*to* SAVAGE): **Maniac!**

SAVAGE: Don't you want to know! Oh, don't you **want**!

HOGBIN: Helen! (EPSOM *and* GUMMERY *lead* HELEN *away.*)

SAVAGE: You want to save her. But she can't be saved. **I know what Helen is**. (HOGBIN *hurries after.*) She could have reared the child in a garden. She could have stayed in Greece. **Always the possibility of silent life but...** (*He walks through* THE BABIES.) And he throws his pity at her, like confetti in a hurricane...

CREUSA: You know too much.

SAVAGE: Yes.

CREUSA: **Do you know you can know too much**.

SAVAGE: Yes. I know even that. (*Pause.* THE BABIES *begin complaining.*)

CREUSA (*to* THE ADULTS): Clear them out. (THE ADULTS *collect up the bundles and carry them away.* SAVAGE *sees* MACLUBY.)

SAVAGE: How many selves have we got, MacLuby? (MACLUBY *looks at him.*) Old self, grab it, can we? Old self off the shelf? (*He stops.*) Show us an old self, MacLuby!

MACLUBY: Trembling...

SAVAGE: Yes...

MACLUBY: Shuddering...

SAVAGE: Yes, but not with horror! How you would love that!

MACLUBY: Me? No.

SAVAGE: How philistine and trite! My grappling with conscience, my submission and supine apology, suicide from a borrowed rope, no. (MACLUBY *shrugs, sets off.*) Show us an old self. (*He stops.*)

MACLUBY: Wants to reach into the wardrobe —

SAVAGE: Yes —

MACLUBY: Take an old self off the hanger —

SAVAGE: Yes —

MACLUBY: Blow the dust off and —

SAVAGE: Why not? How else can I see if I've travelled? (*Pause.* SAVAGE'S SON *enters. They stare at one another.*)

BOY (*tossing a bar of soap*): Ashes of roses... (*Pause.*)

SAVAGE: What...?

BOY: Ashes of roses... (*Pause.*)

SAVAGE: Good... (CREUSA *enters, gesticulating wildly to* EPSOM *and* GUMMERY.)

CREUSA: He said —

EPSOM: We 'eard what he said —

CREUSA: He said — **She was not a Mother** —

GUMMERY: We —

CREUSA: **Listen — exact words — Therefore she should not look like one** —

EPSOM: She doesn't —

CREUSA: **What!**

EPSOM: She doesn't look like one. (*Pause of exasperated disbelief. To* GUMMERY.) Does she? (GUMMERY *shakes his head.*)

CREUSA: What's a mother got?

EPSOM: What's a —

CREUSA: **Yes, what?** (*They stare at one another in bewilderment. CREUSA tears open her garment.*) **It's breasts she's got!** (*Pause.*)

EPSOM (*at the point*):   We'll go back and — (CREUSA *catches sight of* THE BOY, *standing. She stares at him. Pause.*) Shall we? (*She goes to him, smells his hair, his skin. Pause. She sits on the ground.*) Go back and — (*She does not reply. A wind grows from a whisper.*)

Scene Five

HOGBIN *enters with a dish on a pole, which he extends to the cage. He waits. He grows impatient.*

HOGBIN: Dinn — er! (*The wind. Pause.*) Dinn — er! (*Pause. He puts down the pole, flashes his torch at the cage. It is empty. He turns the torch off, then on again. He falls heavily to the floor.*) **Ed — u — cat — tion!** (*He seizes the pole. Wields it.*) Against irrationality the pole of knowledge! **Off!** (*He prods at the air. Pause. He approaches the cage.*) Are you in there? (*Pause.*) Are you, though...? (*Pause.*) Come again...? (*Pause.* HOGBIN *emits a cry of horror. A tiny laugh from the cage. He sinks to the floor. Daylight.* HELEN *enters, armless, legless, pushed by* HOMER *in a chair.*)

HELEN: I've missed you! I really have! I went to brush my hair, and where were my arms? I went to get out of bed, and where were my legs? Fortunately my creator appeared and lent me limbs, but he can't do a woman justice as you can, look, he's got my blouse on back to front. I didn't criticise. He is at least a hundred, aren't you. One hundred at least. Gay says you love each other, but how can you, there is nothing to love, or do you love that? Do you love her vacancy and plan to write your signature across her void? My stumps hurt when the wind is in the East, which is the prevailing angle **The more they injure me the more they hate,** can you explain that? You're educated. (*He looks at her.*) They want to pity me, it is their only hope,

but I am not pitiful, am I? I cannot think why they neglect my
face, it is the obvious starting point, but perhaps they need to
see me weep. I do weep. Or shout an accusation. They long to
be accused. **I won't satisfy them.** (*Pause.*) My clothes are so
exquisite, I found a woman who understands the trunk, as
form, its own aesthetic, and her hemming is magnificent. I
think in future we shall all be mutants, we shall be born so,
and all limbs will be knobs, and some will have more, and some
will have less, and there will be such a wonderful variety! It will
happen in the womb, how I don't know, some fine powder will
fall from the sky, or something in the water, and we will be
such a fascinating menagerie! I set this fashion, as I did in
Attica, I was slavishly copied there, but now I am rather too
progressive. Do you know what Doctor Savage says, he says I
am two mouths, that's all. **Two mouths!** And I ran every
morning in Old Troy. While Paris kipped his coital kip I was
up and tearing through the market, the porters' bawdy in the
slipstream of my arse! They pelted me with fruit and once I let
them cluster me, on sacks. But only once. Royalty is loved for
its transgressions but not habitually. (*Pause.*) Are you deserting
me? (*Pause.*)

HOGBIN: I am losing my mind...

HELEN: Which mind? The one you brought to Troy with you?

HOGBIN: **Which mind?**

HELEN: Yes. Which? Do you think you lose your mind? You
find others. Do you think you lose your sight? You see by
other channels. And the legless also manoeuvre! I once saw a
fingerless woman with twelve inch thumbs. **Of course I say this
to console myself.** (*Pause.*) You want your mind, but why? To
document your pain? To put order in it? To fix its mayhem,
why? **Welcome Pain I always was expecting you.** Even in copulation, even in the madness of torrential fuck I knew my
agony awaited me. Is Gay delivered of her monster yet?

HOGBIN: It's not a monster.

HELEN: How do you know?

HOGBIN: Because we're healthy.

HELEN: Healthy? What's health to do with it? Of course it is a
monster but it merely lacks the strength **Shh! I was punished for
saying this last month, Shh!** (*She looks at* HOMER.) This man
is a monster, aren't you?

HOMER: Yes.

HELEN: I believe he would torture the world to death, for
disappointment.

HOMER: Yes.

HELEN: Poets' Troy will be the worst yet. **Poets' Troy, duck you innocents!** (*Pause. To* HOGBIN.) Hold me, and tell me what I feel like. I cannot hold myself.

HOGBIN: I can't.

HELEN: Why ever not?

HOGBIN: I'll only — I'll get all — start to —

HELEN: Go on, then —

HOGBIN: No.

HELEN: **Hold me...!** (*He goes to her, puts his arms round her. Pause.*)

HOGBIN: I want —

HELEN: What? What do you want?

HOGBIN: A clean, white shirt... (*Pause.*) A tie... (*Pause.*) And trousers, with a perfect crease... (*Pause.*)

HOMER: When Troy fell I followed Odysseus. I followed him because I could not bring myself to look into the ruins. We all knew, there was a history in the ruins. But I thought, there will be no public for a song about the ruins...

HOGBIN: **It's your job, you bastard**. (*Pause.* CREUSA *enters.*)

CREUSA: Your wife's in labour. (HOGBIN *detatches himself from* HELEN, *starts to go.*) The Mums are in attendance. But you may wait. You wait, and pace. Up and down, you pace. Your painless hours. Pitiable thing. (*He goes out. To* HELEN *with joy.*) Another baby! (*Pause.*) My son appeared.

HELEN: Did he?

CREUSA: As if to cleanse me. My lost son. As if to make the juice of kindness flow from my dry and withered ducts. Tears from the baked kernels of my eyes. As if, flinging our arms about each other we would cry, 'Forgive...!'

HELEN: And...?

CREUSA: And I would be washed in pity and walk with a serenity I never found in all my kicked-up life...

HELEN: But...?

CREUSA: It isn't like that. (*Pause. Then* HELEN *laughs.*) Yes, do laugh. You know, don't you, it isn't like that? The redemption? The reunion? All lies? (HELEN *laughs.*) She knows, she knows better than you! (*She looks at* HOMER.) **Redemption fuck**. (*Pause.*) No, we change, we do change. There's the misery. Except for you. (*Pause.*) He told them, tear your breasts off. But they made a torso out of you instead. Men don't grasp metaphors, do they? Not swift to connect. Under the circumstances the babies recommend you may keep the rest —

HELEN: I thank the babies —

CREUSA: Do you?

HELEN: Profusely. (*Pause.*)

CREUSA: I think even as you say a thing, you know it to be
false. You know it, and yet you say it. I think you are the
enemy of all Troys no matter whose. I think you believe
nothing and therefore ought to suffer everything imagination
might conceive. **I am a better person than you.**

HELEN: Yes.

CREUSA: However cruel.

HELEN: Yes.

CREUSA: For all the rotting of my kindness and the crumbling
of my soul —

HELEN: Yes —

CREUSA: **I am. I am.** (*Pause. She runs to* HELEN, *holds her.*)
Oh, you sliced thing, you make me **shudder.** (*To* HOMER.)
Doesn't she? Make you **shudder?** (*She caresses* HELEN.) Say
you deserved it, say you earned it, say it, say…

HELEN: Yes…

CREUSA: I cannot resist you. I, the better person, cannot resist
you, why? When you are so incorrigible, why? This terrible but
honest place. This island of confessions. I long for you, and my
son is earth, is pebble. (*To* HOMER.) Can you explain that?
(*He shakes his head.*) **He doesn't want to know any more…** (*She
lovingly undoes* HELEN'S *buttons.*) And he puts her blouse on
back to front…

Scene Six

SAVAGE *is sitting under the cage.*

SAVAGE: So Alexander the Great came to the barrel where
Diogenes was living **Fuck knows why he lived in a barrel the
poseur** and said I am the most powerful man in the world,
come to listen to you, the wisest man in the world, speak. And
the yob waited. The yob waited for the poseur. And Diogenes
said, timing this ecsquisitely, and **with all the calculation of a
man who knew no autocrat would stoop to tear his bowels out,**

the poseur said, **believing himself secure in his reputation as five Persian armies behind their stakes**, said, **You have to admire the predictability, you really do,** you are standing in my sunlight. (*Pause.*) **Do you call that wit! Do you call that insolence?** (*Pause. A tiny laugh from the cage.*) The intellectual Bajcsy-Zsilinsky had been a racist murderer, an anti-semite, a killer of trade unionists, a scrawler of slogans, a publisher of slanders, an editor of intimidating magazines, anti-pity, anti-intellect, but when the Nazis came he met them with a gun. **He had truly travelled**. And they shot shot him in a cellar. **Bang**. The futility of acquiescence versus the futility of resistance. **Bang**. Why are you dressed like an accountant? (HOGBIN *has entered, and waits.*) Are there accountants in Mums' Troy? How can there be when there's no money? But no, that's logical, that's symmetry, the increase in the level of poverty will be matched by the rise in students of accountancy, and as for poverty we recommend more barrels! (*Pause.*) No, you're worried, I can see you are. I go on, and you're worried. I humour myself and you fret. **That's how we are, John!** I pretend. I act sympathy. (*He pretends to listen.*) The ear — extended. (*Pause.*)

HOGBIN: It ain't normal. (*Pause.*)

SAVAGE: Ah.

HOGBIN: **It ain't normal**.

SAVAGE: Pity...perhaps...

HOGBIN: They say it's me.

SAVAGE: Who does?

HOGBIN: The Babies.

SAVAGE: Say it's you...?

HOGBIN: I said why don't yer let me see it, they said just stand there, I said you're hiding something they said wait, I said it's my kid too, you — and I released a torrent of abuse —

SAVAGE: Well, naturally —

HOGBIN: I was that tense —

SAVAGE: Inevitably —

HOGBIN: And I saw it, and it was — (*Pause.*) They say I am a genetic criminal. (*Pause.*) What's that? (GAY *enters, sits. Long pause.*)

GAY: I do not love it. (*Pause.*) How I wanted to... (*Pause.*) And how absurd to want.

HOGBIN: **A genetic criminal, what's that!** Gay, you testify —

GAY: The testicles can testify.

HOGBIN: Gay —

GAY: **Shh, I am the teacher!** (*Pause.*) Because I know, and always knew, to be born was absurd. So absurd that to be angry was equally absurd. And just as being angry was absurd, so caring was absurd. Quite as absurd. Which left me only — ecstasy. Not my mother's ecstasy, not the fucking-out of consciousness — but the different ecstasy of perpetuating absurdity because what else can you do when you are the victim of a joke but participate in the joke and so outjoke the joker? **Laugh louder, always louder still**. So birth was ecstasy. Through the red blankets of pain I applauded all the blind and inexorable circumstances that brought life into this sticky planet. **More life! And more life yet!** (*Pause.*)

HOGBIN: We'll find a shack. I'll put some flowers round the —

GAY: If only it were malice! The surge of mud that — the earthquakes that — the flood which suffocates the infant and the murderer. If only it were malice...but it isn't...how intolerable...How impossible to assimilate... (*Pause.*) So of course you're guilty. You have to be. And I have to hate. (*She extends a hand to him.*) What's your innocence got to do with it? (*He takes her hand.*) Hide, then. (*She shouts.*) **The Criminal is touching me!** Hide...!

HOGBIN: Gay —

GAY: **Pol — ice!**

HOGBIN: **Hide where?**

SAVAGE: And so, to hide him from his enemies, Athene wrapped him in a mist...

HOGBIN: Give us a mist, then!

GAY: **Pol — ice!**

HOGBIN (*running one way, then back again*): Mist...! Mist ...? No mist!

SAVAGE: Opinion.

HOGBIN: Wha'?

GAY (*hurrying out*): **The Criminal Enemy of Mums' Troy!** (*She points to* HOGBIN.)

SAVAGE: **Opinion** — (*men rush in with sticks*) **is — the — mist**. (HOGBIN *turns to face them. A fraction of calculation elapses.*)

HOGBIN: Helen did it. (*They stop.*)

I mean.

I mean, the misery that woman's.

I mean, her life continues in the same old.

I mean, the very sight of her.

I ask you. (*Pause.*) I am the Accountant and therefore the disposer of all life and death, all marriage, surgery and literacy

hang off my calculation, yes, even the colour of the woman's
pants and the baby's rash (*Pause.*) She is guilty, you know that
as well as me —

EPSOM: I 'ave chopped 'er twice, son —

HOGBIN: And is that sufficient? Two?

GUMMERY: Stood in her blood —

HOGBIN: I ask you. I don't seek to persuade, I merely ask —

GUMMERY: Her blood slopped round my ankles —

HOGBIN: Sufficient, was it? Two? I ask, that's all —

EPSOM: **What more is there?** (*Pause.*)

HOGBIN: What more? What more? Is imagination suffocated
then? Is anger drained? Is all possibility exhausted by four
strokes?

EPSOM: We ain't sophisticated —

HOGBIN: No, but dream a little, you have dark yards of
unthought thought —

GUMMERY: Common soldiers, of the wars —

HOGBIN: Common, no! It is the likes of her have taught you
commonness! You have in you the seeds of every genius who
ever walked, but unwatered, no, don't, don't, it hurts to hear
your nature stamped on, and by you... (*Pause.*)

GUMMERY: I have axed seven Troys. What are you after?

HOGBIN: After?

GUMMERY: **Yer can't manipulate The People**.

HOGBIN: And would I try? Would I? I, scarcely shot of his
virginity, new to the razor, gauche, louche, cunt-mad, cunt-
terrorized, swallower of substances and kicker of cans, would
I aspire to work one over you? You, whose faces are bibles
of experience, would I have the neck? (*Pause. They admire
him.*) Educated I may be, for all that means, and perceptive,
yes, gifted, I grant you, and with skills of certain sorts,
Accountancy and the European Mind, but arrogance, I'm
spared, as you can see. (*He bows.*) All my wits are
fagends, chipbags, and gutter dross beneath your boots...
(*Pause.*)

EPSOM: Thank you.

HOGBIN: No more than your due.

EPSOM: He says so.

HOGBIN: I say so, and repeat as often as you fancy —

EPSOM: **And again!**

HOGBIN: I praise, I praise, but listen to what little judgement I
have assembled, Helen's limbs are neither here nor there —

EPSOM: No, neither. Here nor there.

HOGBIN (*acknowledging*):   You have the sticks, to you the wit
— But Helen still rules Troy, the explanation of your unhappiness. (*Pause.*)

GUMMERY: What unhappiness?

EPSOM: 'ho are you calling un'appy? (HOGBIN *permits himself
a smile.*)

HOGBIN: The unhappy, how slow they are to recognize themselves...! I say instead, unfulfilled. (*Pause.*) A jug half empty.
An engine at low revs. An athlete with bound feet. I ask you,
have you never thought you could do more?

EPSOM: You 'ave the echoing tones of an advert for a
mother's tonic —

HOGBIN: **Well, yes, because great truth shares language with
great error,** and luscious sunsets are reflected in slum windows... (*Pause. HOGBIN waits.*)

GUMMERY (*at last*):   Yes...

EPSOM: Brian —

GUMMERY: **Yes, I said**. (*Pause.*) Because yes, who's happy?
Don't say you are, Les, don't please, your fifteen pints are
testimony to a desperate life —

EPSOM: **And your body**. (*Pause.*)

GUMMERY: My body? What of my body?

EPSOM: I've often thought, why is Brian so very — infatuated
— with 'is body? A woman's, yes, that I cop, but to lavish such
attention of yer own —

GUMMERY: **What in fuck's** —

EPSOM: Evidence of something, Brian —

GUMMERY: **What! What!**

HOGBIN: You see! You see, how once we look, we see! All
points to our restlessness, and why? Because we know, we
know, in every area, we are not whole... (*A profound pause.*)

GUMMERY (*looking around*):   We'll say we couldn't find
you... (*To* SAVAGE.) Could we? Couldn't find him? (*They
go out.* HOGBIN *sinks to his knees, exhausted, ecstatic.*)

HOGBIN: Oh, wonderful, oh, luscious, **Gift of the gab**.

SAVAGE: I see your education was not wasted...

HOGBIN: All your seminars — **Shit on them** — all your criti-
sism — **Piss on it** —

SAVAGE: Yes, yes —

HOGBIN: The Speak. The Speak! **The — Word — Saves —
Life!** (EPSOM *comes back.*)

EPSOM: You do it.

HOGBIN (*horrified*):   What?

EPSOM (*flinging a sickle, which slides over the floor*): What Helen needs. (*He goes out again.* HOGBIN *looks in horror at* SAVAGE. SAVAGE *lets out a laugh.*)

HOGBIN: Laugh. I love laughter. (*He laughs again.*) No, I love it. I do. Laugh. In the death camp. In the execution chamber. Balls to giggling, no, real laughter, please, the cosmic stuff, **Yer think I can't do it, cunt?** (SAVAGE *stops.*)

SAVAGE: I think it's easy. I think there is nothing easier in the world.

HOGBIN: **Flesh, what's that?**

SAVAGE: Quite.

HOGBIN: The jets come down, maim, maim! The rattle of the bofors, **Flesh, what's that?**

SAVAGE: You tell me.

HOGBIN: The stabbing on the Number 3. The wife carved in the basement. **Flesh, what's that?**

SAVAGE: Indeed...

HOGBIN: Two 'undred pounds of murder in the Mercedes boot, **Flesh, what's that!** (*Pause. He is kneeling on the floor with the weapon.*) Shove off, I 'ave to prepare myself... (*Pause.*)

SAVAGE: Will you tell Helen, or will I? (*Pause.*)

HOGBIN: Me.

SAVAGE: I'll send her, then?

HOGBIN: Yes. (SAVAGE *looks at him.*) Go on, then. (SAVAGE *withdraws. A great silence, attended by a movement of sky and light. At last* HOMER *appears, pushing* HELEN. *They stop.*)

HELEN: My boy. My only one. (HOGBIN *doesn't move.* SAVAGE *enters.* HOMER *goes to* HOGBIN, *who is dead. He looks at* SAVAGE.)

SAVAGE: **He refutes the argument.** And how? By counter-argument? Not Hogbin. No, Hogbin chooses to ignore. **No more quotation of the emaciated texts!** The testimony of experts, the beautifully laid bricks of theory, the towering cathedrals of logic, **not for him!** (*Pause.*) I wrote on his report, this student follows arguments, but lives by instinct, but which instinct, **Shame?** (*Pause.*) They'll put this down to love. But is it? (*He grabs* HOMER.) Is it? Is it love? (GAY *enters.* SAVAGE *releases* HOMER.)

GAY: Is my husband dead? (*They look at her.*) We were going to grow old together...! (*Pause.*) We were. When he had done his sentence. I would have waited at the prison door, holding the unloved blob. I would and he — (*To* SAVAGE.) Unforgivable, isn't it? **Unforgivable pessimism!** (*Pause.*) Which I have never suffered from and cannot for the life of me comprehend. (*She looks at him, feigning objectivity.*) Of course the only man I ever loved would choose to kill himself, that was as certain as night follows day, water runs downhill, etcetera, so why I, heaven knows why I — (*she begins caressing his body, kissing him, undressing him*) should be like this — at all — I can't — think — what — (*She moans.*)

HELEN: Gay.

GAY: When I — and — obviously — (*She sobs.*)

HELEN: Gay.

SAVAGE: Let her.

HELEN: Let her, why?

SAVAGE: Mourn —

HELEN: Mourn, why?

SAVAGE: **When Paris died you filled all Troy with mad woman's hollering!** (*She looks at him.*) And pints of your spit ran down the lintels, and your legs were bruised with kicking the inanimate, and servants ran from your flying pans of piss! (*To* HOMER.) He knows! He heard it!

HELEN: In those days I wept over every kind of trivia. (SAVAGE *stares at her.*) How you hate that. How you hate me to pulp the past and look on old fevers with contempt. What are you afraid of? Your coming neglect?

GAY (*rising to her feet*): Better now! (*She straightens her dress. To* HOMER.) Was he a hero? You know what heroes are.

SAVAGE: Coming neglect?

GAY: Heroes have reputations, and these reputations matter more than life itself. Is that correct?

SAVAGE: **What neglect?**

GAY: At crucial points the hero must choose between the death of reputation or death itself. Invariably he chooses —

SAVAGE: **I deny neglect's the consequence of passion** —

HELEN: Why? It happens.

SAVAGE: **I still deny**.

HELEN: Deny by all means —

GAY: **Will you be silent. I'm bereaved!** (*Pause.*)

HOMER: Helen, they will make you smaller still...

HELEN (*horrified*): Will they...? Oh, will they...? Have you seen...? (GUMMERY, EPSOM, OTHERS, *rush in.*)

GUMMERY: New Troy! Don't move, you unfulfilled!

EPSOM (*seeing the body*): Oi! (*He points.*) Accountant. Dead.

GUMMERY (*appalled*):   Wholeness he promised me...

SAVAGE: Yes, but he was in a state of terror. Terror lent him speech.

GUMMERY: Wholeness...

SAVAGE: Speech of a reckless order —

GUMMERY: I long to be whole! (SAVAGE *is silent*.)

HELEN: Whole, yes, but whole for what? Health yes, but health for what? I am neither whole nor healthy and I am in torment if the wind blows from the East but have I ever asked for peace?

GUMMERY: Shut up.

HELEN: I ask you, peace for what? You must ask better questions —

GUMMERY: Shut up!

HELEN: Shh! Helen, not queen now, shh!

GUMMERY: How did he die?

SAVAGE: By choosing not to live.

GUMMERY: What was his name? Accountant, was it?

SAVAGE: He seemed content to be called Hogbin. I never heard him shun it.

GUMMERY (*hurt*):   Hogbin? We can't have that. I prefer he be called — (*He is inspired*.) Hyacinth. (*He looks at him*.) I give up arms today. And punch nobody.

EPSOM: Brian —

GUMMERY: I give up knackering. And bruisery. I preach Hyacinth.

EPSOM: Brian —

GUMMERY: There are hyacinths all along the seashore. We waded through them, coming off the boats.

EPSOM: Remember it...

GUMMERY: **I preach him, then**. I, utterly illiterate, will preach, and where I falter, **praise my effort**. (*He braces himself*.) How much easier it was down the gym... (*Pause*.) Hyacinth says, great sunsets are reflected in slum windows. **I was such a window**.

EPSOM: Oh, fuck it, Brian —

GUMMERY: **I won't desist though speaking costs me blood**.

EPSOM: Daft bugger —

GUMMERY: Or grow wild with you, Les, however ill your criticism. Hyacinth would have me hear!

EPSOM (*indicating* HOGBIN'S *body*):   Corpse of a yob!

GUMMERY: Throw away your liquor!

EPSOM: Bollocks.

GUMMERY: Tip away your beer!

EPSOM: Twice bollocks!

GUMMERY: I forgive this, Les —

EPSOM (*turning*): **You are a murderer**.

GUMMERY: Was, Les, was —

EPSOM: **And a woman butcher**.

GUMMERY: Was, was —

EPSOM: **And a child spitter**.

GUMMERY: Add to my list! Record not one, but every act of unfulfilment!

EPSOM: Unfulfilment? It was your finest hour!

GUMMERY: A slum window, reflecting every kind of filth, and you, on your rotting hinges, also reflect —

EPSOM: Don't call me a slum window —

GUMMERY: Oh, you catcher of bad lights! **Praise my powers and the body, shrivel!**

EPSOM: Goodbye, biceps...

GUMMERY: **Shrink!**

EPSOM: Pectorals, ta ta...

GUMMERY: Yes, muscles waste, because they flexed for evil. (*He waves his hand.*) That's it for today! (*He is breathless from exertion.*) I am tireder than I was from ninety press-ups, but I find myself, my unborn self... coming through the dark...

EPSOM: I shall miss you, my ol' mate...

GUMMERY (*wiping the perspiration off his face*): No, we shall —

EPSOM: No, we shan't —

GUMMERY: Seek you out and —

EPSOM: One day... one day... (*He goes out.*)

GUMMERY (*going to the cage*): Listen to me, did you? (*He laughs, shakes his head.*) No, we do change, we do... Make you a new cage... promise! (*He stretches wearily on the floor.*) To lie down... and know... what comes up behind me finds me... vulnerable... since I was a boy soldier, I always stood with my back to walls... (*He sleeps, vulnerably.*)

GAY: He's asleep.

HELEN: Oh, his little freedom... I could put his whole consciousness into my ear, and it would fit. Or up a fingernail, if I had fingernails... his entire knowledge would lie like greasy dirt between my toes...

GAY: Her arrogance... I do admire her arrogance, without admiring her at all...

HOMER: No one admires Helen. It is not admiration Helen wants. If I had made her admirable, who would know her name? (*He goes out.*)

SAVAGE: She is worn down. She is a butt. A scrag. She rubs out virtue **but the rubber also shrinks**...

GAY: How I detest you. The things you say to make your smoked-out lives seem purposeful!

SAVAGE: **My life is purposeful**. (HELEN *shrieks with a shrill laugh*.) Shriek, yes.

GAY (*goes to* HELEN): Oh, your dirty furrows...! I think of you two as fields deep in unrotted litter, ploughed and ploughed again and yielding less with every harvest **I am a perfectly beautiful and fertile woman** and I would not exchange one fallen hair for all your consciousness. (*Pause. She looks up.*)

HELEN: How you hate us.

GAY: Yes. Now someone cart my husband to the beach and let crabs chew his bits, this ten-day funeral nonsense was only an excuse for fucking, the widow got the males erect, I saw it, child between the laden tables, bewildered child, I saw it all —

HELEN: That's as it should be —

GAY: **Is it!**

HELEN: Yes, fuck the widow out of grief.

GAY: **You won't do anything proper**. (*Pause.*)

HELEN: I don't think we ever shall be reconciled. Neither time nor pain will bring us close.

GAY: Never. Your misdemeanours in Old Sparta were bad enough, but wickedness was fashion as long as there was order. There is no order any more. You're fifty and ridiculous.

HELEN: Oh, Helen, out of date!

GAY: Habitual **naughtiness**.

HELEN: What's worse than being out of date?

GAY: Fatuous **Mischief**.

HELEN: Armless and outmoded, god help me.

GAY: Where is the truth in you? Everything is **gesture!** (*Pause.*)

HELEN: Now, that's unfair —

GAY: Good, unfairness is our atmosphere! I hear my child calling, and though I hate it, I will give it milk. Obligation. Do you know the word?

HELEN: Yes. It's what we owe our feelings. (GAY *rushes to* HELEN, *seizing her head in her hands.*)

GAY: **Truncated and pontificating** —

HELEN: You are strangling me —

GAY: **Slut**. (*She detaches herself.*) You do — you really do — bring the violence out...in us... (*She goes out as* MACLUBY *and* FLADDER *enter with a cart.*)

SAVAGE: My student's dead.

MACLUBY: But not without his uses...

SAVAGE: I thought he'd learned a trick or two, but no, he's dead...

MACLUBY (*lifting the body onto the cart*): Dead in one sense.

SAVAGE (*looking at the body*): And once he jolted to cheap music...

MACLUBY: Persistent in another...

SAVAGE (*holding the dead youth's ankle*): His foot could not keep still — (*He shakes it.*) **Jive now!** Still now. **Throb now!** Still now. (*They begin to move away.*) Regret his death? No, a teacher must, a teacher worthy of the name, must welcome all the horror, such as — **Death calls in all our cavities** — And once he drummed his fingers in tutorials — (*He seizes* HOGBIN'S *hand.*) **Drum now!** Still now. **Twitch now!** Still now. But he emerged, he crawled from underneath the ruins of the rhythm, to know such things as — **Death calls in all our passages** (*They start to move.*) Don't go, don't go, let a man converse, eh? (*To* MACLUBY.) Regret his death, did you say, no, no, you see, he wanted through his fog, his pulsing fog, not knowledge but **Morality,** which I don't teach... (*They push the cart out.*) **Where are you taking him?**

BOY (*entering*): Hyacinth... (*He tosses a bar of soap to* SAVAGE. SAVAGE *catches it. Pause.*) New Troy of Cleanliness. (THE BOY *looks at his* FATHER, *then turns and follows the cart.*)

HELEN (*a sudden access of horror*): Do you love me?

SAVAGE: Are you afraid?

HELEN: **I said do you love me**.

SAVAGE: You are, you are afraid...!

HELEN: Say, then!

SAVAGE: Love? We have burst the word... (*He looks after the departing cart.*) He looked at me and thought — I'm sure he thought — I could boil that... (*He smells the soap. Pause. He smells again. An expression of horror.*) **Hogbin! His very odour! Hogbin! His vest and socks!**

Interlude

A German archaeologist, circa 1902.

SCHLIEMANN: I came in search of Troy. I came in search of Helen's bed. Why? Because I am a European, and Europe begins in Helen's bed. But could I find Troy? I found Troy upon Troy upon Troy.

ASAFIR (*off*): Effendi! Effendi!

SCHLIEMANN: I hired labourers. I hired Anatolians, the finest diggers in the world. To see him dig! They talk of the coolie, but see the Turk!

ASAFIR: Effendi!

SCHLIEMANN: The Asiatics took Helen into Asia. The Europeans took Helen back again. At that moment they became a culture!

ASAFIR (*entering with an object*): Effendi... (*the labourer thrusts the object at* SCHLIEMANN.)

SCHLIEMANN: Oh, Johnny, will you never learn? Dig, Johnny! (*the labourer is disconsolate.*) The peasant does not discriminate between the spewings of industrial society and the most precious artefacts of the ancient world. **This is a bar of soap!** (*He hands it back to him.*) Please, bring me only good. *Nein gut, ja?* (ASAFIR *tosses the soap away.*) You could wash with that! Don't you want to wash? (*He goes out.*) These Troys, clustering upon real Troy, called themselves Trojans, but were they Trojan? Was Troy not dead?

YORAKIM: Effendi!

SCHLIEMANN: Desperate and ever-less viable imitations of a cultural entity expunged by history —

YORAKIM: Effendi!

SCHLIEMANN (*patiently*): The Turk, avaricious and notoriously cruel, is also a natural gentleman. In this, he astonishes us, who think of cruelty as alien to manners, what have we here? (YORAKIM *holds out a* A BABY *in a cloth. Pause.*) Are you trying to be funny? (YORAKIM *thrusts it at* SCHLIEMANN.) No, I do not wish to handle it. (*And again.*) Thank you, take it to its mother.

YORAKIM: No mother.

SCHLIEMANN: Well, that's unfortunate. Did its mother die?

YORAKIM (*thrusting again*): **No mother.**

SCHLIEMANN: Then it must be taken to the Ottoman authorities. We are not an orphanage, we are an expedition.

YORAKIM (*pointing to the ground*): Dig! Dig!

SCHLIEMANN: Yes, good, dig until the light fails.

YORAKIM: **In dig.** (*Pause.*)

SCHLIEMANN: The child was in the dig? (YORAKIM *nods emphatically.*) Now, this is silly, how could it have been in — **It doesn't help for you to shout and wave, it does not help**. (*He uncovers* THE CHILD, *then sways with horror.*) Its arms are missing...! (*He thrusts it back at* YORAKIM.) What are you — what the — **You are trying to sabotage my mental stability** — it is hard enough to work in climates of this kind without — **I have never liked your face it is a screen of cunning** —

YORAKIM (*indignantly*): **In — dig.**

SCHLIEMANN: Liar! Asiatic liar!

YORAKIM: **No liar!** (*Pause.*)

SCHLIEMANN: What is a lie to you in any case? Scarcely a stain upon your soul, deceit is the weapon of the underdog, nothing can be credited where race rules race, but **I am an academic and truth is my** — (*Pause. He sways.*) All right, very well, thank you, this was bound to be a testing time, one cannot expect, seeking the bed, the seed and womb of Europe, can't expect, the womb of Helen being, no, you can't, and I certainly do not expect, so — (*Pause.*) Listen, my friend — (*Pause.*) No — you are not my friend, I apologize — listen, whoever you are, no baksheesh for baby, *nein*. (*He waves his hand.* YORAKIM *starts to leave, then suddenly stops, shouts.*)

YORAKIM: Effendi! (SCHLIEMANN *turns, alarmed.* YORAKIM *chucks the baby at him.* SCHLIEMANN *catches it, instinctively, as* YORAKIM *runs off.*)

SCHLIEMANN: **Aaaah!** (*He holds it at arms' length, in disgust. Darkness is falling. The sound of the evening prayer fills the stage as* THE LABOURERS *kneel towards Mecca.*) Your imperfection horrifies me...creeps along my wrists... (*Pause.*) Soon, so soon, the birth of monsters will be an impossibility, such will be the sprint of science...and all pain abolished... **You were born too soon.** (*He puts it on the ground.*) Even if my wife fell ill I could not sponge her face all day, I could not change her linen and remain a genius, it is a full time occupation, **You only come to me because I am a Christian**, but I also owe a duty to my soul. **I refuse to have my morality exploited!** (*He kicks the baby.*) **You exploit me!** (*Pause.*) Oh,

God, am I one of your flock? (ASAFIR *appears, holding a sickle*.)

ASAFIR: Effendi!

SCHLIEMANN: The responsibilities of this ethic are too oner-ous, as Christ knew, and incompatible with freedom, **as Christ knew**.

ASAFIR: Effendi?

SCHLIEMANN (*looking at it*): I don't think, I really do not think this is of the least... (ASAFIR *jerks his head towards* THE CHILD) archaeological... (*He does the movement again.* SCHLIEMANN *sees*.) Oh, God, I do think the Turkish mind is of such extraordinary and shuddering cruelty... (ASAFIR *goes to* THE CHILD.) **How can you make carpets like you do?** (SCHLIEMANN *turns his back, resumes his lecture*.) These later Troys, clustering like — (*he hears the blow, lets out a stifled cry*) like — **There would be no knowledge if pity governed, would there, Asafir? You know**.

ASAFIR: Effendi?

SCHLIEMANN: You know. Look me in the eyes and say you know. Look me in the eyes, then... (*He takes him by the shoulder*.)...stare in my European eyes with your Asiatic eyes, go on, stare, **stare...!** (ASAFIR *stares at the ground*.) Off now, Asafir, you casual murderer, you are already late for prayers...

ASAFIR: Baksheesh?

SCHLIEMANN: Baksheesh... (*Pause. He dips in his pocket*.) Baksheesh...

ACT THREE

Prologue

MACLUBY: The exhibitionists!
No, they are though, to wreck our peace.
Refuse to be wrecked
I do
I say
Listen
Copy me
I say
This is just another death I am singularly
Unimpressed I look you in the eye whilst not
Reducing one iota my walking pace
Oh, you are cutting your throat
Oh, you are dying on the steps
Oh, I go,
Fancy,
And if the blood goes surging
If it gushes down the cracks
I lift my leg
With
Such
Exquisite
Grace
No, you have to or they will **get our peace and**
Bite it
This suicide epidemic
This madness epidemic
And the beggars are a lake
A lake of beggars
A pond of suicides

The rapids of the mad
It takes some navigating the contemporary street
But this is a revolution
Who said
This is a revolution
Nobody told me
I am a revolutionary also
Says the millionairess in the two-piece suit
And truth dripped through their jeers
In bloody clots

The weak brains pop
The frail imaginations pop
Like skulls in the boiler
Stalin
Who grew in wit as he grew in cruelty
Lenin
Who later on was rarely seen to smile
Robespierre
Gorky
Brecht
And all the strata smashers
All the rippers of the roots
They knew
That under pressure
They called it
The intensification of the struggle
Excellent
They called it
The growing strains of contradiction
I do love that
Under pressure
Our brains would pop
I hear it, ssh!
I hear it, ssh!
This also is a revolution, then
Nobody said
Oh, yes, a proper
I never knew
Shh!
The youth are popping
But they are always to the fore
Chucking bottles

Waving bayonets
Throwing matches at the poor
They are such ruthless imperialists of the soul
No
Let youth go
Bid youth farewell
Paris
Petrograd
Budapest
Warsaw
Europe's youth to the fore
To the workshops
Let us batter out a modern laugh
A laugh for the era
Not a boring howl
But something growing from the bowel
HAAAAA!
It's only the madwoman skating
Exquisitely skating on the suicide's gore

ACT THREE

Scene One

The gaol in Fragrant Troy. A place of baths and faucets.

HELEN: Where was the fat on him? Even his buttocks would
have earned a greyhound's pity...

SAVAGE: No fat...

HELEN: No fat, and yet boiled down he makes a million bars
to perfume Troy with...

GAOLER (*to* SAVAGE): Wash, you!

SAVAGE: I'm clean.

GAOLER: No one is clean.

SAVAGE: All right, but washed —

GAOLER: Wash again —

SAVAGE: It hurts my skin to wash it hourly —

GAOLER: The lather of Hyacinth brings only comfort to the
sore —

SAVAGE: Yes, but —

GAOLER: Wash, then —

SAVAGE: Again?

GAOLER: Again. (*Pause.* SAVAGE *goes to the basin.*)

SAVAGE: I could go joyfully to a tramp's groin now —

GAOLER: And do it thoroughly —

SAVAGE: Or suck great lungfuls from whores' cavities —

GAOLER: Front —

SAVAGE: Every crack would be a garden —

GAOLER: Back —

SAVAGE: The rank old human odour flooding the tortured
nostril —

GAOLER: Now do her —

SAVAGE: Fart's paradise and sweat's apotheosis!

MACLUBY (*entering*):   Today, you are fifty! (*He drapes a garland on him.*)

SAVAGE: Fifty...?

MACLUBY: And Helen fifty-five!

SAVAGE: But I was born in August!

MACLUBY: Why shouldn't dates be flexible! What's wisdom if it can't burst calendars? What's a system if it can't call this the New Year One and abolish stacks of squalid centuries?

SAVAGE: Let us out of here, we die of disinfectant...

MACLUBY: Fifty! An age without distinction! Fifty, and no solutions! (*To* HELEN.) **Don't stare at his parts, Desire is soaped out of existence**.

SAVAGE: Fifty...?

MACLUBY: Fifty, and the ground shifting, fifty and the air thick with falling categories! It snows old faiths, it snows old dogmas! Fragrant Troy forgives your misdemeanours, how clean are you?

SAVAGE: Not clean yet...evidently...

MACLUBY: But washed? (*He sniffs him.*) You have the odour of the will to compromise, which is acceptable... (*He goes out.*)

HELEN: I have this horror we will never fuck again... (*Pause. SAVAGE is staring.*)

HELEN: I said I have this horror we will —

SAVAGE: Heard...

HELEN: Not because it is forbidden but because —

SAVAGE: Fifty...!

HELEN: You have lost the will — are you listening?

SAVAGE: **Fifty and no knowledge yet!** (*Pause. She stares appalled.*)

HELEN: No knowledge? Look at me. Sliced. Minimal. Reduced. Hacked. Slashed. Incapable. How dare you say no knowledge. **I am it**. (*Pause. He fixes her with a look.*) That isn't looking it's a fence.

SAVAGE: **What's a look, Helen?** (*Pause.*)

HELEN: What it is, I don't know. What is was, I will tell you. It was a thing as solid as a girder, down which streamed all the populations of our forbidden life... (*Pause. SAVAGE sobs.*)

CREUSA (*entering*):   I have to tell you this. I am to be your wife again. (*They stare at her.*) Do you think I wanted it? (*Pause.*) **Well, speak, because you know it's possible**. Hatred could not prevent it. In that pit of contempt called bed we reached out sometimes like the drowning in the dark. **Even copulation we could do**.

HELEN: **Shut up**.

CREUSA: **It's possible and it happens in every place**. (*Pause*.)
Clean Troy is to make divorce the only capital offence. And I,
for all my maggot life am not ready to die just yet **We are to be
a Show Marriage**. Life, yes, life in any mould, **speak then**, you
must admire me above all martyrs, I am a martyr to nothing
but life itself, and in the end **one male bit is much like any
other** —

HELEN: **I vomit your** —

CREUSA: You would, you are a monument to pain —

HELEN: **Vomit your tolerance**. (*Pause*.)

CREUSA: The smell of Hyacinth...! In every bath and prison
tub...Hyacinth, who could not make an entry while he lived,
in tablet form swims through the lush of every woman's
parts... (*To* THE GAOLER.) Let me out, please...! (*She
goes. Pause*.)

HELEN: You did not deny. (*Pause*.) Did you? You did not
deny? Or are my ears defunct in sympathy with other parts —

SAVAGE: I was so —

HELEN: Deny it then.

SAVAGE: Overthrown by —

HELEN: Indeed, but now —

SAVAGE: Disbelief —

HELEN: Now, though?

SAVAGE: Appalling and grotesque resuscitation of —

HELEN: So you won't —

SAVAGE: And yet it's possible. (*Pause. He looks at her*.) It's
possible... (*He is aghast*.) Is it? (*Pause*.) **Horror!** (*Pause*.)

HELEN: I am indifferent who — with which bitch you —
devour time — all skirt's your garden, out and plunge there
by the armful, and if I discover you fat and naked in the
compost, red from exploration, good but **No renunciation,
please**. (*Pause*.)

SAVAGE: I am exhausted by —

HELEN: Yes —

SAVAGE: **The plunging lift of this infatuation**.

HELEN: It's not infatuation —

SAVAGE: Floor after floor of —

HELEN: **I have neither arms nor legs, it is not infatuation**.
(*Pause*.)

SAVAGE: I think...let me speak...I think...you are a barrier to knowledge now, when once you were the absolute condition... (*Pause*.)

HELEN: All my life I was afraid I might recant, but never did. Always, it was the man who suffocated passion in the puddle. (*Pause.*) Don't be the grey-arsed priest, I beg of you, don't hide under the arch, squatting on your heels and with a withered finger trace the ancient hieroglyphs, all intellect and sterile. Let me be the board you chalk your meaning on, chalk screaming on the wet slate of my wounds... (*He doesn't respond.*) All right, renounce... (*Pause.*)

SAVAGE: Helen —

HELEN: No, shh, all words suddenly redundant —

SAVAGE: Helen —

HELEN: Can't hear you —

SAVAGE: I have to know what —

HELEN: Words, aren't they weapons? Aren't they wires? Keep your weapons off me! Look out, wires!

SAVAGE: **Renunciation also must be knowledge.** (*Pause.*)

HELEN: I don't persuade. I never have persuaded. They persuaded me. Helen never urged a man, he came, he drenched her in his fever, (*with a sudden wail*) oh, undress me, no one's looking, I am maimed without you, and fuck all limbs, this is the torture...! (*He stares at her.*) What have you learned, then? That you hate Helen?

SAVAGE: Yes —

HELEN: Hate her, and could punch the sight out of her eyes —

SAVAGE: Yes —

HELEN: The feeling out of her lips —

SAVAGE: **All right...!**

GAOLER (*entering*): Go home, now, citizens...

HELEN: **Oh, the gross intrusion of banality...**

GAOLER: Thank you, and take your bowls —

HELEN: Persist...

GAOLER: Towels to the laundry —

HELEN: Persist...! (*The infusion of the city.*)

Scene Two

A Public Place. The cage is no longer visible. FLADDER *enters holding a gong and sits.*

GAY (*entering*): The Concentrated Thoughts of a Great King Deposed, Reviled, Neglected and Eventually Rehabilitated in the Interests of Universal Harmony! (*To* FLADDER.) Beat the gong if you deny my version. (*He gongs.*) Not yet, silly. (*Pause.*) My catastrophic marriage to a — (*He gongs.*) No, let me get started, gong at the end if you have to. (*She composes herself.*) My catastrophic marriage to a libidinous woman inexorably led to the death of thousands — (*He gongs.*) How can you gong that? Everybody knows that! It's a Historical Fact. If you are going to gong everything we will take the gong away from you. You abuse the privilege of age. (*She proceeds.*) When I was destitute I came to truth — (*He gongs.*) Give it to me! (*She snatches it and tosses it offstage.*) **You are trying to ridicule the Government of Fragrant Troy** — (*He shakes his head.*) You are and we are not obliged to tolerate it! (*She rehearses.*) In poverty I discovered twenty truths —
One! In limitation lies the source of satisfaction.
Two! The question leads only to the next question.
Three! You have to die some time.
Four! The final end of equality is universal plastic surgery. (FLADDER *makes a noise in his throat.*) Shut up —
Five! To suffer is to be without soap! (*He gurgles.*) Shut up, I said —
Six! Dig your garden till the sun sets.
Seven! And when the soldiers have gone, plant it again.
Eight! (*To* FLADDER.) **I shall not desist, no matter how you gurgle**. (*Pause.*)
Eight! If you must kiss do it with your eyes open.
Nine! The greatest joy is to concede.
Ten! Don't grieve after midnight.
Eleven! (*To* FLADDER, *who is frothing.*) **This is what you discovered, isn't it? Keep still, then**. (*Pause.*) Eleven! Fornication is the aptitude of mongrels.
Twelve! Swans mate for life.
Thirteen! Violence is no solution.
Fourteen! Nor is justice.

Fifteen! Soap is experience. (*To* FLADDER.) **You are dribbling on my leg**.

Sixteen! (*Pause.*) Sixteen! (*To* FLADDER.) **You see, I am not sabotaged by you!** (*Pause.*) Sixteen! The majority are sometimes right.

Seventeen! It is perfectly natural to hate.

Eighteen! It is love that's artificial.

Nineteen! Marriage is the government. (*To* FLADDER.) **No, I won't stop!**

Twenty! (*Pause.*) Twenty! (*Pause.*) The Past never occurred! (*She pushes him off his knees.*) I did it! I did it, and I was not stopped by you! (*Pause. She looks at him.*) What does it matter if you thought those things or not? What does it matter? Clean Troy is not about truth. It's about me. Now, get off your knees and scarper. (*He climbs to his feet.*) Take your gong. (*He moves.*) Do you still love my mother? (*He stops.*) You do... You do love her...! (*Pause. She looks closely into him.*) Is there anything she could do — anything — would stop you loving her? (*Pause.*) Extraordinary. (*She walks a little, still looking at him.*) I once put corpses in her bed. Arms and things. By this I meant to say, this wrist, this bowel, you caused to howl, you caused to wither. But she was only irritated by the smell. Is that the reason for her power? (HOMER *enters, senile now, and with two sticks.*)

HOMER: Please, don't let them bath me again...

GAY: You must be bathed!

HOMER: Not so often, surely?

GAY: Yes, often and often! Do they scrub you?

HOMER: Yes!

GAY: That's good, I told them, scrub him in every crack and pore because that's where his misery collects, and his misery makes him sing those songs, oh, so miserable your songs are now, and anyone who hears you, they get miserable too! Why did Odysseus go back to Penelope? (HOMER *stares, bewildered.*) I asked you a question. I mean, hadn't he met this girl, this perfect girl? So why did he go back to Penelope? **She must have been a proper hag by then**. (*Pause.*)

HOMER: No more soap!

GAY: Oh, take him away and wash him...

HOMER: No more soap!

GAY (*turning on him*): **I think you must defend your fictions and not take that arrogant stance**.

HOMER (*as he is hurried out*): Oh, God, not soap...!

GAY (*to* CREUSA, *who enters with* SAVAGE): I don't believe he has the slightest interest in art any more. He is interested in soap, and only soap. (*She smiles.*) Now, are you reconciled? You must consummate the marriage, and in public. And to think we once had public executions! No, this is progress —

CREUSA: I wonder if I can —

GAY: Please, don't throw up objections...! How girlish you are...!

CREUSA: Yes...

GAY: When you have been so — used — and flogged — and flung around like soldiers' baggage... (*She kisses* CREUSA *on the cheek.*) Your cheeks are maps of sordid life... (CREUSA *goes out.* GAY *watches her.*) The Troys are slipping away. So many errors... your sacrifice is a small thing compared to our survival.

SAVAGE: Sacrifice? I could not do it if it were a sacrifice.

GAY: What is it, then?

SAVAGE: An education, obviously.

GAY: I might also be an education... (*Darkness falls on the stage.*)

SAVAGE: On Monday I washed the body of the old woman.
On Tuesday I cut the throat of a stranger.
On Wednesday I lifted potatoes from the allotment.
On Thursday I seduced the mother of my lover.
On Friday I was ashamed and unable to act.
On Saturday I read the works of great authors.
On Sunday I lay and wished I was a baby.
On Monday...
On Monday I washed the body of the old woman....

GAY: I'll take my clothes off, shall I?

SAVAGE: It's night...!

GAY: I will, if you will...

SAVAGE: The dictator stirs inside his bunker...

GAY (*removing her shoes*): Shoes first...

SAVAGE: The executioners are checking their weapons...

GAY: Then socks...

SAVAGE: And intellectuals rip the membranes of humanity in their shuddering cots... **All right, undress!** (*Pause.*)

GAY: If I am naked and you are not, what then? (SAVAGE *shakes his head.*) One of us has the advantage, but who...?

SAVAGE: You ask questions like a man throws stones. You talk to fend off silence.

GAY: I have the advantage! (*She flings off her last garment. She stands naked. Pause.*) Stare at me, then. (*Pause.*) Stare. (*Pause.*) Consume me. (*Pause.*) Are you consuming me? (*Pause.*) You're not, are you? Or are you, I can't tell from — (*She sees* FLADDER, *sitting.*) Oh, God, there is a man still here! (*She covers herself with her hands.*)

SAVAGE: What's the matter? He can't speak.

GAY: He can see me — he — **sees me**.

SAVAGE: But what he sees he can't put into words. So what he sees he sees as the stars see. Or the stones. Do you hide yourself from stones? (*Pause.*)

GAY: If you do not respond to me, I shall be damaged. I shall be damaged and the onus will be on you! (*Pause. Suddenly she goes to grab her clothes but* SAVAGE *seizes them first.*)

SAVAGE: You look ridiculous. Beautiful and ridiculous. (*She goes to snatch them but he whips them away. She looks, uncomprehending. She attempts to smile.*)

GAY: What's this? Desire?

SAVAGE: **Desire!** Do you think beauty makes desire? Do you think you only need to **stand and be observed**? (*She looks alarmed.*) It's night... (*She looks nervously to* FLADDER.) Don't look to him. He is a stone.

GAY: Are you going to — **cut me into bits**? (*Pause. He is bemused. He sinks to the ground. Extends a hand limply.*)

SAVAGE: Shh...

GAY (*horrified*):   **Are you?**

SAVAGE: Shh... (*He shakes his head.*) Oh, pitiful...Oh, unknowing... (*He beckons her with a gesture. Timidly she goes to him. He encloses her chastely in his arms. A figure enters from the darkness. It is* GUMMERY, *carrying* SHADE *in a small cage at his belt. He looks at* GAY. *He looks at* SAVAGE.)

GUMMERY: No anger but. (*Pause.*) I walk along the shore so full of kindness for the world. (*Pause.*) No anger but. (*Pause.*) We have our nightly stretch so kindness-sodden and we see his widow and our queen. No anger, obviously. Undressed. (*Pause.*) Much as old Helen might have been. (*Pause.*) Kindness is bruised and Hyacinth demeaned... (*He turns to go, stops.*) How hurt we are. No anger but. (*He starts to leave*).

SAVAGE: How hideous you are. Without your anger. How crippled and deformed. So kind you make all kindness loathsome not that it seemed a very precious thing but now it stinks the corpse of undone actions all tumours in your lung you passive and colourless licker of fallacies I see when I look at you why heroes have to die, Homer was right in this at least he did not pursue the Greeks to their retirement, shuffle, stagger away you offend the landscape and my vocabulary withers in describing you, I, a doctor, too. Speechless, and in revulsion... (GUMMERY *is terribly still.*) Cart your shrunk mate off, you spoil a decent night. (GUMMERY *remains.*) And yet you stay. To test what, I wonder? (GUMMERY *is still.* SAVAGE *climbs to his feet.*)

GUMMERY: Once, I made my body iron. To hurt. And now it's iron to suffer... (*Pause.*)

SAVAGE: Suffer? For what? My student's gabble? There was panic in his trousers.

GUMMERY: **Test me**.

SAVAGE: And you were cruel...they told me... (SAVAGE *goes to* GUMMERY, *who is still motionless. He stands behind him.*)

GAY (*suddenly*):   **Can't watch!** (*She grabs her clothing, runs to* FLADDER.) **Can you?** (*She rushes out.*) **Can't watch!** (*Wind. Darkness. The peculiar voice of* SHADE, *tunefully.*)

SHADE: Intellectuals also kill! Intellectuals kill!
Intellectuals also kill! Intellectuals kill!

Scene Three

Bells. MACLUBY *besuited.* CREUSA *gowned. They look over the city.*

MACLUBY: Troy isn't what it was, when you last wed.

CREUSA: Nor Creusa, either.

MACLUBY: Troys have been, and Troys have gone...

CREUSA: And Creusas, they have been and gone, too...

MACLUBY (*smiling*):   This is the proper spirit for matrimony.

CREUSA: Yes.

MACLUBY: Accommodation.

CREUSA: Yes.

MACLUBY: No more climbing the greasy pole of personality, but —

CREUSA: Yes. Because I fell, and fell, and fell again... (*A blast of rattles and cheers as a massive bed descends. It is upholstered with twig or flint.*) **What's that...!**

MACLUBY: No one said it would be easy...

GAY (*entering*): The territory of epic adventures! The poor man's empire! I am a romantic, at least I have kept that alive! (*To* CREUSA.) On the bed now, and good luck in the maze! I think it is a maze, with its dead ends and repetitions, but at the centre of which is — must be — for those who persevere — I don't know what! (CREUSA *is helped to the bed. Crowd applause.*) How Troy needed this! Listen! When all was disintegration and morals were exploding nebulae! The young particularly will appreciate this **Affirmation,** hurry, make yourself comfortable, your husband is **imminent.** (CREUSA *lies on the bed.*) This shows as nothing better can, the utter **Circularity of life,** the fact we teach in school that if you walk defiantly away from a fixed point, the earth's roundness ensures you will return to that same spot, no matter how terrible the journey! **The loop of knowledge**. He's coming! (*Whistles.*) I could weep with that strange weeping women do at weddings! I could! (SAVAGE *enters, in a motheaten and devastated suit. Applause. She looks at him. She kisses him chastely on the cheek. He stares at the spectacle of the bed. Silence falls.*)

SAVAGE: It's twigs...

CREUSA: Not as bad as you might —

SAVAGE: It's twigs...!

MACLUBY: Climb in, Dr Savage...

SAVAGE (*a terrible connection*): **It's a pyre!**

MACLUBY: You are the one who wants the knowledge —

SAVAGE: **A pyre when I'm not dead...!**

CREUSA: All right, all right...

SAVAGE: **Not dead...**

CREUSA: Shh...shh... (*He mounts the bed. He sits rigidly and apart from her. The occasional rattle from* THE CROWD.)

MACLUBY: And Odysseus went to Penelope, and slew her suitors, and having washed the blood from his hands, undressed her, and she undressed him, and as she did, his eyes travelled her worn and imperfect body, and her eyes saw his decay, and they wept, and pity was the source of his tumescence...what else could it have been?

CREUSA: Look at me with new eyes, or we shan't do it...

SAVAGE: I can't.

CREUSA: It can be done...

THE BITE OF THE NIGHT

SAVAGE: Anything can be done, but not with new eyes...

CREUSA: Hold my hand, then —

SAVAGE: Trying —

CREUSA: Hold it — (*She extends hers.* THE CROWD *whistles and claps.*) **Hold it**... (*With a spasm of pain,* SAVAGE *thrusts his hand into hers. More applause.*) It's all right...! It's all right...!

MACLUBY: The Political Fuck! Not for the first time, the Political Fuck! (*As* THE CROWD *chants its approval,* HELEN *appears pushed by* HOMER.)

HELEN: What can you see?

HOMER: You've got the eyes, not me —

HELEN: To the left!

HOMER: Some agony —

HELEN: The right then! (THE CROWD *obscures her view.*) Oh, shift you fragrant lawyers!

MACLUBY (*watching* SAVAGE'S *agony*):   He squirms, he sweats, but that's the pain a rebirth brings, if birth was painless, would a child be loved?

HOMER: What do you see?

HELEN (*straining*):   A bed —

HOMER: A bed —

HELEN: A terrible bed...

MACLUBY: This is the union from which all stale and mothy marriages will suck their consolation!

GAY (*like a trainer*):   Kiss him, kiss him, do! **More lamps, they are obscure!** (*Spotlights heat the bed.*) The lips release the tongue, the tongue unlocks the fingers, the fingers free the fastenings, the fastenings ungate the flesh, oh, claim her, do...! (*With a desperate effort of will,* SAVAGE *flings himself on* CREUSA. THE CROWD *surges as the bed is drawn out of sight.*)

MACLUBY (*laughing*):   Knowledge...! Knowledge...!

HELEN: Oh, my own madman, does he grin or weep...?

Scene Four

HELEN *is alone*, SHADE'S *cage at her feet*. THE BOY *enters, no longer a boy.*

BOY: My father and my mother have been reconciled. And in spite of her advancing years, she has conceived. They are calling it a miracle.

HELEN: Miracles happen when desire's dead...

BOY: My father wanted me to be an intellectual, but I lean towards business. (*Pause.*)

HELEN: You are the soap maker.

BOY: I wash out minds as well... (*He peers into the cage.*) Is there meant to be a bird in here?

HELEN: Yes. He sings all day long.

BOY: Can't hear him.

HELEN: Really? I find him deafening. Why are you dressed like an undertaker?

BOY: An undertaker? No one has ever said that before. I think of myself as a bridegroom. May I tell you about soap? It is my obsession.

HELEN: How lucky you are to have an obsession. And you can't be more than thirty-two.

BOY: Oh, dear, I think you are going to interrupt me all the time.

HELEN: Isn't that allowed?

BOY: It breaks the flow.

HELEN: I don't like flows. The best things can be said staccato.

BOY: Nevertheless, I will persist.

HELEN: How can I avoid you? My nurse is old and falls asleep, and it's not as though an amputee has anything to block her ears with —

BOY: I came to soap thinking it a product —

HELEN: You would not believe the sheer variety of human innocence that foists itself on me! Poets, infertile women, men with agony inside their trousers, I have to tolerate the lot —

BOY: But it is not a product, it is a culture. For example —

HELEN (*conceding*):   **All right, flow.** (*Pause.*)

BOY: There has never yet been a society that could tolerate the smell of human flesh, can you explain that? The individuals who live with most intensity the odour of mankind have always been the outcasts, the vagrant, the dispossessed. We are born with a profound revulsion for our own scent, an antipathy formed during some nightmare travel down the birth canal — I speculate — but certainly the odour of the mass can turn the stomach and I believe the essence of the human smell to be a lethal toxin. This is soap's justification and the fulcrum of an honourable career. (*He smiles.*) But my concentration on the subject led me further, as indeed all concentration will, no matter how banal the subject. The great banker also knows the human heart. So soap revealed its laws to me. (*Pause.*) Your eyes are shut but you hear everything, I know —

HELEN: You have his voice, but without the edge of panic that clung to all his vowels...

BOY: My flow, please... (*Pause.*) Soap makes harmony, and made with proper inspiration, lets imagination compensate for impossibly demanding life. Which brings me to my point, that you might understand the need for what I hope to call Essential Helen, as Hogbin's body, all kindness and purity, pervades the Trojan spirit now. (*Pause.*) Respond, by all means. (*She is silent.*) Sometimes the horror of an idea is only the boom of its essential truth... (*Pause.*) And now you won't talk...! (*Pause.*) We see in your life spectacularly the price of Eros. I don't stoop to criticize, but simply draw to your attention the fifteen thousand orphans of the Peloponnese, the wail of widows and wounds of conscripts whose total ache would lift the mountains off their feet, I am not judging, you understand I am not ethical, the children of these wars eat murder with their breakfast. I don't judge.

HELEN: What you describe is consequence. I refuse the blame. Every conscript had his choice and every widow could have blocked her man. But if they died for Eros, where's the tragedy in that? In other wars they'll scream for flags, sometimes for banks, or even books, I've heard. No, cunt's a worthy cause as slaughters go.

BOY: You grab the argument! Beauty has this effect, it stirs the blood, and yes, it is a truth of sorts.

HELEN: Truth...? Oh, don't drag truth in, I'm over sixty —

BOY: Very well, but whether it's a truth or not, it cannot be a lie —

HELEN: Beauty is a lie! Of course it is a lie! (*He shrugs.*) It is simply the best available lie on the subject of truth... (*Pause. He smiles, shaking his head.*)

BOY: My flow... my flow... (*Pause.*) But I proceed. However great the pain your Eros brought, we cannot dispense with Eros. It lives in all of us. It cries, and breathes.

HELEN: In you? It cries, and breathes?

BOY (*charmingly*): Now, that is sabotage —

HELEN: Preposterous claim —

BOY: All right, it cries in varying degrees, but because I don't stand out at passing skirt is no —

HELEN: He must defend his sprig!

BOY: Really, you will not disorganize me by —

HELEN: I won't disorganize him —

BOY: By some phallic contest which —

HELEN: He's not disorganized —

BOY: Is both grotesque, pernicious and —

HELEN: He's not, he's definitely not disorganized —

BOY: No —

HELEN: And I don't want to disorganize you, God knows the mayhem if you were, I shrink to think, the uncaging of, the swollen veins, no, no, you stay as you are! (*Pause.*)

BOY (*coolly*): You are piqued.

HELEN: The flow, for pity's sake.

BOY: You are piqued and I know why.

HELEN: Me? Helen? Piqued?

BOY: Because I look at you with cool and level eyes. (*Pause.*)

HELEN: You do. I grant you that.

BOY: Which you are unaccustomed to.

HELEN (*pause. Then with inspiration*): The story of the Actress in the Penal Colony! The star who had made a million men throb in the stalls found the interrogator unyielding and her breasts showing though the dirty quilted jacket moved his lust his pity his ambition **not one bit** so solid and so thick the plating of his **ideology,** and this made her weep. But when she had been returned to the cells he locked his door and stropped himself. **At that moment the soul of The Party died.** (*Pause.*) You are so oblique and so well-mannered, a proper skater, as black as a fly and impossible to swat. A man for the age. Why do you want my body?

BOY: To give all women, so all women may be, at moments of their choice, Hellenic... (*A terrible howl comes from HELEN.*) You howl — yes — you howl but —

HELEN: **My — opic Per — fumier!**

BOY: The lending of transgression to the ashamed, the loan of passion to the guilty, the licensing of total love to the domestic —

HELEN: **Fastidious sycophant!**

BOY: **You don't like people —**

HELEN: No —

BOY: You scorn their simple pleasures, you mock the scale of their imagination —

HELEN: Yes, every day!

BOY: **It's unforgivable!** (*Pause.*)

HELEN: Could I ever forgive myself if I were forgivable? (*Pause. He looks at her.*)

BOY: Your lonely and malevolent life... (*Pause.*) We terribly want to help you —

HELEN: Afraid —

BOY: Who —

HELEN: You. Afraid.

BOY: Afraid, of what?

HELEN: Afraid I'll cling in the imagination of a girl, or in a boy's head, make all his thoughts unscholarly... (*Pause.*)

BOY: Helen — if I may call you Helen —

HELEN: Well, don't call me anything else —

BOY: Helen —

HELEN: That's it, though you say it oddly —

BOY: You have not seen yourself for years.

HELEN: No. I have no mirror.

BOY: I think, if you were to — examine your appearance — you might understand that your capacity for mischief is now, sadly —

HELEN: You talk like a shrivelled priest, and the language shrivels when you talk it — do you mean I'm ugly? I was born ugly. You think that slipping and sliding word circumscribes my power? You're not — though a lipstick maker and a skin-cream bottler — so bereft of knowledge as all that, surely? (*Pause.*) No, you cannot have my fat to let unsuffering women play at deepest life... better the crabs get dinner off me... (*He goes out.* FLADDER *comes in, carrying the gong.*) They want to smear themselves with essence, the new Trojans. Think with a soap called Helen they might temporarily contract desire. Sign nothing. And when I'm gone, in the sea with the remnants, they will boil me otherwise and use my fat to humiliate some unborn class... (*Pause.*) Tell me, is it possible for Helen to be old? (*He gongs. Pause. A* CHILD *enters, without arms.*) Oh, look, she has in her the same appalling gift...! (HELEN *grins.*) It's in her hip... the tilting of her head... **Oh, the wreck of domesticity and the tearing of men from regular employment...!**

CHARITY: What?

HELEN: Shh! Your mother!

CHARITY: Tear men from regular employment? How?

HELEN: It can't be told, it happens!

GAY (*entering*): Listen! The Festival of Families! And we'll be late! (THE CHILD *runs off.* GAY *follows, then stops.*) May I kiss you?

HELEN: Kiss me...?

GAY: Yes. (*Pause, then* GAY *kisses her, goes out. Pause.*)

HELEN (*apprehensively*): I think I am going to be killed. (*Pause.*) Beat the gong, then... (*Pause.*) So they are killing me, **Who is.** (*Pause.*) You know and you're not telling me! (*Pause.*) **Who is.** (*Pause.*) You? (*Pause.*) Well, why not you? Because it isn't in your character? **What is your character?** To think any one of us is knowable, when personality is only crystal grinding between stones, **don't come near me yet.** (*He is still.*) I want to be killed. But in a gush of violence. I wanted to be beaten out of life by some mad male all red about the neck and veins outstanding like the protesting prostitute in the bite of the night, discovered all brain and sheet and stocking. **Not this cold political thing,** hacked to shreds among the bed-things **Not this,** the wonderful gore that trickled underneath the door, **Not this though!** (*Pause. He is still.*) Who signed the warrant? (*She looks at him.*) **The entire population did?** Oh, come on, even the children? **And the as yet unborn?** (SAVAGE *enters, stops. She glimpses him.*) Don't come near. I would rather be blind than see you again. Oh, suddenly the air is thick with stale longings, and sweats gone acid with betrayal, **Old husband and old lover,** I would prefer to be slashed by a passing killer than you two set about me kindly, considerate in strangling, considerate in suffocating, **The considerate lover was always the worst** — (SAVAGE *makes a move.*) **Don't come into my eyeline, I would ram my sight out rather on a branch!** (*He freezes. She averts her face.*) Oh, this purgatory of flowerbeds, in Old Troy temper was the rule, I don't belong and — **Where's Homer!** (*Pause.*) Oh, my maker's gone... Someone has extinguished him... what for? **A poet's soap?** (*She looks at* SAVAGE.) It must have been you... what was it? Did his weeping anger you? We do feel bitter, don't we, towards the genius whose final statements are so trite? But he was silent at the end... the sight of me... robbed him of speech... Whereas you... are shameless... which I loved... (EPSOM *enters, with a cloth. She sees him, from the corner of her eye.*) The knacker comes. (*She grins.*) One for the soap yard!

EPSOM: Got a job to do...

HELEN: A job, he calls it! Magnificent monster! And for a terrible hour I thought there was no one left who hadn't changed!

EPSOM: Change, for what?

HELEN: For what! Exactly! Look at him, as unredeemed as when a dirty boy he worked his snot between his tutor's teeth... (*Pause. EPSOM goes to HELEN.*)

EPSOM (*intimately*): Be yer mate...

HELEN (*not grasping his meaning*): Why not be my mate! What's a little strangulation between friends? I have seen torturers play chess with their victims, and the mothers of drowned infants fuck the perpetrators, no, it's all right, it is! (*He goes to cover her.*) **Sav — age!** (*Pause.*) Can you watch this? (*Pause.*) You can. You can watch this... (EPSOM *silences her by dropping the cloth over her face. He puts his hands about her throat. He exerts. He stops. Pause.*) No, that's wrong, surely... (*He grimaces, as if at effort.*) The way you handle my neck, Les, I've been loved better —

EPSOM: **Die!** (*He exerts.*)

HELEN: Yes, I long to, but —

EPSOM: **Die!** (*A pause, her head drops forward. An immediate cacophony of factory whistles.*)

FLADDER: The revolutionaries are flunkeys, too! The terrorists transport dominion in their handshakes!

We know but we still act!

We know but we still act! (EPSOM *drives away* THE AUDIENCE *which has gathered at the scene.* FLADDER *runs out.*)

EPSOM: Fuck off! Scarper! (A WOMAN *is going near* THE BODY.) Off, yer vermin!

WOMAN: Cures tumours, whore's blood!

EPSOM: No, it's 'angman's spit yer thinkin' of! (*He gobs at her. She flees. He laughs. Others risk his blows to touch* HELEN *for luck, and run.*)

SAVAGE: I can watch. I can watch anything.

EPSOM: It's a gift, mate... (THE PUBLIC *are repulsed by* EPSOM.)

SAVAGE: I think to believe in every lie is better than to see through every truth...

EPSOM (*fetching a broom*): Sweeping up...

SAVAGE (*draws near* HELEN): In passion, the woman births the man. The convulsions of her flesh are births...

EPSOM (*sweeping*):   I wouldn't know... **Clear of the body, please!**

SAVAGE: Imagine, then.

EPSOM: Who, me?

SAVAGE: Why not you? (EPSOM *shrugs*.) **I insist that you imagine.** (EPSOM *stops sweeping*.) To have had Helen, imagine it...

EPSOM: Trying...

SAVAGE: Yes, but to have had Helen, and to have no longer, **Imagine that.** (EPSOM *shrugs*.) The greater the love, the more terrible the knowledge of its absence. No sooner did she love me than I longed for her death, **And you call yourself a monster!** (*Pause.*)

EPSOM: I think —

SAVAGE: **Yes!**

EPSOM: I think —

SAVAGE: **I am what you are only in your dreams.** (*He goes to* HELEN, *and takes her in his arms*.)

EPSOM (*horrified*):   **Clear of the body!**

SAVAGE: Down the tunnels of her ears, I whisper... (*He mutters.*) Down the chasm of her throat I murmur... (*He draws the cloth from her mouth and kisses her.*)

EPSOM: **All right...!** (SAVAGE *lets the cloth fall, goes out. Pause. Then* EPSOM *goes to* HELEN *and removes the cloth. Pause.*)

HELEN: Not dead...
          Until he spoke...
          Not dead...
Why not, bastard...!

EPSOM: Search me —

HELEN: Any death I would have welcomed and you spare me to hear that!

EPSOM: I thought —

HELEN: What was it, pity?

EPSOM: I suppose —

HELEN: Pity...!

EPSOM: I take life and I'm criticized, I give life and I'm criticized, **can't I pity sometimes, too?**

HELEN: Oh, utter decline... Helen pitied... And I thought... for a moment... I dared think you had spared me for lust... (*She laughs.*)

Scene Five

CREUSA *comes in, an old woman pregnant.* SAVAGE *is alone.*

SAVAGE: It's time. (*Pause.*) It's time to write the book.
CREUSA: On what? Soap wrappers?
SAVAGE: Your interventions were always so mundane.
CREUSA: There is so little paper here and one time it was blowing down the gutters, wrapped around the lamp-posts, fine cartridge, too, but who remembers Paper Troy? Collect today for tomorrow may be barren! As for pencils...!
SAVAGE: Can't write the book, then...
CREUSA: And reading's out of date...
SAVAGE (*relieved*):   Can't write the book... (*She shrugs, sits on a stool.*) Inevitable. The greatest document fails to exist. (CHARITY *hurries in.*)
CHARITY: Skipped Hygiene! Skipped Good Citizens and Family Love! Don't tell! (*She is about to run out.*)
SAVAGE: Seen a bit of paper?
CHARITY: Paper? What's that?
CREUSA: You see...!
CHARITY: Oh, that stuff the soap comes in?
SAVAGE (*grinning*):   **Can't write the book!**
CHARITY: Write a book? What for?
SAVAGE: To spread unhappiness, of course...
CHARITY (*inspiration*):   I'll be the book. They say that men in concentration camps learned poems of nine thousand lines. I can do that! (*She sits cross-legged.*) Ready! (*She gets comfortable.*) Now, you speak!
GAY (*entering with officers*):   You say you saw it happen —
FIRST OFFICER: Everybody did —
GAY: Where is she, then?
FIRST OFFICER: **I repeat we all saw Helen die.**
GAY: All legless and armless women, fetch them in!
SECOND OFFICER: There's only one in all of Troy —
GAY: Bring her! (THE OFFICER *leaves.*) They say that Helen's dead —
SAVAGE: She is. I kissed her cooling mouth.
GAY: Then where's the body?
CHARITY: **We're trying to write a book!**
GAY: Be quiet you precocious little — and I can see your knickers, you are not to sit like that!

CREUSA: You were the same —

GAY: I was never —

CREUSA: You were just the —

GAY: **It is not possible I was like that.** (CREUSA *shrugs*. THE OFFICER *pushes in* A POOR WOMAN *on a trolley. She is armless and legless*.)

SECOND OFFICER: Do you mean this?

GAY: Yes. How did she lose her limbs?

SECOND OFFICER: She fell under a tram. To be precise, she fell under two.

GAY: When?

OFFICER: When —

GAY: Not you. (*To* WOMAN.) You.

OLD WOMAN: When there were trams, of course.

GAY: She's lying. When were there ever trams?

FIRST OFFICER: During Mechanical Troy.

GAY: Mechanical Troy... I'd forgotten Mechanical Troy.

FIRST OFFICER: It rusts in shady corners...

GAY (*to* THE WOMAN): Well, if you'd lived in Dancing Troy, you'd only have got bad feet.

OLD WOMAN (*creaking with laughter*): Seen some of 'em! I prefer me truck.

GAY: This can't be Helen, she's far too sensible.

SECOND OFFICER (*to* THE WOMAN): Shove off! (*They start to leave.*)

GAY: Wait a minute! (*She stops.*) Which tram?

OLD WOMAN: The 3.

GAY: In which direction?

OLD WOMAN: Empty. To the Depot. (*Pause.*)

GAY: All right. (THE WOMAN *moves.*) Why do you live? (*Her trolley stops.*)

OLD WOMAN: Out of habit. Why do you?

GAY: You are very impertinent for a thing on castors.

OLD WOMAN: Beg pardon —

GAY: What are you trying to make me do? Commit suicide?

OLD WOMAN: No, I just —

GAY: Isn't there enough suicide without you —

OLD WOMAN: All over the shop —

GAY: I could regard that question as an attempt on my life!

SECOND OFFICER: We'll bring charges —

GAY: No, get her out — (SECOND OFFICER *propels her.*) And see she's washed...! (*Pause.*)

SAVAGE: That was Helen...

GAY: Idiot.

SAVAGE: **Helen!**

GAY: Do you think I don't know my own mother...?

CHARITY: **I wish you wouldn't interrupt the book.** (GAY *and* THE OFFICERS *go out. Pause.*)

CHARITY: Chapter One! No! **Introduction.** (*She shuts her eyes.*) Ready. Expatiate!

CREUSA (*suddenly*): It's coming —

CHARITY: Shh!

CREUSA (*stands*): The child —

CHARITY: The book!

CREUSA: **The miracle! Savage!** (SAVAGE *jumps up.*)

CHARITY (*to* SAVAGE): If you go, you will never write the book. (*He hesitates.*) You know that, don't you? You do know that?

CREUSA: **The child, Savage...!** (*He stares, his mouth open.*)

CHARITY: 'This book was so nearly never written...'

MACLUBY (*entering*): Examining your feelings, Dr Savage?

CHARITY: 'So nearly never written because I pretended feelings I did not possess...'

MACLUBY: She only wants her hand held...

CHARITY: Conscience delays all journeys, but especially journeys of the mind... (*She jumps up.*) That's it, first line! (MACLUBY *assists* CREUSA *away.* SAVAGE *watches.*) Refusal. That's the only way we learn. (*A high wind.* SAVAGE *turns impulsively on* THE CHILD *and starts to throttle her. By a twisting motion of her body,* CHARITY *escapes.* SAVAGE *reels.* FLADDER *enters, carrying a rule, a yard long. He places it against a wall and makes a chalk line. He turns, sees* SAVAGE.)

FLADDER: That low. (*Pause.* SAVAGE *reassembles himself.*)

SAVAGE: What...

FLADDER: That low. (FLADDER *goes off.*)

Scene Six

Under the city gate. THE OLD WOMAN, *parked.*

CREUSA (*entering with a mass of bundles*):   I did it.

OLD WOMAN: You did.

CREUSA: And it is whole.

OLD WOMAN: That's something all Troy knows.

CREUSA: Look, it feeds off me . . . its fingers reach for my flooding tit, which, as if to ridicule my age, is bursting. Sixty, and in surplus!

OLD WOMAN: Baldness and abundance. Arthritis and suck.

CREUSA: Don't wonder where these gifts come from . . .

OLD WOMAN: Enjoy your miracles and keep your mouth shut.

CREUSA (*hoisting her load*):   Off now.

OLD WOMAN: And by the same gate, Creusa . . . ! Forty years since you last fled. (*Pause.* CREUSA *looks at her.*)

CREUSA: By the same gate, yes.

OLD WOMAN: Good luck!

CREUSA: Some dithering old peasant will lend me a corner of his sack, and if he don't speak Trojan, all the better, spare me his preamble, and swop dinner simply for the fuck.

OLD WOMAN: No note for the husband?

CREUSA: Once a quitter, always a quitter. Tell him that.

OLD WOMAN: Damn all reconciliations. It couldn't last. They say he had been Helen's man, so really it never had a chance.

CREUSA: It wasn't that.

OLD WOMAN: Once tasted, Helen spoiled a man for others —

CREUSA: **It wasn't that.** (*Pause.*) He had no hope. (*Pause.*)

OLD WOMAN: Hope? Can you eat that? (CREUSA *shrugs, sets off.* FLADDER *enters with his rule and chalk. He marks a wall, is about to go.*) First Troy was burnt by foreigners. But last Troy the people burn themselves.

FLADDER: That low! (*He departs.*)

OLD WOMAN: What . . . ! (THREE YOUTHS *are hustled in.* GAY *enters.*)

FIRST OFFICER: Three more who say they have seen Helen and enjoyed her!

GAY: Where?

FIRST YOUTH: Down the docks.

SECOND OFFICER: When?

FIRST YOUTH: Between seven and eleven, I don't know exactly, time stood still —

GAY: What did she say?

FIRST YOUTH: Nothing.

GAY: Nothing? Neither mm nor ahh?

FIRST YOUTH: She's dumb, ain't she? (*He looks to the others.*) Helen's dumb? (THE OFFICER *thrusts him away. He runs.*)

FIRST OFFICER: You!

SECOND YOUTH: I met her near the botanical gardens and she drew me in —

GAY: To what?

SECOND YOUTH: The lily house, we poured with sweat —

GAY: When?

SECOND YOUTH: Some time between — say, five and nine —

SECOND OFFICER: **Five and nine?**

SECOND YOUTH: I couldn't say exactly, time stood still —

FIRST OFFICER (*elbowing him away, addressing the next*): Where?

THIRD YOUTH: On a bus —

SECOND OFFICER: Upstairs or down —

THIRD YOUTH: Upstairs, of course —

GAY: When?

THIRD YOUTH: Oh, anything between —

SECOND OFFICER: **Time stood still did it?**

THIRD YOUTH: Yer know! He knows, so why —

FIRST OFFICER: And is she dark or fair?

SECOND/THIRD: 'er 'ead is shaved! (*They laugh and run.*)

GAY: Someone is chalking lines. All over Troy, a metre high. Both on the villas and the slums.

SECOND OFFICER: Not some one Mrs. Some many have been caught with chalk.

OLD WOMAN: Where's the harm in a line?

GAY: We don't know, but we think it has a message.

OFFICER: There's one! (*He goes to the wall and taking out a cloth, begins rubbing* FLADDER'S *line.*)

GAY: And oddly, the suicides have ceased.

OLD WOMAN: That's good, if life is...

GAY: Not good! (*Pause. They look at her.*) No, not good, because the hate must go somewhere. The hatred must. If only we had Helen! She could be the object but now it's the state!

SECOND OFFICER (*seeing* A YOUTH *at a wall*):   Oi! (*He grapples* THE YOUTH *to the floor*.)

GAY: Oh, hold him! He stinks of cellars! And don't puncture him! Be careful of his blood!

SECOND OFFICER (*kneeling on* THE YOUTH):   What's this with chalk?

GAY: His spit! Be careful, all their fluids kill!

SECOND OFFICER: What!

FOURTH YOUTH: That low —

SECOND OFFICER: Come again, you —

FOURTH YOUTH: **That — low —** (THE OFFICER *looks at* GAY.)

GAY: Release him.

SECOND OFFICER: Release him?

GAY: Kill him, then, what difference does it make? (*Pause.* THE OFFICER *kills* THE YOUTH, OTHER YOUTHS *pass, running.* SAVAGE *enters.*)

SAVAGE: The Miracle has gone.

GAY: Into the park with its —

SAVAGE: Been in the park. Just dogs. Just starlings. And dirty youths marking the trees with rules.

GAY: And the mother? Where is she?

SAVAGE: Gone. Without a note.

GAY: Deserted you? But she's seventy! (*A sound of disintegration.* FLADDER, *with* YOUTHS, *hurtles in. They stop.*)

FLADDER: **Last Troy.** (*Pause. She stares at him.*)

GAY: I understood — you — had — no — tongue —

FLADDER (*opening a cavernous mouth*):   **No tongue.** (*She stares.*) But I articulate the people. (*A fall of buildings. He thrusts out the ruler.*) **That high.** The ruins. **That low.** The city. (*People pour out the city, with or without bundles.* THE OLD WOMAN *is buffetted.* FLADDER *departs in the surge of the crowd.*)

OLD WOMAN: Oi! Mind my trolley! (*She is knocked.*) That hurt, idiot! (*And trodden.*) Bite your arse! **What's the rush?** It's no different over the hill, I know because I been there! (*She shouts.*) **They built eleven Troys and every one was faulty! I loved eleven men and every one was flawed. But do I surrender?**

EPSOM (*passing with a sack*):   Save yer breath, four wheels...

OLD WOMAN: Oh, my second father!

EPSOM: Ta ta, four stumps...

OLD WOMAN: Don't go, I still got lips —

EPSOM: Fuck it —

OLD WOMAN: Fuck it, yes, what's in the sack?

EPSOM (*departing*):   Daggers.

OLD WOMAN: **Yer can't eat daggers**. (*He goes.*) Teach a man a trade, and he'll find hirers...

SAVAGE (*seeing*):   Helen...

OLD WOMAN: Oi! My trolley! (*Some women start to tip her.*) Come off it, girls, steal from the wealthy if you must — rob yer enemies — (*They lift her off, dump her on the ground and place their bundles on the trolley.*) **Well, that's nothing if not predictable!** (*One slaps her.*) Sorry! Suffer in silence! Sorry!

SAVAGE: Helen...

OLD WOMAN (*now in the midst of the torrent*):   Sorry — can't move... beg pardon... (*A sack is dropped, abandoned. Tablets of soap spill out over the ground. THE OLD WOMAN cranes to smell them.*) Hyacinth! I smell you, Hyacinth!

SAVAGE (*beside her*):   It's you...

OLD WOMAN: No, it's not.

SAVAGE: It is... it's you...

OLD WOMAN: Not me. And never was. (*A shattering of masonry.*) No Helen but what other people made of her. I deny the body exists except within the compass of another's arms... (*A rush of fugitives. CHARITY glimpses SAVAGE.*)

CHARITY: Come on! We've not finished yet!

SAVAGE: No, nor started...

CHARITY: Chapter One! (*He stares at her.*) But I'm the book...! (*He doesn't move. THE CROWD moves on, CHARITY with them.*)

OLD WOMAN: Give us a lift, somebody! Give us a lift! (*She is spun round.*) I go in a pocket! I go in a bag! Oi! (*She is knocked onto her back. She lies, laughing. THE CROWD thins to individual scattering.*)

MACLUBY (*appearing with a sack into which he pops the soap tablets*):   All gone except the cripples...

OLD WOMAN: 'ho are you calling a cripple? (*He looks at her with supreme detachment.*) I suppose if birds shit in my mouth I might be fed... (*She opens her mouth. Pause.*) Come on, sparrow, I chucked pastry at you once... from honeyed beds ... from honeyed balconies... my fingers crumbled overabundant cake... **Short memory!** (SAVAGE *looks at* THE OLD WOMAN. *He looks around him. Pause.* MACLUBY *tosses him a spade*

OLD WOMAN: Terrible shortage of sparrows... come on, pigeons, divest! (*She opens her mouth wider still.*) Crows?

(SAVAGE *goes to her. He flings on a shovel of earth.*) Anyone! (*He flings on another.*) Oi! (*and another*) **I got no power, why must I be dead?** (*He smothers her with earth, breathless. She is silent. He walks back to* GAY, *flings the shovel at* MACLUBY. GAY *wraps* SAVAGE *in her arms. He is still.*)

SAVAGE: All that I know...and all you don't...

GAY: Shh...

SAVAGE: The long length of our quarrel yet to come...

GAY: Shh...

SAVAGE: Shallow reconciliations and lingering angers in the dark...

GAY: That's love, isn't it? (*He looks at her.*)

SAVAGE: Cut that short, then.

GAY: Love...hammered out thing...shapeless thing...

SAVAGE: Cut that short, then.

GAY: Bashed out like copper...warped like yew...

SAVAGE: **Cut that short, then.** (*She kisses him, but silently. He throttles her, letting her body lie over him. Pause. The wind.* THE BOY *enters, with a stiff bag. He looks at his father.*)

BOY: Find what you wanted?

SAVAGE: Thank you, yes... (THE BOY *turns to go.*) Kiss me...? (THE BOY *looks at him, blankly.*) All right, give us the plate! (THE BOY *looks puzzled.*) Broken plate... (SAVAGE *indicates with a nod the shards of broken plate which lie among the litter.* THE BOY *picks up a piece, gives it to him, goes.* SAVAGE *attempts to slash his own throat.*) Can't... (*He braces himself, but fails.*) **Can't!** (*and again*) **How did the old man do it? Can't!** (*He chucks down the shard.*)

MACLUBY: What do you think suicide is, a solitary act? It's peopled with absences.

SAVAGE: I have absences.

MACLUBY: You murdered everything, and long for nothing. Aren't you already dead? (*He picks up his bag and walks away.*)

SAVAGE: That's knowledge, then... (*Pause. Whistling off-stage.* ASAFIR *enters, sees* SAVAGE.)

ASAFIR: Hey! We are having a picnic here.

SAVAGE: Don't mind me.

ASAFIR (*off*): Hey! (JOHN *enters, bowed by hampers.*) This is the picnic place.

YORAKIM (*entering*): Oh.

SAVAGE: Don't mind me.

ASAFIR: But this is a picnic place!

SCHLIEMANN (*as guide*): The University! What a terrible place this was! The little rooms suggestive of a gaol, the —

YORAKIM: Erm —

SCHLIEMANN: The corridors of inordinate length where tortured thinkers thrashed each other in pursuit of a deity they called Truth —

YORAKIM: Erm —

SCHLIEMANN: A deity without shape or form, of course, these were not primitives — (*He looks at* SAVAGE.) Are you on the tour? (*An inordinate pause. Black.*)

SEVEN LEARS
The Pursuit of the Good

INTRODUCTION

Shakespeare's *King Lear* is a family tragedy with a significant absence.

The Mother is denied existence in *King Lear*.

She is barely quoted even in the depths of rage or pity.

She was therefore expunged from memory.

This extinction can only be interpreted as repression.

She was therefore the subject of an unjust hatred.

This hatred was shared by Lear and all his daughters.

This hatred, while unjust, may have been necessary.

'The best and soundest of his time hath been but rash ...'
Goneril, *King Lear*.

CHARACTERS

LEAR	A Child, later a King
LUD	His Brother
ARTHUR	His Brother
BISHOP	A Teacher
PRUDENTIA	A Widow
CLARISSA	Her Daughter, later a Queen
HORBLING	A Minister, later a Fool
KENT	A Soldier
OSWALD	A Soldier
THE TERRIBLE SOLDIER	
BOY	
THE SURGEON	
ASSISTANT	
GONERIL	A Princess
REGAN	A Princess
THE INVENTOR	
GLOUCESTER	A Vagrant, later an Earl
HERDSMAN	
CORDELIA	A Princess
THE EMPEROR OF ENDLESSLY EXPANDING TERRITORY	
FIRST MAN	
SECOND MAN	
DRUMMER	
THE GAOLED	A Chorus

First Lear

Darkness. A Pit in the Kingdom of LEAR's father. The rattle of a bunch of keys. A child's voice, full of apprehension

LUD: Let's play football! Let's fly kites!
ARTHUR: Let's build castles on the beach!
LEAR: Something bad is happening here...!
LUD: Something horrible!
ARTHUR: I dropped my stick!
LEAR: Something rotten, can you smell?
ARTHUR: My stick! My stick!
LUD: Horrid smell!
LEAR: Something's alive, but only just!
ARTHUR: Oh, let's build castles on the beach!
LEAR: Someone's in pain...!
LUD: Let's play football! Let's fly kites!
ARTHUR: I want my stick!
LEAR: That smell is pain! Be careful where you tread!
LUD: A hand! A hand! I trod on a hand!
THE GAOL: **We are the dead who aren't dead yet**
            Ever so sorry
            Not dead yet

The children cling together.

Whatever we did
Whatever it was
How could it justify this?
LEAR: Are you the bad, then? That you smell so badly?
ARTHUR: We are clean children and our mother loves us.
LUD: Are you our father's enemies? If so, however bad this is, it can't be bad enough for you!
THE GAOL: **We never said that we were innocent**
            What's innocence?

> **We never claimed we had no hatred**
> **Who has none?**
> **We never claimed that this was arbitrary**
> **What isn't?**

LEAR: They have no light...!

LUD: We are the royal children, shut your mouths!

LEAR: They have no sheets...!

ARTHUR: **Foot-ball**...!

LUD: Die, you horrid, stinking criminals!

ARTHUR: **Foot-ball**...!

LEAR: Oh, you poor, wet things, I never knew the ground was full of bodies, and you've got no sheets...!

LUD: All horrid things deserve to die...!

ARTHUR: **Foot-ball**...! (*He tears out, followed by* LUD. LEAR *hesitates.*)

LEAR: I shan't be king, because I am not the eldest but... if I were king... for one thing... I'd stop this! (*He runs out. A ball bounces in a field. A bright sunlight fills the stage.* THE CHILDREN *wander, apart.*)

LEAR: No criticism of our father, but I wonder is it necessary that —

LUD: **Don't talk about our doings**.

LEAR: I wasn't, but I find my mind —

LUD: **Don't remind us of it, posts!**

LEAR (*taking off his shirt*): If people were good, punishment would be unnecessary, therefore —

LUD (*pointing*): **Penalty spot**.

LEAR: The function of all government must be —

LUD: We kick that way.

LEAR (*placing* ARTHUR's *shirt as second post*): The definition of, and subsequent encouragement, of goodness, surely? (LUD *prepares a flying kick off.*) Perhaps by making goodness easier, fewer people would — (LUD *boots the ball with terrific violence. It sails high and away.* LEAR *follows it with a look of incomprehension, shading his eyes.*) You've kicked it so hard it's — (LUD *puts his arm lovingly around* ARTHUR's *shoulder*) gone right over the cliff... (*Linked together,* LUD *and* ARTHUR *walk slowly upstage.* LEAR *sits on the ground to wait.*) You would define goodness in such a way that ordinary people — who at the moment are so horribly attracted to bad things and immoral actions — would find it simple to appreciate and consequently act upon — (*He stops. He is inspired.*) No! No! That's wrong! The opposite is the case! That's it! You make goodness difficult, if anything. You make it apparently impossible to achieve! It then becomes compelling, it becomes a victory, rather as acts of badness seem a triumph now! What you need to do — (*He turns. His brothers have stopped at the very edge of the cliff and look down. Pause.*) I think, Lud, when you are king, the correct approach to punishment would be — (*They fall out of sight, together. Pause. LEAR stares, fixedly. A thin wind blows. He utters a cry, terrible and deep. At last, a BISHOP enters.*)

BISHOP: I am your education.

LEAR: I am hard to educate because I was born wise.

BISHOP: That's something everybody knows.

LEAR: I will be relentlessly critical and nothing you say will I take on trust. Why should I?

BISHOP: Why should you, after all?

LEAR: This is not arrogance on my part.

BISHOP: No, indeed.

LEAR: On the basis of mutual study we may answer some questions that have haunted me since birth.

BISHOP: My imagination is at your disposal.

LEAR: I must warn you I am peevish at times and come out in rashes, I suppose you know that.

BISHOP: I know everything about you.

LEAR: Everything? No one can know everything.

BISHOP: I know your brothers killed themselves. I know you think of death yourself. I know you cry for animals but harbour hatreds you yourself do not yet understand.

LEAR: Yes. How will you educate me?

BISHOP: I will educate you by showing you how bad I am. Because I am a bad man you will learn much from me. I will tell you nothing but what accords with my experience, which is not a happy one. Hope, for example, I have dispensed with entirely. There will be no books because you know the books and have digested them. I detest all untruths, but especially those which are sentimental, and I will beat you sometimes, for which I have authority. Almost certainly, these beatings will appear to you unjustified. I will explode in rages and then fawn on you. I may kiss your body and then ignore you for days on end. You will detest me and your innate sense of justice will cry out for satisfaction. When one day, that cry ceases, your education will be over. God alone knows why your father appointed me.

Second Lear

The CHORUS *are disposed about the stage.* LEAR, *a youth, comes among them as if between trees. He drops to his knees. He shudders. He laughs. He clasps his head.*

LEAR: I'm in such
I'm in such
I won't say ecstasy
I won't say

He shudders with emotion. A WOMAN *enters. She extends a hand to him.*

Don't touch! (*He rests his forehead on the ground.*)

PRUDENTIA: Oh, you bastard, you mistreat me, and I a woman of distinction. Oh, you shallow and temperamental manipulator of emotion, do you think I can't see through you? And your love is rough. Your love is **rough**.
LEAR: Yes. Go back to your books now. You are a lawyer, aren't you? Study the laws of infatuation.
PRUDENTIA: Our next meeting, will it —
LEAR: Next?
PRUDENTIA: Meeting, yes, will it be —
LEAR: **Next meeting? No sooner has she. No sooner have we than. What other meetings?** (*She looks at him.*) Memorize me. Store my touch. (*She turns to go.*) **She wants a meeting!** (*She starts to walk away.*) Please come back! (*She stops.*) I am so thin, and boastful, and poorminded, I am so empty and shallow as a tin bowl, ping! Love my emptiness, and don't run to men of quality and honesty, I will execute all men of character if you do, all those of deep soul who command the loyalty of women, the bearded and the bald, the calm-eyed and the knowing, love your tin bowl or it's a massacre. Ping! (*He extends a hand. She goes to put it to her lips.*) Not there. (*She places it on her belly.*)
CLARISSA (*Off*): Mother...!

A girl enters.

CLARISSA: Mother...! (PRUDENTIA *turns to face her daughter.*) You are everywhere these days except where you should be! That sounds silly but. And you smell strangely. Now look at you! This was the last place I expected to. But now I think, where is the last place she might be, go there! And that is always where I find you! (*She laughs.*) And you smell strangely...This is such a miserable corner. No sun! Your law books are quite dusty. What is attractive about these sunless corners? And you smell strangely.

LEAR: I am a tin bowl. Ping!

PRUDENTIA: Do you know, there is a law in life —

LEAR: A law in life!

PRUDENTIA: Which says, she who habitually absents herself is best left undiscovered?

LEAR: Ping! Remember the law! Ping!

CLARISSA: Why does he say that so often?

PRUDENTIA: I smell oddly because I have been in Heaven.

LEAR (*standing*):   I met a poet, and he said —

PRUDENTIA: Heaven clings.

LEAR: Very gravely, very portentously —

PRUDENTIA: It stains.

LEAR: His eyes on mine, how I detested him, how I hate the gravity of poets. '**Great love lasts through winters.**' (*Pause. He pulls a face of contempt.*) I, of course, shrank at the wisdom. I, being a tin bowl, shallowly vibrated at his profound bass notes. I tinkled on the table. Do you not feel oppressed by the wise, their laws and their shuddering complacency, the fact is I am girl-mad, which is shallowness itself, and most becoming in a tin bowl! Ping! (*He looks at CLARISSA.*)

CLARISSA: You are funny, for a prince. I think you can't command yet, much respect, can he? But here is my mother with him! So there is respect, of some kind, obviously. (*She turns to her mother.*) I came to tell you what no longer seems significant.

PRUDENTIA: Why? Tell me.

CLARISSA: I can't. It no longer seems — it has no —

PRUDENTIA: But all the same.

CLARISSA: I would feel humiliated, since it so obviously lacks significance. What delighted me for half an hour suddenly seems pitiful. I suppose because you have been in Heaven and I only thought I was...**I don't see why Heaven needs to stink**. (*Pause*) My bird is found. (*Pause.*)

PRUDENTIA: Bird... (*Pause.*)

CLARISSA: You don't remember my bird.

PRUDENTIA: Yes, I —

CLARISSA: No, you have entirely —

PRUDENTIA: No, I don't think I —

CLARISSA: You have entirely obliterated my bird from your memory, and why shouldn't you? (*Pause*)

PRUDENTIA: Yes. I had. I'm sorry, Clarissa, yes.

CLARISSA: Yes. I am not you, and you are not me, it is futile we rehearse an intimacy which no longer exists, I am not critical, you understand, I only —

PRUDENTIA: Clarissa —

CLARISSA: I only want to be honest. (*Pause*) From this moment I mark the closure of my childhood. I am sixteen, this is farewell and a dismal corner is correct for it. Shake hands. (*She puts out a hand.*)

PRUDENTIA: Of course not.

CLARISSA: Very well. Thank you for your love. I am most grateful.

LEAR: Ping! I remember your bird very well!

CLARISSA: Why does everybody lie?

LEAR: I don't lie, I exaggerate.

CLARISSA: You think you are amusing, but you are an exhibitionist.

LEAR: I think I am the most melancholy and degenerate character, so sunk in contemplation of myself I walk with stooping shoulders and lids half-draped over my never-sparkling eyes, white-skinned with horror of the sunshine and prematurely bald, incapable of friendship and though wealthy, inclined to theft. I steal the clothes of women and insinuate myself in wardrobes listening to their acts of love. Poverty disgusts me, but equally does wealth. I listen to old men, at least for seven sentences and go early to bed, but your bird has red feathers and was brought from China.

CLARISSA: Yes. But I am looking for a friend now, not an idiot. (*She turns to go.*)

LEAR: If you fuck with a greybeard, I'll — If you go down quiet streets and bed with a musician, I'll — (*He kicks a stone.* PRUDENTIA *goes out with* CLARISSA.)

THE GAOL: **We are the dead**
            We are the cruel
            We no longer need
            To mouth fidelities

FIRST VOICE: **I am the torturer**

SECOND VOICE: **I am the victim**

BOTH: **What brought us into such proximity?**

THIRD VOICE: **I am the philosopher**
FOURTH VOICE: **I am the peasant**
BOTH: **What brought us into such unhealthy intimacy?** (*A peal of laughter. They depart.*)
LEAR: How proud I was, when she did not resist my hand. How its smooth gliding to her heat was uncontested. **Youth — its piquancy!** How she forgives me everything. How she is tolerant of my dog's paws in her liquidity. **Youth — its intransigence!** She loves me not for what I am but for what I will be. To what I will be she believes herself a **significant contributor**. Oh, the vanity! And she complains if I turn her too swiftly on her face. Ow, she says. Some arthritic. Some rheumatic. Ow! (*He covers his face with his hands.*) I must recover. I must shed. I must emerge from this — cruelty...! (*The* BISHOP *enters.* LEAR *hurries to him.*) I have seen a girl I want! (*The* BISHOP *puts his arm around* LEAR.) Of course this may be a passing feeling. It may be slight. It may be trivial. Her hair is gold and her mouth far from luscious but. And gold is not a colour I much care for. It is tangled. Naturally, it's tangled. **Not her hair the emotion**. I don't think anything should stand in the way of my desire, do you? On the other hand, what good can come from it? I think what I want I should have. To be deprived, what good is it? And pain, yes, obviously pain will be experienced, but it is tangled. I am fucking with the mother. (*Pause*)
BISHOP: Have the mother murdered.
LEAR: I considered that! The moment I saw the daughter I considered that. The thought leapt to the very forefront of my mind, it knocked against my skull demanding my attention, one look and I thought, the mother has to die! (*Pause*) But no, I love the mother.
BISHOP: Abduct the daughter.
LEAR: Abduct her, yes! Would you help with that? No, it's not what I want...
BISHOP: You change, my son.
LEAR: I do! I do change! Hourly! The surface of my mind is like the boiling tar vat, God knows what may bubble from the bottom, tar in the eye! (*Pause*) I think I must adore this child Clarissa. I think this is religion. What else is it? Do you recognize religion? My considerateness, my solicitude — what else is it?
BISHOP: I want to show you cruelty.
LEAR: Yes.
BISHOP: I want to teach you indifference.

LEAR: Yes.

BISHOP: Because you are in danger.

LEAR: Am I? Yes, I am.

BISHOP: From your own brilliance.

LEAR: Yes! (*A lamp is lowered on a chain, a cold wind*.) Hold my hand!

THE GAOL *murmurs*.

BISHOP: Look, the gaol is full! Which is excellent!

LEAR: Excellent? Why excellent?

BISHOP: If some are to be free, others must be unfree, or they could not know freedom.

THE GAOL: **Don't turn off the light**
We long for the light
How else can we lodge in your memory?

LEAR: Are they guilty or innocent?

BISHOP: They are all guilty of something, even if it is not the cause of their punishment.

LEAR: But so are we all!

BISHOP: That's perfectly true, but it alters nothing.

THE GAOL: **Lear!**
Ten years since your last intrusion and you are
Now a bigger prince!

LEAR: Yes, and how ugly you are! I may have changed but you have not... my brother could not bear your ugliness...!

BISHOP: The suffering are the least objective, they are swamped in sentiment as they are by sewage. They think, if only others knew our pain, they would cry out, end it! But not so! First error of the conscience-ridden!

LEAR: But isn't this injustice?

THE GAOL: **Injustice yes**
That is the word for it
Remember the word when you go back into the light
Inscribe it on your life

BISHOP: We can go to dinner now. We eat. We drink. We lie on clean mattresses.

LEAR: No, no, that is unthinkable!

BISHOP: Think it! You must think it! (*He seizes* LEAR.) Boy, you must think and swallow it!

LEAR: **Can't eat!**

BISHOP: Must hold these in your head and still pick up the crystal glasses!

THE GAOL: **Lear**
            Soon
            Lear
            Soon
            The King dies

BISHOP: You see, their inextinguishable optimism!

LEAR: I'll act! I'll act, I promise!

BISHOP (*drawing* LEAR *into an embrace*): I am trustworthy.

LEAR (*trying to escape him*): Yes —

BISHOP: I am utterly and wholly trustworthy.

LEAR: All right —

BISHOP: And I love you.

LEAR: Yes —

BISHOP: No one more.

LEAR: Yes, yes! My loved one. My true father. But all you say I can't take heed of. And one day, possibly I'll kill you. Loving you just the same. Loving you undiminished.

BISHOP (*freeing him from his arms*): Yes. (*The lamp is drawn away*.)
What's a life? (*He goes out*).
What's a life...! (LEAR *is alone on stage. He sits*).

LEAR: The poor are not the same as the rich. The poor have got no money! (*He claps his hands*.)
That's an untruth! The truth is, they are not the same as the rich. Having no money, they became different. (TWO FIGURES *enter, equipped*.)
The innocent are the same as the guilty! They were merely looking the other way! (*He claps his hands*.)
Untrue! Another untruth! The innocent exerted themselves to be innocent. Difficult. Difficult. (THE FIGURES *cross the stage, he calls to them*)
Is there a war on? (*He gets up and scuttles to them*.)
I know nothing! I'm told nothing! On the other hand, I don't enquire. (*They gawp at him*.)
Take me. It's unnecessary I know the details, the causes and so on. And stabbing you can teach me on the way. Do you know who I am?

SOLDIERS: Prince Lear.

LEAR: Me, yes. Soon to be. Imminently, your master. What war is this? My father takes a long time dying. Are you making for the frontiers? **Defend them with your life**. No, run away if you want to. I permit it. There. Permission. (*He slaps their hands with his own*.)

Fleeing licence (*He laughs.*)

    I talk gibberish because I'm not the monarch. Come monarchy, all statements I recant. All oaths, in the bin. (*They turn to go.*) He's dying, but so slowly. So laboured his departure it is miserable to watch. **Don't go.** (*They stop.*)

    I know what you're thinking. You are thinking — fuck this for an heir apparent. (*They laugh, frankly. So does* LEAR. HORBLING, *a minister, enters.*)

HORBLING: Your father is sinking.

LEAR: Sinking? Still? How farther can he sink?

HORBLING: I inform you. I inform you, merely. (*He turns to go.*)

LEAR: **I think you should enjoy me**. (HORBLING *stops.*)

    I think you should luxuriate in my infantilism, which undoubtedly must have its rim, the comic preface to unmitigated cruelty. **The heads will make a pyramid to the stars**. (HORBLING *goes out.* THE SOLDIERS *prepare to march.*)

    Listen, I am barmy for a skinny girl and infatuated with her mother — (*They bow and march off.*)

    Yes. I respect that. Yes.

    I wish I had a brother! (FIGURES *appear, carrying a body on a bier.* LEAR *turns his back on it, shrinks.*)

LEAR: Listen, I am playing tennis! Don't attempt to dissuade me because youth needs exercise, it must be flexed about the muscles and I have sat about so long **don't bring him in I can't** — (*They progress. They put down the bier. Pause.*)

    My sense is I shall not do this job well. Is that your sense? (*He climbs to his feet, and goes towards the body with a resolute movement. Suddenly he stops and points.*)

LEAR: Red bird! (*He follows it with his eyes.* CLARISSA *enters, with a cage in her hand.*)

CLARISSA: Gone again...!

LEAR: The first thing is I go to bed early. Please make a note of that, and second — (*He stops, rushes to his father's body and seizes it in his arms, rocking it to and fro and moaning. Pause.* CLARISSA *puts the cage on the floor and walks to him.*)

CLARISSA: You should not do that. Whatever the feeling. You should not do that because in governors extremes of emotion are not liked. (*He continues to sob.*) And anyway, I think you are pretending. (*She sees the bird.*) There it goes! (*She follows it off. Pause.* LEAR *releases his father's body.*)

LEAR: Bury him. I shan't attend (*He walks away. They carry the bier.* HORBLING *attends on* LEAR, *patiently.*)

HORBLING: I was your father's minister.

LEAR: I know the face.

HORBLING: And gave ten years of good advice.

LEAR: Excellent. And yet he died.

HORBLING: On finance, planning, and on policy towards the rival states.

LEAR: We still exist, so excellent.

HORBLING: I had particular regard to harvests, which in all my years were poor, and yet there was no famine.

LEAR: I think —

HORBLING: And land reform was something of a speciality. The draining of the marsh beyond the river yielded fifty thousand acres. Here I propose a settlement for landless peasants.

LEAR: I think —

HORBLING: You ask me how this can be managed? Treaties of friendship with the Irish and the Cornish will reduce the need for soldiers, which will release the necessary labour and save the expense of weapons. Furthermore —

LEAR: I think —

HORBLING: I have prepared in detail plans for the ten years hence which I should like to show you, but in the meantime, this is the summary. (*He extends a sheaf of papers, crisp.* LEAR *looks at him, without taking the papers.*)

LEAR: You are so good at things. Obviously, so good at things. And yet I have no fool. (*Pause*)

HORBLING: Fool?

LEAR: Have I? Lando is senile. Whoever laughs at Lando now?

HORBLING: Well, this is not my field of expertise but Lando could be pensioned and the post advertised, of course.

LEAR: Lando did nothing but make ridicule of women. Their fat arses and so on. So they have fat arses.

HORBLING: Yes... I was never greatly amused by Lando...

LEAR: You do it. (*Pause*)

HORBLING: Do —

LEAR: Why not? Bring to it the same invention as you bring to drainage or economy. And give those to your successor. (HORBLING's *face is aghast.*) Oh, but this is promotion! (HORBLING *is unconsoled.*) And this way, I will have your best, surely? You will, in this function, be unconstrained by duty, conscience, or whatever drives you to make such squiggles on the paper...

HORBLING: **My skills are all in government!**

LEAR: No, that's false modesty and impossible to credit... (HORBLING *looks at the floor, then bows and starts to withdraw.*) Careful...! And be funny...! (*He goes out, passing* PRUDENTIA, *who, alone with him, opens her arms. He runs to her.*)

LEAR: Men hate me!

PRUDENTIA: No, no...

LEAR: Hate me, yes!

PRUDENTIA: No, but bury your father —

LEAR: No!

PRUDENTIA: Think of the people, the people will deduce —

LEAR: **I decline, I decline, and all deductions, pox!** Listen, I think I am alive for one reason, and that is you. But listen again. The you must be as I create her. The you gives no advice. That comes by volume from old men and clerks. Kiss me. Oh, hot and thick skirts, hide me, woollens, linens, silks, hide me, the odour of deep cloths and waterfalls of shift, do you have a centre, hide a mad child there!

PRUDENTIA: My genius. My rare thing. Do not die.

LEAR: Shan't die...

PRUDENTIA: My magician, my liar, don't be murdered...

LEAR: Shan't be.

PRUDENTIA: Promise!

LEAR: Can't. Nothing will I promise, and never anything on oath. (*He detaches himself.*) Why call me a liar?

PRUDENTIA: Did I? I must long to be lied to. (*Pause*)

LEAR: Yes... That also might be a sign of love... go now... (*She goes to leave.*) I must fuck your daughter. (*She stops.*) I must. (*Pause*) And someone will. It must be better it were me.

PRUDENTIA: That would so injure me.

LEAR: I'd best not tell you, then. (*Pause.* PRUDENTIA *grapples with the idea.* LEAR *watches her.*)

PRUDENTIA: This feeling... your feeling for... my daughter... can be explained... can only be explained by... my daughter being...

LEAR: Your daughter, yes. I dare say. (*Pause*)

PRUDENTIA: So in one respect at least... it's... profoundly tied to me... and yet another manifestation... of our intimacy ... couldn't that be said...?

LEAR: It could be said.

PRUDENTIA: It could be, yes. I see your point.

LEAR: My point? But you made it. (*She goes out, thoughtfully. He watches her.*) Oh, kindness...! Oh, decency...!

THE GAOL: **Lear**
Can we address you
Lear
The testament of torturers and victims
Our strange collaboration
The first and terrible discovery
When one lie fails
We are irresistibly attracted to its opposite

LEAR: I was born ancient, and I must discover infancy. I was born wise, and I must find ignorance. Or I will suffer... (*CLARISSA enters, pristine.*)

CLARISSA: I think you want me to admire you. In many ways I do but it would be no compliment if I praised things merely to please you. That would not be friendship, would it? Don't you agree? So I will say — as best I can — only the truth. You will say, of course, what's truth, you do that all the time, but where does that get us? Not very far, I think. (*Pause. He smiles at her.*) I am glad to be invited to your house, but also wonder why. I am not very fascinating. I am sixteen. How can I be fascinating? (*Pause. LEAR goes uneasily towards her.*)

LEAR: Well...it's...well...I...well, now you... (*He smiles, stops.*) Speechless! (*He throws up his hands. SERVANTS appear, carrying a lavish table.*)
Do sit!
And feel —
The absolute and uncommon pleasure of knowing nothing secret exists between us!

CLARISSA (*accepting a chair*):   I do feel that.

LEAR: You do? Excellent! (*Pause. He taps his fingers. Food is transported to the table.*) Commonly I find, alone with a woman, so much unsaid. Much speaking but so much unarticulated. Now, with you —

CLARISSA: I say whatever comes into my head!

LEAR: Excellent! This is an Irish fruit. Don't you feel a long way from me? Not a very sweet fruit but should all fruit be sweet? I don't see why. I can hardly see you! (*The SERVANTS are active.*) Don't you love table-cloths? This one is Dutch and took the woman eighty weeks to manufacture. Am I boring you? When my father died he left three tons of linen. I do not exaggerate. Give her some wine.

CLARISSA: No alcohol!

LEAR: Of course no alcohol. This is a Scottish thing, no grape has been within a mile of it. Why no alcohol, it is not prohibited.

CLARISSA: I like to be myself.

LEAR: Well, she is the one I invited. Isn't this pleasant, and you are excellent company.

CLARISSA: That can't be true.

LEAR: It is true.

CLARISSA: It can't be true, I've said nothing and now I feel foolish. Please don't lie even for kindness. Where is the virtue in it?

LEAR: Do you like this room? It was decorated by Persian gardeners. (*She laughs.*) It was! (*He smiles at her.*) It was! I love to see you laugh. I love your teeth, which are not even, but who likes even teeth? My father brought them here to plant the oriental garden but — (*She suddenly stands, terrifyingly.*)

CLARISSA: **This is fatuous**. (*Pause*)

LEAR: They were surplus to requirements . . . (*She glares at him.*)

CLARISSA: You do not want to lunch with me.

LEAR: No.

CLARISSA: It's something else you want and this is just —

LEAR: Yes. And conversation is a screen. A futile screen in your case, since you are so —

CLARISSA: You are going to flatter me and I hate —

LEAR: I was! I was! All part of my conspiracy to —

CLARISSA: **If you love me say so**. (*Pause*) Or. (*Pause*) What do you want to do with me? Undress me? (*Pause*) I find this difficult but however difficult it is vastly preferable to lies, fruitcake, tablecloths and so on. What do you want to do? Handle me down below? There, I said I would respect you more if you simply told me what it is you want. Now I'm blushing but that is preferable to. Oh, I'm vilely uncomfortable and I have homework to do! (GONERIL *and* REGAN *enter*.)

GONERIL/REGAN: We are the children of the union! Oh, father, Oh, mother, spare us the sights and sounds of struggle! (*Pause.* LEAR *gets up.*)

LEAR: I want to see you naked.

GONERIL/REGAN: Oh, father, this is the spectacle that brought you daughters! Do you not know even a look has consequences?

CLARISSA: I think that is probably the first honest thing you've said to me! I think we can be friends if you are honest.

It isn't difficult, is it? Honesty? (*He looks at her.*) But of course you can't see me because —

GONERIL/REGAN: Only a look!

CLARISSA: A look would only —

GONERIL/REGAN: Give him a look!

CLARISSA: And that would hardly be the end of it so —

GONERIL/REGAN: We want to be born! We want to be born! (*Pause*)

LEAR: I must see you and the door is locked.

GONERIL/REGAN: **We are going to be born! We are going to be born! Insist on it!** (*Pause*)

CLARISSA: Is that expression meant to frighten me? It really is a rather silly face and — (*He slaps her. She shudders, and then masters herself.*) I want to go home now.

LEAR: Impossible.

CLARISSA: I said.

LEAR: And I denied.

CLARISSA: **Then you are an idiot.** (*She glares at him.*) Nakedness can be so cold. Can be so granite. Do you want granite? Here's granite! (*She drags up her dress violently. Her belly is revealed. Her manner humiliates him.*) You foolish man. What use is it? Unless I feel? Unless I want? Dead iron on a mountain. (*She drops her dress.*) Give me the key now, Lear. (*He shrugs.*)

LEAR: Not locked. (*She starts to go out.*)
We must be married. (*She stops.*) It's obvious to me. The pain and. The grinding and. The punishment. Clarissa. (*A wind.*)

Third Lear

A battlefield following a defeat. Figures drift over the stage. HORBLING, in a filthy greatcoat, shaking a bellstick.

HORBLING: Humour.

LEAR (*offstage*): Kill the prisoners!

HORBLING (*sitting*): Humour is the grating of impertinence upon catastrophe.

LEAR (*entering, supported by* KENT *and* OSWALD):   Burn the villages!

HORBLING: Am I academic? I was made that way.

LEAR: And all the infants, massacre!

HORBLING: I bring to foolishness the erudition of a scholar, which is an obstacle, I admit.

LEAR (*as they help him onto a tarpaulin*):   Hang all the citizens! Are the prisoners dead yet?

KENT: There were no prisoners, sire.

HORBLING: But he is tolerant. I have yet to make him laugh.

LEAR: I love to kill! Throat high in killing!

KENT (*to others off*):   Brandy, over here!

LEAR: Who panicked, then? Who fled?

OSWALD: We did.

LEAR: No, surely, we haven't passed this way before?

OSWALD: We fled wrongly.

KENT: The army fled in one direction, and we fled in the other. They fled home, and we —

OSWALD: Deeper still into the enemy's territory.

HORBLING: Humour! Humour is the consolation of impotence! Am I academic? I don't intend to be. (*A* SOLDIER *enters with a brandy flask. They nourish* LEAR.)

KENT: Four thousand miles, if we can make it.

LEAR: Put the lights out! Don't tread on twigs! And make yourselves earth colour. Be clay! This is only the first of my many victories.

OSWALD: We have been warned...

LEAR: Pity the dead, though... pity the common and the uncommon also... there was a singer in the bodyguard who —

OSWALD: Dead —

LEAR: Call him anyway!

OSWALD: Jack! (*Pause*) No Jack.

LEAR: Extinguish all lamps! Is no one listening?

KENT: They are the lamps of the enemy, they are seeking us to kill.

LEAR: Understandable, we have burned their country. But let me talk to them. I don't see grounds for malice.

OSWALD: We have spoiled their peace and happiness!

LEAR: Admittedly, but someone would have done so. So many buildings, such fertile crops. Jealousy alone ensured someone would have put them to the torch. Let me talk to them.

KENT: I shan't stop you.

LEAR (*staggering to his feet*): I'll say Lear's army was no more than fate, no more than hurricane.

KENT: Yes, try saying that.

LEAR: And therefore temper is as appropriate as bawling at the weather, and vengeance as absurd as stabbing wind.

KENT: Do try that argument.

LEAR: As for the dead, they would have died in any case, complaining, sick and senile, which is a burden on the state.

OSWALD (*pointing*): They're over there... (*He points to small lights moving.* LEAR *pulls his greatcoat round him, begins to move off.*)

HORBLING: Majesty! (*He looks back.*) Stay with me.

LEAR: They'll miss us if we don't accost them. They'll pass us by.

HORBLING: Stay, and write your wisdom in a letter. You see I think its truth will numb them, as if, when standing too close to a bell, its boom is staggering, and then they might misuse you. But from a distance, in the quiet of contemplation, the bell is music. Write it in a letter, and then your truth might have a chance. (*Pause*)

LEAR: Yes. That's good. (*Suddenly he lets out a terrible cry, and covering his face with his hands, shudders with the horror.* HORBLING *embraces him, rocks with him.*) I saw so many corpses!

HORBLING: Yes.

LEAR: I saw so many eyes!

HORBLING: Yes.

LEAR: Eyes hopped! Eyes wriggled! **Bang!** And out came eyes!

HORBLING: They do...

LEAR: Clang goes the club!

HORBLING: Out come the eyes... (*Pause. They wait for* LEAR *to recover. He adjusts himself. He looks around him.*)

LEAR: Thank you for your patience. It's obvious I am not yet in all departments fit to govern. (*They look at the floor.*)
I say, demonstrably, I am not, and this disaster is the proof. (*Pause*)
I say you would be well within your rights to put your daggers to my throat and end it. All of you. Now. Not legitimate, but right. (*Pause*)
Rush me if you will and quickly, I shan't lift a finger. (*Pause*)
Leave me tongue-stiff in the dark, who'd stoop to call it murder, I wish I had a brother. (*Pause*)
His body lay in Asia, what a clown... (*He indulges.*)

Stabbed by his lieutenants in the Caucasus, this monarch little
known... (*He watches.*)

But. (*Pause*)

Lear now has this thing in his heart which no successor owns.
A treasure. An ingot, hard beneath the bone. (*He looks from
one to the other.*)

Error.

Oh, the heat of error, and its light... come, warm yourself at
error, who else has this? All this dead, and all these eyes, are
waste if I'm not used for further government. I'm grown. (*He
shrugs.*)

Of course, this argument is difficult, when you're knee-deep
in clot and vein. (HORBLING *breaks the silence with a
compulsive shaking of his bells, a bitter, fury of ringing. He
stops.*)

KENT: Lear is shit. Lear is vomit.

LEAR: Yes.

KENT: Oh, my dead loves out there!

LEAR: Yes.

KENT: Oh, my better-than-any-woman things, my lovelier-
than-cunt brigades, all flat, all pulp!

LEAR: Yes. (*He stares at* LEAR, *but does not move.*
HORBLING *in a paroxysm, shakes the bells again.*)

OSWALD: I should kill you now, and scraping home in rags
from fifteen months of vagrancy, say honour me, for I struck
down the thing that piped us into swamping death, **you chose
that ground**.

LEAR: Yes.

But that was another Lear.

Already I don't know him. He also lies among the
reeds. (OSWALD *wavers.* HORBLING *exclaims.*)

HORBLING: Stab him now! I have the policies! I have
the plans of reconstruction! Stab him now! New currency!
New industry, clothes for the starving, dinner for the
naked. Stab him, then! I predict a marginal increase in
taxes, but silent buses, I've got the documents, why don't you
stab! (*He tears off his cap and holds out the plans.* KENT
stares.)

OSWALD (*Lying flat*): Lights...! (*They all duck, but for*
LEAR, *who climbs to his feet. Pause. Lights flicker.*)

LEAR: Death will either occur, or if not, I shall be better for
having been exposed to it. In any event, it can't be meaningless... (*He walks offstage towards the lights which bob, and then*

are stationary. Pause.) **Clar-issa!** (*A cheer from offstage.*
CLARISSA *enters with new troops,* LEAR *draped about her.*
HORBLING *immediately begins hopping about ringing the bells
febrilely as if to demonstrate his innocuous character.*)

LEAR: She!
    She!
    God's own is there is a God!
    Perfection if perfection is!

KENT (*kneeling*): Oh, Christ in ecstasy, how did this come about?

CLARISSA: We are the Second Army.

OSWALD: Second?

CLARISSA: Who came here by a different route, and found a swamp of corpses, all our colour. Through these we searched for Lear.

LEAR: I was not dead!

CLARISSA: This army will cover your withdrawal.

LEAR: Withdrawal? But we have new troops!

KENT: Withdrawal, yes.

LEAR: **Who says withdrawal! Who!** (KENT *is silent.*)

CLARISSA: The enemy is also tired, and will let us out the country, which this time we should not burn, but tread with exaggerated care, like men who were once drunk, but in the morning rather shame-faced, replace the broken fence posts in the gardens. (*Pause.* LEAR *looks at her, conceding.*)

KENT (*rising*): We'll wash, if you've the patience, and when you say so, march. (*He and* OSWALD *go out.*)

LEAR: Kent likes me. He says I have kind eyes. And when I said destroy me, he hung back...

HORBLING: And me! I said things so ridiculous it made execution improbable. Improbable! What more can you hope for! (*He smiles, weakly.* LEAR *falls into* CLARISSA's *arms.*)

LEAR: Hold me...! I'm real...! I do exist, don't I? Hold me...! (THE GAOL *appear to* LEAR.) I've not forgotten you...! I have you very much in mind...! Time to unlock the gaol! Or maybe not!

CLARISSA: Ssh...I came for you...

LEAR: It is not the circumstance, it is the exposure, it is not the subject but the experience which —

CLARISSA: Shh...I'm here...

LEAR: I mean —

CLARISSA: Shh —

LEAR (*feverish*):   Oh, let me think — oh, let me — disaster was
not the failure — but the purpose of the war! (*He stares at her.
She wipes his face.*)

HORBLING: It's hard to be a fool with this monarch. I meet
many fools now and they say, the job is not what it was. What
was it, then, I say, I am not a trained fool, I am a novice. They
tell me you could do well at one time saying out loud the first
thing that came in your head. Any shit. Any trivia. This was
called Fool's Wisdom. But now . . . you see . . . there's no future
in that one. (*He looks to* CLARISSA.) Take me home, Miss, I
have a longing to sit in a garden . . . (*He goes out.* LEAR *looks
at* CLARISSA.)

LEAR: You are going to criticize me . . .

CLARISSA: Who else will, if I don't . . . (*He shakes his head.*) I
must, Lear . . . (*He nods.*)
I must because to swallow criticism in the interests of false
harmony would be —

LEAR: False? (*Pause*)

CLARISSA: It is my nature and impossible to —

LEAR: Oh, look, your knee! Through all the filth of campaign,
knee! I was ready to die — no — more than ready, yearning
to die — and that knee reminds me — **the momentous loss**.
(*He extends his hand slowly.*) I dare not touch it. How I want to
but I won't. I'll torture my already flogged imagination.
Fingers wait! (*He slaps his hand with the other.*) I won't say
I've missed your sex exactly. It was stiff and — it was board on
sand if I remember, us — a strange collision, grit not fluid,
glass not dew, but I thought again and again, I want what we
can not, I want what we do not, the possibility of you, more
than the plunging pleasures I have on occasions — needless to
relate — indulged elsewhere. Let me touch. (*He kisses her
knee.*)

CLARISSA: You must be sensible, and hear advice. (*He kisses
it again, kneeling.*) You must regard the judgement of others as
equal to your own. I think if this is to be a happy kingdom you
must study good, which is not difficult, and do it. I will help
you. I will criticise you, and I will say when you are childish or
petulant, and you must try to overcome the flaws in what is
otherwise, I am sure, a decent character! (*Pause. He stares at
the knee.*) You are often amusing, which is surely a sign of
goodness! (*He does not meet her eyes.*)

LEAR: How far I've come. They say three thousand miles of
marching, and the villages all roofless where we trod. I am no

longer what I was. But you, equally travelled, are more yourself than ever.

CLARISSA: What was good in me, through seeing, is now more good. What was less good, there is less of.

LEAR: **What is this good?** (*He sways, seized, pained. She looks at him. He uncurls, like screwed paper. Pause.*) And is your mother —

CLARISSA: Yes. She's well... (*He stands.*)

LEAR: Clarissa, if I am a child, it is because a child must know. Its ravings are the protests of the uninstructed. It thinks the sky is a false barrier, and the floor, pretence. It raves less, year by year, as all the barriers are demonstrated to be real, and insurmountable. I am still in my pen, and so I squeal. But thank you. And now I must see you undressed, look at your taut belly and think, childlike, it must be a fruit and a squirming animal, both.

Darkness. A drum taps. In the light of morning SOLDIERS *and* FOLLOWERS *assemble in a ragged line, shouldering their packs.* CLARISSA *walks among them, making her address.*

CLARISSA: I am a queen, and you are peasants. There is the first thing. I am not like you, and cannot call you brothers. So you know me as I am, and never falsely. The second is, when we are home, nothing will reward you but home itself, and this may be poor recompense, or even brutal. I promise nothing, except to be truthful. And the third thing is, many will die on the return as many died in coming. These will have no monument. Lastly, I am pregnant with the king's child. I hide nothing from you, not even the fact I shall eat better, and sleep warmer than you on these freezing nights. When you see my camp fire burning, you will say, she burns the last wood for herself. I am the queen, and that is so. (*They cheer her.*)

LEAR: How well she speaks! And I said such dishonest things! How well she stands! And I was all gesture and false movements. My friends, I said, my darlings, my brothers and such bollockry, no, she is exemplary, she is, and I should commit suicide!

BISHOP: Never say —

LEAR: I should, and she should govern! What's wrong with suicide? More should contemplate it.

BISHOP: You are a great king.

LEAR: Be careful! Such hyperbole leads to further horror.

BISHOP: A great king and she is shallow.

LEAR: She lacked the benefit of your teaching, which only
threw my mind into worse chaos. My head's a sack of clocks,
all keeping different hours. **A sack of clocks**. I blame you for
this, love and blame you, look at her, she sees through me!

BISHOP: She sees nothing.

LEAR: She sees my incurable sophistication! (*He goes to her.*)
I'll speak, shall I? Or not? I thought you exemplary for brevity.
No need, I think just —

SOLDIERS: **Lear! Don't go! We saved you, Lear! We crossed a
thousand miles of desert and drank foul water.**

LEAR: I burned the houses. I poisoned the wells.

SOLDIERS: **Our guts roared like the drainage of the dungeon
and some were sliced by tribesmen. Horribly sliced.** (*They stare
at him. With an inspiration, he jumps onto a chair to address
them.*)

LEAR: Was going to say —
But won't now.
Was going to exaggerate —
But not now.
Had planned such a speech but now won't give it.
Plaster you with gratitude and effusiveness...
But who requires it? (*Pause. They look at him.*)
Or do you...?
When I see a crowd I think —
Oh, horror, they expect banality! (*Pause*)
Which you don't, surely? Grey eyes? Bloody paws, and
stitched-together?
Grown out of futile compliments, surely? (*Pause. He
searches their faces.*)
Or not?
Don't want my wet-eyed exhortations, surely?
Want my tiny thanks, great murderers? (*Pause*)
I am certainly the cleverest king that ever lived and this clever-
ness I wish I had not, I promise you, but there it is, as some
have moles or a sixth finger I have appalling sight, so you must
be patient, **Say what you want and I'll say it**! (*They start to drift
away, unhappily.*)
Who said you could be dismissed? (*They stop, reluctantly.*)

TERRIBLE SOLDIER: Praise us, Lear. (*Pause. They look at
him.*)

LEAR: I pat the dog for bringing me my slipper. And hounds who fetch dead birds. Pat. Pat.

TERRIBLE SOLDIER: But for us you'd be a skin in the enemy's museum.

LEAR: Ask more of me than thanks. That's easy to give and since I don't love life —

TERRIBLE SOLDIER: **You don't love life?** (*The shout is violent. The pause also.*) **He says he don't love life**. (*He looks around.*) **My mates have things stuck in their eyeballs and he says he don't love life.**

BISHOP (*sotto voce*): Thank them. In any words. But thank them.

TERRIBLE SOLDIER: I buried lovely friends and foes alike and this one **don't love life**.

BISHOP: Quickly, satisfy them.

LEAR: I merely meant my nature is too philosophical for —

TERRIBLE SOLDIER: **I crawled through burning schools and am one-eyed for him. And he tells me he does not love his life.** (*Pause.* LEAR *looks with a profound hatred at the* TERRIBLE SOLDER.)

LEAR: If you hate me, fight me.

BISHOP: No, no, he is ten times your —

LEAR: Then at least I can keep pure in my language, which is the heart of me. (*The* TERRIBLE SOLDIER *unbuckles his belt, which falls to the floor along with his packs. Taking a knife from his collection, he flings it to* LEAR.)

BISHOP: He knows nothing of killing...!

TERRIBLE SOLDIER: Then why does he make wars? (*The* CROWD *roars, and forms a ring of curiosity.*)

CLARISSA: My husband is a child. Tell me if he lives, I refuse to watch... (*She sweeps out. The* TERRIBLE SOLDIER *stalks* LEAR.)

LEAR: First, I held my ground...
And then...
I ran in circles! (*He runs. He stops.*)
I thought, I must resort to stratagems. I thought this morally dubious and yet, was not all life likewise dubious? For some seconds I was paralysed by the futility of the ambition to continue to exist. And then — (*Suddenly he lets out a cry and runs, through the watchers. The* TERRIBLE SOLDIER *pursues him off stage. The watchers follow the figures with hand and eyes, groaning or applauding.* HORBLING *squats, not following.*)

HORBLING: The Condolences of History. (*A roar. They point.*) A belief, the holding of which one day appears sheer mischief or eccentricity, on another, shimmers with, rings with, the light of perfect truth. (*They groan.*)

An individual, mocked for his misfortune, acquires, through patience, the attributes of holiness, notwithstanding he hates men. (*They cheer.*)

Your enemy, however great his suffering, and justified in his revenge, will spoil his victory by excess. (*They groan.*)

The oppressor will be pitied, too. (*They cheer.*)

It is a matter of sitting around. (*He cannot contain himself.*) **Kill Him! String his body to the trees! I have the programme! Bury Lear and all his memory!** (*He waves the papers. A silence. He has his back to the direction in which* LEAR *enters, wearily. The silence is suggestive. His hand falters. He slips the papers back under his hat. Pause.*)

BISHOP: My son... Oh, my son...

LEAR: Shh...

BISHOP: Oh, my one son...

LEAR: Shh... (*He is still, allowing no one near him. Pause. The* TERRIBLE SOLDIER, *dying, enters, falls.* LEAR *turns to the body.*)

Oh, awful face, how fate has made a fool of you.

Ridiculous journey of a simple man. (*Suddenly he falls beside the dying man.*)

I want to be good! Get up! I want to be good! (*The watching crowd drifts away as* CLARISSA *returns. She looks at him.*)

CLARISSA: Now we have the child I think...

Now you are soon to be a father it must be time. **Suppose he'd killed you.** (*Pause*)

LEAR: You're right. Everything you say is true. Such a clear mind you have, what I wouldn't give for it.

CLARISSA: You congratulate me all the time.

LEAR: Do I?

CLARISSA: Then persist with your —

LEAR: Yes, I do — I —

CLARISSA: So why admire? What's admiration without imitation?

LEAR: What is it, yes, that's indisputable.

CLARISSA: I believe you have a good character but something is obscuring it. (*He nods. She takes his cheeks in both hands.*) Now, call your armourer. We must set off. (*She leaves. The* BISHOP *is alone on the stage with him.*)

BISHOP: How did you win?

LEAR: I appealed to all that was good in him.

BISHOP: Excellent.

LEAR: Which weakened him.

BISHOP: It does.

LEAR: Which made him — anybody's fool. (*The* BISHOP *takes him in his arms. They embrace. A* BOY *enters with armour. The* BISHOP *goes.* LEAR *looks at the* BOY. *Then he stretches his arms.*) If we are to be friends you must be intimate with me. (*The* BOY *begins to armour him.*) I mean by this, keep nothing back, even offensive things you must articulate because secrets are the rot of friendship, aren't they, don't you find? And I will burden you with mine, that is the price of love, it shoulders all else out the road, it's selfish, it is petulant, it rubs the lovers raw. Do you agree?

BOY: Yes...

LEAR: You are so like me! How you love to care for me. So beautiful the way you tie that sleeve. I think of you a lot. I say a lot, but what's a lot? Always I think of you! What's your name?

BOY: Gary.

LEAR: Oh, I don't like that! Of all the names you might have had, I like that least, but **I must make myself**.

BOY: I could call myself another —

LEAR: No. We cannot turn the world over. We must love it as it is. The helm now. (*The* BOY *puts his helmet on, then runs off. The army begins passing over the stage in its retreat.* LEAR *is quite stationary. The* BISHOP *passes, stops.*)

BISHOP: I found five candlesticks in a burning church. But we must loot. How else can we assuage our impotence? And I'm a bishop! Why do I need candlesticks? (*He goes out. The others pass. At last*, KENT. *He stops.*)

KENT: You want to be the last. But I am. (LEAR *doesn't move.*) They say sacrifice is worthless if the object of the sacrifice is itself unworthy. But they who say that don't understand sacrifice. (*Pause. At last* LEAR *moves off.* KENT *follows, the last to leave a devastated country.*)

LEAR's *Kingdom.* PRUDENTIA.

PRUDENTIA: I wanted my daughter back. Oh, my little daughter. I wanted my daughter dead. Oh, my excellent daughter. I wanted none of them back. Oh, my perfect solitude. I don't know why I like the law so much, I think because it's bottomless, I think because it's interminable, and absolute in five hundred volumes **There a pain can be asphyxiated**. (LEAR *enters, almost on tiptoe.*) A man can lose his hand for theft on Tuesday but not on Saturday. **Don't think that's ridiculous**. On Tuesday he has had time to weigh alternatives, but by Saturday his morality is tired. You're not dead, then? (*He stops.*) To be honest I would not care if you — and she too — alive? If you were three bones in Asia — and I like libraries, they contain on average one truthful book, but finding it! That's the nightmare, and truth's a thing you can grow out of, I — (*Pause*)

LEAR: Any other men? (*Pause. Distant sound of parades and rejoicing*)

PRUDENTIA: My health has been good. Every day I walk. And eating simple food, which is in any case the easiest to find, the shortages have been most exasperating to a scholar but — (*Pause*)

LEAR: Any other men? (*Pause*)

PRUDENTIA: And I plant roses. Only white. Though white is never white. My little garden has a dozen whites, all white and yet — (*Pause*)

LEAR: No others, then. (*Pause*)

PRUDENTIA: Take off your shirt. Obsessionist. (*He removes it, slowly.*) I knew this would be the style of your return. The banners dragging in the dust. The shuffling feet of the humiliated. And your grin.

LEAR: I burned five towns! (*She looks at him, at last.*)
I poisoned all their rivers!
And dragged ploughs through their palaces.

PRUDENTIA: Oh, Lear...I thrive on your insanity. (*She reaches out, touches him with the tips of her fingers.*)

LEAR: Tell me I can do no wrong.

PRUDENTIA: All wrongs are right with you.

LEAR: Tell me my excellence.

PRUDENTIA: All you are is excellence.

LEAR: My sin, even?

PRUDENTIA: Even that is grace. (*He laughs, shuddering with relief. They embrace. GONERIL hurries in.*)

GONERIL: My birth! My birth was far from easy!

CLARISSA *enters, holding her belly.*

CLARISSA: My child comes! (LEAR *and* PRUDENTIA *skip apart. A pandemonium of doctors and midwives. A couch.*)

GONERIL: I was reluctant. No, that's understatement. I was recalcitrant. Even that won't do! **I fixed my heels in her belly and stuck!**

LEAR (*horrified by* CLARISSA's *pain*): I hate this...! (*She cries.*) I hate this...!

SURGEON: Turn her on her side and throw cold water on her back!

ASSISTANT (*calling off*): **Cold water!**

GONERIL: I sensed — out there — was **vile**.

LEAR (*wringing his hands*): I hate this... I hate this!

SURGEON: A dead cat on her stomach!

ASSISTANT (*calling*): **Dead cat!**

LEAR: Is it always like this?

PRUDENTIA (*as a* MAN *enters with a bucket*): Why a dead cat?

GONERIL: I clung — and yet — hearing my father, thought — how kind his voice is... (*A bucket of water is thrown over* CLARISSA. *She gasps.*)

PRUDENTIA: A dead cat, why?

SURGEON: **Why not a dead cat! Didn't you require a dead cat?**

PRUDENTIA: Never.

SURGEON: That is your tragedy —

ASSISTANT: Dead cat! (*An animal is carried in.*)

LEAR: I am to blame! I am to blame!

CLARISSA (*in throes of pain*): **You are to blame!**

LEAR: I said so, didn't I!

SURGEON: Face down, now!

PRUDENTIA: **Face down?**

SURGEON: You talk too much! You create a most unhelpful atmosphere in which the miracle of birth can hardly be —

LEAR: **No more love. No more love**.

SURGEON: **Shut up, you are not contributing**.

PRUDENTIA (*holding his hand swiftly*): Go into the garden.

LEAR: Yes. (*He turns to go.*)

SURGEON: We'll save the child. (*He returns to the patient.* LEAR *is struck, his mind races.*)

LEAR: Save the child — then —

PRUDENTIA: **Get this cat off!**

LEAR: Save the child? You mean —

SURGEON (*grappling with* PRUDENTIA): **You are sabotaging this delivery!**

GONERIL (*as they fight over the birth couch*): **A fight at parturition! How could I have been anything but savage?** And yet... I heard my father... Suffer... (*She skips out*)

Howard Barker

SURGEON: **I take no further part in this, I retire from all, please witness, I withdraw from all, and deny responsibility for all**. Collect my bag, John we are going home.

ASSISTANT (*going out*): You can easily remarry... (*The thought penetrates* LEAR.)

LEAR: Obviously I can remarry...An Asian princess, possibly...I like their eyes... **What is to be done with me? I think I am evil!** (CLARISSA *and* PRUDENTIA *deliver the child. It gives a first cry*)
Evil because...
Evil accommodates every idea...

PRUDENTIA (*bringing the child over*): I think the child wants you...

LEAR: Me?

PRUDENTIA: Look, it does want you...! (*He holds it.*)

CLARISSA: Lear...

LEAR: How beautiful it is! But only beautiful because it owes its life to me...

CLARISSA: Lear...!

LEAR: The nature of beauty, as of goodness, rests in its power to substantiate the self...Which is not goodness at all, is it? (*He wanders off, thinking, still holding the child*)

CLARISSA: Lear...! (CLARISSA *alone with* PRUDENTIA *and a* SERVANT.) Bring my red bird!

PRUDENTIA (*at her side*): Rest, now...!

CLARISSA: I think I am living with a murderer!

PRUDENTIA: Shh, now...

CLARISSA: All kings are murderers, but **I think I am living with a torturer, bring my red bird!** (The SERVANT *hurries out.*)

PRUDENTIA: Shh...shh...

CLARISSA: All kings are torturers, but **why do you always apologize for him?** (*Pause*) That is suspicious, though I hate suspicion. And yet it will occur to me no matter what I.

PRUDENTIA: You are so —

CLARISSA: Delirious, of course I am, **have him if you want to. Naked and**. (*Pause. The* SERVANT *brings the cage and places it by her. He goes out.*) That is a terrible accusation, mother. And I uttered it.

PRUDENTIA: Yes.

CLARISSA: Crossing the desert I felt once — so clearly — no one will ever love me.

PRUDENTIA: That's silly, that's —
CLARISSA: No, don't pity me! I don't mean I wept. I was not
    desolated, I felt — a quality in me forbids it. (*Pause*) A good
    quality, perhaps. (*Pause*)
PRUDENTIA: I want to hold you, and yet I can't.
CLARISSA: That's funny.
PRUDENTIA: Yes. Believe me when I say I want to hold you.
CLARISSA: Yes, but it makes no sense. (*Pause*) I should sleep
    now! Perhaps when I wake up I shan't suffer this oppression...
    (*She sleeps.*)
PRUDENTIA: I also want a child... are you asleep? I also
    want a child... (*She goes to leave. Semi-darkness, out of
    which a white plane suddenly descends.*)

Fourth Lear

THE GAOL: **Lear**
    We are familiar with the lies of politicians
    Their grins and handshakes we despise
    And the freedom fighters
    Who trusts their passionate embraces?
    Their clenched fists which don't unclench
    Look out Freedom's fist in your eyes!
    Lear
    Our calls must reach your bedroom
    On still nights when you sleep alone
    The locks locked
    The bolts bolted
    And the shutters tight
    The moon is walking in the gardens
    And we say
    Lear is thinking of our pain tonight!

The white plane descends, in the opposite direction. The BOY *runs
in. Dogs bark.*

BOY: Fell there! (*He runs off.*) Fell there! (LEAR *enters, with an*
    INVENTOR.)

LEAR: Is this with God's permission? Or is it against God?

INVENTOR: He gave us word. He gave us paper. And He gave us curiosity.

LEAR: But not wings.

INVESTOR: Not wings, no.

LEAR: He did not intend us to be birds, or we should be thick with feathers. But does He resent us becoming birds? There is the question.

INVENTOR: He is eager for us to be so. But He requires we ourselves furnish the means. He says, I give you intelligence. Employ it, therefore. The means I will provide, the will you must discover.

LEAR: I have the will.

INVENTOR: He says the earth is a most imperfect place, go forth and tidy it.

LEAR: Yes.

INVENTOR: After all, did He not have a mere seven days to make it?

LEAR: No time at all.

INVENTOR: He knew even the infant would place his finger in the caterpillar's path. Why? To observe how it altered its behaviour. So every man inflicts himself on his terrain. The horse is placed in shafts. The peasant turns the water's course to his advantage. And even in the death cell the prisoner tutors the mouse. God smiles at this. God claps. (*The* BOY *appears holding the damaged plane.*)

BOY: Busted.

LEAR: Correct its faults. (*The* INVENTOR *bows.*)
Then make the full-sized version. (*He bows again.*)
I'll fly myself. (*He goes out.* LEAR *seizes the* BOY *in an embrace.*)
Here's peace! Here's goodness, surely? Here's truth without contradiction?

BOY: You're hurting me... (LEAR *looks at him. Pause.*) Yes... (KENT *enters. The* BOY *runs out.*)

LEAR: Ah, I do so hate to see you sometimes. Always grave. Always responsible. I never had an uncle but you must be what uncles look like. I never had a friend, but you must be what friends aspire to. You are going to reprimand me. (*Pause*) Or shall I make the speech? I could.

KENT: Everything is neglected.

LEAR: Yes.

KENT: To take a single example, the roads are pits.

LEAR: The people move too much. Look at all these accidents.
KENT: I beg you to be —
LEAR: **People must keep still.** (*Pause*)
        What connection is there between movement and
        knowledge? None, I promise you. Anything else?
KENT: The river burst its banks.
LEAR: It's the rain does it.
KENT: Obviously, but —
LEAR: If we control the river, we shall control the lake.
        If we control the lake we shall control the weather.
        If we control the weather we shall abolish rain, for no
        one likes to get his head wet. Then we shall starve. No,
        it's better we endure floods.
KENT: We? The castle's on a hill.
LEAR: It is much closer to the lightning.
KENT: **All these unnecessary deaths!**
LEAR: Unnecessary deaths? And what is a necessary one?
KENT: **You irritate my loyalty with such fatuous —**
LEAR: **And you my patience with inanity!** (*Pause*)
        No, we must be friends. Mustn't we? If friends we are.
KENT: I think, Lear, in your case, there is no fitting the hand
        of intelligence into the glove of government.
LEAR: None. And I gave you the chance to kill me in
        the desert... (KENT *walks away*.) They say you are a nice
        man! But wouldn't a nice man kill me, in order to be nice
        toothers? (*A thin bell rings. A pair of* BEGGARS *enter, one
        mute*.)
            Hey! Two of my happy subjects! What, brothers, no clinic?
        No warm house? No hot dinners? There's the man! Protest!
        (*He points to* KENT.)
            He says you should not die — unnecessarily! (KENT *goes
        out in disgust*.)
            I feel you ought to live to ninety, but what's ninety?
        No, that's unjust, seven hundred would be better, **ugh, that
        sore is vile...!** (*He turns in horror, then slowly, turns back
        and compels himself to examine it. The* BEGGAR *rings the
        bell*.)
            You have the sore...I have the coin...I give you the
        coin...you still have the sore... (*He holds out money*.)
BEGGAR: Give you the sore with pleasure.
LEAR (*as the* BEGGAR *pockets the coin*): Do you believe in
        anything?
BEGGAR: Yes. Tomorrow.

LEAR: Is that so? I fear tomorrow. I fear tomorrow I may
doubt the few things I succeeded in believing in today. (*The*
BEGGAR *sets off.*)
   Don't go I'm the monarch. (*They stop.*)
   I do think it's funny, that you and I have nothing in com-
mon. Less even than a cow and a crow. Or a worm and a horse.
Less than them, even.
BEGGAR: They share the field, at least.
LEAR: They share the field, yes. (*The* BEGGAR *sets off with a
ring of his bell.*)
   Don't go I'll stab you! (*They stop.*)
BEGGAR: I'll starve to death if I must listen to your logic —
LEAR (*cruelly*): **I need it. As you need bread, I need it.** (*Pause.
The* BEGGAR *shrugs.*)
BEGGAR: At least give us another coin. (LEAR *spins one.*)
LEAR: I'm sure we must have one thing in common. Don't we?
One thing?
BEGGAR: I shit.
LEAR: Yes, well there is a beginning.
BEGGAR: And piss.
LEAR: There's another, but don't be coarse I'll have your
tongue out. This is a polite society.
BEGGAR: I was born, and I must die.
LEAR: The first yes, the second we don't know yet.
BEGGAR: Must die, obviously.
LEAR: **What's obvious about it**? (*Pause. He spins another
coin.*)
   All we know is that all others die. From that it cannot be
deduced we also shall. Perhaps you are immortal. It would be
like immortality to bestow itself on something so grotesque and
unbenign as you. **Don't ring the bell, I'm talking.** (*Pause. The*
BEGGAR *is patient.*) How greedy you are. I have already
given more than you could hope to beg in seven days and far
from creating in you a sense of gratitude you are ringing now
from pure avarice! (*Pause. The* BEGGAR *is so uncomfortable
under* LEAR'*s examining gaze, he fumbles for the money in his
pockets and flings it down.*)
BEGGAR: I can't stick this! Take it! Can I go now, monarch?
(*The coins roll over the floor. The* BEGGARS *get up to
go.*)
LEAR: A duke has died without an heir. Of some place known
as Gloucester.
BEGGAR: Tramped there...

LEAR: Good. You are his successor. (*Pause. The* BEGGAR *stares at* LEAR.)

BEGGAR: What is this? Torture?

LEAR: **You think you are the only one who's tortured?** (*A smile comes over the* BEGGAR*'s face. He grasps his mute companion.*) Not him.

BEGGAR: I've tramped with him eleven years.

LEAR: This is a journey you must make alone.

BEGGAR: He has no tongue and — (LEAR, *mocking dumbness, shakes his head. A pause of sufficient brevity. Then the* BEGGAR *disburdens himself of his bags and satchels and drapes his companion with them. He kisses him swiftly on the cheek and gives him the bell. The* CHORUS *enters.*)

LEAR: Let no one say I hide things from myself.

THE GOAL: **Lear**

LEAR: Let no one say I do not see all sides of the argument.

THE GAOL: **Lear**

LEAR: All consequences and connections.

THE GAOL: **Lear**

LEAR: Ramifications and —

THE GAOL: **Lear**

LEAR: I had not forgotten you. One whim could liberate you. So small an action on my part. And yet. (*An effect of sound and light. An airplane is revealed.*) For this a hundred children starved. For this, four thousand went without arithmetic. And groves of soft fruit perished... (*The* BOY *enters holding* LEAR*'s flying kit.* LEAR *extends his hands for the gloves.* PRUDENTIA *enters. She looks at him.*)

INVENTOR: The wings rotate at seven revolutions to the minute, the mean average of the herring gull. The thickness of the air will cause the craft to float as boats do on water and possibly you may effect a landing on the clouds, the upper sides of which it is believed by us contain estates of lush cultivation.

PRUDENTIA: My body is a better medium to move in, did I not praise you enough, I am forever praising you, this is an affront to me, this is a criticism, or rather a pique, a little criticism worthy of an infant and not a solution.

GONERIL (*entering*): Do go, and hurry, I love you!

PRUDENTIA: The things you have called me, the abuse and the superlatives, my coarse hound, you raised me up against the factory gates one night, there was flight if ever flight was.

GONERIL: And bring me something!

PRUDENTIA: **Have I no power over you!**

GONERIL: Something big and lovely!

PRUDENTIA: I shan't plead! I shan't wheedle! If you fall dying to the ground I'll put up my skirts and piss your face with anger, do you hear me? Do take the gauntlets off you look an idiot but I'm the only one who'll tell you, it takes love to properly humiliate, die for all I care, but not absurdly, please, it mocks me also...! (*CLARISSA enters, pregnant with REGAN.*)

CLARISSA: Don't fly.

PRUDENTIA: He flies because he hates us.

GONERIL: Be quiet, I want a present!

CLARISSA: Don't fly.

LEAR: If I discover paradise, I shan't come back. At least until I discover paradise is wanting. Kiss me all those who loved me, and the rest, pretend. (*The COURTIERS gather round, but PRUDENTIA and CLARISSA remain still.*)

LEAR: Clarissa, always you make me feel ashamed. And to escape shame, I try to rise above it...

GONERIL: Oh, do go and hurry! (*The INVENTOR goes to a wing, the BOY to another. A drum is tapped. LEAR, in the pilot's seat, cranks a handle to the rhythm. GLOUCESTER, the elevated beggar, appears resplendent. He goes to HORBLING.*)

GLOUCESTER: On Thursday I was a tramp, on Friday I fucked rich women. There's a joke, surely? Don't tell the other tramps! (*He goes to PRUDENTIA.*) Have you a lover?

PRUDENTIA: I am learning to go without one.

GLOUCESTER: Excellent. (*He goes to CLARISSA.*) And you?

CLARISSA: I led an army into Asia...

GLOUCESTER: I saw them. They were on the bridge and I was underneath it.

CLARISSA: I led an army into Asia...

GLOUCESTER: So you said, but I would love to see your belly.

CLARISSA: **For this**...! (*The drum beat rises. LEAR cranks faster.*)

HORBLING: The king became a bird, have you heard this one? The king stuck feathers on himself. And the queen said — **I so hate comedy it makes men cruel!** (*The cranking and the drumming reach a climax at the end of which LEAR falls exhausted over the handles. The drumming slows, the wings cease to flap. In the stillness, GLOUCESTER goes to the DRUMMER, takes his sticks, and tosses them onto the floor.*)

GONERIL: Oh, he is not perfect, my father...! (CLARISSA *goes to her child. She puts her hands on her shoulders.*)

CLARISSA: Lear wished to fly, and could not. And I wish to be happy, and cannot. Always less. Less always. In lessness we must discover plenitude. Less always. Always less. (LEAR *climbs off the plane and flings himself to the ground. He flattens himself, as if struggling to be drawn into the earth. He writhes. He moans.*)

INVENTOR: It's weight.

CLARISSA: **It is not weight it's purpose.**

INVENTOR: The king, though much reduced by fasting, also reduced his energy, thereby demolishing the ratio of power to wing area —

KENT: Shh...

INVENTOR: The necessary combination can be achieved by —

KENT: Shh... (*He goes to usher the* INVENTOR *away.*)

LEAR: My boy is light... (*They stop.* LEAR *straightens himself onto his knees. Pause.*)

CLARISSA: Lear, accept the sign.

LEAR (*to the* BOY): You're light, aren't you?

CLARISSA: Accept the sign, that also is a proof of wisdom.

LEAR: **Sil-ence!** (*He blocks his ears. Pause.*)

BOY: I'll go. But I'll be late for dinner! (*Pause.* LEAR *gets to his feet.*)

LEAR: We'll keep some back.

INVENTOR (*moving to the wings*): Drummer!

CLARISSA: Oh, you are intolerable to a kind mind!

LEAR: **And you are a guillotine on lips or fingers!** (CLARISSA *takes* GONERIL *out.*)
    Steel mouth and steel body! (*Pause. The* BOY *climbs up on the plane.*)

BOY: Ready!

INVENTOR: Drum! (*The* DRUMMER *beats the cranking rhythm. The* INVENTOR *and another return to the wings. A wind. The* BOY *cranks.* LEAR *hurries forward as a torrent of feathers descends over the stage, obliterating the plane.*)

LEAR: Oh, who loves kings!
    Oh, who loves thrones, somebody must!

THE GAOL: **Ha, ha, ha, ha, ha, ha!**

LEAR: Oh, kneel before his severed head, it was so full of passion once!

THE GAOL: **Ha, ha, ha, ha, ha, ha!**

LEAR: The temper of the underdog has its own beauty, but so has the firing squad! (*Silence. The last feathers fall. Sound of the wind. Nobody moves. Their eyes scan upwards.*)

HORBLING: If ever there was need for humour this is. (*Pause*)

Since no one else will I. (*Pause*)

At certain times only an idiot can find the words so.

(*Pause*)

His ineptitude uncannily fills the need of. (*Pause*)

For example, at Golgotha, there was an idiot.

This idiot danced under Christ whilst. (*Pause. The clothing of the BOY falls out of the sky at LEAR's feet*)

Lear has killed his one loved boy! (*He points at LEAR.*)

There is the cause of all our discontent so.

Accuse him!

Overthrow! (*No one moves. HORBLING rubs his face ruefully. LEAR picks up the clothing.*)

LEAR: He did not love me. But when I instructed him, he repeated the words. (*He looks around.*) What more can you ask?

GLOUCESTER (*coming to him*): Let's adjourn to a silent room, and ask an old woman to dance naked...

LEAR: Why...?

GLOUCESTER: Or row a skiff to the madhouse on the rocks...

LEAR: Why...? (GLOUCESTER *shrugs.*) It is not life that's sacred. It is death.

INVENTOR (*picks up a fragment*): The structure of the rudder seems —

LEAR: Did he have time to make his death?

INVENTOR: If anything, too flexible, which is not difficult to —

LEAR: His lost years are nothing but could he make his own death, or did you deprive him? (*The INVENTOR looks uncomfortable.*)

INVENTOR: It is the story of our progress. Grief, and after grief, design. The graveyard and the drawing board.

LEAR: Yes. But we must live our own deaths, and not be cheated. You robbed him with your accident. (*The INVENTOR looks to KENT, anxiously.*) Lock this criminal away, and keep him pencilless. For if he has a pencil, he will invent. And no twigs either, or he'll make charcoal. It is a disease, this rabid invention. (*Pause. Then* KENT *goes, reluctantly, to arrest the* INVENTOR.) You shuffle, which is a mute criticism of instruction.

KENT: Perhaps you know things which a simple man like me —

LEAR: Come, come, you, simple?

KENT: A man of rather plain intelligence —

LEAR: You, plain? Never. Why this incessant apology, you bolt apology to yourself like armour, and you love my wife. (*Pause.* KENT *drags the* INVENTOR *offstage.*)

PRUDENTIA (*going to him*): Make love to me, you wretched, lonely man.

LEAR: Tuck up your skirt for Gloucester, he has more appetite.

PRUDENTIA: Have you no love for me? **I am so glad you are not dead**.

LEAR: It's shallow...

PRUDENTIA: Let it be shallow. **So glad**.

LEAR: It was a lake, and now it is a pool. Soon, it will be a puddle, and the sun will boil it to a dark stain on the pavement.

PRUDENTIA: I have been too loyal.

LEAR: Who knows?

PRUDENTIA: I have made myself a casual possession.

LEAR: Who knows? And once I lay all night on a roof to watch you dressing.

PRUDENTIA: I have no dignity. Come with me. I have no pride.

LEAR: And that's a freedom... (*He puts a hand on her.*) I am waiting to be killed, and no one does it. (*She takes him in her arms. He clings to her.*)

Interlude

The sea shore. The BISHOP *paddles, lifting his robe.*

THE GAOL: **How excellent
To be the executed
How excellent**

To know you caused offence
How painful to be just
The victim of an accident
A piece of historic inconsequence

How good to be an executioner
That also is a skill
Ask those who suffered from the inept
How good to be an executioner
He walks home with a civic sense

KENT *enters, and watches the* BISHOP *from a distance.*

BISHOP (*sensing him*): I have these feet.
And salt relieves them.
Sometimes the feet are twice the size.
Pity me. I do. (*He paddles.*)
The sea!
Sometimes it kills, and sometimes it cures.
Pity me I haven't long to live.

KENT: Nobody likes you.

BISHOP: It's true. I always seem to be thinking something else. Behind good-morning even, there is an altogether different sentiment. No one likes this, naturally.

KENT: They say you spoiled the king.

BISHOP: Yes, and what are you, the vessel of opinion or do you have a —

Oh you have a knife
He has a knife fancy
Fancy
He has a knife

And look at me, too far from anyone, oh, I have chosen a silly time to bathe, no what is your view, or are you just the vessel of opinion? Chuck us a towel.

KENT: Unnecessary.

BISHOP: What, the towel?

KENT: Unnecessary, yes.

BISHOP: Oh, dear, never to have dry feet again. This is the last time I shall get near a vessel of opinion. Who are you doing this for? Everybody? I do love that! You are smothering your personal dislike of violence in the interests of the community. I do love that. Give us a towel.

KENT: No towel.

BISHOP: Time to get rid of the Bishop. Ask Kent. He's free. Seen Kent? I know someone who can stick a knife in. Kent, you mean? Yes, him, but say it's for the people. Oh, Kent, you're in, everybody hates the Bishop, got ten minutes? **Kent you have no interior sight and you pass that off as goodness.** (*Pause. KENT takes out his knife.*)

KENT: You have to die.

BISHOP: Only me?

KENT: I think so, yes.

BISHOP: Only me. Relax, you other criminals. Only me... (*Two children appear, GONERIL and REGAN.*)

GONERIL/REGAN: 'ello, 'ello! 'ello!

KENT: Go away. Your mother wants you.

GONERIL/REGAN: 'ello, 'ello, 'ello!

BISHOP: **Come here, dearies!**

KENT: Oh, you loathsome man...

BISHOP: Yes, but I must be consistent.

GONERIL: What are you doing here?

BISHOP: Not a lot.

REGAN: You don't go to the beach, do you?

BISHOP: No, this is my final visit.

GONERIL: Mummy says steer clear of you.

BISHOP: Difficult, up till now. But from tomorrow, easy. **That's enough wit, this man is out to murder me!** (*Pause. The CHILDREN stare, open-mouthed. Then they hold hands.*)

REGAN: Swim, then. That way.

KENT: How loathsome, to drape yourself in children.

BISHOP: Yes, how loathsome I appear to want to live. I appear to be prepared to annexe anything to hand to perpetuate my miserable life. How loathsome. I really need examining.

GONERIL: Swim for a day and you get to an island.

BISHOP: I haven't a day, unfortunately. (*Swiftly, he grabs REGAN, thrusting her body in front of him.*)

REGAN: Ow! Mummy!

KENT: Oh, you nauseous and —

GONERIL (*rushing off*): Mummy! Mummy!

BISHOP: Oh, vile thing I am, vile bag of wicked thought and physical corruption, I am so ashamed! (*Pause. Gulls cry. REGAN is stiff and white.*)

KENT: If I doubted the rightness of this murder, this action must confirm it.

BISHOP: Hilarious. Your logic. Hilarious.

REGAN: He'll kill me by mistake!

BISHOP: Well, yes, I think he will. He is a man of real convictions, **don't move.** (*Pause. The* CHILD *stares. At last, the* BISHOP *pushes her away. She wanders, then runs off.*) How magnificent the gestures of the bad...I did that, not out of love of infants, who are nothing, but because one day I think she will hunt you... (KENT *goes to him, kills him. The* BISHOP *sinks into the water.* CLARISSA *appears, controlling her horror.*)

CLARISSA: I never thought I would give thanks for murder, but I must not hide behind the fiction that all life is good. How simple that would be. How simple and intransigent. Such absolute moralities are frequently the refuge of misanthropy...

KENT (*roping up the body*): Any thought that Lear produced, this man legitimized.

CLARISSA: **We must protect the weak against the cunning.** (*Pause.* KENT *stops, looks at her.*)

KENT: Yes... (*The* CHILDREN *call, off, she goes, swiftly.*)

THE GAOL: **Oh Kent**
You excellent and permanently servile mind.

KENT: The tide...

THE GAOL: **Even your worst enemy you bury.**

KENT: How swift this tide is!

THE GAOL: **Your mother taught you manners and you can't forget**
Your father said to tell the truth and open doors for women

KENT: Hey! (*A high wind lashes the stage.*) He floats! His corpse is a balloon of gases! (*He clings to the body of the* BISHOP. *Music, which stops with a burst of sunlight.* KENT *climbs off the body.*) God help me...I am on a rock...a fucking rock...and oh...**Nobody!**

BISHOP: There's me...

KENT: No sticks to burn...no fruit to eat...**Oi! I railed Oi!** I railed, and then I sat, for standing was pointless. And then lay, for sitting was pointless... (*He lies. The sun beats down. His hand goes to his crotch.*) Clarissa...If three matrons stood between you and my cock I'd savage them **anybody listening!** (*The sea*) Clarissa...I would bend you across my knee and stare into your cavity...**Anybody listening!** (*The sea*)

BISHOP: Sun...surely?

KENT: I would walk over the mouths of the world's poor to grasp you by the —

BISHOP: Salt water, obviously...
KENT (*prodding the body*):   **Get back!** (*The* BISHOP *laughs*)
   Get back (*Pause*)
   I pushed it away, but back it came, on every tide...my super-
   ior in perception...

Fifth Lear

*A hammering at a door. LEAR, bearded, on a bed. A window, with
a number of kites outside, flying, indicating the height of the room.
HORBLING enters.*

HORBLING: I knock. But that's a formality. I have permission. Permission, and more permission. For what? What's permission if imagination's dead? (*He goes to* LEAR.) Are you
   asleep? I bring petitions. From the inventor, asking for his
   sentence to be halved. And the rest are from the inverately
   cruel. They give them to me because Kent's missing. By the time
   I reach the top of the stairs I am carrying my own weight in
   paper. (*He drops a pile of petitions on the floor. He watches the
   kites move.*) Why don't you give them bread? I don't understand it. There is enough bread. You get the loaf and you go —
   (*He pretends to break it.*) Two people fed! And you take the two
   halves and you — (*He mimes breaking them again.*) Four people
   fed! I really do not understand — (PRUDENTIA *enters.*)
PRUDENTIA: Weren't you the minister under the old king?
HORBLING: Me?
PRUDENTIA: Yes. Horbling, wasn't it?
HORBLING: I don't think so. Or was I? Oh, yes, but briefly!
   (LEAR *sits up. The sound of metallic footsteps outside.*)
   What's that? (*They come nearer.*) Your assassins, I presume...?
   (*Two armoured* FIGURES *appear in the door.* HORBLING
   rushes to them.) There he sits! Eliminate the bloody oppressor
   of widows and orphans! Strike and. (*He stops. He sits.* LEAR
   *comes to the figures, and looks at them. They begin to shake,
   with laughter.*)
GONERIL/REGAN: Oh, Dad, our hearts ache for you! (*They
   throw off their helmets.*)

REGAN: Such trickery to reach our father, so immured is he in his tower!

GONERIL: But love will always find a way!

REGAN: Love does!

GONERIL: Love will!

GONERIL/REGAN: Love always — (*They revolve in an embrace, stop.*)

REGAN: Why is our mother's mother here?

GONERIL: We reach our non-existent dad and —

REGAN: Why is our mother's mother here? (*Pause.* PRUDENTIA *moves to the bed, and sits.*)

GONERIL (*bursting with pleasure again*):   We were going to sing you a song!

REGAN: We learned a song!

GONERIL: But now we're too happy to sing! Do you admire us?

REGAN: We're women of **exceptional initiative** you must admit! (*She kisses* LEAR.)

GONERIL: We're giggling!

REGAN: We're frothing!

GONERIL/REGAN: **How clever to get past the guards!**

REGAN: Do we embarrass you!

GONERIL/REGAN: **Pair of idiots!** (*He holds them to his chest.*)

GONERIL: I passed my exams!

REGAN: And I learned archery!

GONERIL: I can swim the river both ways!

REGAN: Boys we hate!

GONERIL: But horses!

REGAN: We're giggling!

GONERIL: We're frothing!

GONERIL/REGAN: **We embarrass him!** (*A pause. He examines them.*)

REGAN: How warm your hands are, like loved garments ... and the smell... (*She kisses his hands.*)

LEAR: Every moment I yielded up to love ... is lost to my own struggle...

GONERIL (*peering into him*):   What struggle...?

REGAN: Look, his feet point inwards still...!

LEAR: Every excellence of intimacy broke the thin wire of my concentration...

GONERIL: Yes...?

LEAR: I wish to be a saint, and all your charm, and love, and small, round voices, washed like a babbling stream the mortar from the joints of my great arch, I want to be a saint and more so than a father...

GONERIL/REGAN: Yes, yes! And that is why we love you!

REGAN: We said that together!

GONERIL/REGAN: **Do ignore us if you wish!**

GONERIL: And that, too!

PRUDENTIA: I encouraged him. In everything, I encouraged him. Because he is a great man.

HORBLING: She says so, but where's the evidence? She asserts it, but where's the proof? If he is great why are the poor poor? This tower is so tall their dying groans don't reach him.

PRUDENTIA: Yes, he is a perfect man, and you screech like a duck drowned by its companions.

REGAN: Why is our mother's mother here?

GONERIL: She cleans does she?

REGAN: She makes the beds?

HORBLING: Makes the beds untidy, yes, by manoeuvring upon her arse. **Don't punish it's all in the past,** as the killer said to the widow.

GONERIL: Why does the king like you?

HORBLING: Good question. He brought me up this tower and gave me a spoon. That may be fondness, that may be not. If A is sent to gaol and invites B to join him, is that friendship? Ponder. Ponder. If B refuses, is that bad manners?

LEAR (*to his daughters*): Leave us now. You've grown, that's obvious. Whether you're beautiful is for other men to judge, and whether you're intelligent is insignificant, for if you're not, others will be.

GONERIL: You once ran with me the length of the sea-shore. I've never forgotten that.

LEAR: I loved you insanely. But in loving you insanely, I only loved myself.

REGAN: Come out and govern the world.

PRUDENTIA: He had a teacher, but now he teaches himself.

GONERIL/REGAN: **What is our mother's mother doing here**? (*Lights change. The* CHORUS *are seen holding the kite strings and staring up.*)

THE GAOL: **For every child that dies we fly a kite**
Lear
Are you not blind with kites?
For every suicide that leaps into the river
We fly a kite

Lear
How dark your room must be!

CLARISSA *enters, holding a loud-hailer. She puts it to her lips.*

CLARISSA: I most tenderly wish to see you.
I most anxiously want to touch you.
I married you.
I saved you from your enemies.
I will not be dissuaded from you no matter what indifference you show.
My bird is dead but I have learned his patience.
And if you hate my voice it is no more than I hate it myself.

Pause. The strings move in the wind. She gives the loud hailer to a MAN. *He proceeds to reiterate her speech.*

MAN: She most tenderly wishes to see you. She most anxiously wants to touch you. She married you. She saved you from your enemies. She will not be dismissed from you no matter what indifference you show. Her bird is dead but she has learned his patience And if you hate her voice, it is no more than she hates it herself. (*He walks to a new spot to repeat the message.*
CLARISSA: Every day I'm here. Every day the message seems less true. But it is not less true merely from being repeated. (REGAN *and* GONERIL *appear, elated.*)
GONERIL/REGAN: **We saw him!**
GONERIL: And he is beautiful!
REGAN: He wears black!
GONERIL: Aged a little —
REGAN: Considerably aged!
GONERIL: Considerably aged yes —
REGAN: But silent!
GONERIL: Almost —
REGAN: Almost silent, yes —
GONERIL/REGAN: **And there is a woman there who looks as if.** (GLOUCESTER *enters.*)
GLOUCESTER: I go to the brothel. I do not expect to be happy in the brothel. But there at least I am able to suffocate the question whether I am happy or not. (*He looks up.*) What does he do up there? (*He goes out*)
CLARISSA (*to her* MAN):   When she comes down, my mother, hood her, and in the hood, bring her to me. Do it if she cries or

struggles. But hood her. (*He bows.*) **I mean however painful do it**. (*He goes out. She looks to* GONERIL *and* REGAN *half-afraid. But they are bland.*)

GONERIL: What kind of grandmother was that?

REGAN: She never played with us.

GONERIL/REGAN: **At that age you surely should be nice!** (*They run out.* CLARISSA *looks at the* CHORUS *of the poor, as they pluck their kite strings, moving together like tillers of a field.*)

CLARISSA: I so hate lies. But, look, the poor! (*She looks at them silently moving.*) I so hate subterfuge. But, look, the destitute! (*She looks. She hurries away. A clang.* PRUDENTIA *hooded is brought in by* TWO MEN.)

PRUDENTIA: It's all right, I can walk! Oh, let me walk! Why drag me when I have —

FIRST MAN: **Legs!**

PRUDENTIA: Legs, yes —

SECOND MAN: **We see your legs!**

FIRST MAN: And wonder —

SECOND MAN: **Where have they been, those legs?**

FIRST MAN: **Where have they thrashed the sky, don't we?** (*They place her on a stool. Pause.*) The pleasure it give us to grab a lawyer. We were so abused by you in courts. You and your vocabulary. You and your wit.

BOTH MEN: **You called us things and it stuck like spit to our expressions. Admit our pleasure. No human could resist.** (*Pause. They stand back from her.*)

PRUDENTIA: Do you know who I am?

FIRST MAN: Yes.

PRUDENTIA: Do you realise the perilous position you have placed yourselves in?

SECOND MAN: We realise your legal language is quite dead.

FIRST MAN: Oh, immaculately exercised legs. Grandmother ... (*They creep away, silently.* CLARISSA *appears. Pause.*)

CLARISSA: Oh, mother, thank you for years of love... (*She collapses onto another stool, holding her head in her hands. Pause.*) I must leave you hooded because if your eyes meet mine, no thing that is correct could be articulated...

PRUDENTIA: Take it off.

CLARISSA: Your eyes would make all crime like passing showers.

PRUDENTIA: Remove it, then.

CLARISSA: Precisely what I cannot for the reasons I have just —

PRUDENTIA: Excellent reasons.

CLARISSA: Are they, though?

PRUDENTIA: Yes, it's truth which burns out argument.

CLARISSA: **I will not have you uncovered all my life I have been dominated. Words. Axes. Looks. Clubs.** (*Pause*) Pity me, because this is so difficult.

PRUDENTIA: I pity nobody.

CLARISSA: **Not even the poor**.

PRUDENTIA: Not even them. (*Pause*)

CLARISSA: You have been seized because — (*She stops, shakes her head.*) No, I seized you. I did. Because things can't go on.

PRUDENTIA: They can if no one puts an end to them.

CLARISSA: They can't go on and —

PRUDENTIA: **No one has to act**. (*Pause*) This acting. This intervening. This putting stops to things. Who obliges you, Clarissa?

CLARISSA: My conscience.

PRUDENTIA: Put it to sleep, then. Strike it with a shovel. Like a senile dog, one swift and clean blow kills it. I was spun by conscience like a top. And when it died I came to life. The top ceased spinning. Look how you shiver. Look how manifestly you are inferior to me. Do I shiver? You are in the blindfold.

CLARISSA: **I think you lie in bed with my husband and** — (*She shakes her head like a cat in a bag.*)

No!

No!

Do what you wish, I am not censorious, do what comes to you, but out there is all starvation and mismanagement and you encourage him!

PRUDENTIA: I could have read this diatribe off any wall.

CLARISSA: Yes.

PRUDENTIA: When a child dies they fly a black rag.

CLARISSA: Yes.

PRUDENTIA: And for every suicide a white.

CLARISSA: You notice, then?

PRUDENTIA: You think the recitation of their agony could alter his pursuit? The sky could be thick in kites and the sun dead. (*Pause*)

CLARISSA: I think your passion, which was magnificent, perhaps, has gone misshapen with obsession, and your love has failed, for love must also be correction —

PRUDENTIA: Ha!

CLARISSA: Yes, love says because I love you I forbid you this or this —

PRUDENTIA: Ha!

CLARISSA: Ha! as much as you like, I am not deterred — a proper love is a matter of fine balances —

PRUDENTIA: **Fine balances**.

CLARISSA: And equilibrium —

PRUDENTIA: **Equilibrium!**

CLARISSA: Yes! And how you hate those things, how you strangle the clean things in yourself —

PRUDENTIA: **This is clean**. (*Pause*)

Shh!

That's him! He calls me from the tower! (*She stands, head tilted.*)

CLARISSA: I think you are guilty. Of smothering your self. Which also is a murder.

PRUDENTIA: He is a great man, and I gave him birth. More so than his mother. (CLARISSA *sobs violently.*)

CLARISSA: How your reproaches twist my stomach, and pulp my little heart... (LEAR's *distant cry is heard. In a spontaneous gesture*, PRUDENTIA *reaches out her hands to* CLARISSA. CLARISSA *does not accept them.*) **No love without criticism!** (*She looks at her mother.* PRUDENTIA's *hands fall.*) And I must see you. I must not hide. (*She pulls away* PRUDENTIA's *blindfold. She stoops in front of her, looking into her eyes.*)

How hard this is.

But I.

And I.

Can.

THE GAOL: **Oh, good!**

She's evil if the word has meaning

Oh, good!

We do hate punishment but some it must be said

Deserve

Oh, good!

In this case human dignity cries out for

One of those rare occasions when everybody must

Agree

**Collectively we must respond
Mustn't we**

An effect of sound.

LEAR *runs in to an empty stage, bright as day.* GLOUCESTER *is shambling.*

LEAR: Hey!

GLOUCESTER: Shh, I'm depressed...

LEAR: Have you seen a woman?

GLOUCESTER: I'm so depressed...

LEAR: In a red skirt and —

GLOUCESTER: **I'm too depressed**. (*He sits.* LEAR *sees another.*)

LEAR: Hey! (*The* FIGURE *stops.*) Have you seen a woman?

HERDSMAN: What do you want a woman for?

LEAR: I want her because — (*He ponders.*) I no longer have her.

HERDSMAN: But when you had her —

LEAR: None of your peasant wisdom. I am Lear. Nothing you can tell me I did not already know at birth. She wore a red skirt.

HERDSMAN: I could have been a monarch. I was born in the wrong room however. (*He laughs coarsely.*)

LEAR (*going close to him*): I said none of your profundity you ambling and complacent self-regarding parcel of banality, if she's dead I also with to die. (*Pause*)

HERDSMAN: She is.

LEAR: She is, is she?

HERDSMAN: The king's whore's dead.

LEAR: The king's whore, yes, that is the one I am referring to. The slag. The man-lover whose parted limbs are ridiculed in public places.

HERDSMAN: Dead yes, what more can I say?

LEAR: No more. Now murder me.

HERDSMAN: I would, except it's treason.

LEAR: I give you permission, here. (*He scrawls on a scrap of paper.*) Command, it says, and that's my signature.

HERDSMAN: I'd rather not.

LEAR: Piss your preference, do it, here's the knife.

HERDSMAN: Look, there's Jack over there —

LEAR: Fuck Jack, you are the chosen — (*He thrusts the knife into the* HERDSMAN's *hand.*)

HERDSMAN: There are more women than — (LEAR *seizes him by the throat.*)

LEAR: **Liar! He tells me there are more women than one! Liar! There was only one!** (*The* HERDSMAN *wriggles free and runs.*) Thrash him for lying! Break him on some wheel for lying! I never lie! Every word I look at, both from the front and back...! (*Pause*)

GLOUCESTER: I go to the brothel. I say to the girl, act naturally. As if I were repulsive to you. 'You, repulsive?', she says. **You are** such a bad interpreter of my needs, I say, with an artificial grin. I do detest you. I do resent your ignorance. If I wanted love, I'd find it... (KENT *enters, slowly. He looks at* LEAR.)

KENT: I have been six years on a rock.

LEAR: And I six in a tower.

KENT: I thought of a woman. This kept me sane.

LEAR: And I through one. This maddened me.

HERDSMAN (*returning*): Changed my mind. I thought, I'll do this. How my neighbours will congratulate me. Michael, they'll say, it is a privilege to shake your bloody hand. Wash it never.

LEAR: Too late.

HERDSMAN: No, surely? (LEAR *goes to him, and swiftly kills him.*) Hey...! (LEAR *goes out.*)

KENT: **The things we quarrelled over now seem**
The things we stabbed for suddenly aren't
The books we carried high
Are only
Fit for arse paper

The genius we thought had understood reality
His eighty volumes now I say are
His beard I wish
His tomb I could

The little man from China with the answers
Was a torturer I never knew
I never knew
I never knew
Did you

And the poet in the tower who we called a
Fucking snob

Has relevance

Sixth Lear

A table. CLARISSA, GONERIL, REGAN *seated.* LEAR *enters. He looks into her. Pause.*

LEAR: Nearly stupid. (*Pause*)
          But not quite. (*Pause*)
          I am shedding thought as a lout shakes scurf. (*He scratches his head violently, stops.*) Nearly fit to govern. (CLARISSA *extends a hand to him across the table.*) I killed a man and Kent's back. (*Ignoring her hand he sits. The table is an image of domestic silence. Her hand remains until it agonizes her.*)
GONERIL: Oh, take that hand back . . . !
REGAN: Mother! (*It stays, until at last she falls into her chair, her eyes on the floor.*)
CLARISSA: I can't apologize for what was proper. Or that's madness. But for pain. I share that. (*She looks at* LEAR, *who extends his arms over the table, so his hands reach for his children, his cheek to the table. They take his hands. They look at their mother. A sound of martial music, light and popular. A* BOY DRUMMER *enters, drumming and goes out, followed by* LEAR, REGAN *and* GONERIL. *The music fades.* KENT *appears, behind* CLARISSA. *He is still.*)
          Dear friend, it must be you. And thinking, as usual, how excellent my nature is. (*She shakes her head ruefully.*) At least you are not dead, and anything else is tolerable.
KENT: No one ever gave me a greater compliment.
CLARISSA: No?
KENT: You are truth itself and never need embellishment.
CLARISSA: I bask in your respect but don't make my life more painful.
KENT: How could I do that?
CLARISSA: By showing kindness, which cracks my armour.
KENT: You need not wear armour.
CLARISSA: No? What's life without armour?
KENT: I was on a rock. I travelled to this rock on the corpse of a bad man, bloated by his gases. So there I was, a good man, saved by putrefaction. Every day he came back, on every tide, viler and viler to behold. And then one day, he did not.
CLARISSA: He sank?
KENT: Inevitably, he sank. (*She senses his movement.*)
CLARISSA: **Do not undress.** (*Pause*)

KENT: I entertained such thoughts of you, which if I described, would make you shrink. These thoughts absorbed whole days, and kept me sane, though they were insane thoughts.

CLARISSA: How? Love's kindness.

KENT: Love's not, love never was, and if I'm vile you also are responsible — (*She goes to move.*) **Don't turn like that your hip** —

CLARISSA (*amazed*):   What —

KENT: **Your hip** —

CLARISSA (*horrified*):   What —

KENT: **Does such** —

CLARISSA: I cannot help my hip — (KENT *covers his eyes.*) I must have caused this and forgive me, or how could you be so bad? (*He lets his hands fall.*) Your eyes are narrow with a cruelty that distorts your normally kind features, dear friend... (*Pause. He shakes his head laughing.*)

KENT: Oh, words, oh, words kill words...! (LEAR *returns. He looks at them.*)

LEAR: I spend whole days with Gloucester. He shows me the other kingdom. **You think there is one kingdom only?** Under the kingdom, the kingdom...

KENT (*going to him*):   Take your wife, and love her.

LEAR: Why, don't you?

KENT: Yes!

LEAR: Then she's over-loved, because you love her and I am occasionally kind, which is more than most get.

KENT: I love and suffer her.

LEAR: Good! Now have a picnic on the hill! Take some poems and a rug.

KENT: You ought not to...!

ILEAR: She reads classics — in translation — at least, the minor works —

KENT: **Ought not to**.

LEAR: And sings a bit to the guitar, a sort of wail she learned in adolescent solitude —

IKENT: **Ought not to piss on innocence**. (LEAR *stares at* KENT.)

LEAR: What word is that? I'm nearly stupid now, what is that? (THE DAUGHTERS *enter. They are impatient.*)

GONERIL/REGAN: Our picnic with our mum and dad!

LEAR: Not me! I have a headache!

GONERIL/REGAN: **Oh, not another headache**!

LEAR: Yes!

CLARISSA: Yes, we need some air!

LEAR: Indeed, take Kent! (*A pause*)

CLARISSA: I think it's better if we three —
LEAR: Yes, and take Kent!
CLARISSA: The three of us merely —
LEAR: In case of wolves.
GONERIL/REGAN (*disbelief*):   **Wolves?**
LEAR: Cats, then.
GONERIL/REGAN: **What cats?**
LEAR: Angry ones who once were petted. You know, or hawks
with debts to settle. (*He smiles.*) Do. I hate to think of danger
from the wild. (*Pause. They go out.* KENT *following.* LEAR *is
left alone.*)
THE GAOL: **Lear...!**
Oh, Lear...!
May we disturb you?
**So many problems but we have suffered beyond
Measure**.
LEAR (*kneeling to them*):   You say this often, as if pain had
measure.
THE GAOL: **We harp on justice here**
Until the word
Eats tunnels through our brains
LEAR: The word's abolished, then, since it grieves so many.
It must be cut out of the dictionary. **Scissors!**
THE GAOL: **Oh, Lear**
You were so much kinder as a boy!
LEAR: Yes, but he was so intelligent, that boy. And he knew
philosophy.
THE GAOL: **What is philosophy unless it dissolves pain?** (LEAR
sits, contemplatively, among them.)
LEAR: Surely, it is melancholy...be assured, I think of you
often...and need you...oh, how I need you... (*He gets up.
The picnic party returns. They look at* LEAR. KENT *flings
himself to* LEAR's *feet.*)
KENT: Execute me, then! (GONERIL *and* REGAN *go to*
LEAR.)
GONERIL/REGAN: We found these flowers! Leaving them
with poems, we found you flowers!
KENT: Execute me, then!
GONERIL: Execute you?
REGAN: Why is he so silly?
GONERIL/REGAN: **Execute yourself!** (*Pause.* LEAR *runs his
fingers through* KENT's *hair, absently. The* DAUGHTERS
drape LEAR *with the wild flowers, and skip off.*)

LEAR: When people loved me — and many have — I felt burdened. When they ceased to love me — I felt cold...

CLARISSA: I can't talk of love because I know so little of it. So I'll talk of necessity instead. And how — through so much — silence — I have longed to be clamoured for. And even how, perhaps, whoever clamoured would have earned my — **You are smiling and I am trying to be honest**. (*Pause*) I am pregnant without question, and not by you. (*Pause*) Oh, listen, I had a bird once but the bird died! (*Music. The* DRUMMER *appears again, crossing the stage. They watch him pass.*)

LEAR: What is he...!
Hey!
What is he...!

Pause. He runs out. A wind and light change. LEAR *enters edging a barrel painfully onto the stage. The barrel is massive. He steadies it, stops. A newborn child is heard.* GLOUCESTER *enters holding a bundle.* LEAR *looks at him over the rim.*

LEAR: Gin.

GLOUCESTER: Bastard. (*Pause.* LEAR *lifts the lid.*)

LEAR: Love...! (GLOUCESTER *comes slowly to the barrel. He holds the bundle out, then drops it in.* LEAR *replaces the lid.*)

GLOUCESTER: Cordelia, she calls it.

LEAR: Thank her. I have seen it, say. And add, Lear was not more arbitrary than rain. Or earthquakes. Or weapons badly aimed. (GLOUCESTER *turns to go.*) **We crawl on the earth like worms**. (*He stops.*) But she knows that. Leave the last line out. (*He goes.* KENT *enters, bows.*)

KENT: The Emperor of Endlessly Expanding Territory. (*He bows as a* DIGNITARY *enters, robed. Pause.*)

LEAR: I greet my visitors in casual dress, which is a compliment, given my inclination to be naked. (*The* EMPEROR *looks. Pause.*) I have no throne but this and you must be happy with a stool, or did you bring your own? (*He hops onto the top of the barrel and sits.* KENT *extends a stool to the* EMPEROR.) They report you very wise, which I was as a child and now am merely arbitrary. The difference is of no significance, the people will substantiate. (*Pause*) What do you want? (*Pause*)

E OF EET: There are not enough bodies in the world. (*A pause of gathering comprehension.*)

LEAR: My wife sleeps with another man. I do not love my wife. What then, is the cause of my anxiety? (*He hops off the*

barrel, leans on it thoughtfully. A sound of tapping from within.)
My wife will tell me everything because she cannot lie. Her
inability to lie is agony to me. If she were a liar I could tolerate
her. I might love a liar. If she fucked secretly in cellars with
bald men I'd applaud her. I cannot help the feeling her honesty
is an attempt on my sanity. (*Pause*) What do you mean, not
enough bodies?

E OF EET: For the faith. (*Pause*)

LEAR: What faith?

E OF EET: There is only one faith. (*He looks into* LEAR.) Are
you not tired from walking in the dark?

LEAR: Yes.

E OF EET: Are you not weary knowing all you know is
false?

LEAR: Weary beyond imagination, yes.

E OF EET: And do you not ache for the solution?

LEAR: The solution's death. (*Tapping on the inside of the
barrel.*)

E OF EET: But after death? (LEAR *stares.*)

LEAR: **Hor-bling!**
          Oh, be careful, you will explode my skull and send the
          splinters in your eyes!
          Hor-bling! (HORBLING *enters, springing as best he can
          and shaking a bell.*)

HORBLING: I'm getting better!

LEAR (*to the* EMPEROR):   They say you executed seven hundred in an afternoon, I don't criticize, they say you blind
adulterers, I don't criticize!

HORBLING: Better, but still not good! (*He skips.*)

LEAR: **He talks of after death.** (*He stares at* HORBLING.
Sounds from inside the barrel. HORBLING *hears it, amazed.*)

E OF EET: I come to you, when being the greatest power in the
world, it was more fitting you should come to me. But I have
no pride. I never conquer. I only deliver. (HORBLING *scrambles to the side of the barrel, listens.*)

LEAR (*still reeling*):   **After — death?** (REGAN *and* GONERIL
enter.)

GONERIL/REGAN: Our mother says the baby where is it?

LEAR: This man says there are not enough bodies for the faith.
This man has seven million soldiers on the frontiers.

GONERIL/REGAN: Cordelia, she says, where is she?

LEAR: **Seven million unafraid of death!** (*The* DAUGHTERS
look at the EMPEROR.)

REGAN: Stab him.

GONERIL: Hang him up by his heels.

LEAR (*to the* EMPEROR): Children! Aren't they miraculous? Do you have children? **I've thought of that**.

GONERIL: He would look different naked. Where's the baby, our mother says.

HORBLING (*flinging himself at the* EMPEROR's *feet*): Seven million? (*He point to* LEAR.) There is the enemy of the faith! There is cynicism and apostasy! (*He drags off his cap and takes out the now decaying papers.*) This plan requires five years to change the kingdom from a lair of beasts to Paradise! Five years, and I revise it frequently, these corrections are illegible I will admit, no — the wrong way up — here — no, that's smudged, it says — I translate — do you have a minute, I — that's the introduction, skip that — it's — this page goes there — (*He falters as* CLARISSA *enters. Pause.*)

LEAR: She does not put on lipstick, Clarissa. Or any false thing. (*Pause*)

CLARISSA: Where is my baby?

GONERIL/REGAN: We asked and he —

CLARISSA: Cordelia? (LEAR *chooses to be silent, walking a line in silence, and returning to the spot, thoughtfully.* CLARISSA *lets out a mournful cry. She falls to her knees and beats the ground with her fists.*)

CLARISSA: **I've done nothing! I've done nothing!** (*She stops. She straightens herself.*)

LEAR (*to the* EMPEROR): Do you do dinners? That is what is wanted here. (*The* EMPEROR *stares at him.*) I loved a woman. She made death possible, and yet to die would be to lose her, therefore she kept me living... (*Pause*) Bring your armies. And I'll be burned. Or skinned. Or whatever it is you do. (*Suddenly, as if on an impulse,* LEAR *rushes to the barrel and flings off the lid, which rolls. He plunges in his arms and pulls out the dripping bundle of* CORDELIA.)

Gin!

Gin!

And she still lives! (*He holds it up, smothers it with kisses.*)

Oh, was that good?

Oh, was that a good thing, hey? (*The* EMPEROR, *in disbelief, rises to his feet. The baby cries.*)

GONERIL/REGAN (*jumping up and down*): **Oh, Oh, our sis-ter! Oh, Oh, our sis-ter!** (LEAR *thrusts the dripping baby at the* *girls, and kneeling at the* EMPEROR*'s feet, tears open his collar to expose his throat.*)

LEAR: Seven million daggers.
     Seven million knives! (*The* EMPEROR *stares.*)

CLARISSA (*to the* EMPEROR):   You see how terrible we find life? How it maddens us? Don't offer us another ... (*Pause. The* EMPEROR *places a hand on her, in a gesture of profound pity.* HORBLING *tears up his five-year plan, gazing on* LEAR, *and withdraws. The light changes, the* EMPEROR *goes out.* LEAR *remains in the posture.*)

LEAR: I wanted to die. And you saved me. I was ready to die. **The third time you have saved me!** (*He stares at* CLARISSA *in horror. A second light change.* CORDELIA *enters.*)

CORDELIA: I think if he had drowned me, I should have forgiven him ...!

KENT (*entering*):   You are at an age when the agonized seem beautiful. Yet there are thousands curse him every day.

CORDELIA: I call them vermin for it!

KENT: I am not trying to make you hate your father, merely — (*He shrugs.*)

CORDELIA (*to* KENT):   I do think, when you speak, it is as if each word had weights attached to it which catch your teeth. You are utterly kind to me but. Perhaps you harbour some sex thing for me, in which case I wish you'd say — (KENT *seethes.*) Is that wrong? I'm often wrong. I get that from my father, not from my mother, who is never wrong and can't be, it seems.

CLARISSA (*extending her hands as if conducting a walk*):   **Children!**

CORDELIA: But if it is so, I wish you would admit it. A thought is better born that smothered, **there now I sound like her!** (*She grins.*)

KENT: **Nothing of the sort.** (*Pause*)

CLARISSA (*enters*):   **Chil-dren!**

CORDELIA: Oh, good. (*She smiles.*) Oh, good! (REGAN *and* GONERIL *hurry in.*)

GONERIL/REGAN: We're going to a dance.

CLARISSA: Later.

GONERIL/REGAN: Going to a dance and now we're late! (*They stare at* CLARISSA. LEAR *is motionless.*)

CLARISSA: I must show you something I have found. (*The sound of the* GAOL CHORUS.)

THE GAOL: **Where's Lear?**

**No one comes here but Lear
You hurt our eyes with strangeness!**

GONERIL/REGAN/CORDELIA: Let's play houses! Let's fly kites! **Let's build castles on the beach!**

CLARISSA: Hold hands, I said!

THE GAOL: **He does not licence visitors!** (*Pause.* LEAR *at last abandons his posture, and rising, comes to them.*)

LEAR: You have found the one place I can discover sanity...

CLARISSA: Free them.

LEAR: You have trespassed in my garden... (*Pause*)

CLARISSA: Garden...? (*Pause. With infinite slowness, a chain swings twice, like a pendulum, between them. A wind.*)
                Free them. Lear.
                Free them.

THE GAOL: **Our suffering is over
Our bodies are returned to us
Do you remember how it felt to own your body?**

They laugh madly, uncontrollably, and stop

LEAR: I said to the inmates of the goal, when I have done a crime sufficient to dwarf not only what you did, but what you have imagined, then daylight's yours. The gaoled are only in the gaol by being worse than their gaolers. How else? (*Pause. The chain swings again and stops.*) **Oh, who will correct me when my wife is gone?**

CORDELIA: I will... (REGAN *and* GONERIL *look at each other with profound realisation.*)

GONERIL/REGAN: Let's go to the dance!

CORDELIA (*releasing the hand of* CLARISSA):   How hard it is to say this, but I do not pity you. I think you never did a bad thing in your life. Or let a false emotion slip through your net. Or postured. Or ever were corrupt. And I think — shall I go on?

GONERIL/REGAN: Do go on!

CORDELIA: I have a deep and until today, an unstirred hatred for you. (*The chain swings again.*)

GONERIL/REGAN: **It's true! It's true! She does say things which we find impossible to express!** (*Pause*)

CLARISSA: Don't hurt me. Someone must do good. And of all people I've done least to — (*Pause. She breaks into a sobbing laugh.*) What's that to do with anything! (*Pause*) I've never exaggerated. And I am not going to now.

CORDELIA: **Do! Oh, Do exaggerate...!** (CLARISSA *shakes
her head defiantly. The chain passes again. A cacophony breaks
in.*)
ALL: **Mummy/Daddy/where are my/going to a dance I said/have
you seen my/comb your hair you look/Daddy/shoes and socks/
Christmas is so/we love each other don't we/Mummy/love each
other so/and holidays are/will you stop quarrelling/and my Dad
says/I said stop that/I said/I said/get out the photographs!** (*It
stops. The chain again, observed this time by* LEAR.)
LEAR: God wants her for the comfort of His solitude...We
can't be blamed... (*With a sudden access of energy,* LEAR
leaps and clings to the chain, usurping it.)
        Raise Me!
        Raise me then, God!

He swings to and fro, pitiful and absurd. The light on CLARISSA
fades. After some minutes, GLOUCESTER *appears.*

GLOUCESTER: May I have her, do you think? (*They look at
him.*) I mean, there can be no particular requirement
for...When I was a beggar I made lovers of the dead since I
was...scarcely a proper suitor for the living... (LEAR
swings.) And they are — perfectly passionate...
CORDELIA (*to* GLOUCESTER):   Take me away. To some
corner of the wood. And do whatever you do to young
women. (*The* DRUMMER *is heard, and the band music.*
LEAR *jumps down. The* THREE DAUGHTERS *crowd to*
LEAR *and embrace him. The* DRUMMER *comes nearer.*)
LEAR: Hey! (*The* DRUMMER *enters, passing.* LEAR *chases
him.*) Who are you?
DRUMMER: Happiness!
LEAR: But I never wanted happiness! Why do I follow you,
therefore? (*A sudden and terrible wind. Snow fall.*)

Seventh Lear

The CHORUS OF THE GAOL *lies heaped and dead.* LEAR *is sitting in overcoats on a folding stool. Through the wind* KENT *staggers on with a chess table. He places it before* LEAR *and unfolds his own stool. He sits. They study. A long time passes.* KENT *goes to make a move.*

LEAR: Erm! (KENT *stops in mid-movement. Pause. He continues to move.*)
        Erm! (*He stops again.*)
        If I may say so.
        Begging your.
        Etcetera but. (KENT *finishes the move.*)
        Erm! (KENT *looks resentful.* LEAR *turns aside.*) I do think cheating is peculiar, so peculiar, because even when the cheat might win on skill alone he still prefers to cheat. It is impossible to satisfy him. I have watched you cheating for eight years.
KENT: Eight years...?
LEAR: Eight years to the day and never once protested.
KENT: I admit nothing. But why today?
LEAR: Why, indeed? Yes, why today? If only we were constant, if only we were! But today I felt it necessary to protest — no — not protest exactly — but to announce my knowledge of your cheating, which I had detected on the first day.
KENT: If only you had said.
LEAR: If only I had, but what difference would it have made? Do continue cheating, I merely wished to acquaint you with the fact I knew — (KENT *suddenly rises to his feet, pointing to the* CHORUS *and letting out a moan.*) Now you are trying to change the subject — (*He groans.*) I apologize for spoiling what was a perfectly innocuous and trivial practice — (*He points.*) I am pedant! I am a pedant! I admit it! (*Pause. The wind blows.* LEAR *seems shrunken in his chair.*) Please move...
THE GAOL: **We knew/How else could we be free?/But knowing/ How could we be allowed to live?**
LEAR: Please move... (KENT *looks at him, then in a spasm of love, reaches out his hand and clasps* LEAR's *across the table.*)

THE GAOLER'S ACHE FOR THE NEARLY DEAD

INTRODUCTION

Those whom the state wishes to destroy must first be vilified. Because revolutions are sexually reactionary, the most efficacious calumny is that of sexual delinquency. Thus Marie Antoinette, last Queen of the French, not sufficiently guilty by virtue of her birth, required to be revealed as a debauchee to ease her progress to the guillotine. The state is obsessed with the visible, and the police are the least of its instruments in the melancholy passion for exposure. Neighbours inform; children are endowed with innocence to act as mirrors in which popular sin may see its hideous image reflected. With the French revolution came the vital ingredient in the new world of total transparency — an uncensored press. Journalists became, and remained, the revolution's favoured sons, the finest instrument of surveillance, the dubious agents of dubious truths, incessant explorers of the underneath.

Yet the rumour — inevitable consequence of privacy — is never merely dream, but conjured from common fears and the product of inspirations. More ambiguous still, all accusations are concealed invitations, and what is popular indictment may be private refuge. For the *Queen* is first and foremost body, object of popular desire, site of myth and incessantly fetishized. This is the woman who cannot be woman alone, but whose private desires are nailed to public function and for whom all acts of love — bar one, perhaps — are stained by mischief, adulation and curiosity. The Revolution and its agents collude in this extravagance, for it knows that to execute a queen is to enhance her divinity. If Revolution is the apotheosis of a myth, Marie Antionette, slandered by the Revolution, must be the myth of its opposite — depravity against cleanliness, licence against order. In incest — invented, imagined, confessed — the crime of crimes, the ultimate transgression over the collective, hope and horror become inextricably mixed ...

CHARACTERS

CAROLINE   Queen of France
LITTLE LOUIS   Her son
WITT   An Aristocrat, Her Lover
TREPASSER   A Demagogue, formerly a Tutor
GAOLER
BIG LOUIS   King of France
HAIRDRESSER   To the Queen
PORTER
FIRST   Female Servant
SECOND   Female Servant
THIRD   Female Servant
FIRST   Doctor
SECOND   Doctor
BALANCE   Member of the Tribunal
QUEEST   Member of the Tribunal
NOTE   Member of the Tribunal
OFFICIAL   Of the Revolution
A CROWD

The Exordium

Darkness. A panel opens, high in a wall. A face appears in the aperture. It surveys. It disappears. The panel shuts with a clap. A wind blows. A panel opens in the floor. A head appears, surveys, is lost in a crowd which surges over the stage, animated, quarrelsome. As they depart, a vast eruption of messianic, triumphant music. The rear wall divides to expose a throne, baroque, gilded, situated at the top of an extravagant flight of steps. On the throne, an infant king, carapaced, crowned and holding a sword. To the thunder of the orchestra, he descends the stairs. He approaches the head which still protrudes through the floor, and with a single swipe at ground level, decapitates it and sends it flying away into the wings. The effort exhausts the child. He sinks to the floor in the sudden silence. The aperture in the wall opens. The face appears, surveys. The wind blows...

Scene One

A Queen enters, in a froth of muslin

CAROLINE: Boy...
                Boy... (*He looks up, wearily*)
                I am making love...
LITTLE LOUIS: Yes...
CAROLINE: So run away and hide...!
LITTLE LOUIS: Yes... (*He climbs to his feet*)
CAROLINE: Find a little temple or an urn, and face the wall.
LITTLE LOUIS: Yes, Mother...

CAROLINE: And if you hear me making — oh, uncommon noises — Don't look...!

LITTLE LOUIS: No, Mother...

CAROLINE: Of course, you will want to look...! These are just the sort of noises boys long to hear, but you must fix your gaze firmly on the wall.

LITTLE LOUIS: I will, Mother.

CAROLINE: Or count the petals on a flower...

LITTLE LOUIS: Yes.

CAROLINE: But whatever you do, you must not look because I shall be in a strange posture. (*He looks at her*)

One you have never seen me in before. It is a posture I am never seen in except for this one thing. You would not want to see it, I expect...!

LITTLE LOUIS: I expect not, no —

CAROLINE: You would not want to see your mother in such a state, her clothes dragged over her head and uttering these little cries which could be misinterpreted as anxiety or even pain...

LITTLE LOUIS: I'll play in my laboratory...

CAROLINE: And an expression on her face of such intensity you might think...poor woman...she is suffering an ordeal ...! (*He stares at her. A man appears, silently. He bows to* LITTLE LOUIS)

Play in your laboratory and — (*Pause. She shrugs*)

Play... (LITTLE LOUIS *goes out. She follows him with her gaze. Pause*)

I do not really want to... (*Pause. The man walks to the front. He looks out, as if over a park*)

I did...

And now I don't... (*She lifts her shoulders, helplessly*)

WITT: When we initiate a course of action, and recoil from the consequences...when we conduct experiments, so to speak, with our sensibilities, and the sensibilities of others, and having struck a flame, flee the fire we ourselves ignited, I wonder if we do not unwittingly rehearse the abdication of our power...? (*She shrugs*)

CAROLINE: I'm not very clever.

WITT: Are we not by this irresolution making manifest the sources of our own extinction, Caroline...?

CAROLINE: I'm not very clever, Julien —

WITT: You always say that...

CAROLINE: Do I...?

WITT: When you are perfectly able to comprehend the most complex metaphors...

CAROLINE: Am I...? Possibly, I — (*He turns to face her*)

WITT: And the extraordinary aspect of this is, not only are you unsure if you want, but I am equally unsure if I am resentful of your not wanting...! (*She laughs nervously*)

Your reluctance is not greater than my apathy! Where is my temper? Where is my will?

CAROLINE: (*With a shrug*) I don't know... (*And again*) I don't know where your will is...

WITT: What is it but authentic decadence...? If your love is tepid, my ambition is lukewarm...! (*He turns, walks a little*)

The Death of the erotic indicates with its lifeless finger, the mortal sickness of the state... (*He looks at her. Again she shrugs*)

I think we will shortly be replaced by those for whom — absurdly facile in our estimation — an action is merely an action, Caroline... (*The aperture opens. The head of LITTLE LOUIS appears...*)

CAROLINE: Undress me, Julien... (*Witt stares at her*)
Undress me, please... (*Pause*)
Explore me... (*Pause*)
Anything... (*Pause*)
I am not very clever and I insist you feel me underneath my clothes... (*He stares coolly at her*)

All you do is speak in these long sentences which I think is a way of making me feel foolish. I am not to be made foolish, am I? I insist you touch my body. (*Pause*)

Listen, this is not any body. It is the Royal Body. Don't you want to touch the Royal Body? Everybody else does. **Hurry up it wants to be touched** . (*WITT removes his hat and lays it down. He then removes his wig, exposing a bald head, shining. CAROLINE giggles, seductively. WITT deposits the wig on the hat, and goes to her. She takes his head between her hands and kisses its top. Her eyes rise to the aperture, which shuts with a clap. A sudden eruption of movement as the argumentative CROWD floods the stage*)

The first Ecstasy of the Persecution

The CROWD *surges away, leaving an isolated figure. He goes to the foot of the royal staircase and looks up. He laughs, shakes his head.*

TREPASSER: I forbid myself... (*He bites his lip, musing*)
             I strangle the urge...
   And strangling the urge, I demonstrate my absolute compatibility with History, which abhors the fatuous delight of desecration... (*He closes the large doors*)
   Look at me. Do you know another man of such immaculate self-discipline? (*A* PORTER *enters with a padlock*)
PORTER: I would have nipped up them steps and shat upon it, Citizen.
TREPASSER: Shat, yes, shat would have been the minimum.
PORTER: (*Locking the doors with chains*) Pissed...
TREPASSER: Yes...
PORTER: Vomitted...
TREPASSER: The entire spectrum of organic contempt...
PORTER: My naked arse I would have —
TREPASSER: Certainly, you are refreshingly human and I, if anything, a trifle too objective, is it a good feeling to urinate on something you dislike? Or does it not suggest a certain reverence which is only fleetingly concealed by desecration? (*The* PORTER *looks at him*)
   To smother with ordure, is it not to bless? (*Pause*) Lock up after me. It is of course, the People's right to demolish all that offends their eyes, but — (*He suddenly seizes the* PORTER *in a vicelike grip and marches with him*)
                        You are incorrigible
                        You are a liar
                        A snob
                        A lackey
                        An inveterate flunkey (*He marches back again, the* PORTER *struggling*)
                        Servile
                        Parasitical
                        And
                        Love your bonds (*He thrusts him away, disgusted*)
PORTER: (*Staggering, clutching his throat*) My throat you — my fucking — (*He chokes*)
                        Throat, you —

TREPASSER: (*Flinging himself to the* PORTER's *feet*)
Report me...! Denounce me to the Tribunal...! I am in such a **blizzard of emotion at the spectacle of man...!** I stagger...! I fall...! I drag my punished body to the clifftop of the future and **gaze out...!** the horizon **boils...!** (*The* PORTER *looks at him.* TREPASSER *sobs*)

PORTER: All right, Citizen...

TREPASSER: How can it be all right...in what way is it all right...I surrender myself to the police and admit my assault upon you...

PORTER: No need, it's — (*He shrugs*)

TREPASSER: There is a need...

PORTER: These times are —

TREPASSER: A pressing need...

PORTER: I don't know... (*He rubs his throat*)

TREPASSER: To thrash my soul until it bleeds a pure essence of inviolable truth...an appalling need... (*He climbs to his feet*)
Very well, since you refuse to indict me...there is no more to be said. (*Pause*) You understand I cannot possibly apologize. (*The* PORTER *looks at him*) What is there to apologize for? We are all of us, are we not, at one another's throats? It is a symptom of our present condition. (*The* PORTER *swiftly, cleanly, slaps* TREPASSER *over the face.* TREPASSER *accepts the blow. The* PORTER *goes out*)
That carries a sentence of death...!

Scene Two

Silence. A wind creeps down the corridors. TREPASSER *walks a little, stops*

CAROLINE: Boy...!

LITTLE LOUIS: (*Offstage*) I am playing a game...!

CAROLINE: (*Entering*) You are always playing a game...!

LITTLE LOUIS: (*Entering from the opposite direction*) It is an aspect of my education. Isn't that so, Doctor Trepasser? (TREPASSER *nods*)

The mind is formed from such apparent trivialities. And in any case, how trivial are they? I find them rather complicated, as the times we live in are complicated, are they not, Doctor Trepasser? You often say so. (TREPASSER *bows and goes out.* CAROLINE *goes swiftly to little* LOUIS *and kisses him. He giggles*)

> You have been with a man...!

CAROLINE: I have not!

LITTLE LOUIS: Yes, I smell him.

CAROLINE: Beast...! He has no smell...! (*She giggles. She examines him, studiously. He looks at her, for a long time. The figure of* LOUIS XVI *appears, and gazes at them in turn. Then he goes off*)

> Hunting again...!

LITTLE LOUIS: It distracts him.

CAROLINE: It distracts him from the melancholy task of governing a state.

LITTLE LOUIS: It relieves him.

CAROLINE: It relieves him from the intolerable pressure of reconciling interests which are not reconcilable.

LITTLE LOUIS: And in the saddle he experiences the peculiar illusion of irresponsibility... (*He stares after his father*)

CAROLINE: Yes... that must be what it is...

LITTLE LOUIS: My own feeling
May I say this
I say this out of love
He ought to ride
And not stop riding
For seven days and seven nights
With or without the servants
Moonlight softly
And the clatter of the hooves on bridges
Moonlight softly on his collar
Like a mother's hand
And not dismount until
Some foreign shop sign loomed above his head
Some fountain fluttered by a breeze
Spilled water on his hand
And
Live
There... (*Pause.* CAROLINE *gazes at him*)

Why did you call me? (*CAROLINE goes to him, and taking his head in her hands, kisses his mouth. He submits to it. The kiss is lingering . . .*)

For no reason, I suppose . . . (*He wanders away in the direction he came from. CAROLINE wipes her mouth tentatively. A CROWD OF COURTIERS floods the room, anxious, seething. They pile at the window, repelled, fascinated by a spectacle below*)

Scene Three

A SERVANT enters with a mirror. As the COURTIERS bubble and boil, CAROLINE sits, her back to the window, and examines her hair, plucking it in the glass. The COURTIERS rise to a climax of exclamation and stop. A peculiar silence. CAROLINE tugs with a frustrated expression.

CAROLINE: I think shoot
I think shoot and shoot again
I know you hate it so do I but hating is irrelevant
Hating does not alter
Hating things is frequently the sign of (*with a bitter gesture at the mirror*)
This curl is conspiring against me . . . ! (*she and the servant laugh*)
It hovers
It hangs on the edge of my vision like an assassin waiting to rush in (*the SERVANT laughs again*)
It is . . . exactly like that . . . !
Cut it off
Go on
Cut it
You see, you are afraid to . . . !
You think it can be persuaded, don't you?
Trained and so on?
I have never liked this curl
What's wrong with cutting it?
Cut silly cut (*The SERVANT pins it. The COURTIERS froth in a sudden eruption, pressing each other, and cease again*)

We do an action we dislike
We are reluctant but this reluctance is not
Surely not
Can't be
Conclusive evidence of
I'm stupid possibly
Of wrongness can it
Isn't that where God comes in?
You are determined not to cut this curl
Claudine (*She laughs*)
All right don't
God it is who deals with afterwards
I love God
I cling to Him
If you do not love God and deny him as so many do nowadays then obviously you cannot deal with afterwards
Afterwards is a nightmare for you
That is why you cannot shoot
You are afraid you'll hang yourselves... (*The* COURTIERS *seethe, press, shriek, and subside again*)
If the soldiers do not shoot they will be disembowelled
Does anybody care about the soldiers? (*The sound of shattering glass.* CAROLINE *tugs her hair both sides*)
You see they are not tight enough
I know you hate tight curls
You like them tumbling
So do I but
Tumbling to the sides (*And another shattering of glass*)
Horrible to be shot I know it is
I saw a bird once
Not a common bird either
Ornamental it was
Which a poacher had wounded
And oh, its feathers were all
And this part of its insides
Oh, I can't possibly describe
Hanging all
Oh
So I do know what I'm talking about
A little bit
A monarchy must rule (*To the* SERVANT)

I don't know why I bother
You're determined to
You have your own (CLAUDINE *giggles*)
Yes, you do
I never knew a hairdresser who had the least
Concern for what her customer required
Not the least concern (*A further shattering of a window*)
And if the monarch will not rule then someone else will do it
Very simple really
I think you are not masculine as my father
Was
I think you want to die at the hands of screaming women
They piss the mouths of dead policemen
Did you know that?
Is that what you want?
A throatful of revolutionary urine?
Please yourselves (*She gets up*)

What I really want is fields of hair cascading down my shoulders, fragrant cataracts of chestnut curls... Claudine...

A man I think adores that plenitude of hair
As if he wandered in a forest
A forest which might also be his grave, Claudine ...

They are born in hair are they not? They pass through hair to life...? (*A door slams.* LITTLE LOUIS *rushes in, distraught*)

LITTLE LOUIS: Mother...!

Oh, Mother, my laboratory is full of dirty women...! (*He is still. He trembles. A wind blows down the corridor.* CAROLINE *extends a hand to him. He walks fearfully, tentatively towards her. Darkness falls. Their hands touch...*)

Scene Four

A swing passes across the stage. The sound of laughing female
SERVANTS *is heard. The aperture flies open. The head of*
TREPASSER *is glimpsed, looking, and withdrawing. The*
COURTIERS *mutter incoherently and disperse. The swing is illu-*
minated for a summer's day. Three women SERVANTS *appear,*
CAROLINE *greets them ecstatically.*

CAROLINE: I have this boy...!

I have this boy and I am going to bore you rigid
talking of him! (*They laugh*)

Yes...! You laugh, but I am...! How you will complain in
the privacy of the servants' hall...! How you will grumble...!
(*They protest*)

You will...! You will...! She does go on, you'll say, she
nauseates us...! (*They protest again, laughing*)

Yes...! I know you will, but this boy took **fifteen hours to be
born**...I was a sodden rag of pain...**swing**. (*They catch it.*
CAROLINE *mounts it prettily*)

A sodden rag. (*They gather*)

Push! (*They push gently*)

And those obstetricians...! Did you see them?
Those great big calipers!

Higher...!

The dimensions of those instruments....!

And one word...one word...filled my mind...as if on
granite obelisks...the one word... **Caesar**...!

LITTLE LOUIS: I heard it.....!

CAROLINE: He heard it and he **clung**...! (*They laugh and
push*)

Who was to blame, you ask, the boy who did not wish to
emerge, or the mother who could not part with him?

LITTLE LOUIS: You!

CAROLINE: We were both scared!

LITTLE LOUIS: Both of us, yes!

CAROLINE: The word of words...! The name of names...!
(LITTLE LOUIS *laughs*)

You laugh!

LITTLE LOUIS: Caesar...!

CAROLINE: You find it funny now, and so do I, but then!
(*She looks to the* SERVANTS)

Oh, are we boring you...? (*They protest*)
Too bad if we do!
  We are entitled to bore, aren't we? After what we went through? The thing I dreaded fifteen hours dreaded was — (*She stops the swing. Pause*)
Articulated... (*Pause*)

LITTLE LOUIS: Who said it?

CAROLINE: Oh, I don't know.. (*He bounces a ball. She ponders, she revives*)
  Who uttered it I don't know, but it was uttered, **My death sentence!**

LITTLE LOUIS: (*stops playing*) **Her death sentence!**

CAROLINE: My body was without significance...! It was merely **an impediment to his birth**...!

LITTLE LOUIS: It's true...!

CAROLINE: Constricting flesh! A sea of flesh and mucus called — **A Queen!** (*The servants laugh, but nervously*)
Push! (*They re-start the swing*)
The boy was to be extracted with a knife!
Hacked out of the suffocating flesh of love! (*She flies*)
And love it was...! Love that held my boy against my bowel!
Push!

LITTLE LOUIS: Love, yes!

CAROLINE: **Love that fixed him to my spine!**

LITTLE LOUIS: I clung!

CAROLINE: **He clung like a waif in a storm!**

LITTLE LOUIS: My little hands went round her vertebrae!
I say that metaphorically
I say that in full knowledge of anatomy (*He bounces the ball on the ground*)

CAROLINE: A battle raged...!

LITTLE LOUIS: Ferociously...

CAROLINE: And then — (*She lets the swing slow*)
And then —
So subtle was he...
So attuned to me...
So perfectly one with my flesh... (*It stops. Pause*)
He conceded...
One way or another...
He had to emerge... (*She bites her lip. The SERVANTS look uncomfortable...*)

> And I was a sodden rag of pain and perspiration...vile to behold...
> **A rather ugly sight my husband said** (*The* SERVANTS *disclaim*)
> Yes...

He could not come near me after. Who could blame him? I was meat... (*She climbs off. The ball stops*)

You see, my body was nothing but the chamber of a king... (LITTLE LOUIS *goes to her, kisses her tenderly*)

I was under no illusions...they looked at me, those obstetricians, as a butcher must stare into the eyes of cattle... mutual incomprehension...horror...and pitiless **Exigency**... (*Pause*)

LITTLE LOUIS: So I got out!

CAROLINE: (*Brightly*) Yes! He knew these things as well as I! He could see we were together in the hands of **Political fanatics**! Doctors, yes, nurses, yes, but governed, impelled, by one solitary ambition...

LITTLE LOUIS: **To smack my arse...!** (*He and the* SERVANTS *laugh)*

CAROLINE: Yes! And our resistance ended...they parted us...

LITTLE LOUIS: (*Bouncing the ball again*) Physically...

CAROLINE: Physically parted us, yes... (*She looks at the* SERVANTS)

> And God was satisfied. God, whose one commandment is to reproduce... (*They look puzzled*)
>
> Well, isn't it? I'm not clever, but who could fail to recognize the sheer imperative of this aspect of the divine will?

LITTLE LOUIS: Nobody!

CAROLINE: (*Retrieving the narrative*) And the applause!

FIRST SERVANT: I was there...

CAROLINE: You were there, were you? Who wasn't there?
>   **The globe was represented!** (LITTLE LOUIS *laughs*)

FIRST SERVANT: We were so — relieved...!

CAROLINE: Relieved, were you...? Yes, well, the monarch had an heir...

LITTLE LOUIS: **Heir! Heir! Heir!** (*They laugh. He turns on the* SERVANTS)

>   What is it like, being a child...? (*They frown*)
>   I ask because I've never been one. (*They are lost for words*)

This swing for example, where's the satisfaction in it? It goes one way, and then the other ... so what ...? (*They shrug, they lift their hands*)

And when I pass your rooms ... these cries ... and groans ... what are you playing ...? (*The women look to* CAROLINE, *who is seated on the swing and idly treads the ground. She chooses not to assist them*)

And then you curse ...! Why do you curse? So abusive sometimes, the same word over and over again ...! (*Pause. He joins his fingertips, in a posture of profound curiosity*)

What are you doing? (*Pause*)

SECOND SERVANT: The Prince would surely not expect us to — (*She shrugs.* CAROLINE *laughs*)

LITTLE LOUIS: You see, I think so much of our behaviour is quite silly, but at the same time this silliness is necessary, it appears. (*He strains*)

I wonder if everything is not silly ... if silliness ... does not ... attach to everything, including death ... and the only reason we do not call death silly is because it hurts, but this hurting can't be construed as a sufficient reason *not* to call it silly, can it ...? (*Pause. He looks up*)

Do you follow me, or are you too childish?
(*They stare*)

So what is it that you do in bed ...? (*He erupts into a rush of laughter, stops, puts a hand to his mouth. Pause. The women relieved by this, look to* CAROLINE, *who is smiling, then they too, break into giggles.*)

THIRD SERVANT: I leave my clothes on ...! (*The others laugh*)
I do ...!

FIRST SERVANT: Not all of them?

THIRD SERVANT: Not all of them silly! I leave sufficient clothes on to make him curious because —

SECOND SERVANT: I don't —

FIRST SERVANT: Me neither —

SECOND SERVANT: I'm naked straight away! (*They laugh*)

THIRD SERVANT: If you show too much it's —

SECOND SERVANT: I show everything! (*They peel with laughter*)

THIRD SERVANT: You keep him in suspense, you show this little bit —

SECOND SERVANT: I can't wait! (*She squeals*)

THIRD SERVANT: And that little bit, you leave some bits covered and some bits —

FIRST SERVANT: That's all very well but they don't —

SECOND SERVANT: **Tear the garments off you, don't they!**

LITTLE LOUIS: (*Who has been turning from one to the other*) Wait...! (*They pause*) You are revealed, but only in stages...?

SECOND SERVANT: She lets a bit of herself show —

THIRD SERVANT: Breasts first —

SECOND SERVANT: She lets her breasts show, and the man goes all —

THIRD SERVANT: I'm telling, aren't I?

LITTLE LOUIS: The man goes what...?

FIRST SERVANT: I show my arse...! (*They squeal*) I do...!

SECOND SERVANT: That's because you think your arse is something special —

FIRST SERVANT: Best bits first —

THIRD SERVANT: It's a matter of opinion which bit should be shown, it could be any order, couldn't it?

SECOND SERVANT: I lift my nightdress and my breasts go —

FIRST SERVANT: **Night dress...!**

LITTLE LOUIS: (*Dimly*) The man goes what...

SECOND SERVANT: Why not a night dress...! I have this little candle burning and I put myself a little bit in shadow —

FIRST SERVANT: I bend over, I keep bending over and he sees that I have got this gorgeous arse — (SECOND SERVANT *squeals*) It is! It is gorgeous!

SECOND SERVANT: Men like nightdresses!

FIRST SERVANT: I don't say it's gorgeous, they do...! (*A peal of laughter*)

LITTLE LOUIS: (*Distraut*) Wait...!

FIRST SERVANT: They do say it, you know they do and —

LITTLE LOUIS: Wait! (*Pause*)

If everybody talks at once I cannot possibly benefit from the description, can I? What use is it if you merely indulge yourselves in these bewildering — (*He shrugs*) One at a time. (*Pause*)

SECOND SERVANT: I lie with my limbs a little but not too far apart.

Not vulgar.

LITTLE LOUIS: No...

FIRST SERVANT: Far enough apart to —

SECOND SERVANT: Suggestively apart — and look.

LITTLE LOUIS: Look...

SECOND SERVANT: Yes, it's looking really that —

FIRST SERVANT: The proper look can work miracles...

SECOND SERVANT: I just keep looking —

LITTLE LOUIS: At what? What do you look at?

SECOND SERVANT: Him.

FIRST SERVANT: In the eyes, you look right in the eyes with this suggestive look —

LITTLE LOUIS: Suggestive...

FIRST SERVANT: And move a little bit, and lift one leg —

SECOND SERVANT: It's me who's telling —

FIRST SERVANT: An inch or two, or stretch... suggestively ...

LITTLE LOUIS: What do you mean, suggestively? Suggestive of what...?

FIRST SERVANT: And then I might turn, to show my rear —

SECOND SERVANT: I let my hair down —

THIRD SERVANT: Hair, oh, yes, the hair is so important, I —

FIRST SERVANT: I was coming to the hair —

THIRD SERVANT: I make the hair the whole point of it —

SECOND SERVANT: I lift my arms, and loosen it, and down it comes very suggestively over my shoulders —

LITTLE LOUIS: What is so suggestive about it...

SECOND SERVANT: Great waves of it...! And all the time I'm looking —

THIRD SERVANT: You have to keep looking —

SECOND SERVANT: It's so important looking — not rudely — not impertinently but —

LITTLE LOUIS: Looking at what...!

THIRD SERVANT: And then I just turn over! I do! I flip over in a posture of complete abandonment...! (*They laugh*)

LITTLE LOUIS: Abandoned to what...?

FIRST SERVANT: I do that...! I hide my face! Stuff it in the pillow!

SECOND SERVANT: I breathe deep, so my shoulders heave...! I do! I can't help it! I'm sometimes suffocating with suspense!

THIRD SERVANT: **Or I mount him!** (*They squeal*) I do! I just scramble over and mount him!

FIRST SERVANT: I bite!

THIRD SERVANT: I can't bear to wait, not after I'm naked I just have to —

FIRST SERVANT: I'm a terrible biter!

SECOND SERVANT: I pull his head towards me and smother him with my —

FIRST SERVANT: I just drool —

THIRD SERVANT: Shut my eyes and go —
SECOND SERVANT: Saliva everywhere —
FIRST SERVANT: Slaps me round the face!
THIRD SERVANT: Pinned down on the floor —
SECOND SERVANT: Hair everywhere and legs all —
LITTLE LOUIS: (*Who has glanced from one to the other*) **I cannot follow any of this idiocy!** (*They are alarmed, silent. They look at the floor*)
>   Surely it can be described...? (*They are still, ashamed*)

Why can't it be described...? (CAROLINE, *still seated on the stationary swing, observes this. A wind blows. The* SERVANTS *curtsey and depart.* LITTLE LOUIS *stares at the ground...* CAROLINE *observes the abatement of his confusion. His eyes rise to meet hers. Pause. She hops off the swing and goes out. His eyes follow her... at last he is made aware that he is watched by another. He turns to see* TREPASSER, *who drops an armful of books with a clatter. The action is deliberate...*)

Scene Five

The Second Ecstasy of the Persecution

TREPASSER: The suicide of the books... (*He emits a high laugh*) The book outlives its author. Is that its tragedy, Louis? (LITTLE LOUIS *stares. A long pause, before* TREPASSER *kicks a book violently offstage*)
   Sorry...! (*He laughs again*) The author dies...and the words go haywire...a startled flock of birds...in all directions go the words...! (*He kicks another, with calculation*) Phrases lifted from a book of love are chiselled on the lintels of a gaol...
LITTLE LOUIS: Yes. It's only to be expected...
TREPASSER: (*Kicking another*) Sorry...!
   (*He mimics cruelly*) 'I never meant that...' wails the author, seeing his poetry has graced the despot's tomb...
LITTLE LOUIS: The author should have known. (*Pause. They exchange a stare*)

> Silly author... (*Pause, then* TREPASSER
> *kicks another*)

TREPASSER: Sorry...!

LITTLE LOUIS: Why do you keep apologizing to the books?
They don't feel anything. What are we studying today?

TREPASSER: Nothing...!

LITTLE LOUIS: Nothing...? But I have to be educated, if
only to — (TREPASSER *takes a flying kick at another*)
appreciate — (*And another. He shakes with subdued laughter*)
ignorance... (TREPASSER *turns his gaze at* LITTLE
LOUIS)

TREPASSER: Who is worthy to be the subject of your labours?
Who? The sanctimonious Socrates? Erasmus the vain? I
really cannot continue to collude in this grotesque charade
in which I, admittedly afflicted with a most poisonous
and degenerate character, affect to transmit to you, ostensibly
an innocent, ostensibly a blank sheet of dazzling credulity,
mangled and pulped versions of the apercues of yet
more poisonous and degenerate characters thankfully dead
whose amalgamated tempers constitute your education, all
right, get your Virgil out, where were we, no, it can't go on,
book seven, was it, I wish time would stop, I wish all
things would stop, if I don't kill myself others will die,
Odysseus puts wax in his ears... read on... (*Pause. He gazes
into space*)

LITTLE LOUIS: That's Homer... (*He still stares, vacantly*)
> Homer   wrote   the   Odyssey... (*Pause.*
> TREPASSER *looks to* LITTLE LOUIS)

Virgil wrote the... (*Pause*) It doesn't matter, does it...? In
my case? (*Pause. The wind blows*) You think it's the end of the
world... (TREPASSER *sobs into his hands.* LITTLE LOUIS
watches him for some time. Suddenly he runs out. WITT *is
discovered, watching* TREPASSER. *He walks idly towards
him...*)

WITT: What is the future of the monarchy, Dr Trepasser?
(TREPASSER *uncovers his face. He recovers his demeanour*)

TREPASSER: What is the future of the university, Count Witt?
(*He starts to collect up the scattered books*) All I know is what I
read in the newspapers.

WITT: But you write the newspapers, Dr Trepasser.

TREPASSER: Ah, that persistent rumour... (*He diligently collects off the floor*) That unextinguishable calumny...I can
hardly resent what cretins alone could possibly believe

> You are standing on my Descartes
> Write the newspapers
> Really, the style is quite beyond me
> Monosyllabic trash

My Descartes.... (WITT *does not move.* TREPASSER's *hand is on the book. He is trapped in a crouching posture*)

I tell you what I do believe. I believe queens need to be cautious where they copulate... (*Pause*)

WITT: You care for queens then, Doctor...?

TREPASSER: Care for them...? (*Pause. He looks up*)

It's adoration... (*Pause.* WITT *removes his foot from the book.* TREPASSER *sweeps it up, stands*)

Their flesh is not the same, you know... (WITT *looks at him*)

WITT: What...?

TREPASSER: The skin. It's different. (WITT *stares...*)

> And the hair....it's made of different stuff. (WITT *is bemused*)

As a doll is not authentically a child, however cleverly it resembles one, nor is a queen a woman, however convincingly she masquerades as one... (WITT *smiles, is about to speak*)

> Don't tell me you know otherwise. (*He puts a finger to his lips*)
> Please.
> Be charitable.

Spare me the tedium of your first-hand knowledge... (WITT *acknowledges* TREPASSER *with a slight nod of his head and turns to go.* TREPASSER *finishes collecting up his library*)

> Going abroad soon, Count? To study in a foreign country? (WITT *looks at him*)

I would. (*Pause, then* WITT *goes out.* TREPASSER *also leaves, but passing* BIG LOUIS, *pauses, bows, proceeds. Instantly, the stage is swept by a procession of insanely loquacious citizens, who obliterate* BIG LOUIS *for some moments. The aperture flies open with a clap. The face appears in the dim light, observing. The crowd passes, leaving a single note on the air.* BIG LOUIS *is facing* CAROLINE *across the width of the stage*)

Scene Six

BIG LOUIS: My head is coming off and I wondered if you wished to hold it...? (*Pause*) Tomorrow this fat head will be —

CAROLINE: Shh —

BIG LOUIS: So would you like to fondle it? (*Pause*) I could place it in your lap. (*She looks...*)

> Please say you want to fondle my fat head... (*And looks...*)

I shall try to make those last few paces dignified, and unforgettable to those who witness it. I think to rant or howl would be to play into the hands of those who... (*Pause*)

I have asked for the head to be returned to you, perhaps in a box, but they said what box, I said the carpenter might make one, they said why should he stoop to make a monarch's box, a decent artisan, a son of the people humiliate himself making a headbox for a tyrant, so I suspect it will come in a bag or even newspaper, they are not conciliatory at all **give it a hug when it is dead then** I asked them wash it first but I can't be sure they'll do that Caroline...

CAROLINE: Shh... (*Pause. He frets*)

BIG LOUIS: Caroline, if you don't receive it, ask. And if it has a pained expression please forgive me, it is not my wish to show a pained expression, not at all, but most are, most heads have pained expressions, it is the seizure of the muscles following the blow and not a true expression of emotion, not at all, brush the hair, would you, or not if you don't want to.... **I wonder where the ideas go?** (*He yearns to her*) And memories...?

Where do they go...? (*Unable to contain his longing,* BIG LOUIS *runs to* CAROLINE *like a child and smothers his face in her clothes. She takes his head in her hands, as he kneels at her feet, a sobbing, apologetic figure. Pause. The aperture shuts.* LITTLE LOUIS *observes....*)

LITTLE LOUIS: Watching this conversation I must say I am filled with a strange apprehension regarding my parentage... (CAROLINE *comforts her husband*)

Despite all physical resemblances I am compelled to at least examine the possibility that my father is not the man who is at this moment a wet and crumpled heap at your —

CAROLINE: Shhh!

LITTLE LOUIS: **He would not be like that.** (*Pause*)

He would at all times maintain the necessary appearances of divine monarchy... (*Pause*)

This monarchy is obviously appearance. I am perfectly aware it is appearance, but an appearance which cannot lapse and which therefore, whilst being appearance is nevertheless **authentic appearance.** (*Pause*)

The king fears death. We know the king fears death. But by not admitting it, by insisting on his immunity to commonplace emotion, he inspires us with... (*He looks...*)

I am inclined therefore to conclude either this man is not the monarch... or the monarch is not my father... certainly he can't be both, can he?

Mother? (*He bites his lip*)

CAROLINE: This is your father's last night on earth.

LITTLE LOUIS: I understand that, but why can't he — (*He turns away, frustrated, confused...*)

BIG LOUIS: I was a decent husband, wasn't I, Caroline? My family was everything to me...

LITTLE LOUIS: (*Crossly*) You see, that is just what I mean! How can his family have been everything to him? He was a monarch! He might as well say hunting was everything to me! Or backgammon!

CAROLINE: **Sit quietly Louis... please...** (*Her eyes meet his. He concedes, bitterly. He sits on the floor. He watches CAROLINE stroke her husband's hair...*)

I dreamed such scenes as this... and always in the dream emotions flooded my brain for which the words and phrases flowed in perfect order, perfect symmetry... but now...

BIG LOUIS: Never mind...

CAROLINE: I could compose immortal sentences of farewell and I think they even rhymed...!

BIG LOUIS: (*Kissing her fingers*) Never mind...

CAROLINE: I mean, these perfect words — (LITTLE LOUIS *stamps the floor loudly*) these perfect words were probably just bits of songs... awful songs from the gutters, which is why they rhymed...!

BIG LOUIS: Yes...

CAROLINE: I don't think people who are silly as I am can even dream things of high quality, do you... though we recognize the thing in others, which is our pain... (*with sudden vigour*) After your death, when we are exiled to some foreign city I am making hats!

BIG LOUIS: Hats?

CAROLINE: Yes! People say I am artistic and being a widow I
shall not be short of time, shall I?

BIG LOUIS: You are artistic, I always said so ...

CAROLINE: I have always rather envied widows, they seem to
blossom, to surge into new life, and their laughter — have you
noticed it — is different from the laughter of their married life —

BIG LOUIS: I hadn't particularly noticed that —

CAROLINE: I expect they grieve, but you wouldn't know it.
I shall try not to grieve, I think it ages you ... (*She looks at*
BIG LOUIS. *Pause. Suddenly,* LITTLE LOUIS, *keeling over,*
erupts into a terrible wail)

LITTLE LOUIS: Don't die ...!
Don't die ...! (*He writhes.* BIG LOUIS
extracts himself from CAROLINE'*s embrace*)
Don't die ...!
My father ...! Oh, my father ...! (BIG
LOUIS *goes to his son. He kneels beside him*)

BIG LOUIS: I'm so sorry ... I'm so sorry ...

CAROLINE: Everything I say is wrong! Everything!

BIG LOUIS: (*To* CAROLINE) Shh ...

CAROLINE: No, it is, I'm not made for these occasions, I am
just not —

LITTLE LOUIS: Hide, Daddy ... Hide ...!

CAROLINE: It isn't that I haven't the feelings, I have them,
but ...

BIG LOUIS: (*His hand on his son*) Shhh ...

CAROLINE: **The feelings will cost me my mind!** (BIG LOUIS *is*
caught between them. LITTLE LOUIS *clings to his ankles.*
CAROLINE *thrusts her fist into her mouth but cannot stop the*
eruption of choking tears. In this agonized hiatus, the aperture
opens. The face dimly appears)

BIG LOUIS: How I wish I had killed my enemies ... when
I look at you ... I know I should have killed my enemies ... and
then we might have said ... over the dinner table on a night of
love ... how sad it was to have been obliged to be severe ... (*He*
kisses his son. LITTLE LOUIS *ceases his plaints* ...)

LITTLE LOUIS: We shall be perfectly happy, mother and I ...

BIG LOUIS: (*Profoundly*) Yes. ...

LITTLE LOUIS: So as your big head rolls away, it need not be
full of despondency!

BIG LOUIS: Good ... Good ...! (CAROLINE *opens her arms*
to LITTLE LOUIS. *He runs to her. They embrace, they turn to*
BIG LOUIS)

CAROLINE: Look at us! Take this picture with you, to the end .... (*Pause*)

BIG LOUIS: I will...I will... (*He blows kisses to them. He departs, watched by them. Pause*)

CAROLINE: I was cruel...

LITTLE LOUIS: Not really cruel...

CAROLINE: I was cruel...

LITTLE LOUIS: No, because to utter false sentiments is surely —

CAROLINE: Very cruel indeed... (*Pause*)

LITTLE LOUIS: A bit cruel, yes... I sensed not only did you lack the necessary sentiments, but neither were you prepared to imitate them, which would have been a charity, and —

CAROLINE: Yes! Yes!

LITTLE LOUIS: And this suggests to me a somewhat infantile desire —

CAROLINE: Oh, dear —

LITTLE LOUIS: Yes, an infantile desire to injure another even in the midst of his despair —

CAROLINE: Yes! Yes! **Little beast!** (*She bites her lip*) Yes. And you —

LITTLE LOUIS: Oh, me...

CAROLINE: **And you were no better!**

LITTLE LOUIS: No, worse if anything!

CAROLINE: Worse, yes, because.... because.... (*They look into one another. LITTLE LOUIS turns his back*)

Boy...

Boy...

LITTLE LOUIS: (*Distracting her*) In my view a woman finds it relatively simple to forgive a man his infidelities but hard to overlook his failure to provide. I mean, that is the contract, isn't it? She yields her body, her womb, her progeny, but only on specific terms. That he protects her... not only from wild beasts... (*A man is detected waiting in the shadow*)

But from the wilder beasts... (*He turns to face the man*)

Of politics...

OFFICIAL: The king is dead. (*Pause. CAROLINE is still, then her shoulders appear to shake, the effect of stifling a giggle ...LITTLE LOUIS also is seized by the same infectious, nervousness*)

LITTLE LOUIS: Long live the king...!

LONG LIVE THE KING...! (*The OFFICIAL bursts out with a throaty echoing laugh. All three are convulsed as music surges over them*)

Scene Seven

The music ceases suddenly. Two men have entered, holding a bag, folding screen, stool. Pause.

FIRST DOCTOR: Undress, Louis, please. (LITTLE LOUIS *looks at them*)

LITTLE LOUIS: Undress yourself...

FIRST DOCTOR: We want to look at you.

LITTLE LOUIS: You are looking at me and in a most impertinent way.

SECOND DOCTOR: (*To* CAROLINE) Tell him, please, you are his mother.

LITTLE LOUIS: She cannot tell me I am the king. (*Pause. The* FIRST DOCTOR *is patient*)

FIRST DOCTOR: If the king were ill...imagine it...and his condition required him to be examined, without his clothes, the king I think would not protest.

LITTLE LOUIS: I am not ill.

FIRST DOCTOR: It would be a consequence of his sickness that obliged him to be naked. Thus arguably, the king is subject to — let us say, fevers, microbes, swellings and so on...diseases impose themselves upon the king...do they not?

LITTLE LOUIS: Obviously.

FIRST DOCTOR: What is the revolution but a disorder, an eruption, a fever and a sore....? (LITTLE LOUIS *looks at him*) It also commands your nakedness. (LITTLE LOUIS *smiles. The* SECOND DOCTOR *unfolds the screen.* LITTLE LOUIS *goes to parade about the room when the* FIRST DOCTOR *seizes him in his arms*)

CAROLINE: **Don't hurt him!** (*They are still. Her shrill cry freezes them.* LITTLE LOUIS *watches her*)

LITTLE LOUIS: Very well...the revolution is disease...the question which follows from this indisputable premise, given that the concept of disease entails the notion of good health, must be... (*He falters...*)

CAROLINE: Do as he says... (*Pause*)

Louis... (LITTLE LOUIS *unbuttons his shirt the* DOCTORS *enclose him behind the screen, which conceals him below the waist. He watches* CAROLINE *with an unsweerving gaze...*)

LITTLE LOUIS: It follows does it not, that if the revolution is a sickness, the counter-revolution must be medicine... (*His shirt is flung over the screen. One of the* DOCTORS, *makes notes, the other, invisible, sits on the stool at* LOUIS' *feet*)

You introduced these concepts, not me... (*He stares. They examine. His trousers are flung over, then his drawers. He endures it*)

Are you not therefore obliged to admit the only ethical procedure on diagnozing sickness is to — (*Pause*)

I don't think he should...he cannot touch a king there, surely... (*He stares, horrified*)

He cannot touch me there ...! (CAROLINE *smothers her face in her hands.* LOUIS' *eyes fill with tears. Her hands slowly come away...their eyes meet. The* FIRST DOCTOR *emerges, wiping his hands.* TREPASSER *has entered. He draws a sheet behind him, taken from a bed*)

TREPASSER: The fall of gates...! That was a music...! (*He inhales the sheet*)

The very symphony of revolutionary creativity! (*He reflects*) Who could forget it? Day and night, the peck of crowbars and the roar of falling iron? (*He inhales*)

It was as if the public had, with extraordinary unanimity, decreed that henceforth nothing was to be concealed...no place...no crevice...immune to the inspecting eye... (*And inhales again*)

What's privacy after all, but the pretext for a sordid criminality...? (*He looks at* CAROLINE)

This child has been the victim of diabolical malpractices... (*She returns his stare, wavering...*)

CAROLINE: What are you doing with my bed-linen...

TREPASSER: You recognize the monogram...!

CAROLINE: You have stolen my bed-linen...

TREPASSER: Steal? It's public property, Caroline...! Most of it laundered, more's the pity. Most of it boiled to a deceptive and sepulchral whiteness, more's the pity, but some...! Oh, the eloquence of stains...!

CAROLINE: **What diabolical malpractices...!**

TREPASSER: (*Inhaling*) The sweet murmuring of stains... (*She stares fixedly. Suddenly the aperture opens with a clap. She looks up*)

CAROLINE: Do we have to be observed! What is this constant observation...?

TREPASSER: Observation...?

CAROLINE: Day and night we are observed!

TREPASSER: (*Turning to look up, as if surprised*) Observation...? Perhaps it is not observation, Caroline, but —

LITTLE LOUIS: **Do not call my mother Caroline!** (*Pause*)

TREPASSER: (*Patiently*) Perhaps the thing you experience as observation is not observation at all. Perhaps in actual fact ...it's love... (*She sways*) The gaze is never without its ambiguities... (*Pause*)

CAROLINE: What diabolical —

TREPASSER: One cannot overlook the possibility —

CAROLINE: What diabolical —

TREPASSER: The very real possibility —

CAROLINE: Practices...! (*He turns to look at her*)

TREPASSER: The State is infatuated with you, Caroline...

LITTLE LOUIS: **She is not Caroline...!** (*He bursts out sobbing, naked. With a loud clap, the aperture is shut. The* DOCTORS *who have watched as spectators, pack up their equipment and go out, leaving* LITTLE LOUIS *clutching his clothes. All are still. A wind blows. His sobs turn to giggles...*)

Scene Eight

The stage darkens. The giggling continues. TREPASSER's *urgent voice comes out of obscurity.*

TREPASSER: Piss on me...
              Piss on me...! (*Pause.* LITTLE LOUIS *still giggles*)
              Piss on me...!

Scene Nine

Music, strained, dissonant. Light is revealed in the aperture. Something is lowered on a string, an object badly wrapped in newspaper. CAROLINE watches its descent. It stays suspended half way down the wall...

CAROLINE: I tell you what I think...
    I think if I... (*She moves a little towards it, pauses, then reaches to take the package. It is jerked out of reach*)
        I knew...!
        Now, that is utterly and
        Oh, the purely infantile
        Because I am a child they think I can be teased by fatuous
        I can be teased
        I know what's in there
    I shan't have a tantrum much as they would like it legs waving in the air etcetera I know what's in there I said
        Snot and little fists going
        No
        No
        No (*She resolutely walks away. Pause. The package descends again to arm's reach. She senses this...*)
    I don't know who you are I do however understand perfectly well my husband's head is in that filthy bag — (*It is dropped to the floor. The string hangs limp. She hums loudly a snatch from Handel's Messiah and stops abruptly. Pause*)
        I do not actually want it (*She smiles. She turns, triumphantly*)
        This parcel of discarded affection you can keep ... (*Pause. She laughs, low, wickedly*)
        Really, the things they — (LITTLE LOUIS *comes in, hurries to pick up the package*)
        Don't touch...! (*She goes to sit*)
        The poverty of their imaginations... (LITTLE LOUIS *goes to look at the package*)
        Dirty...! Don't...! (*He stands away*)
    When it comes to cruelty they have what can only be described as singularly **amateur** inclinations-(*He is drawn towards the package again*)

Boy...!

Don't...! (*He looks at her darkly*)

LITTLE LOUIS: I know what's in it... (*Pause*)

CAROLINE: Do you...?

So do I... (*Pause. He smiles*)

Oh, Boy, we are such clever children... no wonder they hate us... (*She kneels, kisses him*) And I don't mind, do you? This hatred which slops around our ankles like foam on a slobbering tide...?

LITTLE LOUIS: I don't mind...

CAROLINE: Can you imagine the spiritual contortions we should need to endure to make ourselves even tolerable to them...? The amputations? The sheer butchery of our personalities? We should be **monsters of compromise**...!

LITTLE LOUIS: Heads off...!

CAROLINE: Heads off to start with because of our terrible thoughts...!

LITTLE LOUIS: Bit of charm instead —

CAROLINE: Bit of charm, no head —

LITTLE LOUIS: Lungs out and a barrel organ stuck in there which —

CAROLINE: Barrel organ...?

LITTLE LOUIS: Plays revolutionary music —

CAROLINE: Excellent...!

LITTLE LOUIS: (*Warming to the game*) No belly, obviously —

CAROLINE: No belly, why?

LITTLE LOUIS: It might rumble!

CAROLINE: Well, yes —

LITTLE LOUIS: **During a patriotic speech!**

CAROLINE: God forbid! Belly out, then —

LITTLE LOUIS: Belly out and the complete works of Voltaire there instead...! All fifty volumes...!

CAROLINE: Yes! Fifty at least!

LITTLE LOUIS: And as for feet, no feet because —

CAROLINE: No feet because —

LITTLE LOUIS: I'm talking —

CAROLINE: Listen —

LITTLE LOUIS: The feet might make us —

CAROLINE: No, listen, listen!

LITTLE LOUIS: **Turn our backs on the** —

CAROLINE: That's what I was going to say!

LITTLE LOUIS: **Turn our backs on the future!** (*Pause. She admires him*)

CAROLINE: No, I wasn't going to say that...that's good...
no feet because... (*She shakes her head in profound love of him*)
I hope they will not leave that there... (*She looks at the
package. LITTLE LOUIS also. The sound of urgent whispering
of many voices, growing in volume. They stare. CAROLINE
suddenly stands and appeals to the aperture*)
I wouldn't mind a mirror...!

Scene Ten

The Third Ecstasy of the Persecution

*The doors that concealed the throne fly back on their hinges.
TREPASSER is seen behind a prosecutor's desk at the top of the
steps. Pressed all the way up, the PUBLIC, who instantaneously
erupt into mockery.*

CAROLINE: Yes
A mirror
Why not a mirror
I like mirrors they reflect my beauty back (*They
howl and jeer*)
Yes
And water would be nice
Let alone soap (*They explode*)
I like soap (*They are enraged. TREPASSER
merely observes, his chin on his hands...*)
Queens stink if they're not washed (*Howls*)
They do
They do stink it's a fact
They are in many ways identical to you
Not in every way silly (*They roar. She shakes her
head*)
Not in every way but certain functions of the body we must
reluctantly admit queens and commoners — (*Uproar*)
Yes —
I was coming to that —
Yes —

Horrid word but — (*Her bravado fails her. She covers her face with her hands*)
Stop
It
Please (*A silence descends at once.* CAROLINE *sways on her feet. The aperture opens with a clap.* LITTLE LOUIS *looks up*)

LITTLE LOUIS: She isn't here... (*The face appears, dimly, silently. Pause*)

She isn't...!
I am...
However
Here... (*He peers up... a wind...*)

TREPASSER: You have chosen to appear in a very simple dress...

CAROLINE: (*Taking her hands from her face*) Yes...

TREPASSER: This simple dress...the very much exaggerated simplicity of this dress...is an attempt on your part to influence us. It is calculated to imply austerity... (LITTLE LOUIS *walks up and down, stops, looks up at the aperture. Pause*)
By parading in this dress you hope to disguise the monstrous and obscene wealth of monarchy. Why did you not come honestly to the tribunal? In hoops? In petticoats? Ribbons? Taffetas and brocades? Why this mockery of the proletariat, Citizen? (*Pause.* LITTLE LOUIS *walks the other way and stops. Again, he looks up...*)

CAROLINE: I have always had a liking for the pastoral style... (*He is silent. She is compelled to go on*)
My designer, he —

TREPASSER: My designer...?

CAROLINE: My designer, he —

TREPASSER: My designer...?

CAROLINE: Yes, he says — (*A ripple of laughter. She shrugs, capitulates*)

TREPASSER: The simplicity affected by you and your designer is a fiction.

CAROLINE: A fiction...? Yes, I suppose it —

TREPASSER: Because you are not a shepherdess, are you?

CAROLINE: I am not a shepherdess, no. (*Pause.* LITTLE LOUIS *parades again. This time he does not look up, but his shoulders shake with suppressed giggles. His eyes rise to the aperture. A ball drops, bounces. He catches it. The aperture closes with a clap. Pause. The* PUBLIC *erupts into laughter...*)

TREPASSER: Oh, this humour
                 Oh, this barbaric atmosphere
                 I long for the austerity of Pilate
The bruised sensibility of the magistrate whose heavy lids will never veil his eyes from sordid and corrosive expediency and whose sleepless nights are trodden out on garden paths relieved but never healed by musky scents of nocturnal allies, roses and the like

                 I wish
                 I do
                 I ache to be a second Pilate and you to be a Christ but (*A laugh cracks the silence*)
                 Don't laugh she might be Christ for all you know (*And again*)
                 Don't laugh I said
                 How horrible that laugh is Caroline the muscular spasm of contempt
                 I'll clear the court if such a sound intrudes again
                 There is a better self in all of us
                 Somewhere
                 Let us excavate this better self
                 Or why exactly was the Revolution
                 Caroline
Explain why you debauched your son. (*Pause. He joins his finger tips, contemplatively. She is bewildered, silent*)

                 No, it's me...!
                 It's me...! (*He covers his eyes*)
                 I am the guilty one
                 I have the very poverty of spirit I profess to find in others
                 And I aspire to the qualities of Pilate
                 My own barbarity impedes your confession
                 Forgive us Caroline
                 Take as your compensation the knowledge that I will my better character
                 I wrestle
                 Tearing up the floorboards of my soul in search of it
                 Perhaps the thing lies obscure in a corner
                 My fingers reach for it... (*Pause*)

CAROLINE: The world's a pigsty, I think. (*Pause. She looks around*)
                 The world. (*Pause*)

A pigsty. (*Pause*)

And everybody in it, pigs... (*She stares at him, then at the* PUBLIC. *Pause*)

TREPASSER: You are not Christ...

CAROLINE: Not me, no. (*Pause*)

Not a bit like him. (*Pause. Then she laughs, shaking her head. Her eyes rise to meet* TREPASSER's...)

TREPASSER: (*Patiently*) Let us.... (*An intake of breath. He seems to struggle with words...*)

Oh, how easy slogans are and how necessary but...

Let us lay aside the slogan...

Always the slogan's there, a weapon in its scabbard but today...

I plead with you...let us turn our eyes elsewhere...let us contemplate what I believe

And I speak only for myself

I incorporate nobody I assure you in my will in my desire

And now I am confessing

I think

No higher do I put it

Think in my solitary way

And dissent if you prefer it

The purpose of our efforts

Or why exactly was the Revolution

Must

Be

Truth... (*Pause*)

And I don't like the word

I wish there was a better

One less stained

One less encrusted

And I am not ambitious I merely say

It can be

Caroline

Must be (*He throws up his hands*)

I try!

Admire me at least for my persistence! (*He struggles*)

The only validation of our melancholy passage ... (*Pause*)

> **Or am I wrong**
> **Are we the bestial exploiters of advantage**
> Possibly
> Possibly
> I am as vulnerable as you... (*Pause*)

CAROLINE: A pigsty... (*The public look from* CAROLINE *to* TREPASSER . *He indicates his permission with a flick of his hand. They erupt into torrents of abuse...*)

Scene Eleven

Dissonant sounds smother the PUBLIC. *The doors are closed. Into the following silence, the footsteps of* WITT. *He stares at* LITTLE LOUIS, *who conscious of his gaze, draws up his shirt to cover his naked shoulder.*

WITT: The gaol has not been built from which it is impossible to escape. It is not the walls of the gaol that keep the prisoner in... (*He strolls*)
          What's in the packet...?

LITTLE LOUIS: Rubbish... (*Pause*)

WITT: No, the walls are in our heads that are so difficult to scale...

LITTLE LOUIS: Obviously... (*He laughs*)
     I say obviously but that's bad manners! It's obvious to me, but an idea even of that elementary kind might have taken you — oh, ages to arrive at and exhausted your intellectual resources! (*He smiles*)
     Forgive me, Count... I have ideas all the time, so many ideas I cannot possibly pretend to appreciate the ordinary ones... (*He stares cruelly at* WITT)
                    I say rubbish, it's my father's head...!
                    (*Pause*)
                    Which is objectively I think we must admit now... (*Pause*)
                    Rubbish... (*Pause.* WITT *stares back...*)

WITT: I drank your mother's piss... (LITTLE LOUIS *sustains his stare*)

Warm from her body... (*With difficulty...*)

Its harsh, deep brine... (*He sways. A long, injurious pause.* CAROLINE *enters*)

CAROLINE: Home...! (*She sees* WITT, *bites her lip.* LITTLE LOUIS *takes out the ball, and bounces it by himself*)

WITT: (*Bowing deeply*) They have given me five minutes...

CAROLINE: But you should —

WITT: Five minutes and for this five minutes I have given them three-quarters of my estate... (*Pause. She is appalled*)

That is the going price... (*Pause*)

Cheap... (*Pause*)

Dirt cheap to see you... listen, the gaol has not been built from which it is impossible to escape — (LITTLE LOUIS, *overhearing this, turns in disbelief*)

It is not the walls of the gaol that keep the prisoner in, but —

LITTLE LOUIS: He just —

WITT: No, the walls are in our heads that —

LITTLE LOUIS: He —

WITT: Are so difficult to scale, Caroline, do you understand me, I have three minutes left —

LITTLE LOUIS: He just —

CAROLINE: Shh!

LITTLE LOUIS: Said that to me and now he's —

CAROLINE: Boy, be quiet...! (*He is silent, resentful. He shrugs*)

I'm not clever, I —

WITT: You always say you are not clever —

CAROLINE: Yes, I do, I —

WITT: You are clever and you pretend not to be, for reasons of your own which —

LITTLE LOUIS: Two minutes...!

CAROLINE: Yes, it's to spare myself from something. Something terrible that being clever would introduce me to —

LITTLE LOUIS: Yes...! That's good...!

WITT: First you must want to escape. Are you listening, Caroline? Do you want to escape?

CAROLINE: (*Aghast*) Do I want to escape? I have a child here and my life is —

WITT: Yes —

CAROLINE: Vile and filthy —

WITT: Yes —

CAROLINE: Look at me — I have been spat upon...!

WITT: Very well, then —

LITTLE LOUIS: One minute, Count —

CAROLINE: I have been humiliated and abused and every moment of my life pryed on — **Do I want to escape he says...!** (*Her eyes meet his*)

WITT: You are the queen. All that is civilized and ordered, and every hope of culture and religion is fixed in you... (*Pause... she wavers*)

CAROLINE: Yes...

And Caroline...what of her? (*He is puzzled*)

The queen yes, but... (*Pause*)

What about me? (*She snorts*)

I thought you desired me... (*Pause*)

Silly...I'm all that's civilized and ordered... (*She laughs*)

WITT: (*Severely*) Caroline...

CAROLINE: Yes...! (*She turns her back, her hand in her mouth*)

WITT: Millions place their hopes in —

CAROLINE: Yes...! (*He seethes*)

Indeed...

Thank you for visiting me. And I'm sorry for your estate, Julien. All those lakes. And all those trees... (*She turns to him*)

WITT: Caroline —

CAROLINE: Caroline...? Who's she...? (*They look into one another. Pause*)

LITTLE LOUIS: Time's up, I — (WITT *slaps* LITTLE LOUIS. *He is aghast. His mouth hangs open for words. At last he masters his shame...*)

Time to leave now, Mr Witt... (*Pause. The aperture flies open with a clap.* WITT *looks up. For a moment he hesitates, then walks out. A wind blows.* CAROLINE *and* LITTLE LOUIS *are quite still...*)

CAROLINE: Boy...

Oh, Boy...

Kiss me... (*Pause. The aperture closes...pause*)

LITTLE LOUIS: I'm pained.

CAROLINE: Kiss me...!

LITTLE LOUIS: **I'm pained I said**. (*He takes his ball and bounces it deliberately, moving slowly in a circle*)

CAROLINE: (*Infinitely solicitous*) We will ask for a priest. (*Pause*)

I don't think they can refuse a priest and I am
sure we will discover —

LITTLE LOUIS: Don't want a priest —

CAROLINE: Looking through the gospels with him —

LITTLE LOUIS: **I don't require the gospels.** (*Pause. He
bounces. She struggles*)

CAROLINE: This head, I can cover it with —

LITTLE LOUIS: **I hate you.** (*Pause . . .*)

CAROLINE: Hate me . . . why . . . ? (*He bounces the ball on a
single spot*)

Hate . . . why hate . . . ? (*He ignores her*)

Oh, don't be cruel to me . . . ! (*He bounces*)

All right, hate! I don't care! Why should I care? Silly, hateful
boy! (*She flounces to where the head is suspended from its wire.
She removes her shawl*)

And stop bouncing that ball. (*She drapes the head.
She plucks it idly, adjusting the covering*)
The priest and I will sit in the corner and you
won't be allowed in. (*He bounces on*)
You will be excluded.
You will hear these whispers and you won't
know what it is we're saying.
Secrets will ooze out
Oh, Boy, don't hate me, please . . . ! (*He ignores
her . . .*)
What have I done? (*The bouncing stops.* LITTLE
LOUIS *stares at the floor*)
Tell me what I have done and I'll apologize

I cannot bear this silence you are torturing me perhaps we
will be dead in a few hours dragged up the scaffold or stabbed
in the middle of the night, Boy —

LITTLE LOUIS: Good —

CAROLINE: Please —

LITTLE LOUIS: **Stab you in the eyes** —

CAROLINE: Boy . . . !

LITTLE LOUIS: **And rip your womb out and all your bits give
them to the dogs** —

CAROLINE: (*Shrieking*) **Louis I cannot bear this** — (*He
explodes into tears, his fists opening and closing. She watches
the floods of his misery*)

LITTLE LOUIS: They
               Drink
               Your

LITTLE LOUIS: Piss...!

CAROLINE: What...

LITTLE LOUIS: They do...!

                    They

                    Drink

                    Your Piss...!

(*He chokes, his shoulders heaving. The aperture opens. For the first time, CAROLINE allows her gaze to travel to the dimly visible face that observes them... her eyes fall again...*)

CAROLINE: Yes...

LITTLE LOUIS: Why...!

                    Why...! (*He recovers...*)

CAROLINE: I think because... (*She shrugs*)

    I was a queen — therefore — (*Sounds, irregularly, as of a violin plucked. The shadows are filled with FIGURES moving slowly.*)

    It tasted differently... (*LITTLE LOUIS stares, agonized. Suddenly, her laugh rings out. LITTLE LOUIS runs to one of the STRANGERS, and accosts him*)

LITTLE LOUIS: Listen —

                    She is — (*The STRANGER ignores him. He accosts another*)

                    My mother —

                    Do not ignore the king — (*He tries to impede a third*)

                    My word is law you — (*He ignores LITTLE LOUIS also*)

                    Hoo — l — gan! (*They drift past*)

                    Do not think for one minute

                    Do not entertain the silly misconception

    That transient political phenomena can release you from the deepest obligations laid upon you by — (*He shakes a finger at their departing backs*)

                    God for example! *He turns, sees that CAROLINE is observing him...*)

                    How can it...? (*He looks unfalteringly at her*)

    Taste differently...? (*Pause. The STRANGERS congregate. Their murmuring builds in volume. LITTLE LOUIS and CAROLINE giggle mischievously, their shoulders shaking until they are helpless. The aperture shuts with a clap*)

Scene Twelve

The STRANGERS *stand in a silent group. The sound of heavy footsteps descending a ladder. Wind. The feet of the descending man appear on the rungs. The* GAOLER *enters the space. He presents himself. He is still.*

GAOLER: She is regular in her habits whereas the boy is not.
She consumes her entire rations but the boy is finicky.
She sleeps the whole night without moving.
The boy on the other hand tosses and whimpers.
They argue.
They are reconciled but only after lengthy silences.
They find a number of things amusing.
They are becoming progressively dirty and unhealthy.
They are not aware of my existence.

CAROLINE: Louis... *She makes a slight gesture...*)
The little door is shut...

QUEEST: Thank you for that admirably concise if somewhat arid and colourless account we appreciate the objectivity you bring to your vocation no one could accuse you of embroidering the facts the facts however sometimes benefit from illumination rather as an urn or treasure lit from one side is thrown into greater relief.

NOTE: You're flat.

QUEEST: You're one dimensional which has its virtues obviously but start again and this time let us share the moments you describe.

BALANCE: It is your day...!

QUEEST: It is your opportunity to shine not only as a reporter but as an artist.

BALANCE: A poet...!

QUEEST: Painter, anything...!

LITTLE LOUIS: (*Staring up*) The door is closed but that is in itself an indication not of the gaoler's absence but —

CAROLINE: Our invisibility —

LITTLE LOUIS: Merely his arbitrariness —

CAROLINE: Louis —

LITTLE LOUIS: An arbitrariness which by definition he might choose to (*Pause*)
You called me Louis...

CAROLINE: (*Shooting out a hand, her eyes still fixed on the aperture*)

　　　　　　　Boy...the little door is shut...! (*He looks at her...she looks at him*)

BALANCE:　Let me give you an example
　　　　　　Not a florid one
　　　　　　Not egregious
　　　　　　There is an egg on the table
　　　　　　Simple
　　　　　　Bald
　　　　　　And I'm not a poet! I'm not a dreamer God forbid
　　　　　　Now

On the table is an object of great frailty which under certain conditions could transform itself into an exotic bird whose plumage would dazzle the eyes with drunkenness therefore the shape and texture is deceptive it is rather than a simple and innocuous egg a **flagrant possibility concealed a trick a throbbing and pulsating simulacrum of inertia** (*Pause*)

　　　　　　She sleeps whole nights without moving. (*Pause*)
　　　　　　Go on. (*Pause. The* GAOLER *looks at* BALANCE...)

QUEEST:　She sleeps whole nights without moving because.. (*Pause*)

GAOLER:　She's tired...?

QUEEST:　Tired, yes...Tired because... (*Pause*)

GAOLER:　Her emotions have been —

BALANCE:　Yes...

GAOLER:　Profoundly... (*He shrugs*)
　　　　　　Profoundly...

QUEEST:　Satisfied —

BALANCE:　The boy on the other hand tosses and whimpers
　　　　　　...

QUEEST:　Because...? (*The* GAOLER *looks darkly at* QUEEST. *Pause*)

BALANCE:　Because far from being satisfied he is — (*Pause*)
　　　　　　What?

GAOLER:　Disturbed...?

QUEEST:　Exactly...! The mother is gratified, the son is disturbed...

NOTE:　He whimpers...

QUEEST:　**He whimpers your own words.**

NOTE:　**From shame and horror possibly...?** (*The* GAOLER *nods...* LITTLE LOUIS *goes to his mother. He kisses her out-*

stretched hand with passion, studied, intense... TREPASSER
enters, and goes to the table where the others are gathered)

TREPASSER: *(To the* GAOLER) And you have seen this...
with your own eyes...? *(The* GAOLER *is still. Pause)*

How pitiful...

And possibly grotesque...

How painful to observe without that exclamation of indignation proper to a moral man we congratulate you on
your citizenship I could not do it I am not so rarified in
my idealism however not to recognize the profound service to
the State you have performed by looking and looking and
only...looking... *(The* GAOLER *meets* TREPASSER's
eyes...)

LITTLE LOUIS: Take off your dress. *(Pause)*

Quick the little door will open

No

Not necessarily

There is no logic in its movements they are not governed by
anything but the most arbitrary instincts it appears

Lift it then

And who cares anyway not me

Lift a little or I will *(Pause.* CAROLINE *hoists her skirts. His*
face registers shock and wonder. A long pause. Suddenly, in a
suffocated giggle, she lets her dress fall again. Her hands fly to
her mouth)

No

No

No

LIFT IT...! *(His face is taut with pleading.*
She hauls up her skirts again...)

TREPASSER: *(Gravely, to the* GAOLER) Do say if any of this
is...too much for you...we should not like to place your
sensibilities under such strain you felt unable to — *(Pause)*

Speak... *(Pause)*

For that's not uncommonly the consequence of
horror...

Taciturnity...

GAOLER: I'll speak. *(Pause)*

TREPASSER: Good. *(Pause)* Good because — (LITTLE
LOUIS, *irresistibly impelled by the spectacle of* CAROLINE's
undress, stretches over the floor, his eyes drawn up, curious,
overwhelmed... TREPASSER, *as if perceiving this...drifts*
from the group of strangers...pondering, impelled...)

What we are embarked upon is more than the exchanging of a system for a system, the tedious and repetitious substitution of one regime by yet another, the grotesque quadrille of classes slithering on the oily floor of power, no... (*Pause. He observes*)

Rather we are engaged upon an exercise of intellectual hygiene... the rinsing from the mind of those corrosive and infectious elements of superstition which have sustained the irrational institution of monarchy for so long and from which — yes — I include myself — not one of us is entirely immune...!

What will you say? (LITTLE LOUIS *kisses* CAROLINE's *ankles, knees, belly. She lets out a cry...*)

GAOLER: I'll say... (*Pause. He shrugs uneasily...*)

I'll say... (*She utters again. Her skirts fall, smothering* LITTLE LOUIS)

She... (CAROLINE *wraps his head in her arms...*)

Is...

Unnatural... (*The strangers bang on the table with their fists with a wild, irregular beat, talking ferociously and incomprehensibly at one another.* CAROLINE *and* LITTLE LOUIS *sink to the floor in their ecstasy. The doors fly back on their hinges, and a stab of light leaps from the void. The banging stops abruptly. A single, uncomfortable note. A toy horse on wheels rolls from the obscurity and stops.* CAROLINE *slowly uncouples from* LITTLE LOUIS, *draws down her skirts, goes to attend to her hair*)

CAROLINE: (*To no one*) Can I have a mirror...! It is so unfair to have no mirror...! (*Pause.* LITTLE LOUIS *is sleeping. With a now faint clap, the aperture opens. The vaguest suggestion of the observing face.* CAROLINE's *gaze rises to it...*)

I...

I... (*She shrugs. She remains looking*)

Are you one or several? (*Pause*)

Although I cannot see you I have a very clear impression of you whereas you who has an unimpeded view of me know nothing do you take turns is there a rota you can watch for hours and then by turning away to sneeze miss the very thing the very significance that is the entire purpose of your duties and the dullness of it the tedium I pity you it is hardly a career or if it is hardly an honourable one to watch a woman doing — (*Pause*)

the rather ordinary things I do... (*Pause*)

You vile impertinent and surreptitious man do you like squalor I think only because I cannot see your face you dare

do this and anyway who is in prison you or me I say man
perhaps you are a woman shut the door when I tell you shut it
shut it all right don't I think of you as rainfall I think of you as
weather so what it's raining I say I liked the rain I never hid
under umbrellas rain seemed to me a gift from God I lifted up
my face like this and I hid nothing from the rain so why hide
things from you you are nothing you are innocuous as water
you are mineral as the wall like this like this (*She tilts her face*)

it seems to me you must be bald and with eyes rather close
together... (*She shuts her eyes. The aperture closes. She turns to*
LITTLE LOUIS)

        Boy...

        Boy...

        This place is Heaven to me...

Boy...! (*She stares at him, and in a passionate gesture covers
his head in kisses, then tears free, moves a few paces, stops,
laughs deep and long.* LITTLE LOUIS *rises to his feet and
wanders a little way, thoughtfully. He stops. She turns to him.
He does not meet her eyes...*)

I think if the blade came down now it would not hurt my
neck... (*He does not respond*)

But shatter into a thousand fragments, jagged shards sent
spinning into the rancid crowd

        A real queen does her will...

        Surely...? (*He is silent. She looks at him*)

        Oh, listen, what we have done is —

LITTLE LOUIS: Yes —

CAROLINE: Is

        Perfect

        and

        Magnificent

        I

        Say... (*She stares. Pause*)

        Oh, listen, don't retract, I beg you don't —

LITTLE LOUIS: I'm not —

CAROLINE: Disclaim me...! (*He looks up*)

LITTLE LOUIS: I'm not disclaiming, Mother... (*Pause*)

CAROLINE: Good...

LITTLE LOUIS: But thinking. (*Pause*)

        May I think?

CAROLINE: Think, yes...! Do think! Be on your own if you
want to find a corner in which to think you are so contemplat-
ive which makes all spontaneity difficult for you a price to pay

in complication I do understand if only this gaol had a little yard a flower pot to ponder I won't pester you a rose tree I am burning with the intensest heat for you to enter me again and any little curiosity I'll satisfy no thing you can invent will I deny you promise it's the beginning promise promise and I won't pester you . . . ! (*His eyes rise to meet hers*)

LITTLE LOUIS: The beginning, yes . . . (*She turns, as if to go, stops*)

CAROLINE: I shall continue to seduce you, obviously. (*Pause*) I shall respect your silences but also, I shall present my body to you . . . sometimes subtle . . . sometimes crude . . . in the certain knowledge you require it. (*Pause*)

Alpha and Omega. (*Pause*)

In me. The murmur of a body of people. A crowd flows over the stage between them, obstructing their gaze)

Scene Thirteen

The Fourth Ecstasy of the Persecution

This CROWD *assembles with chairs, which they place as if for a meeting. They engage in animated conversations, straightening their clothes.* TREPASSER *enters. He stands, his head bowed. Little by little, the murmuring subsides. They attend on him.*

TREPASSER: I am in love . . . (*He does not raise his head. He allows them to giggle, gasp . . .*)

I am . . . ! Terribly, wretchedly in love . . . (*He shakes his head wearily. A giant photograph of* CAROLINE *falls on wires, stops with a jerk, swings a little like an inn-sign in a breeze. He lets it permeate the consciousness of his audience*)

So now you know . . . (*Nervous, subdued giggles . . .*)

How could I continue . . . staggering beneath the burden of a secret so injurious to you, so reprehensible in me . . . ? (*His eyes rise to them*)

I confess . . .

And already a draught of pure and sweet air ventilates my lungs!

I plunge in your rebukes
Silent
Silent
Rebukes
Peculiarly refreshing as clean knives might be to
a dictator at the termination of his dream...
(*He puts his hands together*)
So now you know...
And the enemy is at the gates! The enemy is at the gates and
his allies are within! All is nearly chaos and I announce I am in
love,

Preposterous egotism yes
I implore two minutes of your time (*Pause*)
Which is an imposition on your patience I admit and one I
dare to make for this one reason only

The peculiarly poisonous nature of my infatuation
Yes
I recognize the injury
I feel it as a wound
Grant me at least the lingering power of discri-
mination
This love humiliates my soul (*Pause. He looks
around*)
So now you know... (*Pause*)
The sick man contemplates his own disease...
Two minutes more
I
Am
Not
The
Solitary
Sufferer... (*He leans on his right hand. He peers
into his audience, examining them...*)
Am I not, rather, the victim of a plague...?
**For that reason alone I claim your continuing
indulgence**
I the thinker of new thoughts I the dreamer of new dreams
whose intellect and imagination are the secure houses of the
Revolution's tenderness I admit to infection
How much less immune are others
Think... (*Pause*)
How much longing this pitiful woman draws to
herself...

I have heard water running into a well...from every stratum it cascaded down the mossy side...so she drains pity from us...high and low...

I am... (*He emits a half-laugh, half-sob*)
myself in tears... (*He wipes his eyelid*)
Yes
Authentic
Tears...!

And pity's powerful...with one blow of her hand she lays logic low... (*Pause. He strokes the table...*)

How fortunate for us therefore...how fortunate for the continuing enlightenment of mankind...that she is criminal...

And always was you say
Yes
Yes
Criminal by birth my loved one

Branded by privilege and the impertinence of power hysterical religion arbitrary authority clerical and mystical obfuscation badges mottos axes yes but more... (*Pause*)

She takes her child into her bed... (*Pause*)

Oh, Caroline...so spoiled by that peculiar and suffocating separation that distinguishes the institution of the monarchy from common flesh...her very instincts are diseased and infect in turn him towards whom every sentiment of proper maternity compels... (*He seems to choke. He shakes his head*)

I've taken far more than two minutes!

Dismiss, therefore! Dismiss a man who trumpets his devotion to the Revolution whilst harbouring sentiments of the profoundest ambiguity! **Dismiss!** Others queue to serve the future who are untainted by emotions of **this unhygienic character!** (*he flings himself down*)

Dismiss! Dismiss! (*He hangs his head in a parody of execution, conscious of having made the speech of his life. His audience rises to its feet, whistling and howling its approval. He shakes his head, he flicks a modest wrist, still staring at the floor. The hanging picture of* CAROLINE *is pelted, ripped, flung this way and that as they mount the platform and lift* TREPASSER *onto their backs to bear him away. In an apotheosis of self-disparaging, he shrugs...*)

He is human...! He is human...! (*He weeps for himself*)

Forgive so much humanity...! (*They bear him out.* LITTLE LOUIS *is discovered, alone*)

Scene Fourteen

He is gazing at the open aperture, in which the faintest presence of a head can be detected ...

LITTLE LOUIS: There is nothing peculiar in being observed like this. Nor in having one-way conversations, it is characteristic of a monarchy. (*Pause. He stares up*)

> I was born to an audience. (*Pause*)
> And I will die to one. (*Pause*)
> The scale of this audience **I tremble to imagine**
> Tens of thousands
> No, that's modest
> Hundreds
> Possibly a million
> **The entire population of a city**
> Some willing
> Some forced
> Babies
> Dying patients hanging out their beds
> Quite a day and (*He stops*)
> The modern world's like that
> It's (*Pause*)
> Absolute
> And they called us absolute!
> **Don't go away!**

Do I bore you? Too bad! Your job's to listen and it's not as though I'm not intelligent the things I say are well worth hoarding and really you must admire mustn't you, my speaking voice ...? (*Pause*)

> It was trained ... (*Pause*)
> I do know how beautiful it is whereas your own I daresay is ... (*Pause*)

Like carriage wheels grinding in a rut ...! (*He laughs. The aperture shuts with a clap. He laughs even louder. A second door closes.* CAROLINE *enters, swiftly, exhilarated.* LITTLE LOUIS *turns. They grin*)

CAROLINE: I was so good today ...! I was so excellent ...! (*They stare ...*)

Words came to me I've never used before. They flew to my lips as if — like birds! Words I had perhaps heard only

once in my entire existence — flew to my lips — and perched
— and —

LITTLE LOUIS: Sang...!

CAROLINE: The court was — oh, **VENOMOUS** as usual,
HIDEOUS as usual, spewing its, spluttering its, drizzling its
abuse, the **familiar torrent of saliva** — (LITTLE LOUIS *squeals
with amusement*)

> But still I — (*She twirls proudly*)
> Ever I —
> Like the faithful ploughman did not forsake my
> labour nor deviate from my —

LITTLE LOUIS: Furrow —

CAROLINE: Yes — I say ploughman I was — (LITTLE
LOUIS *steps to her, kisses her desperately on the mouth*)

> more inspired...than a ploughman...
> I was — (*He kisses her again*)
> Wait —
> You are too — (*He drives her towards the wall*)
> **I'm telling you something.** (*He desists. They look
> at one another*)

I'm telling you...how powerful I was...how everything I
said filled them with — (*Pause. She kisses him*)

> Shame... (*He is cold*)
> Louis... (*He stares. He turns, and slowly walks
> away. She calls after him*)
> When you think...
> When you go away to think...
> What is it you think...? (*He is still, he does not
> reply. He proceeds. She shouts*)
> **You may not walk away like that.** (*Pause*)
> That is so — (*She lifts her hands in a gesture*)

LITTLE LOUIS: Childish...?

CAROLINE: Childish yes. (*She looks at him*)

And they want to kill us. It is their firm intention. They
cannot bear it that we should exist...

LITTLE LOUIS: No. (*Pause. He turns to face her*)

We, on the other hand...we wish to exist. The question is,
for what purpose?

CAROLINE: (*Puzzled*) Purpose...?

LITTLE LOUIS: Yes.

> We are not human, are we?
> We are the monarchy.

CAROLINE: And monarchy's — a purpose — is it?

LITTLE LOUIS: Supremely, yes. (*Pause*)
                That is what I think of. When I'm by myself.
                (*He starts to go*)
CAROLINE: (*With a short laugh*) And I thought...I thought
   perhaps you...**dreaded**...you were feeling...some... (*She
   shrugs*)
LITTLE LOUIS: Not at all. (*Pause*)
      Caroline... (*He goes. Her attention is suddenly diverted by
   the clap of the aperture opening. She looks up, staring, swaying
   ...the GAOLER enters from one side of the stage,
   TREPASSER from the other. She remains in this posture,
   straining to identify the dim presence*)

Scene Fifteen

GAOLER: Some physical deterioration I would say and she
   does not wash...
TREPASSER: Let her be encrusted...
GAOLER: But in high spirits.
TREPASSER: Really? Why?
GAOLER: Some unidentified euphoria induced by mal-
   nutrition, some might say.
TREPASSER: Never mind the general opinion.
GAOLER: And in the night she laughs.
TREPASSER: Laughs? Why?
GAOLER: The sort of laugh associated with a little privilege.
TREPASSER: What privilege? She's allowed none.
GAOLER: I only interpret, Citizen.
TREPASSER: No, do interpret, interpret freely. What privilege
   is this?
GAOLER: A secret.
TREPASSER: What secret? The Revolution has abolished
   secrets, has it not? That is its first achievement, the elevation
   of transparency, the cleansing of the smoked glass known as
   privacy, privacy for what I always ask, what secret? If it's fit to
   be done, do it in public, or the public will surely find you,
   Citizen — there, now I've made a speech, which is the effect of
   a single word on my vibrating consciousness, I am an instrument, am I not, a tuned instrument, what secret —

GAOLER: The child's no child.

TREPASSER: Is he not? He was when I knew him.

GAOLER: Nor is the mother in the least maternal. (*Pause.* TREPASSER *smiles*)

TREPASSER: Your delivery captures the elevated tone of a Rhetorical Republic, and you a common gaoler...! But leave the fashioned sentences to me, or the court will think I've tutored you. (*Pause*)
                    Oh, come on, you —

GAOLER: I am reluctant to —

TREPASSER: Yes, but —

CAROLINE: (*To the aperture*) Have you ever been in love? (*She bites her lip*)
                    I have...! (*She giggles*)
                    So often you would not believe it
         That much of my reputation was certainly deserved! I was frankly **undiscriminating!**

TREPASSER: Go on, I said...

GAOLER: He kisses her... (*Pause*)

TREPASSER: Yes... (*Pause*)
                    Listen, I may be many things. What I am not is prudish. (*Pause*)
                    Continue, please...

GAOLER: Where her thighs join her belly. There especially he kisses her. (*Pause*)
         The odour, he says...and smothers himself...the odour ...and would climb right in her tunnel if he could...would ease himself against her dark pumping heart, listening to the torrent of her kidneys and the slow traffic of her bowel...the odour, he says —

TREPASSER: All right —

GAOLER: And turns her whole beneath to daylight, staring with a microscopic —

TREPASSER: Excellent, I think with —

GAOLER: Concentration like an archivist who —

TREPASSER: **All right, I said.** (*Pause. He rebukes the* GAOLER *with his stare*)
                    I think, with fictions of this sort, we must be careful to —

GAOLER: It's no fiction. (*Pause.* TREPASSER, *joins his fingertips*)

CAROLINE: Look, they won't give me a priest so you will have to do, and too bad if you resent it, it's not as if I can see you yawning up there, picking your nose and so on, I take all that for granted, no, the important thing is you **exist and hear.**

TREPASSER: You play your part quite brilliantly, and I anticipate you will not remain a gaoler very long —

GAOLER: I saw it, I said. (*Pause*)

TREPASSER: Saw it...

But it's a calumny . (*Pause*)

What are you saying...

That he fucks his mother...! (*The* GAOLER *stares back.* TREPASSER *shrugs*)

Now I'm —

Now I'm all —

Obviously you're saying that

That is precisely what we agreed upon you have to say

Must say

Will say

Etcetera

But... (*He is frustrated*)

GAOLER: I was required to see, and consequently, the imperative opened my eyes... (*A wind...* TREPASSER *examines the* GAOLER *with profound curiosity...*)

CAROLINE: The fact is it doesn't matter who you are. When we confess, we should not ask the identity of the confessor, would that not entirely destroy the sincerity of the confession, for we should think, how might I win his pity how might I win his admiration, no, it would inevitably lead to **exaggeration** or even **circumspection** yes, that would be — (*She abruptly ceases. She seems to sway.* TREPASSER *walks slowly out...*)

To erect yet another barrier between oneself ... and God... (*Pause. The voice of* LITTLE LOUIS *is heard from the obscurity where he sits*)

LITTLE LOUIS: What God...? (*She turns*)

CAROLINE: What God...

LITTLE LOUIS: I am your God. (*Pause. She is perplexed*)

There can be no other. (*She looks at him. He walks to her*)

CAROLINE: You are my son —

LITTLE LOUIS: Your son...? (*Pause*)

CAROLINE: You are my son and —

LITTLE LOUIS: How, Caroline...? How am I your son...? (*She dithers*)

No, I have been thinking —

CAROLINE: **You think too much it is unhealthy all this thinking.** (*Pause*)

LITTLE LOUIS: Obviously, there are risks in exposing the most sacred things to microscopic observation but —

CAROLINE: **You are a little boy and shut up** — (*The aperture closes with a clap*)

There, now listen, you do not want everybody to —

LITTLE LOUIS: Why not...? (*She peers at him, uncomprehending*)

A God will be seen. A God will be heard. I do not understand a God who —

CAROLINE: Louis —

LITTLE LOUIS: **Hides and is dumb.** (*Pause*)

He is not secretive. Nor is He ashamed. How else should we recognize Him...? (*Pause*)

Caroline...?

CAROLINE: I don't know, I don't —

LITTLE LOUIS: **You are clever, you are...!** (*He stamps his foot. She stares at him...*)

Shame may be necessary. It is perhaps the single source of discipline. But how can it extend to gods? (*Pause*)

Or monarchs, Caroline? (*Pause*)

CAROLINE: I do not like the way you call me Caroline... (*Pause*)

Or rather...I did like it...and now I don't...

LITTLE LOUIS: You are not listening —

CAROLINE: I am listening but —

LITTLE LOUIS: **You are not agreeing with me, then!** (*Pause. He glares*)

You must

You must agree with me

I am the monarch

CAROLINE: Louis —

LITTLE LOUIS: I am trying to explain to you —

CAROLINE: Yes, but —

LITTLE LOUIS: As patiently as possibly —

CAROLINE: Yes —

LITTLE LOUIS: What I have concluded in the last few days —

CAROLINE: All right —

LITTLE LOUIS: While I have been here on my own and you have been entirely absent —

CAROLINE: On trial for my life —
LITTLE LOUIS: On trial for your life but absent and I do not criticize —
CAROLINE: Thank you —
LITTLE LOUIS: **Do not be sarcastic please**. (*Pause. She is shocked*)

These conclusions were arrived at in perfect solitude. They have the authority that comes from absolute seclusion in the proximity of death... (*He looks at her*)

And you tell me to shut up...

CAROLINE: I'm sorry, I —
LITTLE LOUIS: You try to change the subject —
CAROLINE: I did not actually say shut up I —
LITTLE LOUIS: And quarrel with the way I say your name —
CAROLINE: I've said I'm sorry, Louis —
LITTLE LOUIS: When I am struggling to communicate the most —
CAROLINE: Yes —
LITTLE LOUIS: Complex and —
CAROLINE: **I said I'm listening** . (*Pause....*)

Oh, dear... (*She bites her lip. She looks at him*)

Perhaps I am afraid of what I am about to hear. Perhaps I am doing everything in my power to prevent you speaking words I dread far more than the abuse of any revolutionary prosecutor... silly... when you are quite determined to.... when nothing on earth will stop you —
LITTLE LOUIS: I am the monarch —
CAROLINE: For that very reason, yes... (*He looks at her. She is uncomfortable*)

My eye began to hurt today. I asked for a doctor. A doctor. ...! You would have thought I'd asked for — (*Pause. He just looks*)

All right, I said, an ointment... (*She perseveres...*)

I was offered everything...! Creams for eczema... suppositories for piles... they surpassed themselves... craning over the balconies... axel grease... something they smear on castrated calves... (*She shakes her head*)

The whole lot... it took ten minutes to restore a little calm... not that it's ever very calm... the hatred... so intense... you can't ask for calm... (*Suddenly she is vehement*)

I am not ceasing this with you
You are my love

All day I repudiate
All day I crave
All day I ridicule
All day I ache
Who says I am not clever
There is no one so clever
My belly swells to think what my mouth so vehe-
mently denies
No wonder I am so often faint
No wonder...
Boy... (*Pause. LITTLE LOUIS bounces his ball.*
He does not look at her. She awaits as if it were a
sentence)

LITTLE LOUIS:	Yes...
		But now you must admit it, Caroline... (*He*
		stops, looks at her)
	Must...! (*Pause. He smiles. He runs to her, seizing her in his*
	arms. He wraps himself around her waist, hugging her belly and
	kissing it)

CAROLINE:	Admit it...
		Why...?
		It's Heaven...

LITTLE LOUIS:	Yes...!
	And I'm the King of Heaven, obviously...! (*The aperture*
	opens with a clap. A dim light shows. CAROLINE goes to avoid
	the gaze but LITTLE LOUIS keeps her in place. She does not
	try to move again...)

CAROLINE:	What —
		How —
		Louis —
		I don't know if I'm clever or not... (*The prison is*
		dim... they are barely visible)

LITTLE LOUIS:	You see... I do know what a monarch is...

CAROLINE:	What is it, then...?

LITTLE LOUIS:	It is all that is forbidden... and all that others
	cannot do... the monarch does... here even... I claim privi-
	lege... (*She closes her eyes, with pain...*)

CAROLINE:	Then, it's...

LITTLE LOUIS:	The crime of kings...! (*He explores her cloth-*
	ing. She sobs in the near darkness...)
		Why weep...?
	WHY WEEP...! (*A faint wind blows. The voice of the*
	GAOLER *comes from the aperture*)

GAOLER: Shan't tell... (*She sobs...*)
            Shan't tell...

Scene Sixteen

The Fifth Ecstasy of the Persecution

The CROWD *floods the stage as the doors open to reveal the court. They pile up the stairs, talking wildly, roaring with anticipation. With an access of energy,* TREPASSER *bounds in. They acclaim him. He rises the stairs, taking their salutations as he goes.*

TREPASSER: Share my pain...! Share my agony and enjoy it also! Yes! I understand the pleasure my ordeal bestows on you...! In struggling with my emotions you witness the disintegration of a man, for do I not prosecute this case with more ruthlessness than any living lawyer
   I am destroyed by it...! (*They applaud. They fail to observe the appearance of* CAROLINE, *near the foot of the stairs as he is at the head... he sees her, however...*)
   And here she is... the object of my suffering... laugh if you wish...! I wouldn't deny you...! Laugh... because she is...
   (*He motions towards her. they are quiet*)
   Much fallen in... as splendid pavilions left to the mercy of the elements... still echo with the ecstasies of unrecorded mischief... (*Pause. They observe her.* CAROLINE *observes him...*)
   I shall be hard on you today... (LITTLE LOUIS, *alone in the cell, is startled by the sudden uncoiling of a rope from the aperture. The end dangles at his feet. He contemplates it...*)
LITTLE LOUIS: The dilemma posed to one who is in every sense prepared for death by the sudden appearance of — a ready means of postponement — is in my case diminished by the fact that I have never learned to climb... (*He stares at the end*)
            I was not that kind of boy... (*He shrugs*)
   So thank you but — (*His attention is drawn upwards. A figure is climbing from the aperture in order to come down.* LITTLE LOUIS *laughs with an infectious delight. He claps his hands uncontrollably*)

Oh...! Oh, Louis...! I forgot a rope has got two ends...!
(*He claps again*)

I am ashamed of my vulgarity! I failed to grasp the principle of illusion that attaches to all appearances! I am to be murdered! And I interpreted the rope as the means of escape! How infantile, how inveterately

> **Don't**
> **Kill**
> **Me**
> **My Mother**
> **Isn't Here...!**

(*The court explodes in uproar. CAROLINE, to TREPASSER's horror and disbelief, has uncovered her breasts and stands, her shoulders bare, defiant before the waves of contempt and abuse*)

TREPASSER: Cover yourself...! Cover yourself I say! (*He stares, his arms folded until the noise dies down. He pretends to be bemused. He adopts a lawyer's pose. Silence falls, the attention returns to him. The GAOLER descends the rope, hand over hand, until he touches the bottom...*)

Very well. You have exposed your breasts to the People. The reason for this eccentric exhibition is not far to —

CAROLINE: Not my breasts. (*Pause. He stares*)

TREPASSER: Not your breasts —

CAROLINE: Not mine, no. And did you discover a physician for my eye? I say my eye. I see through it but is it mine? I don't think so. (*Pause. There is discomfort in the court. She suddenly laughs*)

How should I feel modesty for nakedness that is not nakedness at all? To be naked is to reveal that which was yours. And these breasts were never mine, for the simple reason that I don't exist

> **I'll strip to the waist...!**
> **Hips...!**
> **Arse...!**
> **Anyone...?** (*There is a burst of protest and derision*)
> **It's all right...!**

TREPASSER: May I remind you —

CAROLINE: Remind me of what you like —

TREPASSER: This is A People's Court —

CAROLINE: Excellent —

TREPASSER: And the People is Moral —

CAROLINE: It has opinions, certainly —

TREPASSER: The People is Judgement —

CAROLINE: It has eyes, certainly —

TREPASSER: And it will not be mocked!

CAROLINE: **Do you think I am afraid to die...? Do you really think it...? I require it nothing less** . (*Pause*)

To be parted from a body which never for a moment did I possess...can only be...deliverance, surely...? (*Pause*)

TREPASSER: Yes. And you will be parted. I am certain of it, Caroline.

LITTLE LOUIS: I think you do not like the door because you are ashamed... (*Pause*)

You thought...what I am doing...is something not fit for the door...even this door...which is not a nice door would... protest... (*The* GAOLER *stares at* LITTLE LOUIS...)

GAOLER: How right you are...

LITTLE LOUIS: As always...

GAOLER: Yes...

LITTLE LOUIS: Believe me, there is no special pleasure in this — inevitable correctness that I —

GAOLER: It must be quick —

LITTLE LOUIS: How I long to be mistaken — on this occasion obviously, but also —

GAOLER: You talk too much —

LITTLE LOUIS: I know, it's —

GAOLER: Quick because I am expected somewhere —

LITTLE LOUIS: Are you? Well... (*They exchange a long look. The* GAOLER *suddenly covers* LITTLE LOUIS' *mouth with a hand and forces him on the floor, face downwards. The court instantly erupts.* CAROLINE *repudiates their outrage with a stare...*)

CAROLINE: I've changed my plea
Is that not permissible?
Why not change it?
Don't you require me to be guilty?
I'm confessing, aren't I?
I did it
You bewilder me
More than once
As recently as
Yes
With my son
The child

The innocent and
Exactly as indicted
Yes
Debauched
Corrupted
Call it what you like
Infant
Offspring
Of my loins
Fruit of the womb
Yes
Mischief
Copulation
Moisture
Ecstasy
What more can I

TREPASSER: (*Who has watched with horror*) **You may not
             speak** (*He draws breath*)
             You calculating and degenerate hag there is
             something running out your eye... (*Pause*)

CAROLINE: Is there... (*She is embarrassed*)
             Is there — how horrible, I — (*She extends a hand
             aimlessly*)
             A handkerchief or — someone — I — (*No one
             offers. She gropes. She pulls her skirt to her eye ...*)

TREPASSER: (*Having watched her ordeal*) Fortunately, this
    transparent fraud, this imitation of insanity not very convin-
    cingly performed
             You fucking bitch
             Yes
             Has failed in its design
             We are not mocked by your pathetic stratagem
             Your nakedness
             Your lying
             Which is not lying but the flagrant abusing of
             the truth
             We have a witness madam

CAROLINE: There was no witness... (*She dabs her eye*)

TREPASSER: Oh yes there was you fucking bitch... (*The
    gaoler, climbing off the prone body of* LITTLE LOUIS, *adjusts
    his clothes and walks into the court. He looks at* CAROLINE ...*)
             Are you a gaoler at the Prison of La Fierté?

GAOLER: I am.

TREPASSER: And what has been your duty since the prisoner
and her child were placed under the protection of the State?
GAOLER: To look.
TREPASSER: Only to look?
GAOLER: To look and nothing else.
TREPASSER: Sliding back your little door —
GAOLER: It's hinged — (*Pause*)
TREPASSER: Opening your little door — (*Pause*) arbitrarily,
as you do, by day or night, what did you see? (*Pause*) What in
particular lodges in your memory? (*Pause*)

> Something unpleasant to relate, perhaps...?
> (*Pause*)
> Something your natural modesty shrinks to
> relate...? (CAROLINE *bursts out laughing*)
> **Well may you laugh you bitch**
> **You're dead**
> **You're dead**
> Please go on... (*Pause*)

GAOLER: Nothing out the ordinary. (*A shocked silence...*)
TREPASSER: Nothing out the ordinary, what does that...
(*Pause. He swallows*)

Let me assure you, no man or woman in this room feels
anything but the profoundest gratitude to servants of the State
obliged to carry out such tasks as you — (*He stops, looking
from* CAROLINE *to the* GAOLER)

Let me warn you now of the dire penalties attaching to —
**What do you mean is it ordinary to copulate with your child to
take his body in your own his organ in your mouth**

> **Because**
> **Yes**
> **Yes**
> **These are the facts and you**

GAOLER: Never saw it. (*Pause*)
CAROLINE: (*To the* GAOLER) Are you mad....? They'll
tear your eyes out....and I have confessed.... (*The*
GAOLER *merely looks at* CAROLINE. *She shrugs...*)
TREPASSER: His eyes... well, yes.... what use are his eyes in
any case?
GAOLER: (*To* TREPASSER) You invented it. I imagined it.
And she — (*He turns to* CAROLINE. *The wind blows.*
TREPASSER, *as if exhausted, leans on the desk...*)
TREPASSER: Piss on me.... Piss on me....! (*A sharp, metal-
lic note.* LITTLE LOUIS *enters pushing the horse on wheels...*)

Scene Seventeen

In the silence, CAROLINE *looks at* LITTLE LOUIS. *The court is frozen. At last she walks down the steps. She goes stiffly towards him. She extends a hand.*

CAROLINE: Shake hands. (*He looks away*)
Shake hands with your mother, please. (*Her hand stays outstretched*)
I have always liked formality. In my own way I was profoundly critical of the degeneration of formality at court, the bedchamber and so on, please... (*He extends a hand.* TREPASSER *walks out of the court... He watches this. She senses him, turns*)

TREPASSER: Who could discover the will for such frigidity who had not been intimate beyond belief...?

LITTLE LOUIS: Push me! (*He climbs on the horse*)
Push me!

CAROLINE: (*Ignoring her child*) I do believe... (*She laughs*)
One cannot escape the feeling, Monsieur Trepasser... that you have not entirely eradicated... some... lingering nostalgia... for... the truth...

TREPASSER: It's all appearances, Madame...

CAROLINE: Is it...?

LITTLE LOUIS: Push me, I said...!

CAROLINE: Appearances...? (FIGURES *appear dimly in the distant door.* CAROLINE *swiftly seizes* TREPASSER *in her arms and kisses him fixedly on the mouth. He staggers, she clings. Discordant notes. An absurd dance. The figures observe,* TREPASSER *sees that they observe. He forces her away from him. He spits. He chokes...*)

TREPASSER: Monarchic — saliva...! (*He ostentatiously wipes his mouth with the back of his hand*)
Monarchic — spit...! (*The* EXECUTIONERS, ASSISTANTS *etc, advance on* CAROLINE. *One extends a strap...*)

CAROLINE: Thank you, I do not require the strap. (*The* MAN *shrugs*)
No, I'll have the strap... I've nothing against the strap.

ASSISTANT: It was your husband's strap.

CAROLINE: (*She snorts*) But I did not love my husband...
(*She extends her wrists to him*)
Look, I proffer my hands as if in prayer...!
Who gets the strap after? (*Pause*)
ASSISTANT: It's my property, Madame —
CAROLINE: Yes, but you intend to sell it —
ASSISTANT: Sell it...I don't know if —
CAROLINE: **Auction it you fetishist** . (*Pause*)
ASSISTANT: Perhaps. (*The sound of a euphoric crowd floats
down, chanting, impatient. She looks from one face to another,
swaying with horror. The noise grows. Suddenly, with a surge of
will-power she launches herself out of the room, leaving the
OFFICIALS behind, obliged to run after her. TREPASSER
seizes the handles of the horse on wheels and propels LITTLE
LOUIS up and down the room, obsessively. LITTLE LOUIS
shouts in triumph...*)

HE STUMBLED

CHARACTERS

DOJA	An Anatomist
SUEDE	His Assistant
PIN	His Assistant
BERLIN	A Nun
LAYBACH	A Priest
TODD	A Courtier
BALDWIN	A Prince
TURNER	A Queen
NIXON	A Servant
FIRST/SECOND PRIESTS	A Chorus
TORTMANN	A King
KNIGHTS	
A CROWD	

A high wall. The grieving of masses. A rising sun fingers the top. An aperture appears. A naked arm emerges and tips a pan of fluid onto the ground. It disappears again. The grieving continues. A second aperture opens, and a second arm tips a pan of fluid onto the ground. No sooner has it withdrawn than a low door opens in the wall. A novice, fugitive from the miasma of death, flings herself onto the stage. She gasps the fragrance of uncontaminated air. She is restored. Her hands explore the surface of the stone. A third aperture opens. A bowl of blood is flung down the wall. The novice, stiff with disgust, slowly draws up her clothes until they are gathered over her head. She maintains her posture as, at intervals, further containers splash dark fluids down the wall. A second door opens. A novice emerges, retching, his hand clasped to his mouth. He also inhales the morning air. He also recovers. His gaze falls on the motionless nakedness of the girl, pressed to the wall and flecked with visceral muck. He stares. He is inexorably drawn towards her. His hand reaches, withdraws, extends again. He touches her, at first tentative, then more confidently. She chooses not to welcome or deny him, but remains with her head covered, motionless. At the moment he flings up his cassock to take her, the intoxicated cries of a maddened crowd flood the stage. The novice drops his garment and turns his face to the wall. A mass of figures surges past, streaming banners and bawling. Their impetus blinds them to the two novices, who stand stock still. As their cries fade, a further pan of sickness cascades down the wall. The grieving continues. The youth peers sideways to see the girl in the identical posture she had adopted before the interruption. He tears up his garment, exposing his own nakedness, and goes to embrace the girl from behind. He is stopped in his rush by a single shout. Slowly, with a profound reluctance, he allows the robe to fall. He sits, and with an air of resignation, draws up his knees. Blood runs down the wall. A man enters, grey, powerful. He goes to the naked girl, and lifting her in his arms, carries her away. The youth stares fixedly ahead. At last he climbs to his feet, pulls his cowl over his head and returns through the little door to the death chamber. The sound of grief swells, and falls as the door is closed again. The running mourners pass in a frenzy. The girl, now covered by her cassock, returns and opens the door by which she entered. The sound of grief swells but is suddenly silenced. She freezes in her movement.

BERLIN: You're God.... (*The* GREY MAN *inches onto the stage, adjusting his clothing....*)
                From now on... (*He looks at her...*)
        God's you... (*She slips through the door. Immediately the other door opens. The grieving surges as a woman emerges, closes the door swiftly and leans against the wall, flattering her hands behind her*)
TODD: Still not over... (*A pan of fluid cascades.... The* GREY MAN *looks at her. She walks forward....*)
    By no means over and you're premature or possibly he senses your presence rather as a collapsed heifer smells a wolf and struggles miserably to rise from its puddle of excrement slips slides falls again do you like to be a wolf be a wolf if you want and kiss me I must go back soon kiss me your wolf smell I will transport on my skin perhaps he will die inhaling you perhaps it will abbreviate his agony... (*He looks without moving*)
    Don't kiss then obviously your tender sentiments are bruised by such a proposition why should you kiss a stranger when your nerves are strung perhaps more tightly strung even than my own after all your task is delicate infinitely more delicate than anything I am obliged to do I am ashamed to have described you as a wolf far from it no wolf is not the animal not the animal at all will you wait for the body to be cold or slice warmly through the lungs the bowel the viscera I've heard the flesh comes swiftly from the bone but only if the blood still moves whereas cold flesh adheres (*A pan of fluid is tipped out*)
        As if you'd tell...! (*She laughs, falsely*)
    Never mind the kissing then and next time you see me you will say could that be surely not not possibly the woman who and I shan't even meet your eyes or if I do with such a grey indifference you will thrash your memory for lying not her not her surely you'll

The running mourners stream past, yelling. When they have gone, TODD is revealed against the wall in the same state of undress as the novice. For a few seconds she is still. A pan of fluid is thrown down. The GREY MAN goes slowly to her and proceeds to penetrate her. His hands reach to the wall over hers. They are still, intimate. The second door opens with a crash and two PRIESTS *emerge, gasping for air, light and liberty. The surge of mourning accompanies them. They do not observe the lovers in the ecstasy of their relief.*

FIRST PRIEST: I was
SECOND PRIEST: I was
FIRST PRIEST: Up my throat came
SECOND PRIEST: Torrents
FIRST PRIEST: Flooding
SECOND PRIEST: Saw your mouth go
FIRST PRIEST: Saw yours
SECOND PRIEST: Choking
FIRST PRIEST: Sick
SECOND PRIEST: And laughter
FIRST PRIEST: You too
SECOND PRIEST: Laughter
FIRST PRIEST: You too
SECOND PRIEST: Sick and laughter
FIRST PRIEST: Both at once
SECOND PRIEST: Everyone
FIRST PRIEST: Christ
SECOND PRIEST: Stench and
FIRST PRIEST: Agh
SECOND PRIEST: Stench and
FIRST PRIEST: Agh
SECOND PRIEST: Agh (*They collapse in a fountain of laughter during which* TODD *departs through the door they had left open. The sound of mourning is muffled. The* GREY MAN *is immobile. The running mourners stream by, but on their departure, one remains. She gazes at the* GREY MAN . . .)
FIRST PRIEST: And then
SECOND PRIEST: Teeth all
FIRST PRIEST: And then
SECOND PRIEST: The teeth
FIRST PRIEST: Horrible teeth
SECOND PRIEST: Snap
FIRST PRIEST: Snap
SECOND PRIEST: His teeth and we were
FIRST PRIEST: Agh
SECOND PRIEST: C Minor
FIRST PRIEST: In Deo
SECOND PRIEST: Snap

FIRST PRIEST: Fidemus
SECOND PRIEST: Snap
FIRST PRIEST: Agh
SECOND PRIEST: Saw you
FIRST PRIEST: Snap snap

*They collapse again, in each other's arms, wheezing and hooting.
The* WOMAN *goes to the* GREY MAN *and draws up her skirt,
revealing herself. He looks at her, without visible enthusiasm, then
goes to draw her against the wall. The apertures in the wall open
simultaneously, with a clatter, the grieving is instantly silenced and
the projecting heads of a chorus of* NUNS *announce the end of the
king's ordeal. Simultaneously, a surgical table, suspended from
chains, is winched downwards. On this table, the naked body of
the monarch lies ready for dissection. Two* ASSISTANTS *appear
from the wings, holding bags of tools, aprons, buckets. They attend
politely on the master. The chorus ceases. The two* PRIESTS *hurry
away. The grey man draws down the skirt of the* WOMAN *with an
attitude of resignation, and turning from her, goes to the table and
leans on it. The* ASSISTANTS *wait. The* GREY MAN *looks from
one to the other.*

DOJA: Even I
        Yes
        I who so assiduously removed himself
        Who so undressed himself of all things kind and
        gracious
        Shedding the clinging garments of politeness
        And stepping out of manners as a woman lifts her feet
        lightly from shoes
        Even I
        Remain susceptible to
        Obligation (*He turns to the* WOMAN, *who hurries
        away . . .*)
        Why (*The* ASSISTANTS *hold out an apron*)
        Why
When this obligation both left her wholly dissatisfied and created in me a sense of profound resentment (*He extends his arms*)
    It was as if I had submitted to a discipline the rules of which my
entire nature found repellent and under whose arbitrary regulation my soul writhed (*They tie the strings*)
        Bitter
        And

Recalcitrant (*The* ASSISTANTS *proceed to unfasten cases of instruments*)

No

Obligation I must learn to recognize (*They extend the open cases*)

And recognizing it resolutely (*He takes a sharp-bladed knife, but fumbles and lets it fall to the floor*)

You see I am distracted (*He leans on his hands...*)

My infamy whilst making me an object of desire must not create in me some nagging and reciprocal responsibility to those who suffer that desire surely (*He recovers, and takes a second blade*)

I am not after all a monarch

Only

The

Disemboweller

Of

Monarchs (*The* ASSISTANTS *fetch buckets, pails, pans*)

Did you get a decent lunch?

PIN: Thank you we did...

DOJA: And your room?

PIN: Clean, thank you...

SUEDE: Flowers

PIN: On the window sill

SUEDE: Austere however

PIN: And the view

SUEDE: You could not honestly

PIN: Describe it as a view

SUEDE: The flowers being

PIN: As so often

SUEDE: A substitute for views

PIN: And the corridor

SUEDE: Yet again

PIN: The corridor

SUEDE: Unoccupied

PIN: Remote

SUEDE: And cold

PIN: As if we were

SUEDE: A disease... (DOJA *smiles... he goes to the head of the table, and adjusts the head of the corpse...*)

DOJA: My room by contrast (*The* ASSISTANTS *laugh*)

Yes

Yes

You anticipate the luxury of my surroundings
My room is (*He is about to make an incision in the neck
but stops short, the blade in the air...*)
Plump with furnishings and scented like a whore... (*He
is still...*)
Why is that? (*He reflects, then draws the blade exquis-
itely from the base of the neck to the navel...*)
Because
Surely
Because
I am perceived to be like flesh itself
Corrupt
Malodorous
And
Indiscriminate (*He throws the knife into a bucket*)
I don't disagree (*He walks away wiping his hands on a
cloth*)
Open him

*The assistants proceed to draw back the walls of the thorax. A youth
stumbles into the room. He leans against the wall.* DOJA *bows from
the waist. The eyes of the youth are fixed on the table...*

BALDWIN: What's that...? (*The* ASSISTANTS *look at one
another*)
            On the table what is it...
DOJA: It is the degenerate and spoiling prison of a dead man's
soul...
BALDWIN: **Man**
            What
            Man
            Man
            You
            Call
            My
            Father
DOJA: It is in his mortality that a great king —
BALDWIN: **Butcher**
DOJA: Yes
BALDWIN: **Cleaver**
DOJA: Yes
BALDWIN: (*Covering his face*) I have to be here sorry but I
must I must ignore me do your work sorry but it's my desire

my desire's law I won't distract you sorry but I need a stool...
(DOJA *indicates to* SUEDE *that he should fetch a stool.*
SUEDE *goes off*)
                    I loved him...
DOJA: It's a famous love...
BALDWIN: Is it...
DOJA: Legendary...
BALDWIN: Legendary, is it...
DOJA: But I must cut him all the same...
BALDWIN: You must do, obviously...
DOJA: And you must watch without exclaiming...
BALDWIN: I will I said so didn't I...
DOJA: The flesh is not the man...
BALDWIN: Don't lecture me and we will get on very well
    (SUEDE *enters with a stool*)
                    There (*He indicates a place*)
                    Thank you
                    Sorry
                    Thank you
                    I am
                    All
                    A mass of
                    Carry on
                    Sorry
                    I (*He climbs on the stool, adjusts his posture, is
                    still*)

    Monarch silent on a stool... (DOJA *returns to the table. He
lifts a blade from the case of instruments. He is about to make an
incision*)
    Stop...! (DOJA *holds himself rigid. A pause...* BALDWIN
slips off the stool, walks contemplatively in a circle, stops...)
The flesh is not the man...? (*He looks at* DOJA)
    The flesh is not the man...? What is the flesh, then? Is the
flesh not this man's and no other's? If the flesh is not the man,
why are you here? I am a boy and vastly ignorant but we have
spent huge sums on your services, you are not cheap, your fees
are thought by some to be exorbitant, why if the flesh is not the
man? A cat would do, surely, a goat ripped off a butcher's
hook? A goat's heart in the casket would certainly suffice and
let a hundred knights stand guard over a skewered bullock if
the flesh is not the man I am a boy and vastly ignorant parks of
ignorance distinguish me from you but why if the flesh is not
the man...?

DOJA: (*Patiently*) I am sorry if my price is thought too
high —

BALDWIN: By some, I've no opinion on the subject —

DOJA: My skills such as they are have earned a certain reputation —

BALDWIN: Yes —

DOJA: And as a consequence of this reputation I am not
infrequently obliged to choose between one mortality and
another —

BALDWIN: Obviously —

DOJA: I had made detailed plans to visit Sicily when the news
of your father's imminent decease reached me —

BALDWIN: So I gather —

DOJA: The Queen of Sicily did not protest when I proposed a
sum appropriate for this expedition, on the contrary, so
anxious was she to acquire my services I was embarrassed by
the gifts forwarded to me —

BALDWIN: Yes —

DOJA: It was with the most profound reluctance I bowed to the
tide of pleas and promises flowing from this place and can-
celled my visit —

BALDWIN: Yes —

DOJA: I was able to propose a substitute —

BALDWIN: Good —

DOJA: But this substitute has sufficient modesty to acknowledge the body of the King of Sicily is unlikely to receive the
final privilege of a dissection so refined as that about to be
bestowed upon your father —

BALDWIN: Yes —

DOJA: Cheap I would not wish to be for fear of causing
embarrassment —

BALDWIN: Yes —

DOJA: Not to myself, but to those whose grief compels them to
bid for my services —

BALDWIN: Of course and I —

DOJA: Acknowledge this, I'm sure, as for the flesh, my own
opinion can be stated very briefly. It is everything and nothing.
May I continue? My arm aches and if I cannot exert the fullest
concentration on my task the perfection for which I am
renowned will certainly be compromised, to everybody's detri-
ment... (*Pause*)

BALDWIN: Yes, I (*Pause*)
                 Yes, you (*Pause*)

Please do, I (*He returns to the stool, climbs on it,
and rests his chin in his hands...*)

DOJA: (*To* PIN) Dextra...

Inflexit...

Contortum...

Occlusit...

In axio...

In axio...

Dixi...

PIN: (*Working deep in the chest*) In axio... (*An atmosphere of
tranquillity surrounds the work of the clinicians, cutting and
cleaning with a practised routine, hypnotic to* BALDWIN, *who
sways on his stool...*)

DOJA: Et implacit...

PIN: Sub sternum...

DOJA: Implacit...

PIN: Implacit...

DOJA: Testoria...

PIN: Fluvio...

Fluvio... (SUEDE *holds up a pan.* DOJA *lifts out the
heart and suspends it in the manner of a priest raising the
host. It leaks blood.* BALDWIN *is a miracle of balance as
he inclines in fascination...*)

BALDWIN: My father's heart...

My father's heart...

DOJA: Yes... (*A door closes...*)

BALDWIN: Mother...! (*A woman appears, advances into the
room, stops.* BALDWIN *clings to the stool. She looks...*)

Mother...

This man has turned my father inside out...
(*Pause. The* QUEEN *looks without flinching...*)

DOJA: I hesitate to continue... (*Pause...*)

I hesitate because whereas the extrusion of the heart is
relatively clean, I must proceed to lift the bowel from its
— (BALDWIN *emits an audible gasp. Pause. The*
QUEEN *does not move...*)

BALDWIN: Continue...!

Continue, do...! (DOJA *looks at the* QUEEN...)

TURNER: I did not love my husband's bowel. (BALDWIN
giggles with anxiety...)

Nor his lungs.

Nor his liver, either.

BALDWIN: The lungs are going to Jerusalem...!

TURNER: All that I loved was visible, Mr Doja.

BALDWIN: And the bowel to Constantinople...! Or the other way round, is it...?

TURNER: It must be the same with the character. We love what we see. But that is rather little of it. Really, life is solitude. We collide with others. We attach ourselves to surfaces. But what is intimacy, Mr Doja? A fiction, surely...

BALDWIN: No, the lungs are staying, it's the brain that must be going to Arabia...

DOJA: Intimacy I know rather little of.

TURNER: Is that so?

BALDWIN: No, that's completely wrong. The bowel is meant for Rome.

TURNER: Perhaps it frightens you.

BALDWIN: I forgot Rome.

TURNER: Certainly it frightens me.

BALDWIN: Can we get on, now...?

TURNER: Knowing how little intimacy there is, we are correct to fear it, Mr Doja...

BALDWIN: We cannot keep talking, we have so much to do...! (*He looks crossly at* TURNER...)

TURNER: You might give the heart to the dogs for all I care. (*She walks out... Pause...*)

BALDWIN: My mother...! (*He makes a gesture of hopelessness*)

> Never mind my mother...
> She...
> Her...
> Never mind my mother... (*He arranges himself on the stool*)
> Do the bowel, please...!

Bowel, next...! (PIN *lifts a container.* DOJA *places the heart inside.* SUEDE *puts a lid on the container*)

And label everything...! Because how silly if how idiotic and infuriating if the organ having been at huge expense in life and labour transported through so many hostile territories should on arrival be discovered to have accidentally been exchanged the lungs in Lapland and the brain in Ireland for example or the liver somewhere altogether inappropriate the rage the indignation just imagine it so write it very clearly or do you do that anyway here am I reminding you of what is probably a routine probably you do that the label writing is that your task I don't know your name Mr —

SUEDE: It's not my function —

BALDWIN: Whose function is it then not Mr Doja's surely he would not stoop to label writing or possibly he —

SUEDE: Each vessel is a particular shape —

BALDWIN: Yes...!

Yes, that would obviate the necessity for labels I do so admire you Mr Doja I want us to be friends I think at this moment you have a terrible attraction for me and my mother also finds you likeable which is odd she likes so few people I put it down to your silence you do not speak more than is necessary which means that those who would dislike you have little evidence for their offence shrewd and calculating Mr Doja and more effective than whole books of poetry I'm leaving I cannot stomach another minute of this butchery I shall know you better in time and hope oh so sincerely hope you do not disappoint my profound intuition that we shall be friends... (*He slips off the stool and walks smartly from the room.* DOJA *proceeds as if the interruptions had never occurred...*)

DOJA: Focasit...

PIN: (*Giving him a tool*) Focasit...

DOJA: Enterritur... (SUEDE *goes out...*)

Et excisit... (*He draws a long incision down the wall of the dead man's abdomen...*)

Tentastes...

PIN: Mihi...?

DOJA: Cum clavi... (DOJA *withdraws to the head as* SUEDE *returns bearing a substantial pan to contain the bowels.* DOJA *takes a saw...*)

Of course this surge of intimacy comes as no surprise. (*He throws down the first saw and selects another...*)

This deference mingled with desire... (*He rejects that, also...*)

This morbid appetite for nakedness and the profane... (*And picks another...*)

I think if any of us is to leave this place alive I must fuck with the Queen... ubi serrula...? (*He tosses down the last saw...* SUEDE *hastens to sort through the tools.* DOJA *is patient...*)

I am not attracted to the Queen... (*The clatter of instruments..*)

There is an odour clinging to her which...

Ubi serrula minor est...!

SUEDE: It's here, I know I —

DOJA: **Ubi**
         Ubi
SUEDE: (*Sifting the instruments in a desperate manner*) I saw it,
         it's —
DOJA: **Ubi**
         Ubi
         Dixi
SUEDE: Out of sequence, it's —
DOJA: **Cur not sequentia est** ...?
SUEDE: I don't know, I don't know, I... (*He is close to sob-
         bing. He extends the saw to* DOJA... *Pause*...)
DOJA: So what if I do not like her odour? My partiality is
         scarcely relevant. Of far greater importance is the necessity to
         fuck with her in such a way as to satisfy her curiosity without
         awakening a passion the extent of which may be more threat-
         ening to our survival than if I had never aroused her in the first
         place, but that's too late, she's aroused already...
SUEDE: Serrula...?
DOJA: Trepannit...
SUEDE: Mihi...?
DOJA: **Trepannit**... (SUEDE *looks at* PIN *in horror*... *he goes
         to the head of the corpse*...)
         And the boy's inflamed also...
SUEDE: Trepannit...? (DOJA *walks away from the table*... *he
         contemplates his situation*)
SUEDE: Trepannit, Magister...?
DOJA: Yes, why not you...? (*The* ASSISTANTS *exchange
         anxious glances*...)
     No, it's complicated. The boy does not like his mother. The
mother does not like her son. Each of them has discovered in
me the alleviation of his solitude. It calls on all my resources to
satisfy these competing claims. But do I possess the resources? I
am not young any more. Recently I have become susceptible to
moods of irritation which make even common politeness an
effort for me, let alone the affectation of desire, amicability and
the like, I think we erred in coming here but how was I to know
the depth of passion my very appearance would cause to stir,
like some turbid pool a hound had splashed in, throwing up
decaying matter, exotic coloured weed and God knows what
fragments of — (*The* ASSISTANTS *are looking at him. He
meets their eyes. Pause*)
         Very well I knew
         Yes

Obviously
It was entirely predictable (*He walks back to the table*)
Retract the scalp...
SUEDE: (*With relief*) Magister...
DOJA: (*Taking a blade*) Cum fasces, placit...
SUEDE: (*And pleasure*) Magister...!

They proceed to expose the dead man's skull, while PIN *works on
the abdomen. Two of the high windows fly open and the heads of the*
PRIESTS *emerge. Their dialogue is punctuated by the musical
effects of the surgical instruments...*

FIRST PRIEST: Everything's
SECOND PRIEST: Ourselves included
FIRST PRIEST: Everything's
SECOND PRIEST: Peculiar
FIRST PRIEST: As if some miasma of
SECOND PRIEST: Some putrescence possibly
FIRST PRIEST: And this interminable mourning
SECOND PRIEST: Makes me
FIRST PRIEST: You too...!
SECOND PRIEST: Want to scream
FIRST PRIEST: Scream what
SECOND PRIEST: Scream
FIRST PRIEST: **Torrents**
Of
SECOND PRIEST: We seem
FIRST PRIEST: Not only us
SECOND PRIEST: Things seem
FIRST PRIEST: Even the trees
SECOND PRIEST: The tiles on floors
FIRST PRIEST: Have been seen to move
SECOND PRIEST: **Torrents**
Of
FIRST PRIEST: As if in a profound embarrassment
SECOND PRIEST: Embarrassed tiles...?
FIRST PRIEST: And when we pass each other
SECOND PRIEST: **Torrents**
Of
FIRST PRIEST: People avert their eyes
SECOND PRIEST: They do
FIRST PRIEST: It's universal this suffocating
SECOND PRIEST: Kiss me

FIRST PRIEST: This asphyxiating
SECOND PRIEST: Kiss me
FIRST PRIEST: And airless
SECOND PRIEST: Kiss me I said
FIRST PRIEST: I heard
SECOND PRIEST: Or I will scream
FIRST PRIEST: **Torrents**
              Of

*They laugh. Their laughter falters. Their eyes go dim. Simultaneously
their bodies are launched from the little windows and plunge towards
the floor. They swing by their feet, to and fro in a breeze . . .* DOJA
and the ASSISTANTS *continue with their labours, unconscious of
their fate . . . the* NOVICE PRIEST *enters. He stands politely, waiting to be observed.* DOJA *wipes his hands on a clean towel and goes
towards him. Pause. They examine one another . . .*

LAYBACH: Obviously I hate you but I must speak. (*Pause . . .*)
        I have been here on three occasions. (*Pause . . .*)
        I stood there and — (*He indicates . . .*)
DOJA: I saw you.
LAYBACH: Yes and what I have to say is very hard to say so
   on each occasion I chose instead to leave, thereby avoiding the
   actual purpose of my visit . . .
DOJA: What you have to say offends you . . .
LAYBACH: Yes, and I feel even now a powerful desire to
   avoid your sight but she would not forgive me a fourth time
   there is a limit even to her tolerance and if it offends me so
   what so much offends me in this life I am bruised by everything
   she pleaded with me so I came bitterly I came I offend even
   myself you see she is stricken with you utterly stricken and
   cannot move her limbs you have to go to her. (*Pause.*
   LAYBACH *stares at the ground . . .*)
DOJA: Who . . . ? (*Pause.* LAYBACH *still stares at the
   ground . . .*)
LAYBACH: Oh, God . . . (*He shakes his head in disbelief . . .*)
        Oh, God . . .
DOJA: Do look me in the eyes. I find this place odd. But the
   oddest thing is the impossibility of meeting any other's eyes . . .
LAYBACH: I cannot . . .
DOJA: Why can you not . . . ?
LAYBACH: I am too . . .
        I think . . .

If I contrived to meet your eyes I would kill you.
(*Pause... He shrugs...*)
I exaggerate...
Certainly I would try to kill you...
And almost certainly I would fail...
She is paralyzed with her infatuation and you (*He turns on his heel, begins to walk resolutely away, but freezes. He sways, like the* DEAD PRIESTS *in the wind...*)
Why should you know, why should the identity of an obscure girl whose face I doubt was even registered by you, why should you stoop to —
Yes I could kill yes (*Pause*)

DOJA: This obscure girl whose face I did not register is loved by you... evidently...

LAYBACH: You are so perceptive, Mr Doja — (DOJA *slaps him swiftly over the cheek.* LAYBACH *reels, horrified... He stares...*)

DOJA: I think...
By and large I think...
Whilst I did not wish to strike you...
The blow has saved us... infinite... perambulations of sarcasm and —

LAYBACH: Yes, probably... (*Pause. He rubs his cheek*)
I am dreadfully unhappy...

DOJA: Yes...

LAYBACH: Perhaps to be unhappy is my fate. She is at the infirmary. May I tell her you will come...?

DOJA: Yes. (*Pause...*)

LAYBACH: Pity...
I would much have preferred to carry back your cold contempt.

DOJA: Obviously. (BALDWIN *enters, stands between the* DEAD PRIESTS. LAYBACH *leaves...* DOJA *turns to* BALDWIN ...)

BALDWIN: They laughed... (*Pause...*)
Not on this occasion only... (*Pause...*)
Frequently they laughed... (*Pause...*)

DOJA: One must be cautious where one laughs. It is a thing to be rationed, laughter.

BALDWIN: You don't laugh, Mr Doja.

DOJA: I laugh but sparingly. And in the strangest places.

BALDWIN: I've not heard you...

DOJA: Still, I do laugh...

I should not wish you to think me incapable of laughter
...

BALDWIN: But not like them...!

DOJA: I have not actually heard the manner in which they —

BALDWIN: **Not like them I'm certain...!** (*Pause...*)

DOJA: No, if you're certain, then I think, probably not like them...

BALDWIN: Oh, good... (*He seems suddenly shy...*)

When one admires someone... how important it is that he should not in any detail of his character... ever disappoint you... (*He looks at the ground...*)

A tall order, but... (*Pause. He extends a paper towards* DOJA...)

You are invited to — (*He stops*)

Who was here just now...?

DOJA: Just now...?

BALDWIN: As I came in you were in conversation with someone —

DOJA: A priest, yes —

BALDWIN: A novice, surely...?

DOJA: I didn't notice that he was —

BALDWIN: A novice, certainly —

DOJA: Yes, he was — I'm not sure who he was —

BALDWIN: I see... (*He offers the paper again...*)

You are invited to —

No —

No —

There was an atmosphere of cordiality between you, a manner of —

Not cordiality —

Intimacy —

DOJA: I don't think intimacy —

BALDWIN: Something very like it —

DOJA: Far from intimacy, I assure you —

BALDWIN: **All right the opposite of intimacy then but still a —**
(*Pause. He sways a little on his feet*)

Profound passage of feeling, Mr Doja, which I should dearly like to have shared with you myself... (*Pause... He extends the paper again*)

This invitation is — (*Suddenly, he screws up the paper into a ball and tosses it down*)

Not an invitation any more... (*He turns on his heel, takes a few steps, stops again...*)

                    I must be helped ...

DOJA: Yes ...

BALDWIN: **You see that, do you, Mr Doja, that I must be helped?** (*Pause ... The* ASSISTANTS *watch ...*)

DOJA: Yes, someone must certainly — (*He is tentative ...*)
            Certainly ...

BALDWIN: What? (*Pause ...* DOJA *takes the initiative of retrieving the ball of paper, unwrapping it, smoothing it, and reading it*)

DOJA: Oh, it's an invitation addressed to me ...! (*A fractional, crucial pause. Then* BALDWIN *laughs*)

BALDWIN: Yes ...!
            Yes ...!
            That's exactly what it is ...! Say you will ...!

DOJA: Certainly I will ...!

BALDWIN: I knew ...! I knew however smothered with attention Mr Doja might be still he would —

DOJA: Oh, yes —

BALDWIN: Find time to —

DOJA: Yes, indeed —

BALDWIN: Thank you ...
            Thank you ... (*He stares at* DOJA, *smiling, then walks away.* DOJA *goes slowly to the table, leans on it ...*)

DOJA: Take the horses, now, and ride. Not by the way we came. Find another road. Or rather, do not use a road at all.

PIN: What ...?

DOJA: I will finish the dissection ...

PIN: What ...?

DOJA: Go now. Do not even return to your room.

PIN: What ...?

DOJA: Do not say what again. Wipe your hands and leave.

SUEDE: Impossible, we —

DOJA: This is my final kindness, believe me. If it is a kindness. Most likely it is no more than the shedding of an onerous responsibility, and therefore, far from kind, rather another manifestation of my inexorable selfishness. All the same it is the best advice you will ever receive. Leave at once.

PIN: (*Tears rising in his eyes*) Magister ...!

DOJA: **Get out ...**

PIN/SUEDE: Mag — ister ...! Mag — ister ...!

DOJA: **Get out I said** ... (*The* ASSISTANTS *fall to their knees, and clutch at* DOJA's *clothes ... he observes them ... pause ...*)
            Very well, die ...

PIN/SUEDE: Magister...
DOJA: Die, die, if you must...
PIN/SUEDE: Yes...
              Yes...
              Beside you, Magister...
DOJA: Yes...
         Beside me, yes...

Pause. He touches their heads lightly. A SERVANT *passes bearing a massive covered tray. A table, identical to the anatomical table, descends. A* SECOND SERVANT *appears, staggering with a second tray. And then a* THIRD. *This new table is rapidly piled with meat and offal until it resembles a cornucopia, overflowing, preposterous. The passage of servants is accompanied by the staccato chant of the* DEAD PRIESTS

FIRST PRIEST: Killed for nothing
SECOND PRIEST: For nothing
FIRST PRIEST: Not that something
SECOND PRIEST: Would make it satisfactory
FIRST PRIEST: Would it
SECOND PRIEST: Would it
FIRST PRIEST: Be altogether better if
FIRST/SECOND: **We'd sinned**
FIRST PRIEST: Or if
              Of it
              Or if
FIRST/SECOND: **We saw the executioner**
FIRST PRIEST: That would have helped
SECOND PRIEST: Or
FIRST PRIEST: Or if not helped then possibly
SECOND PRIEST: Lent us an object of resentment
FIRST/SECOND: Oh yes
              Oh yes
              Oh yes
SECOND PRIEST: **How the dead hate**
FIRST PRIEST: We do
              We do
SECOND PRIEST: Admit it
FIRST PRIEST: Yes we hate
SECOND PRIEST: And sadly must confess to wanting the extinction of the human race
FIRST PRIEST: I do

SECOND PRIEST: Me too
FIRST PRIEST: Admit it
SECOND PRIEST: Yes
FIRST PRIEST: Yes
SECOND PRIEST: How lovely to admit it
FIRST PRIEST: Hold my hand (*The* DEAD PRIESTS *reach out*...)
And laugh...

In the stillness and silence that follows, the footsteps of a MAN. *He stops. He bows towards* DOJA. *He is formal, dark, as if a servant*...

NIXON: I'll take your coat.
DOJA: I didn't bring a coat.
NIXON: Something else, then.
DOJA: Something else...?
NIXON: Gloves, perhaps?
DOJA: I have no gloves...
NIXON: Please.
DOJA: It's warm, I —
NIXON: Please. (*Pause.* DOJA *examines* NIXON. *He removes a handkerchief from his pocket, and extends it to* NIXON. NIXON *takes it, thrusts it into his own pocket and walking away, positions himself at a distance from the table.* DOJA, *lacking a destination, aimlessly crosses the room. He stops. He crosses it in the opposite direction. Again he stops, then with apparent decision, goes as if to leave*)
You are also a monarch. (DOJA *stops*)
In your own way, also a monarch. (*Pause*)
DOJA: Arguably...
NIXON: Yes, I feel the quality of monarchy in you... (*Pause*)
DOJA: And you... what are you...? (NIXON *is silent*...)
NIXON: Sometimes the king's assassin bears in himself the very characteristics of dignity, ambition, and so on, that characterized his victim. I have observed this time and again.
DOJA: I am not an assassin...
NIXON: You? No... (*Pause*...)
And yet how rarely the assassin is permitted to occupy the vacancy he has himself created...! (*Pause*...)
That seems absurd to me. Surely he is the candidate most qualified. (*Pause*...)
DOJA: I am not however, an assassin...
NIXON: You? No... (*Pause*)

The assassin is put to death. And horribly. As if this would deter all others. Frequently I think, oh, how wasteful this execution is ... we have compounded the loss ... two monarchs are extinguished when we might have suffered only one ... (*Pause* ...)

But you are not an assassin ... (*Pause* ...)

DOJA: Me? No ... (*They examine one another ... a large door opens in the wall, sufficient to permit the entrance of* TURNER, *in an extravagant dress.* NIXON *bows to her* ...)

TURNER: I put this on. I then wished I had not. I had it taken off again. I raged before the mirror. Poor mirror. It is party to such. Silent witness of so many. I pity it. I then — (*She laughs, a long laugh* ...)

Concluded my first instinct was correct. It so often is. But these instincts are always subject to examination, judgement, inspection, and so on, which contaminate the purity of spontaneity. How I would love to rid myself entirely of my second thoughts. And how difficult it is ...! (*Pause* ...)

DOJA: Certainly, in this instance, your first thought was immaculate ... (TURNER *seems to examine this compliment* ... *Pause* ...)

TURNER: Failing to keep faith with my instinct, I paid the price of my unnecessary exertions ... (*She looks at* DOJA ...) I'm dishevelled ... (*Pause* ...)

And perspiring ...

DOJA: This can only have contributed to the striking quality of your overall appearance, I feel sure ... (*Again, she seems to weigh his compliment ... his eyes meet hers* ...)

On the other hand ...

TURNER: Yes ...?

DOJA: Inevitably one cannot but think — excellent as this garment is —

TURNER: You know about garments, do you ...? (*He smiles, thinly* ...)

DOJA: One cannot but think, how fortunate the mirror was to have —

TURNER: What do you know of garments, Mr Doja ...?

DOJA: (*Persisting*) To have witnessed your impatience, since the very excess of material compels imagination to contemplate what lies beneath ... (*Pause. He shrugs* ...)

I ... (*Pause* ...)

Do you wish me to continue in this vein or not ...? (*Pause* ...)

TURNER: Yes...
          A little longer...
DOJA: I think...
          In certain cases...
          The bereaved are peculiarly enhanced by grief...
          (TURNER *looks at him*...)
TURNER: What grief...? (*She regrets her words. A pause of
painful exposure*...)
          Listen, I do not like clever men... (*Pause*...)
DOJA: My cleverness I promise you is nothing but the brittle
shelter of my soul... (*She stares, bemused*...)
TURNER: Is that so...? What quality of soul, Mr Doja...?
(*She whirls away*)
          Perhaps you do not have a soul at all...! (*She
          laughs*)
   Some don't...! Some are quite simply, soulless...! And we
should envy them, we should envy their extraordinary capacity
for happiness, they live like birds, they leave no imprint on the
ground and death, when he collects them, finds them insub-
stantial as fallen leaves, which satisfies his idleness, my husband died a death of such reluctance, Mr Doja, clinging to life
by every thread, as if the banner of one of his regiments were
gnawn down the middle stitch by stitch, I did not think it
possible, but he made death rage, he made of death a ranting
exhibitionist... (DOJA *examines her... she looks down*...)
   I put this on for you... (BALDWIN *enters, hurried, then
stopping, ebullient, and suddenly constrained... pause*...)
BALDWIN: I so wish us to succeed... (*Pause... he bites his
lip*...)
   If you knew the scale of that wish... you'd shrink...! (*He
grins. He lifts his arms, in a gesture of helplessness*...)
My mother...! Her body...! (*He smiles*...)
   I'd intended to bring a present. But what? What present
could possibly gratify a man of your discrimination...? I
dreaded, more than the shame of giving nothing, the slightest
hint of disappointment in your face that what I did give was
inadequate in any detail...! Obviously, you would conceal this
disappointment! —
DOJA: I should conceal it, yes —
BALDWIN: You would...! You would conceal it, and brilliant in concealment I am certain that you are, still I should
detect it, so attuned am I to every nuance of your character...
(*He stares... smiling*)

Not really... (*He smiles on...*)

Not really but I intend to be... (*He turns*)

How does she have this body...she's not
young... (*Pause*)

DOJA: It's me, surely, who as the guest, should have cudgelled
his brains to find the perfect gift, alas, I —

BALDWIN: For example, her legs... (*Pause...*)

To which she devotes inordinate attention...

Her legs are... (*Pause...*)

You say, Mr Doja... (DOJA *looks from* BALDWIN *to*
TURNER. *He is visibly in the process of constructing a suitable
response when* TURNER *cuts him short*)

TURNER: Mr Doja is a clever man and far from embarrassing him, which is obviously your intention, you merely
provide him with further opportunities to demonstrate his
cleverness —

BALDWIN: I am obvious, I admit it —

TURNER: What is the point of it, when what we require of Mr
Doja is that he lays aside his cleverness, which he assures me —

BALDWIN: Horribly, horribly, obvious —

TURNER: Is nothing more than a means of fending off his fear
of intimacy —

DOJA: Did I say that...?

TURNER: *Say...*? I don't know about *say*, you expressed it,
and you express it now, Mr Doja...I am the same, which is
why I am able to recognize in you the preposterous evasions we
undertake in order not to —

BALDWIN: Kiss the legs, then... (*Pause...*)

If you can't describe them, kiss them. (*Pause...*)

Oh, am I obvious...? (*Pause...*)

But it's quicker...! (*He laughs*)

And she washes them in milk... (DOJA *hesitates...*)

DOJA: I... (*He lifts a hand in a gesture of bewilderment, lets it
fall...*)

I... (*He looks at* TURNER)

TURNER: He... (*She also makes a helpless gesture...*)

He...

BALDWIN: Lost for words, the pair of them... (*He chokes a
laugh, bites his lip...*)

Or not...? (*He watches their stillness. He
turns...*)

Nothing

Nothing
Nothing
Is lost on me
I am
Oh, misery
Oh, melancholy
Intuitive to an inordinate degree
My skin
So thin
I feel a thought alight on me
I feel the mothlike footsteps of a curse uttered in
distant places
And vision
Vision, oh
My sight is such agony to me I could court blind-
ness for a day's relief from this
Pitiful transparency of others
I dread maturity
The nakedness of things will scald my soul
God shield me with a clever liar soon
God give me a liar
A great liar

Oh, a tower of prodigious mischief, please (*He clicks his fingers at* NIXON, *who surges forward with a plate and serving tongs*)

NIXON: Pike from the high pools of the Isonzo poached in the pale wine of the Carnic Alp —

BALDWIN: Yes —

NIXON: Served on a field of primrose dashed with honeyed oil and kernels of —

BALDWIN: Yes —

NIXON: The Tyrolean pine and swept in sauces —

BALDWIN: Whatever you say — (*He turns back to* DOJA ...)
Can't kiss, Mr Doja ...? (*Pause* ... DOJA *looks at the floor* ...)

DOJA: However much my instinct urges me —

BALDWIN: Instinct ...? (*Pause* ...)

DOJA: However much my will commands me to —

BALDWIN: Will ...? (*Pause* ...)

DOJA: However much my appetite is stimulated by your invitation, some modesty restrains me ...

BALDWIN: What modesty is this ...? (*Pause* ...)
Oh, it's me ...! (*He feigns surprise* ...)

You —

My —

The — (*He laughs, as if in disbelief*)

NIXON: (*Touring the table and piling a plate*)

Haunch of venison in a light-baked sleeve of polished pastry garnished with pressed anchovy, drained, smothered and sun-dried in —

BALDWIN: You put your hands inside my father, Mr Doja... (*Pause...*)

DOJA: Yes... (*Pause...*)

And you are now proposing... (*Pause... NIXON clears a serving spoon by tapping it against a plate... DOJA looks to TURNER...*)

NIXON: Or breast of guinea-fowl marinaded in a flood of Grappa, cherry and Swiss cheese, reclining on a lawn of finely-chopped red peppers of Trieste —

BALDWIN: Yes... (*Pause...*)

I witnessed one, why not the other...? (NIXON *makes the same sound with the spoon...*)

And my mother's warm... (*A fraction of a Pause...*)

Oh, Mr Doja, everything conspires to make me intimate with you...! (*He turns to* NIXON)

Stool...!

DOJA: Wait...

BALDWIN: No, don't wait, Mr Doja —

DOJA: Compliments aside, I — (NIXON *goes to fetch a stool*)

Profound as my respect both for your father and your mother is —

BALDWIN: I know, I know these things —

DOJA: To require of me such an appalling trespass of —

BALDWIN: **Trespass and be damned**... (*Pause...*)

DOJA: (*As* NIXON *returns*) You violate my liberty... which is not proper in a king... (*He looks at* TURNER...)

Though in this instance... (*He shrugs... he is in a crisis of diplomacy...*)

Violation might be... the doorway to a different liberty...

BALDWIN: (*Climbing on the stool*) Yes...! Oh, excellent, that is so typical of you... if I may say — at this stage of our friendship, if I may dare to say what's typical of you... that is so... typical of you...! (*He clasps his head in his hand, crossing his legs as he did in the anatomy clinic...*)

NIXON: (*Returning to his function*) And a mousse of birds, lark, thrush and capercailie —
BALDWIN: Yes, but little...!
    Don't pile the plate... (*Pause... NIXON serves the mousse of birds. DOJA, with infinite tact, advances towards TURNER, who is still, observing him, he extends a hand, stops...*)
DOJA: I —
BALDWIN: Sh... (*He yearns...*)
              Don't you see how beautiful this is...?
              How proper...?
    How correct...? (*DOJA places himself behind TURNER, his hands spread on her torso. He kisses her neck. NIXON taps the serving spoon...*)
                      Shh... (*They are all still,* NIXON's *spoon in the air...*)
DOJA: Manifestum...
          et...
          Mammarum...
          Exposito...
          (*He unhitches her dress... her breasts are exposed... she is immobile...*)
          I've no desire to...
          I've no —

TURNER *kisses him, placing one hand behind his head and drawing his mouth to hers...* BALDWIN *is a miracle of balance for the second time, a picture of curiosity and repulsion, in which by degrees, the repulsion triumphs until he throws himself from the stool and, close to suffocation, runs offstage... the light fades on the scene, to the sound of a distracted youth hurling objects about a room.* NIXON *removes the handkerchief given him by* DOJA *from his pocket, and holds it to his nose...*

SUEDE: We carry on
PIN: We carry on as if
SUEDE: Precisely in the manner we are used to
PIN: Calmness
SUEDE: The triumph of routine (*They are placing the organs of the dead king in containers with a peculiar urgency*)
PIN: Being the finest antidote to
SUEDE: **Horror**
PIN: **Horror**
SUEDE: And anyway he would have wished

PIN: It was his rule

SUEDE: No job should last more than — (*Dropping a lid with a clatter, clasping himself in his arms...*)

Twenty...four...hours... (*He watches the lid roll idly over the floor...*)

PIN: I've done nothing with my life... (*Pause... PIN stares at SUEDE...*)

SUEDE: We have seen several cities...

PIN: I had planned to do things, but later...

SUEDE: We saw a thousand geese fly overhead...

PIN: Later, when I was more prepared...

SUEDE: Five thousand, possibly —

PIN: When I was qualified I was waiting to be qualified —

SUEDE: Few can have seen that many geese —

PIN: Then I would have —

SUEDE: The sky was full of them —

PIN: Certainly then I would have —

SUEDE: Wings beating —

PIN: Done extraordinary things I was merely waiting to be —

SUEDE: Racket in the sky —

PIN: Qualified... (*They stop, forlorn... DOJA enters... they lift their eyes to him...*)

Oh, Master, we were talking of you in the historic tense... (*He looks at them, silent. PIN goes to collect the dropped lid but before he can retrieve it, DOJA sends it flying with a kick. The ASSISTANTS stiffen...*)

SUEDE: We waited on you at your door... three times we knocked but... (*Pause*)

PIN: You weren't there... (*Pause... DOJA goes slowly to the table, leans on it with both hands...*)

Talk with us, master...

DOJA: Talk with you...?

PIN: Why not, master...?

DOJA: How should I be the master, if I talked with you...? (*They shrug their shoulders... LAYBACH enters...*)

LAYBACH: You didn't come...

(*DOJA's head turns slowly to him...*)

You assured me you would come and then did not come which only confirms my instinctive antipathy for you what kind of man —

SUEDE: Shh —

LAYBACH: Knowing the misery to which his careless action has reduced a harmless girl —

SUEDE: Shh —

LAYBACH: Would stoop to further injure her by —

SUEDE: (*Going to usher him away*) Shh —

LAYBACH: (*Avoiding him*) **Hush yourself** — (*He goes to* DOJA)

   I came to abuse you and I will abuse you my fear of violence notwithstanding I find it vile that someone so arrogant, malevolent, so — so —

   I've forgotten what I was going to say — (*He shakes his head furiously*)

   Please see her I don't think I can come here again... (*Pause...*)

DOJA: There is a smell on me... (*Pause...*)

   A smell which nauseates me and yet...

   A smell I —

LAYBACH: Death...

DOJA: Is that what it is...? It's from a woman's body... (LAYBACH *struggles with an impulse to strike* DOJA, *but turns and hurries away, passing* TODD *as he does so...*)

TODD: I have to speak with you.

DOJA: Do you...?

TODD: Now. Yes.

DOJA: This urgency to communicate with me appears to have afflicted the entire population —

TODD: Is that so?

DOJA: People cannot stay away, they are driven by some terrible compulsion, children climb on the roof, old women put their eyeballs to the cracks, and the excuses, the preposterous and exaggerated fictions just to get one foot inside the door, my assistants are exhausted, they go to bed wrung out from their exertions, and they are specialists, they are anatomists, not doormen, the flesh of monarchy, what is its fascination and I only

   What is it you want I have no time (*Pause... she looks at him...*)

TODD: You are in danger...

DOJA: Is that so, I have always been in danger, one gets accustomed to such things, now forgive me, I must finish —

TODD: God help you when you do... (*Pause...* DOJA *looks at her... He is still...*)

DOJA: The removal of the organs is only the first stage of a —

TODD: Good —

DOJA: Complex and exacting series of procedures which —

TODD: Good —
DOJA: Might take anything up to — (*Pause...*)
        A year...
TODD: A year...?
DOJA: At the very least...a year... (*Pause...the*
        ASSISTANTS *gawp...*)
              In some awkward cases....five or... (*Pause...*)
              How many years do you think what danger I cannot sleep
              with everybody woman man and boy what danger
              Very well
              I'll come to you
              I know your room
              I've seen it
              Lit all night
              Perhaps the danger's you
              Oh yes
              Quite possibly
              Red curtains
              Never drawn
              I don't miss anything
              Eyes peeled
              Thin skin
              A butterfly of nerves
              That's me
              Yes
              I'll come
              And washed
              And fragrant
              All you require I'll be and
TODD: We don't require your nakedness, Mr Doja... (*Pause...*)
DOJA: Don't we...? (*Pause...*)
        Who's we...? (TODD *goes out. A wind shakes the doors. The*
        sound of children laughing and jeering. A cry. Piercing...)
BERLIN: God...!
              Oh, God...!
DOJA: If ever I was God I think I am not now... (*He walks*
        past LAYBACH, *who stands sentinel-like, some yards from the*
        bed on which BERLIN *is sitting*)
        God is not coerced, surely?
BERLIN: Pity coerces Him. Pity is His weakness. Why did your
        pity take so long?
DOJA: I thrust it away.
BERLIN: From those who love you...?

DOJA: Those especially. There is a youth there who adores
  you...
BERLIN: Yes.
DOJA: Relieve him, then. His life is a furnace of frustration.
BERLIN: I used him. As a means to you. His frustration is no
  concern of mine.
DOJA: Is it not?
BERLIN: None. You are the sole object of my life.
DOJA: Pull the blanket over you, it's as cold as death in here —
BERLIN: No —
DOJA: No, why no —
BERLIN: You will warm me. You or nothing. If I die, so be it,
  I am in God's hands.
DOJA: This is blackmail...
BERLIN: Blackmail...? Why, it's love...
DOJA: **People manipulate me and I won't be** (BERLIN *laughs
  ...shaking her head...*)
BERLIN: That is the proof...!
DOJA: Of what? The proof of what?
BERLIN: Your divinity...! It is the very cry of Heaven...!
DOJA: Yes
  Well
  God
  Also
  Squirms
BERLIN: He does...! He squirms to know the depths of abjec-
  tion that His creatures plumb to know one second even of His
  intimacy...! Kiss my hands, they have waited too long for
  your blessing...!
DOJA: I —
BERLIN: Do kiss...! Do kiss...!
  (*She extends her hands to him...*)
DOJA: (*Hesitating*) This is precisely what I —
BERLIN: Oh, kiss...! (*Pause. He leans forward and taking her
  hands, kisses them...*)
DOJA: (*Retaining a grip on them*) I must tell you... I must
  warn you... that whilst I may be God... I am not kind...
BERLIN: No...
DOJA: No, and furthermore, to put the least faith in me would
  be to open yourself to an appalling wound...
BERLIN: Yes...
DOJA: A martyrdom...
BERLIN: Yes...

DOJA: A crucifixion...

BERLIN: Yes, because whereas many have faith in you, you have none in yourself... (*He leans over her, kissing her mouth...*)

DOJA: I exist...

BERLIN: You exist, and to ask more of you than mere existence would be... heresy... (*He covers her with his body... in the silence, the footsteps of* BALDWIN... *he appears, stops, examines* LAYBACH *from a distance... the* ASSISTANTS *cut, swab, displace lids and pans...*)

BALDWIN: It is so horrible, being me... (LAYBACH *inclines his head a little...*)

When I come near people they undergo some change, some mineral disintegration, colour, structure, odour, a puddle underneath my gaze I hate it whole individuals men of character women of integrity pulped to a goulash of apology I don't require it what possible pleasure could there be in such a spectacle for me...? (*Pause...*)

Why are you standing alone in the night? (*Pause...*)

It is so excellent being me... (LAYBACH *inclines his head for a second time...*)

The pride, the posture, even the vulgarity they must shed as thieves ditch treasure when encountering the law, they shiver like shaved hounds in the chill wind of my interrogation, I love to see it fall, the crust of practised personality, the manners and the see-I-have-no-manners, artifice and calculation, flung to the floor, they are so naked, oh, so naked and so poor, I'm certain I should cease to find such pleasure in it, speaking from a moral point of view, but I am not moral and I do (*He pauses...*)

Find pleasure in it... (*The sound of a woman in coitus, faint, recognizable.* BALDWIN *reacts with a slight move of his head...*)

You love someone...

Oh, let me sit...! Oh, let me study you...! (*He snaps his fingers. A figure emerges from the obscurity, places a stool behind* BALDWIN, *and withdraws again.* BALDWIN *sits, crossing his legs in a rapture of anticipation.* LAYBACH *is mortified...*)

LAYBACH: I —

BALDWIN: Shh...! (LAYBACH *sways. Out of the silence, the faint sound of* BERLIN...)

Oh, is that terrible...? (LAYBACH *suffers...*)

Is that the most terrible sound in the world...? (*Pause...*)

LAYBACH: Yes...

BALDWIN: And that is why you stand alone...I knew...! He does not stand alone for nothing...! Oh, I knew...! (*Pause. He concentrates. The sound of* BERLIN, *notes and breath, barely audible. The sound of the* ASSISTANTS, *faintly accompanying*... BALDWIN *stands, goes to the anatomy table, and returns with a cruel knife. He tosses the knife at* LAYBACH's *feet...he then sits to contemplate the effect*...LAYBACH *stares at* BALDWIN...BERLIN *gasps*...LAYBACH *studedly turns his back on* BALDWIN...*he lifts his hands and covers his ears*...)

Exquisite man...! You love your pain...! (*He jumps up, lifting the stool by a leg and is about to leave*...)

Who is in there? (LAYBACH *turns, uncovers his ears*...)

Who...? (LAYBACH *lifts his shoulders in mock-ignorance.* BALDWIN *goes into the obscurity. The* ASSISTANTS *clang lids as they heave the metal buckets of remains into a descending order of size*...)

LAYBACH: Stop now...
                       Stop now...
                       Stop now... (BERLIN *is silent.* DOJA *still*...)

I'm after all a youth which whilst not an excuse yet still might be an explanation for — no, curse youth, pulp youth, rot youth, never again shall I parade the thing called youth as vindication for my tempers — I would rather perch on a bough, a hen, a parrot, squawking and shitting my indignation — no, less whining, less pleading, less everything — **I heard every breath of your what shall I call it fornication fornication yes what else is it and —**

DOJA: Fornication, it must be —

LAYBACH: Yes and —

DOJA: The word's good —

LAYBACH: Perfectly —

DOJA: The act good also —

LAYBACH: Possibly —

DOJA: Assuredly —

LAYBACH: I couldn't say —

DOJA: Being a youth —

LAYBACH: **He offered me a knife and I declined to use it why**.
                       (DOJA *looks at him, for the first time*)
                       Why when
                       Why if

Why

It was my instinct and I (*Pause*...)

DOJA: Offered you a knife...? (*Pause*...)

LAYBACH: Somebody... (*Pause*. DOJA *gets up*...)

DOJA: I must not come here again...help me not to come again... (BERLIN *sits up*...)

BERLIN: Tomorrow.

DOJA: There is not the least chance I —

BERLIN: Tomorrow. (*Pause*. LAYBACH *laughs, a peculiar laugh, which is unrecognizable to him...he stops...* DOJA *departs, pulling his coat round him...the* DEAD PRIESTS *erupt*)

FIRST/SECOND PRIEST: **Hey**

Hey

Death's an education

DOJA: Is it? Then there's something to look forward to.

FIRST PRIEST: Sarcasm —

SECOND PRIEST: Is the first thing we dispensed with —

DOJA: Pity, I find great comfort in it —

SECOND PRIEST: And humour, that is useless too —

DOJA: It's not the place for me, that's obvious —

FIRST/SECOND: **Death is the end of freedom, Doja...** (*Pause*...)

DOJA: The end of it...?

FIRST/SECOND: **And the beginning of** (*Pause*...)

DOJA: What...? (*Pause*...)

The beginning of what...? (*The* PRIESTS *sob, in a subdued, suffocated way*...)

I don't think you should be —

These —

Left —

Unburied, I — (TURNER *appears, also in a dark coat*...DOJA *shrugs*...)

It's not my country but... (*Pause*...)

I don't criticize...

TURNER: Have you been looking for me?

DOJA: I —

TURNER: I was looking for you —

DOJA: You were looking for me...!

TURNER: You weren't in your —

DOJA: No —

TURNER: Me neither, so —

DOJA: Absurd —

TURNER: Both of us —
DOJA: Out looking — (*They laugh, as if with modesty...*)
TURNER: I've —
I've —
I so want to tell the truth —
For the first time, possibly, in my existence, wanted
to tell the truth and — (*Pause...*)
It's like being naked but —
No, worse, God knows I have been naked and with
many so that's such a redundant metaphor, no, not
naked — (*Pause...*)
Flayed...
However, I... (*Pause...*)
I interpret your silence as permission, I — (*She
laughs shrilly*)
Flayed I said
Now that's
Flayed
You see even the word I choose is yours, an aspect
of your own profession
I have thought of you since you parted from me
Never mind exaggeration
Thought of
Adequate
Adequate
Word
You say something now, will you
Too bad if I'm humiliated... (*Pause... her eyes rise
to meet his for the first time...*)
DOJA: Too bad for whom...? (*She frowns...*)
TURNER: I have no sense of humour...forgive me, it is not
something I — (*She shrugs...*)
Ever required before...
DOJA: It is not compatible with...
TURNER: It is not necessary —
DOJA: Not necessary, no —
TURNER: In queens...not being weak...we scarcely need to
laugh **I do feel weak with you however** how shall we make love a
second time how you say I find the second time a problem the
second anything a problem do you want me here now possibly
the landscape its cruelty its indifference being such a contrast
to the last luxurious and private place how hard it is to know
you everything I say may be offensive everything a false step

and driving iron bars between us but if you refuse to speak I
must I must articulate the feeling or strike you yes I can do that
(*She slaps him*)

Which is preferable to a sense of humour in my judgement
(*Pause.* DOJA *rubs his cheek . . . they exchange long looks . . .*)

DOJA: I'm circumspect . . .

TURNER: Yes . . .

DOJA: Because I am a slave . . .

TURNER: Yes . . .

DOJA: And slaves live only at the whim or possibly the indifference of their masters —

TURNER: Very well, I'll do the talking —

DOJA: Anything I say —

TURNER: Or fail to say —

DOJA: That also, yes, might cause offence and therefore —

TURNER: **You have kissed me where the daylight has not visited.** (*Pause . . . she shrugs . . .*)

Even so, one might, such intimacies, and still, the most
profound, and then, next day, despite the, with a new sunrise,
even

> **Everything that occurred was novel to**
> **Me**
> **Everything**
> **The dress**
> **The manner**
> **The conversation**
> **Never**
> **Never**
> **Before**

I was a stranger to myself (*Pause . . .* DOJA *looks into her
stricken face . . . he leans into her and breathes the odour of her
body . . . the* ASSISTANTS, *with a clatter, wash the instruments*)

PIN: I've no desire to go home . . .

SUEDE: (*Filling a pan from a tap*) Home . . . ?

PIN: Home, I called it home . . . ! The room . . .

SUEDE: The room's not home.

PIN: Not home and I'm peculiarly reluctant to . . . for some
reason unwilling to . . .

SUEDE: It's not a nice room . . .

PIN: It's —

SUEDE: They've tried —

PIN: They've tried but still —

SUEDE: It's bleak —

PIN: Very bleak and in many ways I find this place every bit as congenial as —

SUEDE: Or the room, to put it the other way round, no more congenial —

PIN: No more congenial than this —

SUEDE: Which is a damning verdict on their hospitality —

PIN: Yes...! (*A pause like a stroke of a knife*)
Yes, we'll stay here —

SUEDE: **Put a chair against the door** —

PIN: (*Infected*) **Oh**...!

SUEDE: (*Dropping the pan*) Yes...!

PIN: Quick, a chair, quick...! (*They collide in seizing a chair.* SUEDE *recovers and jams the chair-back under the door handle*)
Christ, oh, Christ...!

SUEDE: The lights...!

PIN: Lights...?

SUEDE: **Off**...!

PIN: Off...? Why off...?

SUEDE: **Lights off**...!

PIN: Wait —

SUEDE: **Surely off** —

PIN: No, on, because —

SUEDE: Oh, quick —

PIN: Because —

SUEDE: **They know we're here** —

PIN: Yes, but — (*He fathoms swiftly*)
All right...! (*He turns off the lamps... A profound gloom settles over the room. A silence also. A pause...*)
I think they should be on because... (*Pause...*)
Where are you...? (SUEDE *taps a knife on the ground...*)
It's all right, we can speak —

SUEDE: Shh...!

PIN: Surely we can — (SUEDE *taps again, as if to silence him... pause...*)
What have you got...?

SUEDE: The eight-inch scalpel...

PIN: I'd better get some — (*He scrabbles...*)

SUEDE: Shh...please...shh... (*The sound of blades shifting on a tray...*)
please...please...

PIN: **They won't come here**...!

SUEDE: (*In despair*) Oh, please...! (*Pause...*)

PIN: They won't come here... (*Pause*...)

Which is why I argued for the lamps...the lamps illumi-
nated because... (*Pause*...)

Because of him... (*Pause*...)

SUEDE: Who...?

PIN: Him.

SUEDE: Who...?

PIN: **Him him who do you think him —**

SUEDE: Shh —

PIN: **On the table him of course him in the buckets —**

SUEDE: Shh —

PIN: **In the pans old offal stinking him who else —**

SUEDE: (*With a new chill*) Be quiet or I will stab you. (*Pause*...)

Light the lights. (*Pause*...)

PIN: What...?

SUEDE: I will. (*He gets up. He kicks a bucket. A muffled oath.
The lights glow.* SUEDE *points an accusing finger*...)

You are the curse.

PIN: Curse...?

SUEDE: Yes, you. You are the origin.

PIN: Of what...?

SUEDE: **The mortal danger we are in. You.** (*He lifts the scalpel*)
Don't come near me. Not that I fear you. But I would think
myself contaminated by your blood.

PIN: Would you, and how should that be...?

SUEDE: (*Going to the door, removing the chair*)

And I was looking outside...! How mistaken, and yet how
quintessentially human to seek the origin of horror in the outside world — (*He tosses the scalpel onto the tray with a studied
nonchalance*)

When always, always it is — (*The door opens.* DOJA
enters)

Near

Oh, very

Near

Proximity is its very character (*He turns to* DOJA...)
Master, I wish to discuss with you the character and
suitability of my colleague —

DOJA: Why —

SUEDE: His long association with us makes me reluctant to
initiate such a —

DOJA: (*Rolling up his sleeves*) Apron...

SUEDE: (*Fetching it off a hook*) Painful and possibly humiliating —

DOJA: I'm working nights —

SUEDE: Inquisition but —

DOJA: My nights have been too free, nights only from now on, the lamp's low — (PIN *adjusts the wick*)
Nights and only nights

PIN: We were thinking the same thing...!

SUEDE: (*Persisting*) He has revealed traits and attitudes —

PIN: We were seriously considering sleeping here —

SUEDE: Quite incompatible with —

PIN: Weren't we...? A mattress on the floor is perfectly —

SUEDE: (*To* PIN) **Be quiet I am indicting you**. (*Pause.* DOJA *looks at* SUEDE...)

Master, my colleague lacks that character of spirituality that you have always insisted is the pre-requisite in any student of anatomy — (*He turns his gaze on* PIN)

It gives me no pleasure to announce —

PIN: **It gives him huge pleasure** —

SUEDE: None at all —

PIN: **Vast** —

SUEDE: None I said —

PIN: **And vicious pleasure** —

SUEDE: **We're under a curse**...! (*He turns to* DOJA)
And he's the reason. He has no reverence for flesh. All these years and we did not suspect —

PIN: Suspect what —

SUEDE: (*To* PIN, *cruelly*) **Suspect your infidelity**...!

PIN: To what —

SUEDE: Oh...!

PIN: Infidelity to what —

SUEDE: (*Shutting his ears with his hands*) I can't listen —

PIN: **To what to what am I unfaithful** —

SUEDE: **Our compact with the dead**. (PIN *screws up his face... in the silence,* DOJA *lifts a tool from the tray... Pause...*)

DOJA: Things are bad here, certainly... (*He throws it down, picks up another... This also he tosses down... He leans on the table...*)

I'm not myself...

PIN: None of us is —

SUEDE: **You say that to protect yourself**...! (PIN *stares at* SUEDE, *horrified by his vehemence...*)

DOJA: I think for example, whilst I am able to lie with my usual dexterity... (*Pause...*)

>I am not certain if these lies are lies at all... (*Pause...*)
>I cannot conceal from myself the possibility... that these lies... are... (*Pause...*)
>Aspects of the truth... (*Pause...*)

The odour of the Queen, which I described as uncongenial to me... (*Pause...* PIN *completes* DOJA's *sentence*)

PIN (*Cheerfully*) You're gasping for...! (*Pause... He regrets his impetuosity...*)

>Forgive me, master, I — (*He drags his hands through his hair*) Oh, I —

None of us is himself... it's true... (*He turns, makes a short, absurd walk, stops... dogs bark in the distance. In despair,* PIN *extends a hand to* SUEDE. SUEDE *ignores it... at last, the hand falters*)

DOJA: It's not too late, you can still —

SUEDE: (*Panicked*) **I'm not leaving this room**...! (*Pause... DOJA looks up at him...*)

If what you're saying is — if you are — whatever you are saying with the Queen I think — no wonder we — of course you are the master and will always be the master in my eyes — nevertheless — the curse I think could be quite adequately explained by — you must sleep where you wish but — (*He waves towards the body on the table...*)

>**The deceased are capable of pain**... (*He looks at the dissected body...*)
>And therefore, surely... of resentment... (*He bites his lip...*)
>He fought death... you can tell that from the condition of the tissue... (*Pause...*)
>I daresay because... (*Pause...*)
>He knew... of your...
>(*He falters...*)

I'll make a bed over there... if no one else wants that... particular... (*He drifts away, throwing a coat onto the floor... the sound of sobbing comes from his obscure corner... slowly, daylight penetrates the scene...* BALDWIN *is discovered with a basket of laundry.* DOJA, *summoned, goes to attend to him. He inclines his head...*)

BALDWIN: Good day for a dry... (*Pause...*)

A dry they call it... the laundry women, how I like to speak their tongue... did you bring the pegs...?

DOJA: Yes...

BALDWIN: They never mind me...! Nor the cooks...! I drift about their premises, and I am not the king in there...!

No, they are the queens of the copper tubs, but so supreme in their authority they do not think to shut their mouths...the oaths...the bawdy...swimming in the steam...! This morning, for example — (*He points to an item in the basket*)

> You take one end — (DOJA *lifts a sheet...shakes it about in search of the hems*)
>
> This morning it was — (*He pauses...*)

The stubbornness of stains... (DOJA *is half-upright...pause ...he rises. He holds out a sheet hem towards* BALDWIN...)

> Not anybody's stains...!
>
> And me there...!

Me, a leaf of tenderness that tumbled on the wave of their extraordinary speculations... (*At last he takes the sheet. They proceed to hang it on the line, pegging it...*)

Don't I have feelings...? Oh, the density of them, the strata of my feelings...but they go on...! I blush, I squirm, and they...! (*He shakes his head...he shrugs...*)

Steam on... (*He returns to the basket*)

You have to admire such an extravagance of coarseness, they are made of leather, and that's the subtle ones, no, they're brick, souls of brick and gobs of clay...!

(*He stoops to the basket*)

I like them... (*He pulls out an item of underclothing...female ...he opens the garment with his fingers...* DOJA, *with an attempt at casualness, extends his hand to take it to the line...* BALDWIN *counters by remaining in possession...*)

She went with many, many men... (*His eyes rise to* DOJA's...)

And these men had to die...they knew it...! Oh, they were fully apprized, they went into it with their eyes open...! They understood my father had no option, they were stricken, obviously but none complained... (*Pause...*)

They knew if she was not to die, then it must be they... (*Pause...*)

Given that my father... (*He throws the pants to* DOJA...)

Doted... (*Pause...* DOJA *proceeds to peg the pants to the line.* BALDWIN *stoops for another item...*)

DOJA: Her skin... (BALDWIN *stays low...*)

> Has that peculiar... (DOJA *pauses to contemplate the effect of his speech*)

That simultaneously... (BALDWIN *stays stooping*...)
I can only describe it as possessing the identical extremes of
fecundity and decay associated with... (*He observes*
BALDWIN's *unyielding posture*...)

Compost...

Manure...

Ordure...

Spoiled fruit...

Drenched hay...

Intoxicating...

Nauseating...

I can only spend a little time with you today my assistants
are not experienced in the techniques of organic preservation...

And opening her legs she... (*He watches*
BALDWIN ...)
Exhales this... (BALDWIN *is fixed*... DOJA *enjoys his
pain*...)

They are not incompetent but whilst the removal of the
viscera is merely the organization of formlessness, the forestalling of corruption calls for altogether... (*Pause... he himself
squirms*...)

This...

This...

Breath of rivers, blood and human floors to which my lips
are drawn as if steel cables hauled me in, a barge inexorably
brought into its berth... (*Pause*...)

I stink of her even now... (*Pause*...)

I stink... (*Pause*... BALDWIN *lifts another garment on the
end of an extended arm, his body still fixed... Pause... then*
DOJA *takes it, and pegs it to the line. Simultaneously, they
both erupt into laughter,* BALDWIN *rising at last and shaking
with the exertion of it. The laughter fades...* BALDWIN *shakes
his head*...)

BALDWIN: It's me you love...! (*He is still. He looks at* DOJA
under his eyes...)

All this —

Oh, I understand it...! I am the same...! This forestalling
and false signalling, I am the same...!

How hard it is to say... (*Pause... his eyes
remain on* DOJA...)

And I don't ask you to say... on the contrary, I would
perhaps forbid your saying, because I know for you saying is

so — practised, such an art, whereas your silence...! There's a tribute to a choking love... (*Pause... his eyes fall...*)

On the other hand, an action, possibly indiscreet... (*He shrugs...*)

> I don't know... (*He bites his lip...*)
> I don't know how to advance... (*He looks up...*)
> Do you...? (DOJA *shakes his head...*)
> Not even you...
> Know how... (*He affects an exasperation...*)
> **And we're kings... the pair of us...!**
> (*He laughs, stops, looks hard into Doja...*)

If kings can't do... what they most want to do... I'm shedding monarchy... and like some crusted quarryman blaspheming from the canteen I'll abuse you... words of one syllable... the thought unqualified by manners or by poetry, **I'm howling, Mr Doja, kiss my arse and I'll kiss yours...**

DOJA *is suspended between politics and revulsion, but* BALDWIN *allows him no time to reflect, flinging himself on* DOJA *and dragging the sheet with him.* DOJA *is the more powerful, however, and in the ruins of the laundry, topples* BALDWIN... *The dead* PRIESTS *squeal with mingled horror and delight...*

FIRST/SECOND PRIEST: **Oh, majesty... oh, reversed majesty ...!**
FIRST PRIEST: The blue sky never was more blue
SECOND PRIEST: The sheets like sails
FIRST PRIEST: On plunging schooners
FIRST/SECOND PRIEST: Crack... Crack...!
FIRST PRIEST: And you
SECOND PRIEST: Are so much closer to your execution
FIRST/SECOND PRIEST: **A fine day for a dry the wind fills skirts as if the occupants were prancing**
SECOND PRIEST: On an avenue...

A silence descends, the wind alone stirring the few hanging garments... DOJA *climbs to his feet, extricating himself...*

BALDWIN: Kiss, I said...
    (*He moans...*)
    Kiss, I said... (DOJA *is aware that another has entered and is observing him...*)

TODD: How you have loved to be beyond...keeping your
intimacy for the dead...and visiting, as it were...just visiting...the living... (*Pause*)

But now... (*Pause*)

How you have stood as crows stand...on the rim...and
watched through unpitying eyes the antics of we who deserved
no pity...untouched by weathers and with each flight casting
memory away as some thing undigested... (*Pause*)

But now...

BALDWIN: (*Wailing*) Kiss, I said...!

TODD: We wait for you...but not infinitely...

DOJA: Yes...

TODD: **Not...infinitely**... (*She turns to* BALDWIN... *with a
pretence*)

Oh, what has happened here...! (*She hurries to him*)

Oh, Lord, the line has come down and the prop...oh, some
wind dislodged the prop and...oh...grass and goose
muck...!

(*She shouts off, to the launderers*)

Boil up, the whites are ruined...! (DOJA *surges through the
disorder to find* TURNER, *who is bathing.* NIXON *holds a
towel...* DOJA *recovers, dictating a silence...at last he speaks*)

DOJA: I came by forty graves... (TURNER *squeezes a sponge,
thoughtfully...*)

Shaded and the whispering descent of pine needles...pol-
ished but unnamed... (*She draws a comb through her hair...*)
You'd know the names...but not the order of the names...I
daresay... (*Pause...*)

Always I have preserved the most clinical and frozen distances between myself and the material remains of the — (*He
shakes his head...*)

Please, this affectation of — (*She stops...*)

This studied and contrived languidity, I — (*Pause. She holds
the comb still in the air*)

Murderers, torturers, cannibals who put whole cities to the
sword and stewed the infants in the ponds, nothing to me...!
Revered archbishops, fratricidal usurpers, guts in the pan and
— (*He stops...his eyes close...pause...*)

In this case however...a profound loathing for this degen-
erating flesh makes me recoil from the most mundane professional activity, I — (*He sees, and is transfixed by, the spectacle
of* SUEDE *murdering* PIN *in the anatomy room...as* PIN
fights for his life, the pans and buckets are swept over, instru-

*ments are strewn over the floor in an appalling ballet which
concludes with* PIN's *death from innumerable wounds.*
SUEDE, *exhausted by his exertions, collapses onto a stool,
head in hands...* TURNER *is not aware of this, but in the
returned silence, her weeping is heard...* DOJA *turns to her...
His eyes travel to* NIXON, *who shrugs his shoulders...*
TURNER *weeps out loud...*)

       Stop that... (*She excels herself in grief*)

       Stop that...! (*He turns to hurry away*)

NIXON: Don't go, Mr Doja...

DOJA: (*Stopping...*) Don't go...? Why not go...? The
Queen's a liar...

NIXON: And can you not be lied to, Mr Doja...? (*Pause...*
NIXON *encloses* TURNER *in a towel, as she emerges from the
bath...*)

   This tenderness with regard to a deception might be seen as
certain evidence of love... (*He dries her body...*)

   But equally, so might the deception that created it... (*He
ceases... leaving* TURNER *enclosed in the towel*)

       Love and the world... (*He shrugs...*)

       The one abhors the other... (*He smiles...*)

       I lecture you...! I, the ignorant and —

DOJA: Don't go on —

NIXON: Servile agent of my master's whims, I —

DOJA: Don't go on, I said —

NIXON: Lecture you...! (*He goes, drawing away the towel in
which* TURNER *is enclosed, she is perfectly still, her back
exposed to him, her head inclined...*)

DOJA: All things here... even the confessions... are manifestly
false... (*Pause...*)

TURNER: Yes...

DOJA: And nakedness... far from being... a testament to
truth is... further —

TURNER: Yes...! (*Pause...*)

DOJA: Manipulation —

TURNER: I manipulate you, yes —

DOJA: Not only you —

TURNER: Not only me?

DOJA: **It's universal I am plucked and pulled as a doll is tortured
by a poisonous child** —

TURNER: **Doll you doll what doll is this...?** (*She is silent...*)
I cannot argue naked if you wish to argue dress me find a towel
my skirt I cannot let my nakedness be spoiled like this —

DOJA: **Spoiled it's a football field of fornication** —
TURNER: My skirt — my towel — (*She extends a hand in desperation*)
DOJA: **A sodden quarry of copulation** —
TURNER: My skirt, I said —
DOJA: **Trodden, slippery and forlorn as gravel pits in winter** —
TURNER: My skirt
        Oh skirt
        Skirt
        Please
        My

(*Her hand hangs in he air. DOJA watches, then seizing the hand, kisses it desperately... SUEDE, climbing with an air of resignation off the stool, begins to collect the scattered lids and implements. He ignores the body of PIN, even when LAYBACH enters... LAYBACH stares at the body...*)

SUEDE: I don't know where the master is... (*Pause...he tidies...*)

He left notes at one time...little notes in this exquisite hand...black ink...and dated...the day fully described...no numbers...Tues-day...the whole word...! (*He wipes a blade on a cloth, places it on the tray*)
        Fri-day...

Excellent, I wish I'd kept them because he not only informed us as to the nature of his absence but announced as well the precise time of his arrival...!

Yes, and he would not fail to appear...! (*He collects, organizes...*)

An extraordinary man I am honoured to have served him at what we must now recognize was his — apotheosis — and it was not brief — no, in this state of perfection he continued many years, I learned so many things from him — (*He stops in mid-movement...*)

Many things...? (*He shakes his head*)

I learned it all... (*Pause...LAYBACH stares...DOJA, parting from TURNER, enters the anatomy room...SUEDE pays him no particular attention...*)

LAYBACH: I —
DOJA: Yes, I was expecting you —
LAYBACH: It's been considerably longer than she anticipated, and her —
DOJA: Health, yes, is deteriorating —
LAYBACH: Health and not only health —

DOJA: (*To* SUEDE) Where's my apron...?

LAYBACH: Her character —

DOJA: Apron...? (SUEDE *ignores* DOJA)

LAYBACH: **You know how I recoil from these humiliating errands but** —

DOJA: **Apron...!** (*Pause.* SUEDE *stops...*)

SUEDE: Are you addressing me...? (*Pause...*)

DOJA: I can't address...the other...

SUEDE: No... (*He shrugs...*)

The other...as you call him...the other's dead...
(*Pause. He busies on, ignoring* DOJA...)

The other...! Funny...! And we were amicable
once...And now he is merely — the other...

LAYBACH: (*Patiently*) Never, never will I allow myself to be
so racked and ridiculed by an unreciprocated love of this
description, never, never —

DOJA: (*Turning on him as if to swat a fly*) **It's the love you
like...!** (*He returns to* SUEDE)

This corpse is for the river... (SUEDE *stops...an iciness
afflicts his mouth...*)

SUEDE: This —

What...? (*A pause settles...*)

This —

DOJA: Carcass... (SUEDE *adjusts his glasses...*)

Sacks...

Stones... (SUEDE *chews his tongue...*)

Or no stones...? (*Pause...*)

No stones... (*Pause...*)

No stones and no sacks, either... (*Pause...*)

There's a bend three miles downstream where every suicide
and unlucky boatman fetch up in the reeds... (*Pause...*)

The sun beats down... (*Pause...*)

The storks go —

SUEDE: I'm so sorry —

DOJA: The storks' beaks go —

SUEDE: So sorry —

DOJA: Sharper than butcher's knives —

SUEDE: **To see you rot like this** —

DOJA: He rots, not me —

SUEDE: **And I revered you once...!** (DOJA *stares into*
SUEDE...)

DOJA: This vile character... (*He indicates the body, his eyes
still fixed on* SUEDE...)

is not for preservation... (*Pause*...)

Tip his bits into the river... (SUEDE *holds out for some seconds, then his face collapses and he stamps his feet*...)

SUEDE: **It's my profession**...! (*He grabs a wicked blade from the table and levels it at* DOJA...)

How sad how terrible how sad and terrible to have to kill not one but two oh what a place oh what an atmosphere we never should have come here but we did too bad too late too everything the poison came from him it seemed but no not only him you too you are the source to call a king a corpse a what a corpse and a cadaver no you're ill so very ill I'm sorry I alone appear to keep faith with an honourable profession if you insult the dead they shout they also have their tempers — (*He nods towards* LAYBACH, *who is staring wildly*...)

Run to the castle run and tell...! (*He makes a lunge at* DOJA, *who steps back, and follows it with another*)

Run and tell I said...! (DOJA *trips in retreating from* SUEDE's *jabs*...)

LAYBACH: (*His ecstasy unstopped by* DOJA's *frailty*)
　　　　　Stab him, stab him, stab...! (*He goes to seize* DOJA *in his arms*...)

God fingers me...! God fingers me...! (DOJA *evades* LAYBACH's *impetuous rush, grabbing up the wooden stool to protect himself*... LAYBACH *takes a knife from the tray. The young men menace* DOJA...)

I am saving a life... (*He advances a step*...)

In taking your life... I am saving a life... (*He advances another step... suddenly he seems to fold at the middle... the knife drops to the floor... he shudders and wails*...)

　　　　　I'll run to the castle...

SUEDE: Go on, then, run...

LAYBACH: (*Incapable of movement*) I'll run to the castle... (SUEDE *is about to rage at* LAYBACH *when* BALDWIN *enters, casually.* SUEDE *replaces his knife on the tray with exquisite composure.* DOJA *places the stool on the floor and perches on it in a single movement*)

BALDWIN: (*Observing* LAYBACH's *wretchedness*)

Always you repudiate the knife, when the knife is precisely your requirement. Always you fail to act, when action is the very — (*He stoops, retrieves* LAYBACH's *knife, and places it on the tray*...)

Or not...? (LAYBACH *sobs*...)

With you, the knife is perhaps, the mirage that shimmers on

the horizon of your life...the alibi for ecstasy never quite attempted

      I talk of ecstasy

      Me

      Me Mr Doja

      Ecstasy...! (*Pause...he wanders to the table, and lifts the corner of the sheet...*)

I have my fifty knights. Ten with the liver to Kiev. Ten with the heart to Riga and so on. **It is a shambles in here is it not** and one of the experts dead dead on the floor what kind of and you are not cheap you said yourself hardly the lowest tender Mr Doja

      I am a changed man

      No

      Not changed

Oh, preposterous and incredible claim is anybody is anything changed no not changed merely reassorted

    I am reassorted (*He flings back the sheet*)

    I was a boy and now I'm reassorted what does that make me Mr Doja last time I looked upon my father I shuddered not today however some reassortment surely...? (DOJA *climbs off the stool...*)

DOJA: I have abandoned my vocation.

BALDWIN: Can you abandon a vocation, Mr Doja? Perhaps it has abandoned you?

DOJA: It's fled, certainly...

BALDWIN: Fled and my father in a dozen parts...!

DOJA: The necessary reverence for the dead I found in this particular instance rapidly diminishing —

SUEDE: **He told me toss it in the river...!**

DOJA: I experienced disgust —

BALDWIN: Disgust?

DOJA: Disgust, which is the —

BALDWIN: Disgust, Mr Doja?

SUEDE: **In the river, tip it in, he said...!** (*Pause... DOJA completes his sentence...*)

DOJA: The nightmare of anatomy... (BALDWIN *lets the sheet fall back on the body...*)

BALDWIN: My knights, however, have their own exigencies. I cannot think your squeamishness will find much sympathy with them, they ache to gallop with my father's bowel, a pennant, a banner flying in the wind, **What sudden horror of a man's interior is this Mr Doja ...!** (*He stares at* DOJA...)

SUEDE: If I may — (BALDWIN *and* DOJA *are fixed...*)
        If I could — (*Pause.* LAYBACH *runs off...*)
    I think I can say without false modesty that I alone possess
the necessary — spiritual authority — for this task, having —
(BALDWIN *goes towards* DOJA, *and takes his head between
his hands...*) discovered in myself the courage to — (*He kisses*
DOJA *on the mouth...*) to murder even where sacrilege had
poisoned the atmosphere, and... (*He moves to the table and
begins work with the knives...*) so on... no... nobody I think
... is better qualified to... (*He works on, with a detailed attention to his craft, as* BALDWIN's *kiss lingers...*)
    Serrula... (*He extends a hand...*)
    Ubi serrula...? (BALDWIN's *kiss ends...* DOJA *goes to the
table and hands* SUEDE *the tool...* BALDWIN *silently withdraws...*)
            Et inflexit... (DOJA *assists...*)
            Dextra...
            Dextra...
LAYBACH: (*To* BALDWIN, *who passes at a distance*) I cannot hurt, it is my problem... (BALDWIN *stops, wipes his
mouth ...*)
                I long to hurt... which some would say... is just
                the same as hurting, but... (*He shrugs...*)
                Perhaps the world is made of those who can and
                those who only wish to... (*Pause...*)
                Hurt... (BALDWIN *moves to go...*)
                **He has your mother and others too numerous to
                mention**
                I merely
                I just
                I
                I
                No that is
                Forget I said
                That is so (*He makes a dismissive gesture with his
                hands...*)
                An utter
                Pure calumny
                I am sick with jealousy it makes me lie
                Preposterously lie
                I perjure myself
        Sick my life is ebbing out of me ... (BALDWIN *cogitates...*
LAYBACH *gathers his resources from the bottom of his soul...*)

Perhaps... (*He shrugs...*)

Perhaps in submitting to an ordeal a man...finds powers which...had he resorted to an instinct...he never could have assembled... (*He shrugs again...*)

Perhaps... (*He turns to leave*)

BALDWIN: The death of Mr Doja is certainly the solution...I am painfully aware of it... (LAYBACH *turns...*)

At my first glance I knew...much sleep would be lost as a consequence of Mr Doja...and sleep's precious, I am an advocate of sleep...

LAYBACH: It is a rare commodity round here...

BALDWIN: It is...! One shuts one's eyes, but on the lids, oh, racing rivers, cascades brighter than the sun, how I wish I could relieve you, it is after all among a monarch's many obligations that he grants his subjects the facility of sleep **Had my mother where exactly** lamps are burning at all hours and kettles boiling in the dead of night it is a plague that Mr Doja brought in with him a plague of insomnia **In what posture where show me** —

LAYBACH: What —

BALDWIN: Now —

LAYBACH: Show you —

BALDWIN: The place —

LAYBACH: The place? I —

BALDWIN: **He took my mother in** —

LAYBACH: I have not personally —

BALDWIN: **The place, show me** —

LAYBACH: I can't, I haven't —

BALDWIN: **Invent it, then**... (*Pause...* LAYBACH *is strung between horror and resourcefulness...*)

The rumour...make it...live... (BALDWIN *is patient...*)

LAYBACH: I... (*He strains...*)

One afternoon...between the abbey and the hospital...was — (*He is aware of a third party standing in the penumbra of the light...*)

On an errand and... (*He swallows...*)

I think this will be the death of me... (*His eyes search* BALDWIN's *imperturbable features...*)

Came upon this — (*The figure enters. It is* TURNER. *She sits on the ground, taking* BALDWIN's *fingers in hers...* LAYBACH *observes this with a terrible unease...*)

Spectacle... (*He covers his face with his hands...*)

This violates my soul — (*The* DEAD PRIESTS *shriek with laughter*)

FIRST PRIEST: His soul goes ow...!

SECOND PRIEST: Ow...! Ow...! His soul...!

FIRST PRIEST: Wrapped round a drum and —

SECOND PRIEST: Ow...!

FIRST PRIEST: His soul is more elastic than —

SECOND PRIEST: **St Elmo's bowel...!**

FIRST PRIEST: Ow...! Ow...! (*Pause*...)

FIRST/SECOND PRIEST: Let out...let out...your soul ...as a fat woman...loosens her bodice...or you...will never be a bishop...but die...a novice... (BERLIN *crosses the stage in a wheelchair, propelling herself. She stops in the vicinity of the anatomy room*... DOJA *senses her patience*...*he goes to leave the room*)

SUEDE: Non exeat... (DOJA *stops*...*Pause*...)

Non exeat... (SUEDE *works on*...)

If every passing bitch can draw you from your labour where's the — (*Pause. He cuts*...)

  The sign of our profession is its immunity to every passing instinct, every transient circumstance... (*He proceeds without looking*...)

This might be a battlefield. (DOJA *is still*)

A battlefield

A kitchen

Or

A

Brothel

BERLIN: **I moved...!**

SUEDE: Still our whole attention would be on the task in —

BERLIN: **My legs refused so I coerced them...!**

My legs declined therefore my arms were forced to serve me and if my arms dare mutiny my teeth will be enlisted

That is the power of my will

DOJA: The master —

BERLIN: Master...?

DOJA: Will beat me certainly if I —

BERLIN: Master...?

DOJA: Unfortunately yes —

BERLIN: You are the master...

DOJA: He's far from kind, and lashes out sometimes with a bare fist, which I put down to his limitless dedication, demanding as he does the same devotion in his assistants that he —

BERLIN: **You are the master** —

DOJA: Shows himself... (*Pause. A low laugh comes from* BERLIN *...she shakes her head... her laugh rumbles on...*)

BERLIN: Oh, Doja, you think... (*She laughs still...*)

You think to smother your... (*And laughs again...*) **I admire it...**

To escape the notice of the world you —

Act dead (*With a swift exertion she rises out of the wheelchair and walks into the room.* SUEDE, *disconcerted, looks up with irritation.* BERLIN *jabs a surgical instrument into him.* THE PRIESTS *erupt into a staccato laugh.* SUEDE, *incredulous, staggers in a grotesque dance...* DOJA *stares...* BERLIN *crushes him in an embrace...* LAYBACH, *intuitively perceiving the murder, rushes into the anatomy room... he stares in disbelief...*)

BERLIN: He's mine...!

I saved him from obscurity...!

He must be mine, therefore...! (SUEDE *crashes into* LAYBACH's *arms and dies...* LAYBACH *holds the body for some seconds, then lets it slide to the ground. Silence returns...*)

And pale...! How pale he was becoming, like a leaf in the first chill of Autumn, no, he would have shrunk, become transparent, disappeared, and —

DOJA: It is not you I love...

BERLIN: Passing carriages could have splashed through his brains unknowingly, as some frail bird's egg fallen from the nest is smothered in their wheels...

DOJA: I said it is not you —

BERLIN: Shh...! I know...!

LAYBACH: (*To* BERLIN) **You are magnificent and I detest you**. (*Pause.* BERLIN *looks at* LAYBACH...)

BERLIN: Detest me...? Why...?

LAYBACH: (*Grimly*) Did you think... (*He wipes his hands on his cassock...*)

Oh, did you really, really think my little fountain of pure devotion could just flow and tinkle day and night like some spring bubbling in a market square, century on century of loyal provision, **Whoever thanks the fountain rather they piss in it** (*She puts out a hand. He dashes it away*)

No...!

I have turned toxic do not drink from me... (*He glares at her. She by contrast, is kind-faced to him...*)

BERLIN: But of course...! How else could you be...? (*She bites her lip... he weeps... his hand goes up and down...*)

LAYBACH: Oh, sick... oh, sick of this weeping... (*He waves in his despair...*)

Cut me open, Mr Doja... take out my liver and plant the place with some black bear's bile instead... (*He walks slowly out...*)

DOJA: How the little priest consoles himself for his weak character... he applauds his sensibility... and asks us to applaud it, also... (*He looks to* BERLIN...)

I've nothing to offer you... neither gratitude... nor love...- even the instinct that our nakedness might **Don't undo your garments** possibly inflame **or let your lip protrude** would be lower than a guttering candle dying in its wax **I've nothing nothing** — (*He stops, as* NIXON *enters with a handcart, which he drops in a business-like manner alongside the body of* PIN...)

BERLIN: Nothing is precisely what I ask... (*She goes out, ignoring the wheelchair...* NIXON *puts his arms under the dead man's shoulders...*)

NIXON: The dead, oh, listen to them...!

DOJA: Yes, they give us no peace...

NIXON: (*Jerking the body onto the cart*) Like wolves behind a wire...

DOJA: Yes, very like wolves —

NIXON: Baying —

DOJA: (*Of the dead monarch*) Him especially...

NIXON: (*Pausing*) The assassin is free in one sense only. He is free to become an assassin... (*He looks at* DOJA...)

It is a destiny... (*Pause. He lifts the legs on the cart...*)

Characteristically, he squirms, for assassination offends him also... (*He looks at* DOJA...)

He shrinks... he shuns the light... (*He picks up the cart handles...*)

Only at the moment when, donning — so to speak — the garments of his destiny — he admits his character, does the assassin experience the calm assurance that attends on all those who have abandoned the struggle to resist what they are chosen to —

DOJA: **Assassinate who...?** (*He points to the body on the table...*)

He's dead...! (NIXON *lifts the handles and pushes the cart away... Pause...*)

Or not...? (*A chill wind rattles tin roofing.* DOJA *laughs...*)

He's dead because I disembowelled him...! (*He shakes his head...*)

What kind of evidence is that? (*He goes to the remains* ...)
And washed his heart's blood off my fingers ...
Evidence, you call it ...?
And splashed the yellow fluids of his brain over my cuffs, my shirt front splattered it with tissue ...
Just the stuff of just the substance which
And put him into seven jars
Diffusion what's diffusion (*He takes a flying kick at a can, which spills as it clatters against a wall* ... *Pause* ...)
It's up the wall ... long fingers of his succulence ... (*He turns* ...)
Call that death I don't ... (TURNER *is looking at him* ...)
How clean you look today each time I see you I say that woman is so clean her eyes even as if they had been taken from their sockets bathed in dew and restored with scented fingers to their places my assistants knew they'd die they dreaded it and so they have perhaps in their anxiety brought down on their heads the very thing they most (*Pause* ...)
Do you still love this (*Pause* ...)
      Man or memory do you still (*Pause* ...)
      Mess or monarch (*Pause* ...)
      And the lying here is —

TURNER: I cannot help the lying ... (*Her eyes meet his* ...)
          The lying is — (*Pause* ...)
          Me ... (*Pause* ...)
So answering your question ... for all that my love compels me to ... might yield you nothing but a further terror to go marching through your sleep —

DOJA: **I get no sleep** —
TURNER: Me neither —
DOJA: (*Seizing her by the wrist*) **I was the monster, me** ...!
(*Pause* ...)
          And this place ... dwarfs my frigidity ... what is that smell on you ...?

TURNER: My flesh —
DOJA: (*Pulling her close to him*) No, your flesh, no, you're smeared with something —
TURNER: Nothing, I assure you —
DOJA: Lying —
TURNER: No —
DOJA: No? Not lying? What, then?
TURNER: In this matter, not —

DOJA: Not lying in this matter?

TURNER: Not in this — you're hurting me —

DOJA: Hurting a liar?

TURNER: Yes —

DOJA: Oh, liar, now it's stronger, oozing from every pore —

TURNER: Fear —

DOJA: Fear?

TURNER: Fear of you, perhaps —

DOJA: Why me, I'm innocent —

TURNER: Innocent, you —

DOJA: **Oh, appalling innocence** — (*He forces her head steeply back* ...)
        Drink your husband... (*Pause... the tin roof rattles in the wind...* TURNER *is rigid with horror* ...)

TURNER: Drink —

DOJA: I'm your physician, do take my advice... (*He holds her still* ...)

TURNER: Drink —

DOJA: I say advice, in cases of this gravity I think advice is not —

TURNER: Drink —

DOJA: The word, advice, no, it's imperative —

TURNER: Drink —

DOJA: Your health depends on it —

TURNER: **Drink my** —

DOJA: **And mine the surgeon's sickness also must be cured**...
        (*He continues to grip* TURNER *with one hand, and with the other lifts a beaker of fluid from the anatomy table to* TURNER's *lips... A long pause* ...)

TURNER: Of course I loved him...

DOJA: Loved him, yes...

TURNER: Obsessive —

DOJA: Yes —

TURNER: And implacable —

DOJA: Yes —

TURNER: Madness of —

DOJA: I have no rivals, drink —

TURNER: Insoluble —

DOJA: I tolerate no rivals. drink —

TURNER: Horror —

DOJA: **Drink**
        Drink (*She gulps the fluid* ...)
        Drink

*The sound of her swallowing. She drains the beaker. It falls to the
floor.* DOJA *sinks to the floor with* TURNER *in his embrace. He
takes her from behind in a faltering light as the* DEAD PRIESTS
whisper . . .

SECOND PRIEST: About Death, now . . .
FIRST PRIEST: The very best perspective . . .
SECOND PRIEST: Believe me . . .
FIRST PRIEST: From which to see . . .
FIRST/SECOND: **The sheer exaggeration of the world** . . .
FIRST PRIEST: Especially with regard to . . .
SECOND PRIEST: Sad to say . . .
FIRST PRIEST: Emotions, Mr Doja . . .

Pause . . . TODD *enters . . . she leans on the back of the abandoned
wheelchair, watches as* DOJA *and* TURNER, *their act completed,
disengage.* DOJA *sits on the floor his knees drawn up . . .* TURNER,
unsteady, moves to go . . . avoiding DOJA's *eyes . . . she stops . . .*

DOJA: Lies, obviously . . . (TURNER *shakes her head violently
. . . goes out . . .*)
TODD: The new . . . (*She walks in . . .*)
       Always made of the old, unfortunately . . . (*She folds
       her arms, gazing at him . . .*)
       We could have been such . . . ! (*Pause . . .*)
       A permanent source of regret to me —
       A Dynasty I think . . . (DOJA *shrugs, lifts his hands . . .*)
    Instead of this less brilliant thing, a **Common interest** . . . (*She
half-laughs, shaking her head . . .*NIXON *returns with the hand-
cart . . .*)
NIXON: I put them side by side . . .
DOJA: Side by side . . . why not . . . ?
NIXON: (*Hauling* SUEDE *onto the cart*) The fact they quar-
       relled violently should not deprive them of the possibility that
       in death they might be reconciled . . .
DOJA: Yes, let them educate each other . . .
NIXON: I think if death is good at all, it must be from the point
       of view that its infinity eradicates all friction . . . (*Pause . . .*)
DOJA: How sentimental servants are . . . I've observed it over
       and over again . . .
NIXON: Yes . . . and a proper servant has no ambition for him-
       self . . . in the deepest places of his heart he feels a loyalty to
       things beyond self-interest, even beyond the interest of his

master ... to order itself, perhaps ... (*He starts to move out the cart, but stops ...*)

    The knights will take three months to escort the royal remains ... (*Pause ...*)

    The sooner they go the sooner ... (*Pause ...*)

DOJA: I've discovered an antipathy for my old profession which —

NIXON: Yes, of course ...! Some greater purpose is asserting its dominance over your soul. ... it was obvious to me from the moment I laid eyes on you, here is a man who cannot be content with surgery for long ...!

DOJA: **I am however dissolute**. (*Pause ...*)

    Skilled

    And

    Dissolute ...

NIXON: Yes ...

DOJA: Hardly the figure who could bring order to a world whose — disorder — appalls your servant's sensibilities ...

NIXON: (*Smiling ...*) Mr Doja, you do not like your life ... (*Pause ...*)

DOJA: Do I not ...?

NIXON: Under your repudiations and disavowals, a stern critic sits ... (*Pause ...*)

DOJA: Does he ...?

NIXON: Oh, yes ...! It's obvious ...!

DOJA: Everything is obvious to everyone, and nothing is obvious to me ...

NIXON: How could it be ... you have for such a long time cultivated a supreme indifference to the panics and pretentions of the governing life ... I admire it, and yet, the nature of perfection is precisely — its own redundancy ... (*He picks up the handles of the cart ...*)

    Do you want any — for these gentlemen — any — solemnities ... or ... (DOJA *hesitates ... laughs ...*)

DOJA: You choose ... (NIXON *bows ... goes out with the cart ...*)

    I love the queen ... the queen I will not have assassinated — **Assassinated ... I have said the word** ... you see, I am drawn in to your ... I think your thoughts when I was perfectly contented with my own — (*He shakes his head ...*)

Get your thoughts out of my head ...!

    I am fifty years old and have a farm with three hundred acres, gardens, fountains and the like, a tessellated pavement,

most beautiful and a wall of blue mosaics I had transported
from an antique site to rest my gaze upon in my retirement, a
summerhouse to make love with my neighbours' daughters in,
I am in all ways —

TODD: You cannot go —

DOJA: Satisfied with my —

TODD: You cannot go, Mr Doja —

DOJA: **I rinse your thoughts out of my head** ...!

TODD: (*Relentlessly*) The question is not whether you will go,
but how you will stay...my own desired one...my own
desired one... (DOJA *slowly extends a hand towards*
TODD...)
        No...
        For us...
        That is not possible... (*His hand falters*...)
        Our union is of another sort... (*He looks at his
        extended hand*...)

DOJA: I... (*He turns it*...)
        Must find a different use for it...

A cry from TURNER...DOJA *turns his hand again... she cries
out again... he looks at it from another angle...* TODD *walks
out*...

BALDWIN: My mother...! (DOJA *immediately begins thrusting the remains of the decreased man into assorted pans and
buckets, banging down the lids with a clumsy indifference*)
        My mother's hanged herself...!

DOJA: Knights...! the knights for Cracow, where are they...?
(*he hammers down the lid of an urn*...)
and Dijon...!

BALDWIN: Mr Doja...!

DOJA: **The knights for Dijon**...!

BALDWIN: (*Entering*) Hanged herself but failed...! (DOJA
stares at BALDWIN... *the hammer in his hand*...)

DOJA: Failed...?

BALDWIN: **Failed**...! (*Pause*...)

DOJA: **The knights for Lubeck, where are they**...!

BALDWIN: Don't visit her.

DOJA: (*Hammering down a lid*) Why not...?

BALDWIN: She's been restrained —

DOJA: **The knights for Estragom**...! How restrained...?

BALDWIN: Horribly, horribly restrained, I can't look at her —

DOJA: Can't look at her — (*He hammers wildly at a lid*)
        But looking's love —
        The knights for Olmutz and for Rome ...! (*He scrambles
        to his feet*)

These knights, they are, if I may say so, hardly clamouring
with impatience for their sacred task, the organs are sealed in
their caskets —

BALDWIN: (*Scrutinizing*) Sealed —

DOJA: Sealed in their caskets and rapidly acquiring those
        aspects of religiosity with which all relics are endowed —

BALDWIN: Not *sealed*, Mr Doja...

DOJA: And where is this blessed band, this fraternity of excel-
        lence whose entire existence has prepared them for this lofty
        honour —

BALDWIN: (*Kicking a can with his toe*) Not sealed at all...

DOJA: Tumbling...! Tumbling on the grass...! (*Pause...*)
        Not sealed, no...the one who sealed...can't seal today...
        (*He turns to* BALDWIN...)
        They insist I kill you...me...whose journeys in the living
        flesh have been...for the most part...fruitful and benign...
        (*He turns the hammer in his fingers...*)

BALDWIN: (*Nervous, Smiling...*) Your — presumably your —
        surgical skills —

DOJA: Second to none —

BALDWIN: And anatomical —

DOJA: Oh, I know where the veins are —

BALDWIN: (*laughing but weakly*) Expertise has...impressed
        itself upon their —

DOJA: **And I'm in two minds about it**... (*Pause...*)

BALDWIN: Are you...? In two minds...? (*Pause...*)

You must love me, then... (*Pause...with a swift move,*
BALDWIN *grabs a chair and drawing it to him, sits in it.*
DOJA's *response is too slow and* BALDWIN *is seated, facing*
DOJA, *and with folded arms and crossed legs almost before*
DOJA *perceives this action...*)

You must know, of all the hands that would now and will
with passing time acquire the itch to send me reeling into
darkness yours alone would I admit to be elected to the deed
Kill what's yours, Mr Doja since you arrived I've not slept a
whole night through **Who's prince here me or you** and I have
hardly governed yet a signature endorsed a regulation here and
there the opening hours of the tennis courts scarcely draconian
but what's the pleasure of coercion if I can't coerce your

thoughts in my direction I think to have my brain sent splashing would be to know I'd moved you have you a first name I've always been afraid to ask... (*Pause...*)

Observe me seated in the puddle of my father I do not exaggerate though exaggeration pleases me the certain sign my life is poor I do not exaggerate however when I say his stains his fragments might cling to my shoe and I would not stoop to scrape them with a stick or wipe the sole on grass **That is the measure of your obliteration Mr Doja memory's dead** and I revered him did you not say yourself my love was legendary it was it was a legend and so are you you fill my brain a tumour a sprouting plant that squeezes my character against the inside of my skull and empties it what character I am only fifteen fifteen and —

DOJA: Stop now — (BALDWIN *ceases...*)

Stop... (*Pause...*)

Do stop... (*The wind rattles the shutters...*)

How brilliantly you lie...how dazzling...you skate on fictions ...you gasp at the craftsmanship of your invention like old women gawping in museums...I've seen it...oh, I've seen it...in dancers...and in athletes...sheer adoration of the self and as you say **Fifteen**...! I genuflect...I...yield to it...

BALDWIN: I'm hurt that you should feel...that in my agony I have attempted to —

DOJA: Shh —

BALDWIN: Mislead or consciously deflect you from —

DOJA: Shh —

BALDWIN: Whatever act you —

DOJA: **Shh**. (*Pause...*)

The perfection of it requires no further elaboration... (*He looks at the hammer...*)

And I have not done... (*He bites his lip...*)

What certainly should have been done... (*He winces...*)

And still

Yes

Still

Might

Yet

Be

Done...(*Pause...they look at one another...with a crash, a door flies back on its hinges. Two armoured men stand in the entrance...*)

Too late now, however...!

*He flings the hammer against the iron wall of the anatomy room.
The* PRIESTS *erupt...*

FIRST/SECOND PRIEST: **The pleasures of the dead**
FIRST PRIEST: Consist in witnessing
SECOND PRIEST: Your passage to oblivion
DOJA: Is that so...? I feel sure you will be thoroughly entertained...
FIRST PRIEST: The heart attack
SECOND PRIEST: The passing peacefully away in sleep
FIRST/SECOND PRIEST: Could not have satisfied you
                               No death on the cheap
DOJA: Nothing less than an ordeal would be appropriate to you ...
FIRST/SECOND PRIEST: **You craved it**...
DOJA: Did I ...?
FIRST/SECOND PRIEST: **Craved it**...
DOJA: Possibly... I craved it... yes... (*He looks to the immobile* KNIGHTS...)
        The knights for where... exactly...? (*They do not reply.*
BALDWIN *gets up from the chair and going to a brimming
bucket, flings water over the anatomy table, deluging it, washing
away the blood and offal. In the following pause,* NIXON *enters.*
DOJA *lifts a hand in disbelief...*)
        But you...
BALDWIN: Apron...! (*Dumping the bucket, he runs to the
hook...*)
DOJA: (*To* NIXON) You are the one who...
BALDWIN: Apron...! (*He extends the apron to* NIXON...)
DOJA: **What does he know about anatomy**
        He's a cook
        A butler
        A bath attendant (*He appeals to* BALDWIN...)
        Honour me with expertise... (NIXON *wears the apron.*
BALDWIN *ties the strings.* TODD *enters, stands with folded
arms...*)
TODD: The assassin, having been nominated, yet declining to
assassinate... so naturally endowed with the necessary qualities, yet defying nature... can only be compared to a great
physician who, possessing the power to heal, withholds his
gifts and with a cruel detachment, studies the sick and lets
them perish... (*She looks at* DOJA...)
        Such things can never be forgiven...

BALDWIN: Oh, let me have his heart...! (*They wait, with repressed impatience, for* DOJA *to submit. He indicates his torso with a finger*...)

DOJA: You cut from here to — (*A woman's cry comes.* DOJA *recognizes it to be the cry of* TURNER... *his head does not turn*...)

From here to — (*It comes again*...)

Oh, perfect liar...

He goes to walk swiftly to his fate, but trips on an abandoned canister of royal organ... he nearly falls, but in regaining balance, turns to see TURNER's *cries are the consequence of an act of love. The lid of the can rolls away*... DOJA, *drawn by the spectacle of* TURNER's *nakedness, moves a few, agonized paces towards her... as he does so, the man who has participated in her ecstasy lets out a terrible cry of solitude and melancholy, shame and despair*...

FIRST/SECOND PRIEST: Doja... (*He ignores them*...)

Doja... (DOJA *strains his eyes and mind*...)

Much easier to die than see... (*He goes nearer, afraid*...)

Who gives the queen... her ecstasy... (*His mind races. He fathoms. He plunges to the depths of an idea. He repudiates, and then submits to the idea... He looks to the attendant group*...)

DOJA: Who could so gratify a queen...? Only a king, surely...? (*A wind. With the excruciating sound of an unoiled winch, the* PRIESTS *are hauled slowly into the air, back to the apertures from which they plunged*... DOJA *turns to the table*...)

And this was... (*He shrugs*...)

Some dog... of... adequate obscurity... on whom my skills could play... uncontradicted...

I cut only kings...! (*He smiles*...)

My own decay had long set in, obviously... or I should have known, through the scalpel's infinitesimal vibration, this was... vulgar flesh... (*The* KING, *leaving* TURNER, *comes down into the anatomy room.* DOJA *bows*...)

Oh, how painful your life must be... (*The* KING *looks at* DOJA...)

I have flayed kings... but in your case, there is no skin that I can see... the nerves are naked... and wind even, gives you agony... (*He remains in the bow*...)

Why don't they bow ...? (*He resolutely refuses to rise.
The assembled court does not bow ...*)
Etiquette
Etiquette
Etiquette
Why don't they ...? (*Pause ... Then he rises swiftly ...*)
Obviously, you don't exist ... outside the bedroom ...
I'm recruited to a game
I who
I the master of
And erudite
Cynic
Sceptic
And triumphant evasionist
I with neither party nor a wife am (*Pause ... A strange
laugh comes from him ...*)
Part of a game ...
And not my own game, either ... (*One of the*
KNIGHTS *takes a single step ...*)
Do I object ...? (*And another*)
No, wait. (*And a further step ...*)
Wait
Wait
Let a man decide if
Wait (*The* KNIGHT *is still*)
If he concedes ... or if he finds it ... humiliating ... and
preposterous ...
I don't know
  For if some weapon loosed at random can splatter my brain
or tripping on an unlit path I topple in a cold canal my screams
ignored by courting couples slippery fingered and
Whose game is that
Somebody's (*To the* KNIGHT)
  No don't rush me I'm half-way to understanding — (*He
drags his shirt over his head, stopping half-in, half-out ... sobs
come from within ... he staggers ... he wails, fighting his horror
in the dark ... the court observes, unmoving ... at last the writhing ceases.* DOJA *completes his disrobing. He is naked to the
waist. Suddenly, the appearance of* LAYBACH, *breathless ...*)
LAYBACH: I stabbed ... (*He looks around, from face to face ...*)
             I stabbed and ....
             Having stabbed ... experienced ... (*He shrugs,
             enormously ...*)

> **Relief**...! (*No one reacts to his passion...*)
> And she was guiltless, guiltless obviously, but this
> guiltlessness was... (*He bites his lip...*)
> **Possibly the cause of my relief**...! (*He looks from
> one to another...*)

Whilst my hatred did not shift from its original and habitual target... while Mr Doja remained the object of my envy and contempt... in stabbing her I sensed, oh, such a draining of my misery, as if some tide had raced away and left me solitary on a wide and undisputed beach, the squeal of gannets and (*he stops...*)

> I expect to be punished with the utmost severity
> ... (*He dares them...*)

This is not to say however, that I admit to even the slightest sentiments of shame or guilt... (*They are still deaf to him*)

> **On the contrary I** —

DOJA: Shh...
LAYBACH: **I affirm my** —
DOJA: Shh...

He looks at LAYBACH, a smile of unfeigned kindness on his face... LAYBACH is stopped... DOJA goes to the anatomy table. He picks up an instrument, looks at the blade, tosses it in a bucket. He repeats this with the next, and so on... the sound is rhythmic, relentless, as the light fades from the scene and rises on two windows which fly open in the wall...

FIRST PRIEST: A King's night...!
SECOND PRIEST: The window open and a light breeze
FIRST PRIEST: Stirs the beeches
SECOND PRIEST: Moon
FIRST PRIEST: Moon and
SECOND PRIEST: The laughing leaves
FIRST PRIEST: Under a single sheet he lies
SECOND PRIEST: White
FIRST PRIEST: Laundered and white
SECOND PRIEST: He lies
FIRST PRIEST: A bell
SECOND PRIEST: Stiller than death
FIRST PRIEST: A bell
SECOND PRIEST: Naked
FIRST PRIEST: The fountain falters in the breeze

SECOND PRIEST: The crawling hours of his agony (*The light returns to the anatomy table, where* DOJA *lies. Seated beside him, head in hands,* TORTMANN. *They are alone...*)

TORTMANN: (*At last*) An obsession... what's an obsession, Mr Doja... but a privilege...? And because I was a king... my privilege was itself privileged... because I was a king my ecstasy has been... extraordinary... an ecstasy akin to God's... (TURNER *slowly enters, and sits at a distance.* TORTMANN *senses her, but does not turn...*)

For she is impossible to own... which for a king... is infinite — is unrelieved — torture... we are so unbalanced by possession... (*Pause...*)

DOJA: Execute her, then...

TORTMANN: That was my first inclination... but you will have deduced I am no common husband, Mr Doja... I hoarded pain as some hoard money... and through hoarding it... I found in pain whole realms of pity and excess that butchering cuckolds know nothing of...

DOJA: And we — while we —

TORTMANN: I kept my distance... oh, distance, Mr Doja, distance is everything... to know... to see... what's that but sordid witnessing...? I walk by the wide river, whose fullness races like my blood... (*He rises to his feet...*)

I'll keep your heart... a thing no doubt you've long since ceased to revere, but I... (*He shrugs...*)

believe me, study... (*He goes out, leaving* TURNER *alone with* DOJA... *she sits in perfect stillness...*)

DOJA: Heart...? (*Pause...*)

What heart...? (*Pause...*)

What heart I've none none nothing the cavity the hollow chamber underneath the rib the vault the crypt that echoed to a woman's heels walk the tiled floor of its absence do walk (TURNER *does not move...*)

I'm impatient
Oddly impatient
To be another remnant of your passion yes another rag of your extraordinary love

I've seen the graves a pleasant spot do you walk there not unlike the cemeteries of war whose occupants must surely grumble more than I shall at the futility of their extinction to suffer for a flag or book oh nothing nothing to my martyrdom I'm not humiliated no to perish for the pleasure of (*He stops...*)

It is not pleasure, is it... you two share... (*Pause*...)
But terror...? (*She remains motionless*...)
What's common love alongside that...? (*Pause*...)
Answer me... (*Pause*...)
Oh, answer...!
No
No
They all say that
They all
They all
They all say that
Don't answer
No
I'll cut
I'll do the cutting
I
I'll cut
The master me

His hand sweeps for an instrument, spilling a tray which clatters. He gropes. The apertures in the wall fly back. Desperately chattering heads appear, horrified, fascinated. The hysteria of the audience rises. DOJA's hand is seen to make the movements of swift dissection, the other assisting it, nimbly, as if inspired, rapid as a concert pianist, an apotheosis of a skill. BALDWIN, entering in a routine manner, sees, stops, is fixed to the spot, his left knee rising, his arms clutching himself in a slow paroxysm of disbelief. At the moment he is in a position of absolute balance, twisted yet erect, the audience drained of utterance, falls silent. In this silence, the sound of instruments exchanged. The frantic activity of DOJA's hands... a spectacle of will, dexterity, endurance... of magic, therefore, which endures until the sudden entrance of BERLIN, uninjured. DOJA's activity ceases, is suspended...

BERLIN: (*Looking at* BALDWIN...) The priest is mad and
   locked me in a hut... (BALDWIN *ignores her*)
          With food... (*Pause*...)
   And great jars of water... (BALDWIN *does not remove his
   gaze from* DOJA...)
   I said — (*Irritably,* DOJA *taps his instrument against a metal
   bowl*... BERLIN's *gaze slowly turns in* DOJA's *direction*...)
          I climbed out through the roof...
BALDWIN: Shh...

BERLIN: This roof —

BALDWIN: Shh...

BERLIN: Was thatch — (*Again* DOJA *taps to silence her... but* BERLIN *is so shocked she can only persist...*)

It seems to me therefore... despite the food and water... he had no desire I should remain in there... on the contrary... he locked me in... precisely in order that I should escape —

DOJA: **He's hanged shut up**... (*This information stifles* BERLIN's *voice. In the resulting silence,* DOJA *reaches for another instrument and proceeds to incise himself...*)

BERLIN: **Hanged but he** — (DOJA *raps the blade against a bowl...*)

TURNER: There is a man there who is making his own death... (BERLIN *sways...*)

And I have not moved one centimetre... (*Her eyes close...*)

> I
> Who
> Love
> Him

Not one centimetre from this seat... (*A collective gasp from the public accompanies a stroke by* DOJA... *a profound groan issues from* BALDWIN... BERLIN *takes a violent step towards* DOJA, *as if to remonstrate or restrain him, but* BALDWIN *is swift and seizes her by the wrist...*)

BALDWIN: The flesh is not the man... (*Pause...*)

BERLIN: The flesh is not the man... **What is the flesh, then?** (*A further gasp from the public...*)

BALDWIN: Oh, Mr Doja is cutting the strings of my own heart...! (*A gasp again, an instrument discarded, another taken from the tray...*)

BERLIN: **I also love**...!

TURNER: Then find a seat...

BERLIN *turns from* DOJA *to* TURNER *in disbelief... in the suspended silence, an instrument chimes against another... the* DEAD PRIESTS *appear from the obscurity*

FIRST/SECOND PRIEST: Are we a little premature?

FIRST PRIEST: Anticipating

SECOND PRIEST: Our impatience is so typical

FIRST PRIEST: Of death

SECOND PRIEST: Which longs for more

FIRST PRIEST: A spoiled child

SECOND PRIEST: More

FIRST PRIEST: Death

SECOND PRIEST: Still... (*They peer, on tiptoe...* DOJA *lifts another tool...*)

FIRST PRIEST: Skill...

SECOND PRIEST: Infinite skill...

FIRST PRIEST: In leaving every vein uncut until (*A public gasp...*)

                    His

SECOND PRIEST: We wait...

FIRST PRIEST: His

SECOND PRIEST: We wait...

FIRST PRIEST: His

BERLIN: (*A cry of revulsion*) **Sit still...?** (*Her cry unleashes a river, a sluice of black fluid which roars like an unlocked lake, streaming in a profusion from beneath the table to a downstage drain. The roar continues, a Niagara of sound as the apertures slowly close, the witnesses withdrawing one after another, leaving* BALDWIN, BERLIN *and* TURNER *in fixed postures... as the last window slowly closes, a sound of running footsteps, descending iron stairs, fills the silence.* LAYBACH, *breathless, comes into the room...*)

LAYBACH: A man...

A man has flung himself into the river...! (*They ignore him...*)

And I —

I wanted to follow him...

But...

But... (*He shrugs pitifully...*)

In the river a man...!

The mass of grieving figures hurries past, frenzied, as in the first moments of the play. The light of the sun descends to the rim of the wall. As the last of the figures departs, TURNER *is discovered on her knees in front of the chair she has been seated in. She is quite still. The mass of figures returns. They pass. The light is reduced to a single blade of light reaching over the wall. An old woman appears with a bucket and a mop. Ignoring the still figures she begins the laborious task of washing the floor. As she finishes a section, she shifts the bucket with one foot. The light, sinking, suddenly drops behind the wall.*

THE HOUSE OF CORRECTION

CHARACTERS

SHARDLO
VISTULA
LINDSAY
HEBBEL
GODANSK
FIRST SERVANT
SECOND SERVANT
THIRD SERVANT

PART ONE

A MESSENGER

A damaged room. A storm of leaflets falls from the sky. They cascade onto and around a standing woman. The storm ceases. A second woman enters, and contemplates the first . . .

VISTULA: How very extraordinary, it is your way of standing that infuriates me now. How extraordinary this hatred is, how volatile . . . ! Yesterday your hair enraged me, I could have torn it out by the roots . . . (SHARDLO *is motionless . . .*)

Millions stand exactly like that, millions, and never until now did I find it in the least offensive. Shift, will you? Sit or something? Obviously it is not the posture — oh, you are uncompromising, you ask for all you get, oh, you are so very adamantine and the less you concede the worse I become, I blame you for much of this . . . ! (SHARDLO *does not move . . .*)

I am not bad . . . (VISTULA *shakes her head . . .*)
I am not . . .
I am not bad . . . (*She clenches her fists . . . she hunches her shoulders in a spasm of pain. She hurries out.* SHARDLO *remains still for some time, then she erupts into movement*)

SHARDLO: (*calling*) **Pick this up . . . !** (*She strides, she fetches.* SERVANTS *hurry in with straw baskets and pluck up the leaflets*)

I can't
I won't
I never do (*She flings a white sheet over an iron bed . . .*)

And sometimes — let us dare confess it — sometimes, yes, the poetry is good, the poetry is not without its qualities, some days rhyming, some days not, all tastes are catered for and whilst it is forbidden to allow one's eyes to drift over the words inevitably one or two stand out good words unusual words that linger in the memory. (*She fetches more linen*)

Paralysis I noticed and cacophony beautiful words in my opinion perhaps I should deny myself the luxury of speaking them but treason can't reside in the vocabulary or can it surely it's the attitude I don't claim to understand these things (*She stops suddenly in mid-movement*)

Now that was false (*She is still*)

That was so false I understand perfectly well why did I affect an ignorance not one of you would attach the slightest credence to you of all people who know the strength of my intelligence why did I (*They continue, as if deaf to her*)

Now of all times

Succumb to

A pretence (*They collect. She reflects... she crushes the linen in her hands. She falters, then swiftly walks out, throwing the sheet to the floor. The servants continue undeflected, moving like crop-gatherers. A figure rises painfully out of the bed, haggard, pale, grasping the iron to haul himself upright*)

HEBBEL: Blood...!

Blood...! (*The servants ignore his existence... The sound of an aeroplane passing low. As it does so, the servants rise from their stooping postures in unison, and look up, then bend to continue collecting...*)

Blood...!

Blood...! (*Leaflets fall in dense clouds over the stage. In an attempt to sustain order, the servants collect the remnants of the first leaflet raid before attempting to gather up the second... A woman enters, briskly*)

LINDSAY: Why do you keep saying blood? (HEBBEL *ignores her...*)

It is not blood, it is paper...

HEBBEL: Blood...!

LINDSAY: You will get all the blood you want, I promise you.

HEBBEL: Never

Never

Never

Enough

Blood... (*Pause... LINDSAY stares at him...*)

LINDSAY: To satisfy whom...? (*The old man's hand lifts off the blanket and falls again. The last leaflets fall to the floor... the* SERVANTS *are waiting an instruction to repeat their operation, and gawp at* LINDSAY, *baskets in their hands...*)

Don't be frightened, he is not an oracle. If anything, it is his own anaemia he is referring to... (*She laughs, quietly...*)

Carry on... (*They gather again.* SHARDLO *returns with more linen. She looks at* LINDSAY...)

SHARDLO: We shall need that bed. (*Pause...*)
Shan't we...? (*Pause...*)
We shall need all the beds we can get... (*Pause...*)

I am opposed to any sort of privilege in beds. He can stay until — (*She stops. Her hand goes to her mouth. She sways a little, recovers...*)

No, it's his bed... (*She shrugs...*)
I'm...
I'm... (*She makes a gesture of futility...*)

I have developed the aptitude for crisis when the crisis has yet to materialize... (*She smiles...*)

Never mind... when it does arrive... how much more prepared I'll be...! (LINDSAY *smiles wistfully... The* SERVANTS *gather...* SHARDLO *extends a hand to* LINDSAY, *impulsively...*)

I do want to triumph... don't you...? I do want to discover the extent of my magnificence...

LINDSAY: Yes...! And certainly this peace could not continue —

SHARDLO: Impossible —

LINDSAY: It was becoming — oh, intolerable... (*They clasp hands...* LINDSAY *looks down at the floor...*)
I cannot wait to see your... (*She shakes her head...*)

SHARDLO: Dear one...

LINDSAY: To share in your... (*She hesitates, shrugs...*)
Can't say it...

SHARDLO: Don't say it, then... wait... witness it... and describe it afterwards... (LINDSAY *kisses her swiftly...*)

I think this room can take eight beds. At a minimum. Obviously, eight is far from adequate. We shall be overwhelmed. We shall be inundated and our resources discovered to be utterly inadequate. We shall move like ghosts. Our characters, our appetites, will be suspended as we stagger under the effects of sleeplessness. Hope will evaporate. Energy will be drained. And the things we shall see...! (*She bites her lip...*)

Things the sight of which might now cause us to sink to our knees under a canopy of horror we shall — (*She stops...*) I

don't know yet... (*She smiles*...) No, let us have ten in
here. Five on each wall and the centre, when we are swamped,
can be — (*The deep drone of a passing plane. The* SERVANTS
*stop and gaze up, having cleared a large part of the floor. The
sound fades. In the returning silence, a snowfall of leaflets
begins*...)

        Do you read these at all...?
LINDSAY: Isn't it forbidden...? (*The* SERVANTS *look down,
as the leaflets drift*...)
SHARDLO: It is forbidden, yes...
HEBBEL: Blood...!
        Blood...!
LINDSAY: It isn't blood, it's paper...
SHARDLO: What it says...the poem...on the paper...might
possibly be true... (*The* SERVANTS *look at* SHARDLO ...)
    There is another truth, however...which is hard for poets to
believe...five times I have tried to commit suicide...five
times...! (*She looks at the servants*...)
    They know...they lifted me from ponds or cut me down
from beams in barns... embarrassing...! For me... ! For
them...! (*She goes to the* SERVANTS. *Kisses one of them on
the cheek*)
    No more of that, I promise you... (*She turns to leave*...)
    When that's done, find me, I shall be in the laundry or if not
there in the conservatory, I thought ten beds in there, but is it
warm enough, it's summer now but if the oil is rationed it will
be intolerable by the first week of September or does that (*She
stops*...)
    Of course the crisis will reverse our order of priorities...
(*She looks at* LINDSAY)
    Won't that be exactly how the crisis will announce itself...?
(*The servants stare at her*...)
    In a sense therefore, to even contemplate the crisis is a
contradiction, illogical, futile, since by definition it makes
havoc of the very conditions under which it could be contemplated... (*They stare*... VISTULA *enters, holding a bucket.
She looks at* SHARDLO. *She looks at the* SERVANTS...)
VISTULA: You hear this voice...
        You're walking down a corridor...
        You're in the orchard...
        Cleaning...
        Polishing...
        Unblocking a drain...

And there's this voice...
It travels...
God knows why it's not so very... (*She thrusts the bucket to the floor. It clatters...*)
Like some tap running in the night some plumbing in a desolated palace
Possibly a bath
Yes
A bath left running by a man who's died
A bath of useless questions
The crisis is just another pretext for you to talk about yourself (*To the* SERVANTS)
Pick this up now
Every bit
I'll help you
I am not afraid to stoop (SHARDLO *goes out. The servants begin again to clear the leaflets...*)
Don't accuse me I can't help myself.

LINDSAY: Is that so?

VISTULA: Can't help myself and if I don't speak I'll strike her.

LINDSAY: You have struck her.

VISTULA: I have and I was sorry.

LINDSAY: She also has a soul.

VISTULA: She has a soul and I hate it.

LINDSAY: You should be ashamed.

VISTULA: I'm not.

LINDSAY: You should be.

VISTULA: I don't deny I should be.

LINDSAY: Frequently I experience an irritation when I deal with you.

VISTULA: Oh.

LINDSAY: Some habit. Some inflection. Anything. But I don't advertize my irritation.

VISTULA: Advertize it if you want to.

LINDSAY: I don't want to, but the tolerance I feel towards you is —

VISTULA: Tolerance?

LINDSAY: Yes, and this tolerance is — (*With a swift movement,* VISTULA *slaps* LINDSAY *over the cheek. Both women are shocked.*)

VISTULA: I'll apologize for that. (*She bites her lip...* LINDSAY *stares...*)

Oh, let me apologize for that — (LINDSAY *strides out...* VISTULA *sways... the* SERVANTS *ignore her...*)

HEBBEL: Shh...

VISTULA: Mmm...

HEBBEL: Shh... (VISTULA *shrugs, wearily...*)

VISTULA: How hateful to be tolerated... (*She picks up the bucket*)

HEBBEL: It's coming to an end...

VISTULA: It is, is it...?

HEBBEL: Oh, yes. (VISTULA *goes out. The* SERVANTS *are picking up. A pause of labour...*)

Oh, yes. (*They move like gatherers of crops...*)

Oh, yes. (*Pause...*)

The fact is I have wisdom but I have no intention whatsoever of dispensing it to you. (*Pause...*)

> What would you do with it, in any case...? (*Pause...*)
>
> Alter bits and claim it was your own. (*Pause...*)
>
> I've seen it...! (*Pause...*)
>
> Seen it, I've suffered it...! The very phrases...!
>
> Oh, the reputations of these plagiarists... dwarfed my own... (*Pause...*)
>
> Plead, by all means.
>
> Hammer on my doors... (*Pause...*)

Like distraught women who suspect their abducted infants are hanging from the stairs... (*Pause...*)

> Bang, bang...! (*Pause...*)

Oh, bang, bang...! (*A figure has entered. He is covered in a fine dust. The* SERVANTS *neither recognize nor acknowledge him. He looks around...*)

GODANSK: I need water... (*They are silent...*)

To be precise, it is not I that needs the water. I have a horse. (HEBBEL *gazes at him...*)

> The horse needs water... (HEBBEL's *stare renders* GODANSK *uncomfortable...*)
>
> It's a dancing horse... (*Pause...*)
>
> It was not bred for distances... (*Pause...*)
>
> Very well, if there is no water, I must — (*He goes to move, stops*)
>
> There must be water here. (*His firm tone causes the* SERVANTS *to look to each other...*)
>
> There is no other building anywhere near here so you must oblige me. (*They are still, afraid...*)

I am a courier.

HEBBEL: On a dancing horse...! (*HEBBEL's scoffing tone draws GODANSK's curiosity. He walks to the bed...*)

GODANSK: You have identified the first of many peculiarities that attend on this particular undertaking.

HEBBEL: Are there others? I don't speak much. I keep my wisdom to myself.

GODANSK: Several.

HEBBEL: Name another.

GODANSK: The stable was full of horses any one of which could easily outdistance mine. Younger animals in good condition and familiar with the road. Mine has rarely been outside the show arena.

HEBBEL: Fascinating but I must not become excited does yours walk on hind legs? (*He scoffs...*)

Oh, dear, I am becoming animated and you will extract something from me I've no desire to impart...! No, there is no water here. (*The SERVANTS, who had ceased collecting, return to their labour. GODANSK watches them...*)

What's wrong with a motorbike...?

(*Pause... GODANSK turns to him again...*)

GODANSK: That also struck me as odd. And odder still is the fact that in the first place I was ordered to walk.

HEBBEL: Walk...!

GODANSK: Yes. The dancing horse was a concession to me, given my long service, a reward for loyalty. (*Pause...*)

HEBBEL: No, it's a pity about the water... (*GODANSK glares at the old man, then turns on his heel*)

GODANSK: I'll find it myself and God help anyone who obstructs me...! (*He strides out... as he does so, LINDSAY surges in*)

LINDSAY: There's a horse in the yard...!

HEBBEL: It dances... (*SHARDLO hurries in from the opposite side*)

SHARDLO: Have you seen the horse?

HEBBEL: It dances...

LINDSAY: Some stranger's here.

HEBBEL: On its hind legs, apparently.

LINDSAY: But who?

HEBBEL: I denied him water but he became coercive.

LINDSAY: Who did?

HEBBEL: The courier.

LINDSAY: Courier?

SHARDLO: Give him water, whoever he is. And tell him to go.
HEBBEL: This horse was considered preferable to a motorbike.
SHARDLO: (*fretting*) This is the problem with the road.
LINDSAY: Is the road a problem?
SHARDLO: It draws strangers.
LINDSAY: Rather few...
SHARDLO: Rather few but we have no time to waste on
strangers. Not now. Not with the crisis — (*The drone of an
aircraft. The* SERVANTS, *who have almost finished clearing the
last drop, gaze upwards in unison*...)
                    Oh, and we have so much to do...! (*The plane
                    passes.   Leaflets   begin   to   flutter   down*...
                    GODANSK *enters... he looks at them*...)
GODANSK: Why do you say there is no water? There are three
troughs and a standpipe in the yard... (*They look blankly at
him*...)
                    **It is against the law to hinder or obstruct a messen-
                    ger.**
        (*Pause... the leaflets trickle down. With a sudden gesture*
GODANSK *plucks one out of the air. He reads it*...)
SHARDLO: That also is against the law. (GODANSK *ignores
her remark and continues reading*...)
                    That also is against the —
GODANSK: Shh. (*Pause. He completes the reading of the leaf-
let. He thrusts it at* SHARDLO)
                    It's a poem...!
SHARDLO: Yes...
GODANSK: I don't like poetry.
SHARDLO: Then they have entirely wasted their efforts.
GODANSK: In my case, certainly. (*He withdraws his hand,
screws up the leaflet, drops it to the floor*...)
                    On the other hand, others may well be suscept-
                    ible.
SHARDLO: That would explain the prohibition on the reading
or dissemination of the leaflets.
GODANSK: Yes. (*He looks at her*...)
        Much of what the government decrees is correct, even if it
does not always seem so at the time. Sometimes its decisions
appear arbitrary, even illogical. One puzzles over the peculiar
and contradictory nature of its decisions, thinking some error
must have occurred, if not at the point of decision, then in the
system of communications, an official misreading a letter in a
word, a typist momentarily losing concentration when a man

she loves appears in view. Invariably, the errors are our own in not possessing the subtlety of mind to match the complex mechanisms of the ministry. At least, this has been my own experience. Others may disagree.

HEBBEL: So there is a reason why you have no motorbike...?

GODANSK: I don't know.

HEBBEL: And being denied a motorbike, you are also denied a horse...?

GODANSK: I have a horse.

HEBBEL: You have a horse but it prefers to dance on its hind legs...!

GODANSK: Yes, but the obvious drawbacks of a performing horse as a mount for a government messenger are in my case amply compensated for.

HEBBEL: By what? (*Pause... GODANSK looks critically at HEBBEL ...*)

By what? (GODANSK *stares...* HEBBEL *shrugs...*)

LINDSAY: I feel sure the Citizen Messenger must —

HEBBEL: What is he saying? On the one hand that the decision to supply him with a dancing horse reflects the as yet undecipherable wisdom of the government department that concerns itself with messengers, but on the other that he has himself discovered means by which to frustrate precisely these complex and byzantine arrangements, for example, by placing the horse on a railway track. Is that what he is saying? I like to know what people are saying.

SHARDLO: Be quiet, you are an idiot.

HEBBEL: All my life I have sought explanations. All my life I have been denied them.

LINDSAY: Yes...! Yes...! It's true, you have suffered...! (*She throws her arms round HEBBEL...*)

GODANSK: I can only say that in selecting me to bear this particularly important message, the provision of an apparently imperfect horse was negated to a considerable extent by my well-known expertize in short-cuts, cross-country riding, the seasonal effects of rainfall in this region on the height of rivers, and so on, all significant factors in determining the choice of courier from among a group some of whom were young and inexperienced. I admit, as we plunged through bracken and galloped over estuaries, I pondered these seeming contradictions, but to no avail. All will become clear later, I have no doubt, if not to me, to others...

HEBBEL: Will it...! Will it become clear, however...?
(GODANSK *shrugs*...)

SHARDLO: We have delayed you by this inquisition on the
nature of things, Mr —

GODANSK: Godansk —

SHARDLO: Mr Godansk, and now you will be obliged to
employ even more of your special skills to compensate for
time lost at this unscheduled stop — (GODANSK *bows very
slightly*)
                    Just as we must now work even harder to assem-
ble all that we require for —

HEBBEL: Was it unscheduled...? (*They look at him*...)
    Or, looked at from another point of view, even if it were
unscheduled, it might nevertheless be true that in stopping he
evaded an encounter with highwaymen, murderers, those who
prey on messengers and devotees of dancing horses who would
most certainly have detected in its prancing style the origins of
this particular and irresistible animal, mud-spattered as it certainly must be, ungroomed and unribboned...!

SHARDLO: **Oh, do cease this, oh, do cease...!** (*She closes her
eyes in her agony*...)
                    The crisis will
                    The crisis must
                    The terrible cleanliness of the crisis

VISTULA: (*Entering, seeing the* SERVANTS *staring idly*...)
    Pick up...! Pick up...! (LINDSAY *holds* SHARDLO *in
her arms. The* SERVANTS *begin again to clear the floor.*
GODANSK *briskly leaves.* SHARDLO *frees herself from*
LINDSAY's *embrace, and smoothes her clothes, wiping her
palms on her skirt*)

SHARDLO: How horrible that man made me. I was unfamiliar
to myself.

VISTULA: You say that as if. Forgive my impertinence but
you are always saying that. Isn't she? (*She looks to*
LINDSAY)

SHARDLO: Am I...?

VISTULA: As if there was another you.

SHARDLO: (*To* HEBBEL) I apologize. I called you an idiot.

VISTULA: As if this other you was — what — immaculate —
and we —

SHARDLO: We must get on —

VISTULA: Dustmen, messengers, pastry cooks, etcetera, we —

SHARDLO: Please —

VISTULA: We spoil this you, we smudge and smear it with our presence. (SHARDLO *looks at* VISTULA...)

SHARDLO: Well, perhaps you do...spoil it...perhaps it should be spoiled —

> **Oh God**
> **Oh God**
> **He has left his wallet** (*She beckons to the* SERVANTS...)
> Run after him...! (*They throw down their baskets and hurtle off.* HEBBEL *is heard to chuckle...* SHARDLO *turns on him*)
> What is funny...! (HEBBEL *is silent...*)

Is it funny that we now must go about our business in the certainty that at any moment some stranger will burst in and throw us into absolute and total disarray, distracting us from all the meticulous and (*She stops...*)

> And you cannot have that bed. You cannot occupy that bed like that.

HEBBEL: Like what? How should I occupy it...?

SHARDLO: I don't know —

HEBBEL: You would prefer me horizontal...?

SHARDLO: I don't know, I only know the bed is (*She stops again...her body heaves...* LINDSAY *extends a comforting hand to her...*)

How absurd...I am unsettled by a single interruption when...the crisis...when it comes...will consist of interruption...will be nothing but perpetual interruption...interruption to the extent that we will cease to recognize it as such... (*She smiles...*)

Order, which we now take as the basis of our life, the very thing that permits so much reflection, will evaporate in the heat of crisis, we will exist not in our heads but in our fingertips...! (*The* SERVANTS *return...*)

> Did you find him...?

SERVANTS: Gone, Miss...

SHARDLO: Yes, no doubt he leapt into his saddle, dug in his spurs and —

VISTULA: He'll be back —

SHARDLO: Of course he will —

VISTULA: Half-way up some mountain pass he'll think —

LINDSAY: To spare him even greater loss of hours I'll —

VISTULA: (*To the* SERVANTS) Pick up...! Pick up...!

LINDSAY: I'll hang his satchel on the gate —

HEBBEL: Peculiar —

LINDSAY: We need not see him, he can —

VISTULA: Snatch it at a gallop...!

HEBBEL: Peculiar —

SHARDLO: (*Irritably*) What is, what is peculiar...! (*They look at* HEBBEL...)

HEBBEL: I'm afraid to speak...! So often, I'm afraid to speak...!

SHARDLO: Good, you have had a lifetime of speaking —

LINDSAY: Shh —

SHARDLO: He has, he has spoken too much...

HEBBEL: Yes, far too much, and everything I said was thieved by others —

SHARDLO: God knows why —

HEBBEL: **Because it was a wealth and all that's wealth is stolen.** (*Pause...*)

SHARDLO: Yes...
         Yes...
         That's obvious...

LINDSAY: (*To* HEBBEL) Don't be — (HEBBEL *sobs...*)

SHARDLO: I'm sorry.

VISTULA: (*To the* SERVANTS, *who have gawped...*) Pick up...! Pick up...!

SHARDLO: I'm sorry.

LINDSAY: (*To* HEBBEL...) Shh...Sh...

VISTULA: I think you are almost entirely without charity. I think that's admirable but also I want to kill you.

SHARDLO: I said I'm sorry.

VISTULA: Yes and not one syllable was from the heart.

SHARDLO: I have no heart. That is something we long ago established.

HEBBEL: (*Recovered in an instant*) Peculiar because what courier worthy of the name ever removes his satchel? Is the satchel of a courier not the vital element of his anatomy? Is it not more intimate to him than his liver or his kidney? He might as well have left his eyes lying on the table... (*Pause...*)

Possibly he is not a courier at all, therefore, but someone masquerading as a courier...

LINDSAY: The enemy...?

HEBBEL: The enemy, certainly they have agents dressed as couriers, it would be the first thing they would think of, but they would not I daresay mount their impostors on circus horses, they would, unless I underestimate their genius for complication, place them on motorbikes, motorbikes of precisely the same manufacture as our own... (*Pause*... VISTULA *reaches for the wallet*...)

SHARDLO: I don't think we should look at it. (VISTULA's *hand is poised*...)

I don't think we should permit ourselves to be distracted from the task in hand by speculating as to whether this intruder was a proper courier or not. Who cares if he is genuine? And if he is an enemy, what is that to us? The crisis will almost at once obliterate any distinction between the enemy and those we call our own. That is surely an aspect of its magnificence? (VISTULA's *hand falls*...)

I think enough time has been wasted on the —

LINDSAY: Anyway, it's locked. (*They look at her*)
The satchel. (*Pause*... *she shrugs*...)
It has a massive lock on it...

HEBBEL: **Who's got the key**...! (*He chuckles*...)

SHARDLO: Shut up or I shall tip you out of bed and you can crawl about on all fours arguing —

VISTULA: (*To* SHARDLO) Why are you such a —

SHARDLO: **He enrages me he is entirely and egregiously the thing that makes me ache for death.** (*She sways*... VISTULA *stares at her*... LINDSAY *breaks the tension*)

LINDSAY: I'll organize the blankets... (*She turns to go.* SHARDLO *turns to her*...)

SHARDLO: Can't you see... (LINDSAY *stops*...)
Oh, can't you see... I'm so... near to... near to something which... (*She bites her lip*...)
Of course you can see...! You see too much...! (LINDSAY *spontaneously kisses her and goes out*...)

VISTULA: (*To* SHARDLO, *cruelly*) And the pain of others is —

HEBBEL: **A Garden.** (VISTULA *looks at* HEBBEL...)
A garden through which she walks stooping to take great lungfuls of sweet odour... (*He sneers at* VISTULA)
You are poor and she is excellent. (*He glares*...)
The more so because she sees through me. (*He turns to* SHARDLO)
I don't require the bed. Chuck me! Chuck me!

SHARDLO: (*To* VISTULA...) This vile old man's endorsement makes me shudder, believe me... (HEBBEL *chuckles*...)

VISTULA: Yes, and you should shudder, it should scald your skin to feel the truth of those appalling compliments shower you... (SHARDLO *stares at* VISTULA ... *She sways a little between temper and resignation*...)

SHARDLO: All right ... (*She gropes with her hands*...)
Go wherever you —

VISTULA: **I am so** —

SHARDLO: Wherever you were going —

VISTULA: **So** —

So — (*She shuts her eyes tightly, then sweeps out. SHARDLO is quite still. The SERVANTS pick up paper. SHARDLO remains thus, observed by HEBBEL, then herself leaves. The SERVANTS, as if by tacit agreement, straighten their aching backs, rub their shoulders. The distant sound of a horse's hooves. The SERVANTS exchange glances. HEBBEL, as if by instinct, disappears into the depths of the bed from which he emerged... The SERVANTS resume their labour as the sound of the courier comes closer and stops...GODANSK enters. He looks at the backs of the SERVANTS*...)

GODANSK: Cease that now. (*They turn to peer like curious cattle*...)
That futile labour. (*They stare*...)
Out. (*He jerks his head... They look at one another, and concede. When they have gone, GODANSK goes to his satchel... He examines the lock. He satisfies himself it has not been tampered with. He looks around him swiftly. He stoops, picks up a poem, reads it. LINDSAY enters, alerted. GODANSK screws the paper into a ball in his fist*)
Why was this not hung from the gate?

LINDSAY: (*Puzzled*...) We —

GODANSK: My satchel. Given the loss of precious time incurred by the error I had made in forgetting my satchel, and the further loss entailed in dismounting, tethering my horse and coming through the courtyards to this place in order to retrieve it, it would seem entirely proper and responsible to have hung it from a nail or better still, driven a stake into the ground so that I might have swept it up into my arms without quitting the saddle.

LINDSAY: We considered all those things. (*She stares boldly at him*...)
Arguments were advanced in favour of hanging it from the gate and driving poles into the ground. Following your tracks in relays and even more outlandish proposals were seriously entertained. We concluded however that the contents of the satchel must be of such significance, not to mention value, that

to expose them to the risk of theft by suspending them from a pole or entrusting them to servants would be a greater reck-lessness than the recklessness of obliging you to return through these labyrinthine courtyards. You ought to be grateful. There was some expense of intellectual energy and even temper entailed in this. We quarrelled. Oaths were uttered. Can I fetch you something? I like your face. It is however, coated in dust. I'll wash it. I'll kiss your mouth. Women must be forever. You left your satchel and I was the reason. Feel me beneath my skirt. Feel me. My name is Lindsay but I know the detrimental quality of names. Give me another, I'll take it as my own. I have a room on the second staircase — (VISTULA *enters...*)

He left his satchel...! But you know...!

VISTULA: The servants have stopped working...

GODANSK: I told them so.

VISTULA: You are a courier.

GODANSK: Yes, but the sight of their futile efforts obliged me to overstep my authority. It happens frequently.

VISTULA: That is an unfortunate characteristic, if I may say so.

GODANSK: I am certain it will lead to my death.

LINDSAY: He is staying for a little — I say little — why not a great deal of — refreshment...

GODANSK: (*with a slight bow*) You are too generous —

LINDSAY: Not at all —

GODANSK: I must however, refrain from losing further time —

LINDSAY: But that's absurd...!

GODANSK: Possibly, but —

LINDSAY: No, that is really, really absurd, to say you must not lose more time when already you have forfeited God knows how long by your own incompetence and now are quite pre-pared to offend the laws of hospitality by — oh, go if you want to, go, go, I've no interest in preparing meals, it's not my vocation, ask her, it's not, is it...? (*She looks at* VISTULA *... Then swiftly back to* GODANSK)

Do you like bread? My father was a wood cutter, but he did not eat bread. (*Pause...*)

I mention that because... (*She shrugs...*)

The outdoor life...air and forests...you'd think — (*He is still, his eyes on* VISTULA*...*)

Bread or not...? (*The sound of an aircraft fills the air. They are quite still as it passes, fades...*)

GODANSK: Possibly the sole advantage in having been provided with a circus animal is its relative immunity to taking
fright. The shrieks of children, the discharge of guns, brass
instruments and so on, have no perceptible effect on her, but
low-flying planes might cause her to rear and jerk the halter
from the ring, or given the antiquity of this place, pluck the
ring out of the wall... (*He turns to go. The first poems cascade
from the sky...*)

LINDSAY: Are you coming back...? (*He looks at her...*)

I ask because... I know I shall be more than a little piqued if
having gone to the expense of time and energy in making you a
sandwich you simply — (*She stops...*)

I say a sandwich, but possibly like my father, you don't like
bread...? (*Pause...*)

Leave your satchel, won't you...? (*He goes out, the satchel
over his shoulder... the two women are still in the falling leaflets...*)

VISTULA: He despises you...

LINDSAY: I don't think so...

VISTULA: Yes, he despises you and the more you —

LINDSAY: I don't think he does —

VISTULA: The more you —

LINDSAY: I don't think he despises me at all —

VISTULA: What does he care for your father's antipathy for
bread?

LINDSAY: I never had a father —

VISTULA: What —

LINDSAY: Silly —

VISTULA: What —

LINDSAY: I want a little happiness —

VISTULA: You just —

LINDSAY: Before the crisis comes from him from anyone —

VISTULA: **You just said you** —

LINDSAY: **Don't slap me.**
Don't.
You must stop slapping people. (VISTULA's *hand is
raised but the blow does not fall...*)

I lie all the time. I have always lied. I feel certain that the
crisis will cure me of lying but will it make me happy?

VISTULA: No.

LINDSAY: Exactly. I am making him a sandwich. (*She goes
out smartly. VISTULA stands in the falling leaflets...
GODANSK returns... He looks at VISTULA...*)

GODANSK: This profusion of leaflets, or more precisely, this
concentration of leaflets, which may or may not be profuse
when considered from the point of view of an overall strategy
of leafleting — the availability of pilots and of paper, of
suitably patriotic poems, etcetera — but which certainly
appears profuse when viewed from this single place, is no
more than the consequence of your isolation... (VISTULA
examines GODANSK ... *The leaflets cease*...)

Your isolation and your position relative to the road, both
of which became evident to me as I travelled here, away, and
back again... (*They do not remove their eyes from one
another*...)

The road being a ribbon of white chalk not only visible but
compelling, hypnotic to a navigator's eye and this building
notwithstanding its decay being a welcome and gratifying subject of human occupation in a landscape which is frankly
monotonous, the domain of cattle and predatory birds...
(*Pause*...)

One must also acknowledge that universal element in the
human character which prefers a safe journey to an heroic
death and see these storms of paper as a reflection of the pilot's
natural inclination to discharge his burden over an unprotected
target rather than expose himself and his crew, some of whom
will certainly be married and others mothers' sons, to the aerial
defences of a town... (*Pause*...)

VISTULA: Yes. (*Pause*...)

Yes. That was my conclusion also. (GODANSK
smiles, strokes his chin... *Pause*...)

She is taking such a long time with that sandwich —

GODANSK: Oh, please don't hurry her on my account —

VISTULA: Don't hurry her?

GODANSK: She might slip, the knife might slice her finger —

VISTULA: That's very thoughtful of you but surely —

GODANSK: Thoughtful? No, I was concerned to forestall an
accident —

VISTULA: **You're in a hurry, aren't you?** (*Pause*...)

What with this — (*She shrugs*...)

Inappropriate horse and... (*She lifts her hands*...)

Important orders, I... (*Pause*... *She shuts her
eyes*...)

People lie and... lie... and... (*Pause*...)

The way they... speak... and stand even is... (*Her
eyes open again*...)

This has to be picked up...this paper...because to be so —
supine — in the face of things is — it's not the orders of the
magistrates, it's a moral and — (*She moves swiftly to call the*
SERVANTS)

Pick up...!

Pick up...! (*She goes out...* GODANSK *does not
move...* HEBBEL *begins to stir in the bed...he appears,
having hauled himself onto the pillows...*)

HEBBEL: Killer...

GODANSK: Who...?

HEBBEL: Her...

GODANSK: Which one...?

HEBBEL: Killer... (GODANSK *turns to* HEBBEL *at
last...*)

GODANSK: What is this place...? It resembles a convent and
like many convents it seems at first glance to be fortified. The
moat, for example, whilst stagnant now, suggests some military
function, but its width is insufficient to discourage access to the
walls, and the walls themselves, whilst inordinately thick, lack
height. A determined thief could make his way into the heart of
it, given he was not discouraged by the puzzling nature of the
courtyards, none of which is connected to another except in a
wholly arbitrary way... (*He waits for* HEBBEL *to
reply...* HEBBEL *merely looks at* GODANSK...)

Notwithstanding this, it might well be a convent, since I have
observed not a few convents are located in buildings the original function of which had little or nothing to do with the
service of God... (*He waits in vain...*)

On the other hand, where is the bell...?
(*Pause...*)

The crucifix...? (*Pause... He resolutely pursues
the argument*)

Unless some persecution has obliged the women to conceal
their practises, it is hard to avoid the conclusion that despite
appearances, this place is not a convent at all, but rather —
(SHARDLO *enters with a sandwich on a plate...*)

SHARDLO: You required a sandwich...? (GODANSK
smiles...)

This is a sandwich. (*He bows his head slightly...*)
Don't please, take too long to eat the sandwich.

GODANSK: Don't take too long to eat it...?

SHARDLO: I want to wash the plate. (*Pause...* GODANSK
nods...)

You are in any case, unlikely to want to eat it slowly, given the even greater urgency that now — (*She stops, as the* SERVANTS, *with their baskets, appear and begin working on the litter...*)

Having gone without the satchel, and been obliged to retrace your steps you must be frantically impatient to make up lost time... (*She extends the plate to* GODANSK)

It stands to reason. (*He takes it...*)

GODANSK: Certainly, it would seem so given your own estimation of the situation. (*He bites into the sandwich, chews it thoroughly, swallows...*)

And I don't criticize. One who is relatively stationary enjoys a perspective of such a different order from that lent to another by his incessant mobility. It is frequently the case with the best couriers that on cresting an escarpment one's gaze detects a vastly shorter route — perhaps through woodland even a few hours earlier impenetrable to the eye — which if taken, might have halved his journey time... (*He bites again, chews unhurriedly, swallows...*)

Just such a case occurred on leaving here. Even in retracing my steps several times I might cover that same stretch and still have time to spare... (*He bites, chews, swallows...*)

But you require the plate... (*He bites again...*)

HEBBEL: Why didn't she wrap it in a cloth? (*Pause...*)

Or paper...? (*Pause... They ignore his interventions...*)

A courier is used to eating in the saddle...

Singing in the saddle... (GODANSK *finishes the final part of the sandwich*)

Dying in the saddle, probably... (*Pause...*)

Yet she provides a plate... (*Pause...*)

It's inconsistent... (GODANSK *goes smartly to* SHARDLO *with the plate. She hesitates. She accepts it.* GODANSK *turns on his heel to leave, goes three paces, stops...*)

GODANSK: This message... (*The* SERVANTS *cease... Their heads turn... Pause...*)

I don't know what it says... (*They stare... A pause...* SHARDLO *lets fall the plate, which shatters... The* SERVANTS *turn, shocked...*)

SHARDLO: Don't just stare... fetch a dustpan... quick...! (*They all turn to leave*)

Not all of you...! (*They hesitate... one goes, still looking back apprehensively...* GODANSK *has not moved... Pause...*)

How should you know...? You are the courier...
(GODANSK *looks bewildered... Then he leaves abruptly.*
SHARDLO *is still, then recovers her animation...*)

The crisis...its peculiar effects...! And that is the merest
indication of the profound and subterranean changes it will
inflict on all of us...! A courier, whose honour and efficiency
is beyond reproach, finds himself troubled by his ignorance of
the contents of his saddle-bag when that ignorance is precisely
what qualifies him for his task...! (*She shrugs, laughs...*)
Everything that seems confirmed, self-evident and beyond
evaluation suddenly is — (*She controls her pleasure...*)
            Not *suddenly...*
It will have *seemed* sudden, when viewed in retrospect... in
actual fact, it will imitate a cataclysm of the natural world
whose origins are subtle and scarcely observed... the first few
flurries of an avalanche... the rising of a river, and the uncommon anxiety of swans... manifestations of overwhelming
alteration which only the most perceptive minds — those pre-
disposed to welcome it — can sense before it topples and
crushes them beneath its debris... (*Pause...*)
If it does crush...! Some will be crushed, but others, they
will — (*Pause...*)
            Obviously emerge... (*Pause...*)
HEBBEL: Me...I... (SHARDLO *looks at* HEBBEL...)
            Shan't emerge...
SHARDLO: Not you, no...
HEBBEL: **Have I ever have I even once**
SHARDLO: (*Fatigued*) I don't know...
HEBBEL: Never
            Never
            Emerged...
SHARDLO: (*With a gesture*) I haven't the time or patience
to —
HEBBEL: And what prevented that emergence...?
SHARDLO: Others...?
HEBBEL: **Others yes**... (*She stares at him, half-pitying, half-
bemused...*)
SHARDLO: Yes...
            Yes, and how... insignificant... that suddenly
            appears...
HEBBEL: Yes, oh, yes...
SHARDLO: (*Tearing her gaze from him*) I must —
HEBBEL: Insignificance itself — (*She is departing...*)

You gave him a plate... (*She stops. She slowly turns back to him...*)

I am not stupid. How much better it would have been if I were stupid. I longed for it. You heard me, I craved stupidity. The stupid are not plagiarized. (SHARDLO *shuts her eyes in her impatience...*)

SHARDLO: You were never, never to my knowledge, plagiarized...

HEBBEL: Ha...!

SHARDLO: (*Patiently...*) As for the plate to which you are according such inordinate significance —

HEBBEL: Me...? I'm not...!

SHARDLO: **The sandwich was handed to me on a plate**...

HEBBEL: Obviously —

SHARDLO: **I did not place it on the plate, I collected it on a plate and delivered it to —**

HEBBEL: So...?

SHARDLO: **So**

So

Oh, all this is (*She shuts her eyes...*)

Going under the avalanche...! (*She strides out... The* SERVANTS *pick up paper.* LINDSAY *enters... she drifts... staring at the two* SERVANTS... *she hugs herself, for comfort...*)

LINDSAY: How splendid to live a life on horseback... (*They ignore her...*)

Of course it is easy to exaggerate the pleasure of an outdoor life... for one thing, in this particular region we are blessed with too much rain... but even rain... if you were clad in oilskins... its faint patter on your hood... might be... (*The* SERVANT *enters with a dustpan and broom and sweeps up the remains of the plate...*)

Music of a sort... I'm certain as he gallops over flooded meadows, the hooves of his white mare flinging —

THIRD SERVANT: (*Unbending again*) He's in the fifteenth courtyard, Miss... (LINDSAY *stares at the* SERVANT...)

LINDSAY: He's...?

THIRD SERVANT: (*Beating the broom on the side of the pan*) Lost. (*She goes out again...* LINDSAY *goes to follow her*)

LINDSAY: Lost...? (*She frowns*)

Lost...?

HEBBEL: I'm not particularly perceptive... (VISTULA *enters.* LINDSAY *turns to her*)

LINDSAY: He's lost, apparently...

HEBBEL: It was never the accuracy of my perceptions that I valued in myself...

LINDSAY: (*Shrugging*) Wandering in the courtyards...

HEBBEL: But all the same...

LINDSAY: (*To* HEBBEL) Shh...!

VISTULA: How peculiar...when on previous occasions he was able to negotiate the entrance he should now be sacrificing vital minutes by —

LINDSAY: I'll go to the tower —

HEBBEL: **Go to the tower yes** —

LINDSAY: (*Turning on him*) Be quiet, I said — (HEBBEL *chuckles*...)
And from the tower —

HEBBEL: **Signal him** —

LINDSAY: (*Furiously*) **Precisely my intention**. (*She leaves the room, as the* SERVANT *returns*...)

HEBBEL: **And wave...if he is unobservant...wave**...
Your skirt...
Your heart...
Your underwear... (*He laughs, mildly*...)

VISTULA: You enrage everybody...

HEBBEL: Yes...

VISTULA: By announcing what is obvious...

HEBBEL: Yes...

VISTULA: When what is obvious —

HEBBEL: Is the very thing nobody wants to hear...! (*He grins*...)

VISTULA: Yes...on the other hand...this tin whistle...this tuneless flute...of your incessant —

HEBBEL: Oh, terrible, I know —

VISTULA: It is, yes —

HEBBEL: I know, I know —

VISTULA: Grates on every —

HEBBEL: Sets your teeth on edge, I know... (*He looks at her*...)

VISTULA: Yes... (*She shrugs*)
You know... (*She is about to leave when* GODANSK *enters*...)

GODANSK: This is ridiculous...! (*She stops. He lifts his shoulders, as if bewildered*)
Since we parted I have been stumbling from one courtyard to another...! (*She turns. The* SERVANTS *look up*...)

The error was entirely mine. For some reason, on my departing here I turned left three times in succession when I knew perfectly well the opposite was the direction I required. As I wandered from place to place I tried to understand the reason for this apparently wilful miscalculation. I could only deduce that having drilled myself so thoroughly to turn right, the very recollection of the fact I had required such discipline in the first place compelled me to opt for the less familiar word —

HEBBEL: This happens —

GODANSK: This does happen, and certainly it can only be the effect of excessive repetition. I had memorized the word when I should have done better to memorize the wall, the paving, the situation of a sprouting weed, though it must be said even here the absolute similarity of things might well have rendered such a mnemonic less effective than you might expect. But this was only the beginning of my troubles... Recognizing the gravity of my error, I resorted to the expedient of whistling my horse —

HEBBEL: A courier would...!

GODANSK: A courier would not fail to summon his horse, if only to enable him to spare his legs by riding through the courtyards, and this I did, I whistled her and certainly she heard, she heard and she obeyed, her loyalty was unimpeachable, but what neither of us understood, or even having understood, would have possessed the knowledge to effectively militate against, was the wholly deceptive nature of an echo in enclosed spaces when the walls are of a certain height relative to the angle of the roofs. Thus, she always sought me in a place, which if I had visited at all, I had certainly left minutes or perhaps only seconds before she arrived there. I suffered the profound frustration of hearing her hooves clattering on cobbles which for all I knew, lined the very courtyard next to that in which I stood, yet running in this direction only rendered us further apart...! (*He looks at* VISTULA, *shaking his head*...)

Predictably, such a nightmare could only be resolved by accident. Coming past here for what may well have been the fifth or seventh time, I saw the broken pieces of the plate on which I think the sandwich had been served to me, or possibly another plate from the same service but all the same sufficient to persuade me I —

VISTULA: Where exactly were the pieces of the plate...? (*Pause*...)

GODANSK: Not far beyond the door, they —
VISTULA: I do find servants odd. (*Pause. The* SERVANTS *hang their heads* ...)

> Odd
>
> And

What is it surely not simple idleness not sullen anger sabotage or anything so malevolent as that it comes from some obscure instinct and it isn't mutiny it's (*Pause* ...)

> I wish I knew what it was ... (*Pause* ...)
>
> And sometimes they are scrupulous ...! (*She bites her lip* ...)

It could be the weather ... I am affected by the weather why shouldn't they be today for example it's oppressive and these little flies ...
HEBBEL: And still he lingers ...! (*He scoffs* ...)

I hate to say what can only spoil the comfortable and collusive nature of this silence but

> Or do I
>
> No
>
> Try honesty
>
> The unplumbed horrors of authentic honesty
>
> I don't hate it at all I like it
>
> I announce the peculiar lethargy of a courier
>
> There
>
> **Hate away ladies** ...! (LINDSAY *enters, sees* GODANSK ...)

LINDSAY: He hasn't gone ...!
HEBBEL: (*Replete with sarcasm* ...) Gone? No, he's still here ...
LINDSAY: I'm breathless ... (*She hangs her head, breathing deeply* ...)
HEBBEL: Far from gone, his footsteps are, as it were, encased in lead, no longer the swift servant of his master Mercury, he has the lumbering instincts of an antediluvian reptile for whom mud, not cloud, is his natural environment —
VISTULA: All right, lie down, now ...
HEBBEL: I will, I will lie down ... (VISTULA *goes to assist him* ...)
LINDSAY: I ran up the stairs, I'd forgotten how many flights there are ...
HEBBEL: I am lying down ...!
LINDSAY: And the view was magnificent, I had forgotten how extensive the view is on a perfect day, but I was not

there for the view...I was there to guide you through the courtyards...

GODANSK: Certainly I was in dire need of it...

LINDSAY: You were...? I looked, but I saw nothing, neither you nor your horse...

GODANSK: At the very moment you flung open the window —

LINDSAY: There isn't a window, it's a —

GODANSK: No window...?

LINDSAY: It's open to the elements —

GODANSK: At the very moment you leaned over the parapet, I discovered a vital clue to my whereabouts —

LINDSAY: Good —

GODANSK: A servant's negligence was my salvation —

LINDSAY: Good —

GODANSK: Or else I might have wandered until your cries alerted me —

LINDSAY: If they did alert you...I must admit as I leaned out it occurred to me that my voice, which is not strong, would have been borne away on the wind...

GODANSK: That's something the architect of this place never thought of...! If indeed, it ever occurred to him that the tower might be employed to guide lost messengers through the labyrinth of courtyards...! (*He laughs...*)

Your father is correct however, in his —

LINDSAY: He is not my father... (*Pause...*)

GODANSK: How strange...I could have sworn...

VISTULA: Nor mine, either...

GODANSK: Not yours, either...? (*He walks a little way, profoundly puzzled... the* SERVANTS *look at him out of the corner of their eyes*)

VISTULA: (*Detecting this*) Pick up...! Pick up...! (*The drone of an approaching airplane. The* SERVANTS *ignore* VISTULA *and gaze into the sky...it passes low... fades...* SHARDLO *enters...a pause...leaflets trickle from the sky...*)

GODANSK: (*Turning*) Whose father is he, then...? (*No one replies. The poems fall.* GODANSK *bends, plucks one off the floor. They stare at him...*)

SHARDLO: If you intend to read that, I must warn you I shall inform the relevant authorities. (*He looks at her...*)

Alternatively, you can put it in your pocket and at your own risk, examine it elsewhere. (*He is quite still*)

Certainly you may not read it here. (*He screws it into a ball and drops it on the floor*)

We have so much to do and you are a distraction (*He is still...*)

What's more, despite your official status, your continued presence constitutes a trespass —

GODANSK: Is that so?

SHARDLO: Certainly, under the law of 1909.

GODANSK: And that applies to government officials?

SHARDLO: They are included in a sub-section.

GODANSK: Sub-section 8?

SHARDLO: Exactly.

GODANSK: Sub-section 8 has always been the subject of controversy.

SHARDLO: It may well have been.

GODANSK: Some clarification was in preparation when the crisis developed, but so many details had accumulated from reports submitted by the couriers, some of whom had been abused and others physically maltreated, pursued by dogs, and even in one case, mauled by a bear that had been educated to identify him by the colour of his tunic, that it required a whole contingent of lawyers to prepare even draft legislation, but these lawyers are now scattered among the many emergency committees that have sprung up to provide for the exigencies of the crisis, causing me to conclude that however pressing the need for unambiguous codification of the law on trespass, we shall for the present need to show considerable restraint in our interpretation of the existing and unsatisfactory paragraphs... (*Pause. They stare at him...*)

Not your father, but what else could explain his... (*The leaflets have ceased...*)

VISTULA: Pick up...! Pick up...! (*The* SERVANTS *continue their task*)

SHARDLO: I am not sure you are a courier.

LINDSAY: (*Dismayed...*) Oh, but he —

SHARDLO: He has a courier's bag —

LINDSAY: Not only that —

SHARDLO: And on the bag, a badge —

LINDSAY: I wasn't referring to the badge —

SHARDLO: He could have stolen the bag —

LINDSAY: It's not the bag that —

SHARDLO: Killed a bona fide courier and —

LINDSAY: **All couriers use motorbikes.** (*Pause*... SHARDLO *is patient. She places the tips of her fingers together* ...)

SHARDLO: Forgive me, but are you suggesting that the fact of this particular impostor failing to procure a motorbike but appearing on a horse instead, is precisely the evidence that satisfies you as to his authenticity? (*Pause*)

LINDSAY: Yes.

SHARDLO: It's illogical.

LINDSAY: Yes. (*Pause*)

Yes, it is illogical, I think I intended to say that **How silly it doesn't matter to me whether he stays here or not** My point was this, that had he killed a genuine courier about whose identity there is no question, he could not have been satisfied merely to steal his satchel but, intending to mislead others, would have carried his act to perfection by appearing mounted on his victim's motorbike, that is my contention —

SHARDLO: It's dishonest —

LINDSAY: What is —

SHARDLO: What you're saying —

LINDSAY: Is it —

SHARDLO: Yes, horribly dishonest —

LINDSAY: Is it, why —

SHARDLO: **You know perfectly well** —

LINDSAY: Do I? I thought I was putting a case for something which needed clarification —

SHARDLO: (*Turning wearily away from her gaze*) Oh...

VISTULA: (*To* LINDSAY) She's right, you're lying. (LINDSAY *looks to* VISTULA, *horrified*)

And that is why she is so offends me. Look at her, quivering, throbbing, incandescent with the satisfaction of exposing your flirtation with a stranger, who, quite possibly, receives —

LINDSAY: Not a flirtation —

VISTULA: A dozen such proposals in a single ride —

LINDSAY: Not a flirtation, I said —

VISTULA: Very well —

LINDSAY: Not a flirtation at all, if you call it a flirtation again I shall do something —

VISTULA: What...?

LINDSAY: I don't know —

VISTULA: I do all the violence round here — (*She laughs, against herself*)

LINDSAY: Yes, you do —

VISTULA: I am the monster —

LINDSAY: The word flirtation fills me with disgust I hate the word and you employ it precisely to humiliate my instinct which —

VISTULA: I apologize —

LINDSAY: Which I do not deny repudiate or suffer any shame for I do not know if I love this man I simply want him to kiss me I have thought of nothing else since he came here. There. Perhaps you feel the same.

VISTULA: Certainly not.

LINDSAY: Very well, you don't. (*To* SHARDLO)

I was moving beds from the dormitory to the conservatory, shall I continue or —

GODANSK: It gives me no pleasure to be the cause of this dissension that has sprung up between you, I assure you, but whilst it might seem obvious that my swift departure would bring it to a close, things cannot be that simple...

SHARDLO: Why not? (*He declines to reply...*)

You are in dereliction of your duty, which, if you are a courier, will almost certainly result in your trial and execution, since the death penalty has been restored for the duration of the crisis and reluctant couriers will need to be made examples of, rightly in my opinion, if only to remind the population of the gravity of their situation and the new energies and disciplines that are required if they are to overcome their passive and dilatory — (*She stops...*)

On the other hand, if you are not a courier but a criminal, it is all the more necessary we eject you now and — (*She addresses the* SERVANTS)

> **Stop picking up papers now** (*They look at one another*)
>
> Yes
>
> Return to that another time (*They straighten up...*)
>
> Escort this man to the gate
>
> He has a horse I understand
>
> The horse also
>
> And shut the gate behind him
>
> Bolt it
>
> Bar it

Unpleasant but we must accustom ourselves to things which in our other life we might have flinched from

> Yes

That is how we recognize the crisis

Then come back and carry on (*The* SERVANTS *shift uneasily, exchanging glances with one another ...*)

Now, please ... (*They put down their baskets and prepare to move towards* GODANSK ...)

GODANSK: I feel sure you are making a mistake ...

SHARDLO: How? In obliging you to carry out your orders ...?

GODANSK: Quite possibly.

SHARDLO: How can that constitute a mistake?

GODANSK: I don't know.

SHARDLO: You don't know why you should not carry out your orders?

GODANSK: I cannot say with any certainty why I should not carry out my orders. On the other hand many things suggest that these orders are perhaps not the most suitable orders, or that, even given their suitability, they are being frustrated by circumstances outside my own control.

SHARDLO: (*With a glance at* LINDSAY) Her, for example?

GODANSK: It's possible that the love she feels for me, sudden and unexpected as it was, is yet another manifestation of that innate obstruction to my mission that began so long ago with the substitution of a circus horse for a motorbike ... (*Pause ... the* SERVANTS *look confused ...*)

LINDSAY: Yes ...! (*She looks to* VISTULA ... *bites her lip ...* SHARDLO *ignores this. She sways a little ...*)

SHARDLO: What you are saying is inconsistent. (*He looks at her ...*)

Every aspect of things that has hindered your journey has arrived in the form of an accident, at least as far as you are concerned. The substitution of a horse for a motorbike, the fact of the horse's unsuitability for cross-country riding, the fact that on leaving here you forgot your saddlebag, and your subsequent confusion in the maze of courtyards, all occurred apparently in contradiction to your will. Your reluctance to continue with your journey is an altogether new factor however, not circumstantial in the least, and motivated possibly by cowardice or desire for a woman who has had the misfortune to pity you —

LINDSAY: I don't pity him —

SHARDLO: (*to the* SERVANTS) Please, now, escort him to the gate.

LINDSAY: Not pity.
SHARDLO: Call it what you like.
LINDSAY: Not pity.
SHARDLO: No... (*The* SERVANTS *edge towards*
    GODANSK, *who bows very slightly to Shardo, and turns on
    his heel. He walks out smartly. The* SERVANTS *follow. The
    women are still, speechless... at last, they move, but aimlessly,
    and stop again...*)

> I felt then... (*Pause...*)
> In the middle of that argument I felt...
> (*Pause...*)

Oh, that bottomless exhaustion of the soul that's like some
vast bay in which the sea has died... is motionless... the
corpse of the sea beneath my ribs...

VISTULA: (*Extending a hand to her*) But the words came...
SHARDLO: Yes, they did... (*She shakes her head...*)

Oh, and the crisis rushes on...! Really...! I exchange these
arid syllables with some pensive stranger, but for the last time,
surely...!

VISTULA: Surely, yes...!
SHARDLO: He drew me, staggering, back towards my sui-
    cide... (*She shudders...*)

> If he comes back, it's you that must — (*She
> stops...*)
> Comes back...? Why should he come back...?
> (*She laughs, crushes* VISTULA's *hand in hers*)

HEBBEL: Of course he will... (*They are still...*)

> He will... (*Their stillness, their silence, is a
> threat...*)
> **Why should I not tell**
> **Why**
> **When nothing else at all**
> **Nothing**

**Can justify my continuing to sit the blood revolving and the
kidneys flushing liquids in their dark and thickening canals gases
excretions squeals in the bowel**

> I leak the truth... (*Pause... they look at him...*)
> From *one* orifice... (*He smiles...*)
> Malodorous commodity... (*He chuckles... they
> stare, bitterly...*)
> It's the horse, you see... (*Pause...*)
> Its musical inclinations... (*He laughs... they
> stare...*)

As long as I was loved, the truth was something I could happily forego... is it not the enemy of love, in any case... but unloved I find it has the fascination of an outlawed faith... I mutter it... I see the countenances of you all obscured by a cloud... you squirm... you look the other way... Christ announced in Mecca... Luther in Rome... (*Pause... The* SERVANTS *return... they stand, uneasily*)

SHARDLO: (*Turning to them*) Has he gone...?

SERVANTS: Yes, Miss.

SHARDLO: You saw him?

SERVANTS: Yes, Miss.

SHARDLO: Riding?

SERVANTS: Galloping, Miss.

SHARDLO: Galloping... (*She smiles...*)

You see, we recalled him to his duty...! He did not look back?

SERVANTS: Never...

SHARDLO: There you are...! The crisis has this effect on individuals, even those of criminal or idle dispositions, that they are rinsed, cleansed, wrung out of their melancholy introspection and — in a straight line, undeviating, was he?

SERVANTS: Straight for the frontier, Miss...

SHARDLO: I should have liked to see him, the cloud of dust raised by his horse's hooves... (LINDSAY *bites her lip*... SHARDLO *goes to her, holds her in her arms... The* SERVANTS *return to their work*)

This is only the beginning of so many pains, pains which will like forest leaves, thickly smother one another in the torrent of their fall... (*Pause... Her expression changes...*)

The frontier...? (*She releases* LINDSAY)

The frontier... which...? (*The* SERVANTS *are engrossed in their labour...*)

You said the frontier...

SERVANTS: (*Aroused, straightening their backs*) Miss...?

SHARDLO: Which frontier...?

SERVANTS: (*Pointing*) It's that way, Miss...

SERVANTS: Of course it is, but... (*Pause... She ponders...*)

He might well be... (*She knits her brows...*)

Why did you say the frontier...?

VISTULA: It lies in that direction —

SHARDLO: (*Crossly*) I know perfectly well the direction of the frontier, I wonder why they specified the frontier as his destination, perhaps he indicated this —

SERVANTS: He said nothing, Miss —

SHARDLO: He said nothing —

SERVANTS: Not one word —

SHARDLO: Not one word did he say and yet they assert without the slightest hesitation that he was making for the frontier, these who, for all their loyalty and capacity for unstinting labour are not known for their speculative capacities —

VISTULA: You are becoming fretful —

SHARDLO: Am I —

VISTULA: Fretful and ugly, yes —

SHARDLO: There are a hundred places to which a courier might be despatched between here and the frontier —

VISTULA: Places of no significance —

SHARDLO: Insignificant places, but who are we to judge their significance in a crisis, quite possibly the crisis has bestowed significance on farms and hamlets whose previous obscurity —

LINDSAY: Shh —

SHARDLO: **I am quite prepared to be ugly**. (*A sullen pause... at last* SHARDLO *shrugs...*)

> They don't know why they said the frontier... obviously, it was an intuition... (*She is uneasy... she lifts her hand, and lets it fall.* VISTULA *looks at the curious* SERVANTS)

VISTULA: Pick up...! Pick up...! (*The* SERVANTS *obey.* VISTULA *swiftly leaves...*)

LINDSAY: I want to see you...I want to witness you...in full possession of yourself...I always have... (*Pause...* SHARDLO *looks at* LINDSAY...)

SHARDLO: Have you...? I'm touched...

LINDSAY: Are you...

SHARDLO: Yes... (*She shrugs...*)
>   No...
>   What is it to me that you —

LINDSAY: But not at some appalling cost...to me... (*Pause...*)

SHARDLO: Too bad. (*She lifts her shoulders...*)
>   It's too bad...! (LINDSAY *stifles a reply. She leaves, bitterly...*)
>   **Am I supposed to cease becoming me for your**
>   She's gone
>   Am I supposed to fade and falter in some airless
>   half-life in order that
>   She's gone

Like some plant which instead of reaching for the sun for fear its leaves might overshadow others willingly wilts droops turns yellow in obscurity

> Anyway she's gone
>
> **I have stood five times at the door of suicide**
>
> No
>
> It's a terrible injustice
>
> Five times
>
> Twice in the moat
>
> Three times in the orchard
>
> Brought gasping from some smothering death
>
> **They prefer to pity me than that I should step into my own character**
>
> Too bad
>
> Really, just too bad
>
> She's gone I needn't (*Her hand waves in the air. She holds her cheeks in a sudden seizure . . .*)
>
> You can go, this —
>
> This —
>
> Picking up paper —
>
> Just go —
>
> Go — (*The* SERVANTS *hesitate . . . they exchange looks and then go to leave*)
>
> This frontier. (*She becomes upright, still, masterful*)
>
> It explains everything . . . (*The* SERVANTS *hesitate, then go out with their baskets, uneasily . . .* HEBBEL, *low in his pillows, observes* SHARDLO . . .)

No, it's hard to resist the feeling that not only my personality but also the objective circumstances of the world militate to bring about my death . . . (*Pause . . .*)

And when I say death I do not mean it literally I do not mean silence lifelessness extinction and so on I mean the very low habit of the morning . . . and the very low habit of the night . . . (*Pause . . .*)

The courier is delivering the message which will terminate the crisis . . . (*Pause . . .*)

It couldn't be otherwise . . . ! (*She half-laughs, she bites her lip . . .* HEBBEL's *long, thin arm reaches for her, hangs in the air. She sees it without accepting it . . .*)

You know . . .

How terrible that you know everything . . . (*She takes the hand in hers . . . she presses it to her breast . . . her hands fall . . . his hand remains . . . his fingers work at the buttons of her dress,*

*exposing her breasts. A pause, of wonder and
contemplation... The* COURIER *enters the room... neither*
SHARDLO *nor* HEBBEL *react, but are still... the*
COURIER *flings down his satchel... he leans against a
wall... a long pause elapses...*)

GODANSK: We encountered gipsies... (*Pause...*)

     These gipsies played violins... (*Pause...*)

     To be precise, one viola and three violins...
     (*Pause...*)

And whereas at one moment we were cantering, the next, the
mare had ceased in her velocity and like a puppet drawn up on
silent strings, was finely balanced on hind hooves. My aston-
ishment was matched only by my frustration when she began
to dance, to sway from side to side and drawing back her lips,
to whinny an equine accompaniment... (*Pause...*)

For a while this was humiliating... I, a courier on urgent
business and carrying a possibly significant dispatch which —
so we were constantly reminded at the Academy of Messengers
— might alter the course of History, I was mounted on a
dancing horse so captivated by the music of a band of peddlers
she would not heed even the most savage application of the
spurs...! (*He shakes his head...*)

So I came back. (*His smile disappears... His stare is fixed on*
SHARDLO. *He defies her to speak. Their gaze holds, second
after second...*)

SHARDLO: (*At last*) Yes... well, you had no choice...
(GODANSK *leans off the wall... he goes to* SHARDLO *and
taking her behind, draws her away from* HEBBEL's *feeble hand.
She emits a single gasp as he sinks with her to the floor...*
HEBBEL's *hand remains loosely in the air...*)

HEBBEL: (*Without anger or bitterness*) And this road... this
road to which the peddlers were fixed like greyhounds to a
track... though less urgently... this road could not be bypas-
sed... four gipsies with their innocuous instruments had
more power to disrupt the course of History than forts
bristling with rocket-launchers and machine guns...! (*A brief
pause...*)

The fields which stretched on either side... the meadows...
firm and flat... the courier deemed unsuitable, a certain sign of
the inevitable deterioration of imagination, I have identified
this phenomenon in other walks of life, and in this instance it is
perfectly exemplified, **The courier's fixation with the road...** (*A
brief pause...*)

You had no choice and who knows these gipsies were perhaps not gipsies at all, or if indeed they were authentic gipsies, nevertheless authentic gipsies recruited by the agents of a government precisely to distract your mare, and who, had you thrashed her into a state of continuing obedience, might have flung aside their musical disguise and shot you, yes, their quaint clothing possibly bulged with weapons...! (*He chuckles...*)

Certainly one must conclude that all things without exception have conspired to delay the delivery of the courier's despatch... even the flesh of these no-longer young young women... (*A pause... SHARDLO haul herself from the floor... she wipes her hands on her skirt... she spits at the still-prone COURIER, who makes no response... she then laughs, half-hysterical... then she spits on him again... and laughs again... she shakes her head, trying to clear her thoughts...*)

SHARDLO: These... vile acts... erupting in the middle of... (*She gestures vaguely...*)

> These... perversities of human relations are... (*She shrugs...*)
>
> Obviously... (*She draws her hands down her skirt again...*)
>
> Manifestations of the crisis...
>
> Repellent...
>
> Degenerate...

Necessary... I feel sure... (*With an effort of will she goes to leave the room. She is unsteady however, and almost collides with a wall. She regains her composure. She walks out. In the silence that follows, GODANSK climbs to his feet. An aircraft is heard approaching, low. It passes, the sound fades...*)

HEBBEL: The crisis will certainly dispose of me... and that I daresay, is its purpose... (*He laughs. Leaflets tumble from the sky...*)

Am I not entitled to view it from my own perspective? Why shouldn't I? Haven't I suffered? I am entitled to conclude that the entire cataclysm that hangs over the world has no other purpose than the disposal of a man who has outlived his time, a man who arguably was never equipped to survive his infancy but who through the untiring ministrations of a possibly deranged parent was enabled to cling to life, to describe life according to his own distorted vision, and to earn the love of certain women. But the game's up. They want the bed. For whom? Some disembowelled wretch who cannot possibly in his final agony comprehend the meaning of his ordeal but believes it to be the consequence of the grinding engines of diplomacy. On the contrary, it is no more than an element of a complex plan for my obliteration. (GODANSK *idly retrieves a leaflet...*)

I look forward to it. Long after I am disposed of, in a world replete with values no more sympathetic to me than those which now wash over the world like urine on the floor of a pitching ferry, some disordered mind will alight upon my poetry — some fragment of which has lodged behind a criminal's library shelf — and declare it —

GODANSK: (*Extending the leaflet limply*) This is yours. (*Pause.* HEBBEL *is speechless...*)

    This is... (*He screws it into a ball and throws it down with studied indifference...*)

The problem surrounding my return is complicated. On the one hand, by submitting to the musical fallibility of my mare I was only fulfilling what must have been known, if not intended, by the ministry, namely, that I should be constantly delayed by the sound of instruments, but by not exerting myself to discover an alternative route, I perhaps went further than anyone might have predicted, for an expert courier, which I was, would not allow himself to be frustrated by a gang of gipsies. On the other hand, I must confess to the magnetic effect this building and its occupants has had on me, almost certainly robbing me of that particular energy in enterprise that characterized me only a short time ago. But even that may have been calculated at the highest level. How am I to know? The fact of the matter is that the woman who was here just now not only expected me, but was glad of my return, notwithstanding my brutality towards her. I cannot deny I am profoundly troubled by this, not to say —

HEBBEL: (*Still gazing at the floor*) What do you mean, mine...? (*The* SERVANTS *appear with baskets...*)

SERVANTS: Shall we or shan't we...? (GODANSK *looks at them...*)

    One Miss says pick up, the other says not to. (VISTULA *enters. They flinch, and start to gather the leaflets into their baskets*)

VISTULA: The gates were barred...

GODANSK: Closed, certainly...

VISTULA: Barred and bolted...

GODANSK: I leaned from the saddle, pushed, and they swung open.

VISTULA: They were not barred, then...

GODANSK: Certainly not to me...but others, leaning against them in an identical way, might have found them unyielding...

VISTULA: What others?

GODANSK: Are there no others?

VISTULA: I shall study servants. I shall keep a notebook in which I faithfully record which orders they adhere to and which they choose to ignore. I shall discover the characteristics of the latter and attempt to classify them. Armed with this knowledge I shall know in advance of issuing instructions the likelihood of them ever being carried out **If we do not bar the gates people come in** (*The* SERVANTS *shrink...*)

The gates are freedom the gates permit us to discriminate between the welcome and the unwelcome they are the fulcrum of hospitality (*The* SERVANTS *are bent double with shame*)

Yes I must keep records or heaven knows my complacency will engulf me, wandering about in the absurd conviction my instructions have been heeded I do so hate to be made foolish other things solitude pain or failure I can tolerate but to be made a fool of I really I (*She writhes, she goes to the* SERVANTS...)

I shan't hit you...I shan't hit you... (*She embraces one... his face is nevertheless a picture of anxiety...*)

GODANSK: Even had the gates been barred I must tell you I think they would not have been effective. Given the narrowness of the moat and the generally poor condition of the walls, my return was probably inevitable, even were the servants as efficient as brutality or loyalty could make them But the question which presents itself is not to do with my arrival but rather the conditions under which I shall be able to achieve my third departure, if I am able to achieve it at all, given the apparent fascination this place holds for me.

HEBBEL: Besides, the mare is dead... (GODANSK *casts a swift glance at* HEBBEL...)

GODANSK: Dead...?

HEBBEL: The dancing horse, sensing how ill-equipped she was for the new conditions that will hold sway during and following the crisis, lost the will to live...and anyway, you galloped her...this heat...

GODANSK: I forgot to water her...!

HEBBEL: Well, you say *forgot*...the watering of horses is surely an instinct in a courier...?

GODANSK: (*Hurrying to the door*) She — I — (*He looks back*) These courtyards are — (*He is still...*)

You're right, I am perhaps no longer a courier. And despite the fact I carried out my tasks effectively for fifteen years this failure was certainly dormant within me, a sickness that the arrival of the necessary circumstances would unleash, like some plague bacillus dormant in the rotting timbers of a barn which an unprecedented heatwave could — (*Pause...*)

Of course I might proceed on foot... (*Pause...*)

HEBBEL: It isn't such a very heavy satchel...

GODANSK: On the contrary, it's... (LINDSAY *and* SHARDLO *enter, hand in hand.* SHARDLO *is dressed in a new, clean garment...*)

LINDSAY: (*Sadly*) Your mare's — (*She lifts her hand...*)
She —
All at once —
A felled tree —
Oh, a never-to-be-forgotten sound —
On to the cobbles of the yard —
And lay —
We ran and took her head —
We lifted it —
This mighty head in which the eyes were wide with a bewilderment and —

GODANSK: What is in the satchel, anyway? (*Pause... they examine him... furrowed with anxiety...*)
A document, perhaps...

Certainly I have always taken it for granted that the thing I transported was, if not a document, an object whose associations were so powerful that it was, so to speak, a substitute for a document, a thing which might articulate more by its very appearance, its revelation, than whole sheafs of correspondence crafted by the finest poets and most subtle diplomats working in tandem. This was the case on one occasion, when I carried nothing but an empty lipstick case, a thing of no intrinsic value or artistic interest whatsoever, but which when presented by me to a certain individual, caused her to display such agitation that I feared for my own life, and looking back to that period, I have no doubt that a number of military disasters, the decimation of promising cadets, and the obliteration of certain villages, could be traced to that transaction, though I have no evidence to substantiate my claim. In this instance however, I suspect the bag is empty. (*They stare... they fathom... SHARDLO laughs, a short half-mocking laugh...*)

SHARDLO: Certainly, that would relieve you of any urgency
   to reach your destination... (*She bites her lip...*)
HEBBEL: Why?
SHARDLO: Because if there is nothing to deliver —
HEBBEL: Precisely that nothingness is what he was required to
   carry — (GODANSK *laughs*)
                Yes...!
                My unfailing vision...!
                Yes...!
                My repellent fingering of truth...!
                Nothingness is eloquent as our masters knew...
VISTULA: (*To* HEBBEL) I think you should shut up...
HEBBEL: Yes...
VISTULA: For your own sake...
HEBBEL: Yes, I should —
VISTULA: Your life is in the balance —
HEBBEL: Is it?
VISTULA: I think so, yes —
GODANSK: Of course, it's possible I am mistaken, that this
   particular item is written on paper of so little substance as to be
   almost transparent, light and fragile as the wings of butterflies,
   but in fifteen years a courier becomes actuely sensitive to the
   minor changes in the weight of satchels and what's more the
   expression on the face of the official who handed me the bag
   was distinctly sinister, pained, clouded, as if he sensed he was
   participating in a deception the outcome of which might prove
   fatal to me but which I was nevertheless already party to. This
   expression had never to my knowledge, been attached to him
   before. (*Pause...*)
SHARDLO: Open the bag.
GODANSK: It's locked.
SHARDLO: Unlock it, then.
GODANSK: The couriers do not have keys. The key
   is —
HEBBEL: **Over the frontier...!** (*Pause.* GODANSK *turns to*
   HEBBEL...)
GODANSK: Yes... (*Pause...* HEBBEL *looks to* SHARDLO
   ...)
        That is exactly where it is. And the individual who holds it is
   almost certainly expecting me... (*Pause... they exchange
   glances with one another...*)
VISTULA: (*Observing that the* SERVANTS *are gawping*)
                Pick up...!

Pick up...! (*They bend at once.* LINDSAY *steps forward to* GODANSK)

LINDSAY: I think you have ceased to be a courier. I think whilst you feel yourself to be an honest servant of the state, loyal and diligent, the state has not been honourable to you —

GODANSK: Honourable...?

LINDSAY: Yes. I think you have been ill-used. Furnishing you with a circus horse, when it is perfectly obvious the poor animal had not been bred to ride, and then to put precisely nothing in your satchel when you are risking life and limb transporting it is a mockery of your profession.

GODANSK: Perhaps...I never thought of that...

LINDSAY: No, you are so dedicated to your vocation such ideas would not occur to you, but your loyalty is being abused and —

GODANSK: (*To* HEBBEL) If this is not a convent, what is it? (*Pause.* LINDSAY *bites her lip.* VISTULA *clenches her fist...* HEBBEL *is silent.* GODANSK *glares round the room*)

Three women and a bed-ridden architect —

HEBBEL: Architect...?

GODANSK: (*Turning on* LINDSAY) No, it is you who is dishonourable —

HEBBEL: Architect...?

GODANSK: The entire character of this place, the eccentricity of its plan, causing me to lose my horse and probably intended to swallow me up in its incomprehensible design in order that I might starve to death or suffocate in some abandoned drain, the persistent coming and going of women so patently obsessed with fornication, nakedness and erotic oblivion, and this recalcitrant and unbiddable family of ficti-tious servants, all confirms my sense I have been abducted, seduced from my proper function and made the victim of a conspiracy, notwithstanding I have chosen three times to incarcerate myself in your — (*He stops...his eyes travel the room...*)

What is that sound...?

LINDSAY: Sound...?

GODANSK: Sound, yes what is it...? (*They strain...they hear nothing...* GODANSK *looks from one to the other....*)

I am profoundly lonely, and detecting my loneliness you thought me vulnerable, whereas —

What is it a sort of ring a clock is it — (*They gawp...*)

A bell a little bell but frantic — (*He prods one of the* SERVANTS...)
Look for it... (*The* SERVANT *looks to* VISTULA *for instruction*)
Look for it, I said...! (*The* SERVANT'S *brows are knitted*...)

VISTULA: There are two hundred rooms here —

GODANSK: Go into every one — (*The* SERVANT *is pitiful*)
And the cupboards, open them —

LINDSAY: It will take all day —

GODANSK: Longer, possibly, he must be thorough, take a candle, light it, and stand it at the head of every stair, then I shall see you are methodical —
It's stopped... (*Pause. He listens, turning his head...*)
Yes... (*He smiles...*)
It's stopped... (*He looks at* HEBBEL)
I must tell you, the depths of depravity that you have plumbed, the arcane and tortuous contrivances your malice has inspired in you to lure and to trap the unsuspecting —

HEBBEL: I am not an architect —

GODANSK: **Not an architect no more am I a courier**... (*He stares fiercely at the women...*)

SHARDLO: Oh, God, you are the crisis... (*She lets her hand travel to her face...*)
It's you... (*She looks to* LINDSAY, *to* VISTULA ...*a short laugh comes from her...*)
My innocence...!
My intellectual lethargy...!
My dismal and somnolent imagination...!
I could rip my face with my nails
It's shame
It is
It is embarrassment
The humiliation of a mundane mind which entertained such — (*She laughs, shaking her head...*)
As if authentic crisis would stoop to represent itself in colours such as I described... (*Pause...*)
I have read too much. This reading inflamed my mind. Perhaps if I had never read I should not have recognized the melancholy nature of my life. I blame him. (*She indicates* HEBBEL)

362   *Howard Barker*

Yes, he is the cause, and having read so much is it surprising
that, encountering, if not the crisis, the rumour of the crisis, I
should picture it as crisis is conventionally presented? The
beds? The blood? The terrible shortages of bandages...? **I
longed to tear my dresses into shreds for some child's wounds**...
(*Pause*...)

The ordeal will not be familiar. The blow will come from the
unexpected place. And the experience will be for all its savagery, cheap... (*Pause*...)

        I daresay...

VISTULA: I nearly pitied you... so nearly pitied you I felt the
warm tears rising in the bottom of my eyes, and then...! (*She
shakes her head*...)

        You lurch from one conviction to another...

SHARDLO: Leave me alone...

VISTULA: For one brief moment I thought, she is beautiful,
she doubts —

SHARDLO: Please —

VISTULA: And then the doubt went out, like a light —

SHARDLO: Please —

VISTULA: Smothered by another galloping intransigence —

SHARDLO: **This man has violated me**... (*Pause. LINDSAY
looks with horror at SHARDLO*...)

        Yes

        And I am believe me tired of drawing your atten-
tion to — (VISTULA *scoffs*...)

        Yes

        It was five suicide attempts and now —
(VISTULA *shakes her head*)

        Yes

        Another triumph of evasion I employ it all to
suffocate your criticism —

GODANSK: **There it goes again**...! (*He listens... he strains his
hearing*...)

        Not a bell... (*Pause*...)

        Water...

LINDSAY: Violated you...?

GODANSK: Shh...! (*He is still... he looks to HEBBEL*)

Water... cascading down the shaft of some... bottomless
well... (*He looks at LINDSAY*)

The bag is locked but since the bag will never be delivered,
since I am already in defiance of the law, it can hardly com-
pound my offence to burst the lock or cut the leather —

LINDSAY: Violated her...?

GODANSK: That also will be entered against me. Fetch a tool, a knife or wrench —

LINDSAY: **But I loved you.** (GODANSK *stares at her.* LINDSAY *suddenly puts her hand to her mouth, gnawing her knuckle...*)

GODANSK: You did but I was a different person then. At that stage I was not fully apprized of my peculiar obsession with this place. I believed I was a courier. My destiny appeared to be bound up with the exigencies of the ministry. But now...! I shall never leave this place again, and your love might come back stronger from its little offence... who knows? (VISTULA *pulls a knife from her belt. For a moment,* GODANSK *falters...*)

Is that... (*He smiles, with relief...*)

For a moment I thought... I was about to remind you of the penalties for obstructing the imperial despatch, yes, that is the official terminology for murdering a messenger...! (*He removes the satchel...*)

Shall I cut it or shall you...? (*Pause...*)

The seal's intact... we only need to —

HEBBEL: **Kill him... kill him...!** (GODANSK *looks with contempt...*)

Kill him I said...! (*No one moves...* GODANSK *is wary...* VISTULA *holds the knife...*)

SHARDLO: Kill him...? But he's the crisis... (*The anticipation lingers until* VISTULA *snatches the satchel from* GODANSK *and kneeling with it, prods the brass lock with her knife, clumsily attempting to burst the lever...*)

HEBBEL: It would seem obvious to anyone who thought about it that the bag is empty, but this very obviousness, the shrillness of the logic, makes me for one suspicious. I would go so far as to say the bag is itself an element in a deception —

VISTULA: (*Nicking herself in her haste*) Ow...!

LINDSAY: What have you —

VISTULA: It's all right, it's all right, I —

HEBBEL: But whose deception? Not the courier's, I think, for whilst we are correct to regard the courier, now no longer a courier, as an ambiguous and possibly delinquent personality —

VISTULA: (*Beating the bag on the floor*) **I can't do it...!**

LINDSAY: I will —

VISTULA: No, I can do it —

LINDSAY: Your thumb's bleeding...!

VISTULA: **I know it is** —

HEBBEL: The greater and more tantalizing prospect which now presents itself is that this courier is himself no more than a whim —

VISTULA: (*Injuring herself again*) Ow...!

LINDSAY: Oh, do let someone else —

VISTULA: **I will do it go away**...!

HEBBEL: A spasm in the universal and irresistible eruption of malevolence which now engulfs the world and which like some ravenous monster emerging from the waves can be satisfied by one thing only — sacrifice —

SHARDLO: Whose?

VISTULA: **I Will do it I will I will**...!

SHARDLO: Whose   sacrifice?   (HEBBEL   *turns   to* SHARDLO...)

HEBBEL: Mine... (SHARDLO *smiles, gasps*...)

SHARDLO: Oh, the vanity of this man...I thought I was vain...but you...!

VISTULA: (*Scrambling to her feet, enraged*) All right, you do it! (*She thrusts the knife at* LINDSAY)

SHARDLO: He thinks the accumulated rage of the entire universe, the friction of the planets, the temper of animals, the boiling of youth, and wailing of widows —

HEBBEL: Yes —

SHARDLO: Storms of violence and howling packs of unrepentant criminality —

HEBBEL: Yes —

SHARDLO: All can be subdued —

HEBBEL: Yes —

SHARDLO: **And by what? His own extermination**...! **You should never have been given poetry**. (*Pause. She shrugs at her own rage*)
Funny, this indiscriminate dissemination of extraordinary qualities —

LINDSAY: I think we ought to cut it —

SHARDLO: He gets poetry, and you —

LINDSAY: Slit the leather —

SHARDLO: What did you get...? (*She stares at* GODANSK. *He shrugs his shoulders*)

LINDSAY: I'll slit it, then — (SHARDLO *slaps* GODANSK *over the cheek. He does not retaliate*...)

I am cutting the bag...! (*She sobs, against her will...*)

SHARDLO: (*Not taking her eyes from* GODANSK) Cut it, then...

LINDSAY: (*Sniffing, as she works*) It's so — I can't make any impression — (*She hacks at it with less and less resolution*)
> Perhaps it isn't meant to be — (*She falls onto her hands...*)
> **Why do you stare at him all the time...?** (*Pause. At last* SHARDLO *removes her eyes from* GODANSK...)

SHARDLO: Because he is a liar... (*Pause...*)
And liars I study with the intensity of connoisseurs transfixed by works of art... (*Pause...*)
> Perhaps I have never ceased to be amazed by it... (*Pause...*)
> The audacity of it...! (*Pause...*)
> Perhaps I like liars... (*Pause...*)
> And harbour secret longing to lie myself... (*Pause...*)
> But on a massive scale... (*Pause...*)
> Little lies I don't think I would have the patience for... (*Pause...*)

GODANSK: A liar, me...?

SHARDLO: Yes.

GODANSK: Everything I have recounted approximates as near as possible to the events as they occurred. Sometimes the order of my thoughts may have become distorted, scrambled by the effort to recollect what was after all, frequently a violent cascade of impressions not always susceptible to methodical description, but on the other hand, no sooner had I recovered my normal condition of calm objectivity but I rehearsed the situation I had recently experienced, knowing that I should at some point have to deliver a report. All this is normal practice for a courier whose accuracy must be relied upon if officials are to arrive at proper judgements yes I am a liar I love to lie the lie is everything to me the facts however are as stated... (*Pause... then* SHARDLO *goes to the satchel and picking it up, rips away the seal and releases the catch. She lays back the flap and inserts her hand*)

SHARDLO: Not empty... (*She does not withdraw her hand...*)

HEBBEL: **I said** —

VISTULA: Yes —

HEBBEL: **Not empty I said** —

VISTULA: We heard you —
HEBBEL: **I said**
         I said
         Oh God
         My
         Terrible
         My
VISTULA: Shh...
HEBBEL: Don't look at it —
VISTULA: Shh...
HEBBEL: **Neither locked nor empty**
         I'm unforgivable
         I'm all the world detests
VISTULA: (*Losing patience at last*) Oh, shut up...!
HEBBEL: (*Grasping her, pulling her close to him*) Is it not extraordinary? Confess it is extraordinary...!
VISTULA: **It's grotesque**... (*Pause*)
HEBBEL: Yes, it is...! It is grotesque... (*Pause...*)
         It is grotesque and must be punished... (*Pause...*)
    Look if you wish... (*Pause, then* SHARDLO *swiftly withdraws her hand. It contains a small and faded photograph. She does not examine it, but lets it hang at her side...*)
SHARDLO: I'm hesitating... (*Pause...*)
    And this hesitation can only be a consequence of anxiety... (*Pause...*)
    Why should I be anxious...? (*She looks at* HEBBEL...)
    When what is in the bag was never — however great its significance for the future of the world — never intended for me...? (*Pause...*)
    Most likely it will be meaningless, a — (*She swiftly, wilfully, casts a glance at it before turning it aside again...*)
                    It is... (*Pause...*)
                    Meaningless... (*She snatches another glance...*)
                    It's... (*She shrugs... she shakes her head...*)
                    A schoolboy... (*Pause...*)
GODANSK: It never occurred to me the satchel was not locked... (*He smiles wistfully...*)
    Always we underestimate the flexibility of the officials, as if routine alone would guarantee the unfailing repetition of an action, but no, still they are able to discriminate —
LINDSAY: A schoolboy...?
GODANSK: I must have made a thousand journeys for the ministry and every time the bag was locked, I'm certain of it,

and locked for the very good reason that the contents were of particular significance, state secrets and so on, and now, on this solitary occasion, which also happens to be my last mission, albeit I was unaware of this on setting out, the item I am the bearer of is of so little import that —

LINDSAY: We don't know that. (*Pause...*)

Whether this document, which happens to be a photograph, is of significance or not, depends on its many meanings. For all we know, this schoolboy's face might be sufficient on its own to cause a revolution, and the fact your bag was never locked might only be a reflection of the terrible anxiety that this official suffered even in handling it, you said yourself he had a strange look on his face, no, the only useful subject for interrogation must be this — what is this child's identity? (*She laughs nervously. She bites her lip...*)

Surely...? (*Pause...*)

You see, I think like you...! Isn't that a certain sign of love? (*Pause...* SHARDLO, *without examining it again, extends the photograph to* LINDSAY. *She collects it. She looks it...*)

LINDSAY: (*To* GODANSK) It's you... (*In the ensuing silence,* HEBBEL's *deep and guilty laugh comes from the bed...*)

HEBBEL: I knew...
                   I knew...

VISTULA: Of course you knew...

SHARDLO: The messenger has nothing to deliver but himself... (*Pause...* GODANSK *takes the photograph from* LINDSAY *and examines it...*)

And this spectacular redundancy is the triumph of the crisis...

LINDSAY: (*Perplexed*) The official looked sad...!

SHARDLO: Obviously he looked sad...! He knew never in his life would he dispatch a messenger again... the crisis will see to that... this sad expression was undoubtedly the melancholy of a man who knows the world had ended... in its existing form... (*She looks at* GODANSK...)

A similar expression no doubt could have been seen inscribed on your face when this building with its spires and turrets came into view... a sense of profound helplessness, such that even to lift a finger to avert it, to effect the slightest correction of the circus horse's rein and thereby pass it at a distance, seemed... (*Pause...*)

Infantile... (*Pause... The throb of aircraft engines fills the air. The* SERVANTS, *exchanging swift glances, fling down their*

*baskets and rush out.... The rest remain motionless, anticipating
the fall of bombs or leaflets. The engines fade ... nothing falls ...)*

GODANSK: They have ceased to value poetry ... at least, as a
means of coercion ... from this moment on, poetry is restored
to its original function ...

HEBBEL: It has no function ...

GODANSK: So you say and yet it was your verses that were
being scattered across the land ...

HEBBEL: Mine ... ?

GODANSK: Yes, and without regard to copyright. The most
powerful and yet most private sentiments of a distinguished
mind drifting in profusion over a landscape inhabited largely
by cattle not one of whom —

HEBBEL: *(Intuitively disturbed)* I am an architect —

GODANSK: Was observed to do more than flick its tail in
irritation —

HEBBEL: An architect, you said so yourself —

GODANSK: As if a swarm of flies had descended from the
heavens to add to their bestial burdens

> **You are a poet and these are your daughters**
> Yes
> The courier discerns
> The courier detects
> Intuitive the courier

You have suffered long enough the indifference the abuse the
plagiarism and now the wholesale dissemination of your work
taken out of context and on paper of such dire quality I cannot
see you squirm a moment longer let us pray the crisis will
destroy a world which could not tolerate your dazzling super-
iority —

HEBBEL: **I am an architect** —

GODANSK: *(Going to the bed)* Up now, your terrible ordeal is
nearly over — *(He flings back the blankets and seizes* HEBBEL
in his arms. The women stare fixedly ...)

HEBBEL: The courier's a murderer ...! *(*GODANSK *hoists*
HEBBEL *over his shoulder and starts to go out with him. At
the entrance, he stops. The horrified face of* HEBBEL, *mouth
open but now speechless, appeals to them over* GODANSK's
shoulder. His lips move. After some seconds, GODANSK *turns,
concealing the old man ...)*

GODANSK: No words, which for a poet, must be death ... *(He
walks out with the old man on his back. The women avoid each
other's eyes ... a pause ... the distant and sudden eruption of*

HEBBEL's *cries... the women remain still, then, by tacit agreement, they go to the bed and strip, folding the blankets and sheets between them in a businesslike manner. The cries fade with distance. The women work...*)

PART TWO

A WELL

The bed is stripped down to the mattress, the blankets folded on top. The women stand posed about the bed. They are silent. GODANSK returns...

GODANSK: I found the well... (*They look at him...*)
The well I first thought was a clock... (*They look blankly...*)
You did not know there was a well...? (*They stare...*)

Peculiar because at first this place was like a maze to me but now it is as familiar as a kitchen must be to a cook... I can put my hand to anything. I found the servants cowering and told them to dig a grave for the no-longer dancing horse. In this heat corruption is accelerated and we must consider — (*He stops... he moves his mouth thoughtfully... he walks a few paces, and turns back to them...*)
Forgive me. (*Pause...*)

I have lived a life of virtual solitude and this whilst not obliterating the natural delicacy of my feelings has to some extent robbed me of the facility of expressing them... (*Pause...*)

Naturally, you will look on me with some distaste for having performed a task which —

SHARDLO: Yes. (*GODANSK slightly inclines his head...*)
On the other hand, it was the very thing that he predicted.

GODANSK: Quite.

SHARDLO: And not only predicted. He craved it.

GODANSK: Yes.

SHARDLO: His horror of death, whilst painful to observe, was nothing more than the apprehension which attends on every moment of decision —

GODANSK: Quite so —

SHARDLO: And if the decision was not, strictly speaking, his own, we all know how frequently he invoked his death as something intimately bound up with the crisis —

GODANSK: I heard him myself —

SHARDLO: I am not without feelings —

GODANSK: On the contrary —

SHARDLO: On the contrary, yes, if anything I am encumbered with an excess of feeling —

GODANSK: Perhaps —

SHARDLO: We all are, we all have this tendency to extremes in our emotions which he separately detected and almost certainly exploited, but in the new conditions of the crisis this feeling of affection rapidly acquired the character of history, I think I speak for all of us when I say the passions we had known for him were not recognizable any more, were impossible to recall, and if by some strenuous effort of imagination one could evoke the actions which desire had driven us to perform, a powerful embarassment caused it to be swiftly repressed again.

VISTULA: (*To* GODANSK) If you had not disposed of him, she would have.

SHARDLO: Yes, I don't flinch to confess it.

VISTULA: She flinches at nothing at all, but why should she, she is magnificent, and the man who both created and subsequently maimed her character, paddling at this moment in a pitch black well from which he never can emerge, has already shrunk to occupy an infinitely obscure corner of her memory, a well itself, down which no bucket of recollection will ever plunge, I daresay —

SHARDLO: Possibly not —

LINDSAY: (*To* GODANSK) Surely you — before you dropped him — slit his throat or something —

GODANSK: I'm not sure that I did —

LINDSAY: Not sure you —

GODANSK: I didn't, no, I tipped him in —

LINDSAY: Alive...?

GODANSK: Alive, yes, I distinctly heard him cry as he —

LINDSAY: **Heard him cry** —

GODANSK: Yes —

LINDSAY: Where...! Where...! (*She goes to attack* GODANSK, *who seizes her wrists to protect himself*)
                    Where...!

SHARDLO: It doesn't matter where —

LINDSAY: I'll call to him...!

SHARDLO: Call what...?

LINDSAY: **Where is the well**... (*She glares at* GODANSK *...She struggles...*)

           The well... (*She struggles. She stops*)

           Where is it...? (GODANSK *does not reply... pause...*)

SHARDLO: I think, looking at it from every point of view, to have you calling over the rim some shame or consolation will only serve to prolong his struggle, lend him hope, or even stimulate him to yet another effort of valetudinary poetry, whereas abandoned and alone, his spirit, like some guttering candle, will be extinguished all the quicker.

VISTULA: That's perfectly true, but how can she forgive herself for suppressing an impulse which, however it might actually contribute to another's pain, is nevertheless spontaneous, human and —

SHARDLO: I don't know. (*She looks boldly at* VISTULA. LINDSAY, *slack, is freed by* GODANSK. *She thoughtfully massages her wrists...*)

LINDSAY: If I have to forgive myself for that, must I not also forgive myself for failing to intervene when the courier, barely disguising his intentions, carried off the old man in the first place? The fact that I love the courier and will continue to love him no matter what terrible acts he perpetrates can't relieve me of —

GODANSK: Shh... (*He listens acutely...*)

LINDSAY: Forgiveness is an aspect of the crisis which —

GODANSK: Shh... (*Pause...*)

           I should have cut his throat... (*Pause...*)

           Another time I — (*Pause...*)

    Purely for my own peace of mind, given the state of my hearing, I ought to have — (*He listens...*)

    Or beat his head against a wall — (*Pause... he is suddenly animated*)

    One must live with the consequences of one's actions, or more precisely, with the consequences of the actions one failed to perform —

SHARDLO: We are in your debt but the crisis alters everything, even the relationship of creditors to debtors. If you set off now, you can find some lodging before it's dark. (*Pause...*)

GODANSK: Set off...? (*Pause...*)

SHARDLO: Yes.

GODANSK: But I am not a courier.

SHARDLO: You are not a courier but —

GODANSK: Absolutely not a courier and I have met my bride.

SHARDLO: Carry her with you. (*Pause . . .* GODANSK *stares at* SHARDLO . . .)

I am not going to be destroyed by you. The man who five times brought me to the edge of self-destruction is drowning in a well. This well he trod over for fifty years not knowing of its existence.

LINDSAY: (*To* GODANSK) We'll go. (*She extends a hand . . .*) We'll go and — (*Pause.* GODANSK *looks at her. A darkness fills her gaze . . .*)

I'm not the bride . . . (*Pause . . .*)

I love you, but the bride's not me . . . ? (*Her hand falls . . .*)

When you were here the time before . . . the time . . . of your first or second visit I can't remember which I made you a sandwich —

VISTULA: Second —

LINDSAY: Second visit, was it, and having made this sandwich I could not deliver it —

VISTULA: She wanted to —

LINDSAY: I wanted to but great as this wanting was I wanted even more for you to suffer the fact that I failed to return with it, I wanted my absence to wound you and in wounding you to inform you of a need that perhaps had not been fully recognized —

GODANSK: It was not recognized at all —

LINDSAY: Not then —

GODANSK: Nor at any other time —

LINDSAY: No, I had entirely misjudged things —

SHARDLO: It was I who delivered the sandwich —

LINDSAY: She delivered the sandwich and as a consequence — it's all so obvious in retrospect — she became the object of your fascination —

GODANSK: Not at all —

LINDSAY: No?

GODANSK: The violence of my actions towards her later on was conditioned by so many things I hesitate to place them in any order —

LINDSAY: Try —

GODANSK: I will try —

LINDSAY: I have said I love you and this love will not be bruised by truth I assure you, rather the truth will strengthen it —

GODANSK: Is that so?

LINDSAY: I affirm it absolutely —

GODANSK: Notwithstanding the fact I never for one moment have regarded you as either my lover or my bride?

LINDSAY: Even so —

GODANSK: Very well, then I can state with certainty that my behaviour was compelled not by any powerful feeling I harboured for her, either as a consequence of her delivering the sandwich or of my recollecting her at any moment during my last attempt to leave, but purely from observing her body fondled by the old man now swimming in the well, a touch of such profound possession, so intimate and yet so unresisted, I was seized by a rage of envy, a passion for usurpation swept over me whose origins lay in my first glimpses of this place. It was a touch which for all its beauty condemned the senile poet to his death. (*Pause . . .*)

SHARDLO: It is impossible to like you . . . but you have perhaps dispensed with liking, or with being liked. So have I. And far from being humiliated by your announcement that I was, in my indignity, merely an instrument of your malevolence, I feel cleansed by it —

VISTULA: Shh —

SHARDLO: Why shh, nothing was more loathesome to me than the idea that this inept and misappropriated courier —

VISTULA: Shh —

SHARDLO: Should have entertained feelings of insatiable desire for my naked flesh —

VISTULA: You are too shrill —

SHARDLO: I am not shrill in the least I am expressing my satisfaction with his account of my ordeal, I might have been a chair, I might have been a cabinet, on which he could wreak some petty havoc with a knife, I assure you I feel wholly and completely disassociated from a sordid transaction which threatened to — (*She stops. A silence imposes itself . . . Pause . . .*)
            I heard him . . .

LINDSAY: Yes . . .

SHARDLO: Calling —

LINDSAY: Crying —

SHARDLO: My name —

LINDSAY: Yours, yes —

SHARDLO: Terrible, I —
LINDSAY: Yours because —
SHARDLO: Mine, why —
LINDSAY: Because you —
SHARDLO: (*To* GODANSK) Has the well a cover?
GODANSK: A cover...?
SHARDLO: A lid, a cover, yes —
GODANSK: I don't recollect a cover, but I was agitated and
   quite possibly failed to observe the existence of an object
   which, whilst not altogether familiar to me, would certainly,
   in other circumstances, have represented itself to me as — (*The*
   SERVANTS *enter, pale with fear*...)
SHARDLO: It's all right, we know — (*They point, with falter-
   ing fingers, to the depths of the house*...)

> We know
> We know
> All about it
> Is the pit dug for the horse
> A deep pit
> Horses are so huge
> So very huge
> And what you've dug is certainly inadequate
> The rains
> The frost
> A little soil erosion
> Up come the hooves
> No
> Deeper, please

VISTULA: Deeper
SHARDLO: Yes
VISTULA: Deeper, please
SHARDLO: (*Turning abruptly to* GODANSK) It's self-evident
   to me that whoever constructed the well would not have failed
   to supply a lid for it —
GODANSK: It is a very ancient well —
SHARDLO: So what — (*The* SERVANTS *have not left. She
   turns on them*)

> Dig...!
> Dig...! (*They edge out*...)

GODANSK: Far older than the house —
SHARDLO: Quite possibly —
GODANSK: I am not an archaeologist but the most cursory
   glance convinced me that the well is Roman —

SHARDLO: Is that so? And did the Romans not place covers on their wells?

GODANSK: I am not an expert in —

SHARDLO: They preferred perhaps to fall headlong into them?

GODANSK: I couldn't say, I am only attempting to suggest that the lid provided by the Roman well-diggers has certainly at some stage in the passage of time either decayed or more likely, been appropriated, possibly for firewood —

SHARDLO: If the lid was wooden —

GODANSK: (*Coldly*) If it was wooden, yes... (*Pause... they glare at one another...*)

Whereas, if it were iron — (*Pause...*)

SHARDLO: I must go to the well —

VISTULA: I don't think you should go to the well —

SHARDLO: **I must do, mustn't I**... (*She appeals to the women...*)

It was my name he called... (*They frown...*)

When I get to the well —

GODANSK: It is a hundred metres deep... (*Pause...*)

SHARDLO: Arriving at the well I —

GODANSK: I discerned the depth more by accident than design. In stepping back from having tipped the poet in I clumsily dislodged a section of the coping stone, which fell away and plunged after him. I counted the seconds, being careful to distinguish the first splash from that which followed afterwards. I calculated the rate of acceleration as —

SHARDLO: Why me, though...? (*Pause...*)

Certainly, in his extremity, he might have many reasons for privileging my name above all others — (*She flinches...*)

There it is again... (*Pause...*)

Certainly it cannot be assumed this choice is a mark of favour, the expression of a deeper love, on the contrary, it might merely be a testament to my greater efficiency... his estimation that I am more equipped to extract him from the well than either you... or you... (*She bites her lip, looking at the other women all the time...*)

LINDSAY: I'll come with you... (*Pause...*)

Standing either side of the well-hole we could lean out, clasp hands and thereby look down directly to the depths whereas alone you could only perch precariously on the rim

You do not wish to join him do you

Say

Say if you do

I don't

Myself I

Speaking as truthfully as possible I must say whereas I now regret failing to prevent

To speak

To anything

Now he is gone I

SHARDLO: I shan't leap in... (*Pause*...)

Or, more precisely, I shall not leap in drawing you after me... (LINDSAY *smiles. She extends a hand to* SHARDLO, *who accepts it. They go out.* VISTULA *remains, still, her gaze on* GODANSK ...*a pause elapses*...)

VISTULA: I'm not certain if I wish to be your bride. (*Pause*...)

What is a bride in any case? I've never been one. (*Pause*...)

Presumably it's ecstasy. (*Pause*...)

I've had ecstasy. (*Pause*...)

Never in a white dress but I've had it

Yes

Let's (*Pause...he does not remove his gaze from her*...)

And afterwards, the grim, slow grind of our degeneration —

Yes —

I —

Why not —

Yes —

Yes — (*The* SERVANTS *enter, uneasily*)

What is it now the hole can hardly have got deeper can it in five minutes you are peculiar it is as if having declared the hole completed no amount of argument or logic can persuade you to return to it I'll look and if it's shallow I will — (*She stops, turning to go. She looks at* GODANSK)

Yes (*Pause*)

The word's —

I like the word... (*She goes out. The* SERVANTS *hang in a group, moving like weed in a current*...)

GODANSK: Say, then...! (*They lift their eyes to him*...)

Say what this place — (VISTULA *enters briskly*...)

VISTULA: Ridiculous...! The hole is... (*She lifts her hands*...)

You saw the horse...

How can you dig a hole which is so completely unrelated to the proportions of a horse...?

I — (*She is speechless with disbelief*...)

Go and measure the horse. (*They begin to move off*...)

Wait. (*They stop*...)

When you have measured the horse, mark out the width and length of it, with chalk, using the excavation that already exists

Do not begin another hole

The depth of the existing hole is more than adequate

It must however be extended

Hugely extended

In all directions (*They start to move*...)

Wait. (*They stop*...)

There is something in your attitude which is so grudging and reluctant I

Why when the necessity of burying the horse is obvious to all

Do you want to be ill

Do you like diseases

Stench

Flies

Maggots

When the hole is finished attach ropes to the horse's hooves and pull it to the hole

Hurry please (*They go off, swiftly*...)

I am not a bad person

I would not hesitate if I were bad to say so

I know what badness is

I've seen it

Oh, the real thing

Kiss me

Kiss me but in such a way I (*SHARDLO enters. GODANSK and VISTULA look at her. She looks boldly at them*)

SHARDLO: This well is peculiar. (*Pause*...)

I know nothing whatsoever about wells but looking at it from a general point of view it would seem to me that falling fifty metres down a well-shaft, suffering the glancing blows that

would inevitably be inflicted during the descent, and plunging
into ice-cold water which might, if shallow, not even serve to
soften the impact, could only impair an old man's grasp on life.
(*Pause . . .*)

    Not so . . . (*Pause . . . she perches on the side of the bed, her
hands loosely clasped . . .*)

    He is if anything, restored to vigour . . . (LINDSAY *enters,
pale with horror . . .*)

LINDSAY: He shouted at me . . .

SHARDLO: I heard . . . (*She shakes her head . . .*)

    This is a crisis, obviously, but not the one I wanted, the crisis
I required was altogether more — universal, horrifying, and
sublime, whereas this is, if anything —

        No, it is —

        It is horrifying —

GODANSK: The water is restorative. (*They turn to look at
him . . .*)

    What other explanation is there . . . ? The Romans built it as
a spa. This well, and possibly others, is situated over a stream,
a spring, whose contents are so rich in minerals that even a
brief immersion is sufficient to —

SHARDLO: (*Standing with decision*) The well must be filled in.
(LINDSAY *looks to* GODANSK, *to* VISTULA)

        Tell the servants —

VISTULA: They are digging a hole —

SHARDLO: The hole must wait —

VISTULA: The horse is putrefying —

SHARDLO: I recognize the odour of corruption just as well as
you — Why does he shout my name . . . ? Why me . . . ? Why not
you also . . . ? He is persecuting me . . . he hates me . . . (*To*
LINDSAY)

        Call the servants . . .

VISTULA: **The servants are fully occupied** (*Pause . . .*)

SHARDLO: Now, wait a minute —

VISTULA: **I am the bride** (*Swiftly, to* LINDSAY)

        Forgive me but I am

        I am

        I am

        And this

        Ask him

        This carries with it certain

        Surely

        Certain privileges

Such as
LINDSAY: But you don't love the courier —
VISTULA: Don't I —
LINDSAY: No, you don't —
VISTULA: **You make too much of love**...! (*Pause*...)

Forgive me, but we are familiar with your claims on this man —
LINDSAY: How can you marry without love? (*Pause*...)
VISTULA: I know nothing of marriage. I only know I am the bride. (*She turns to* SHARDLO)

Take the servants. Possibly the rubble which has been excavated for the horse's grave could be employed to fill the well. I have never set eyes on a wheelbarrow, but he had no antipathy to wheelbarrows that I recall, and if there are no wheelbarrows, let them transport it all in buckets —
GODANSK: Or failing buckets, bowls —
VISTULA: Bowls, yes, or cups for all I care...!
           Kiss me
           I am submitting myself to an ordeal...
           (SHARDLO *hesitates, wavers, leaves*...)
           An ordeal she envies, it appears... (*Pause. She wipes her hands on her skirt.* SHARDLO *enters again, seething*... *She goes to* VISTULA...)
SHARDLO: Kiss you...? (*Her eyes close*...)

You are smothering your responsibilities in the fiction of a life which cannot possibly occur, the spurious propositions of an uninvited stranger who has insinuated himself into the melancholy grave of your ambition and like some thrusting weed has cracked you open, split your walls and tilted you until
           I am not the well
           You also are the well
           The well is all of us

Let us all kiss but with the joy that makes a kiss ignite the soul a blaze a conflagration please
           My name
           My name again (*She raises a fist, clenched, and lets it fall*...)
           His kisses were like that
           Did you think so
           Only in kissing did his horror recede
           Some childlike rage
           Some precious and unguarded extravagance
           Oh

We never exchanged the details of these intimacies
Never in so many years discussed the subject of
our servitude
Until he's dead perhaps that isn't possible ... (*She
goes out ...*)

GODANSK: How hard it is not to be a messenger ... (*he walks
idly across the room, stops, turns back to* VISTULA ...)

Already I feel the terrible lethargy that comes not from
inactivity but from ceasing to occupy a vital function in the
organization of affairs, if it is organization, it is perhaps not
organization at all only the counterfeit of it, but all the same
You did not indicate the old man was your lover (*He turns to*
LINDSAY)
        And yours also it appears
        I should have known
My instincts were keener once a glance was adequate to
know the entire order of a household
                Its contracts
                Frauds
                Defaulters
Perhaps I was already failing perhaps had I succeeded in
delivering the final message and even in returning with an
answer I should have been retired nothing escapes the officials
I have seen retired messengers they grapple always with the
agony that at some point in their careers their unsuitability was
revealed but where the ministry is silent on this point they
cannot sleep they stare at the horizon even retrace the journeys
of their final years sometimes are found dead in their mildewed
uniforms it is only hours since I ceased to be a messenger and
already —

VISTULA: I will give you messages — (*He casts a withering
glance at her ... she is bold ...*)
        Why not
        Why not my messages?
        My messages might be more
        Yes
        Even more
        Imbued with significance than (*He turns away ...*)
        Yes ...! (SHARDLO *hurries through the room, her
        hands uplifted as if she had touched something loath-
        some.* LINDSAY, *shocked at her appearance, hur-
        ries after her. Immediately, both surge back into the
        room*)

SHARDLO: **He likes the well** (*She paces furiously up and down...*)

Not only the well (*She continues pacing, and stops...*)

All that falls down the well

VISTULA: Sit down —

SHARDLO: Sit down yourself —

VISTULA: I'll fetch a bowl —

SHARDLO: Yes —

VISTULA: A towel —

SHARDLO: Yes —

VISTULA: Soap and so on —

SHARDLO: Soap, yes — (*the* SERVANTS *appear as* VISTULA *is about to hurry for a basin and water...*)

SERVANTS: **We can't do this**

VISTULA: Just wait...!

SERVANTS: **We can't**

We can't

We can't do this (*They wail, their hands hanging at their sides...* VISTULA *hurries out...* SHARDLO *lies on the mattress...* GODANSK *observes the spectacle with a certain detachment...*)

LINDSAY: Why not? What prevents you doing it?

SERVANTS: **He's in there, Miss...!**

LINDSAY: He's in there, yes, and the horse is in a similar position —

SERVANTS: **But he's not dead** —

LINDSAY: Don't argue...! Always you argue...! Always you are reluctant...! What have you ever done that you were not driven to...? (*They hang their heads...*)

The horse is dead, and he is so nearly dead that... (*Pause... she bites her lip...*)

There is a difference but... in perfect justice one must say that whereas the horse was an innocent and inoffensive creature... he was so critical of life... so argumentative and recalcitrant... to bury him is not comparable to the burial of any other individual who might happen to have fallen down a — (*She falters...*)

He requires it and so do we. (VISTULA *returns and proceeds to wash* SHARDLO's *hands.* GODANSK *is pondering the photograph...*)

GODANSK: It's obvious that in the bottom of a well a man might be the subject of terrible perceptions that had evaded

him in every other circumstance of his life. This flood of perfect
knowledge would certainly compensate him for the many
terrifying aspects of his situation and with certain men of
intellectual character, render the place preferable to the mundane influences of daylight, nourishment, human company,
etcetera, that he was accustomed to in the world above. I
think — to choose only one among many devastating
truths that must certainly have presented themselves to him
— he can only be luxuriating in the dazzling discovery that
in choosing from a world of women three to adore and be
adored by, he was simultaneously selecting the agents of
his own extinction. What distinguished them and at the
same time delighted him, however it was unappreciated at
the time, was their common capacity for murder... (*He
shrugs...*)

No wonder he is unaffected by cascading bricks. Possibly he
experiences the bricks as massage... (*Pause...*)

LINDSAY: (*To the* SERVANTS) Continue, please. (*They
decline to move...*)

Filling the well... (*They are stubborn, whilst avoiding her eyes...*)

Or you will join him in there... (*They exchange
terrified glances.* SHARDLO *climbs off the
bed*) (*To* SHARDLO) They must do as they are
told —

SHARDLO: Yes —

LINDSAY: Mustn't they —

SHARDLO: Yes —

LINDSAY: (*to the* SERVANTS) Go out and fill the well....!
(*She turns back at once to* SHARDLO...)

I am not happy —

SHARDLO: No one is —

LINDSAY: How can I be? How can I be happy?

SHARDLO: I don't know, perhaps by ceasing to desire it —
(LINDSAY *swiftly, unreflectingly, smacks* SHARDLO... *in
horror, she bites her fingers...* VISTULA, *shaking her head,
faintly laughs...*)

It's all right...

It is — (LINDSAY *makes an uncompleted gesture
of regret...*)

I do enrage...I always have...enraged...the
universe...

VISTULA: The universe...

SHARDLO: Clouds...fields of wheat...yes...boats at their moorings...fret...jostle...when I appear... (*She turns to the* SERVANTS...)

He cannot be recovered from the well, he is profoundly altered and so are we. The world is furthermore, no longer what it was. All this makes it impossible to even contemplate the restoration of the conditions that originally prevailed. On the contrary, we must move with the current of events. That is what she meant by saying you would join him in the well. If you do not embrace the future you will be consigned to the damp dark of the past. That is what she meant and I agree. Now let us finish what we have begun. (*They shift... squirm...*)

You transport the bricks and I will drop them in. (*They twitch... their feet lift and fall again...*)

I can and so can you... (SHARDLO *leads. They follow... The remaining women stare, open-mouthed... the hiatus is ended by* GODANSK, *who goes to the mattress and lies on it...*)

GODANSK: I must confess a certain chill suffuses me when in spite of my reluctance I am at intervals drawn, as if by a morbid fascination, to contemplate the remainder of my life. A peculiar blindness descends on me, such as I have on rare occasions known in blizzards or in fogs. I cannot discern what lies ahead. This does not in itself prevent my making progress, only this progress is predicated on an act of faith, namely, the existence of the road. Quite possibly the road has finished, or worse, leads into a gravel pit...quicksands...or over a cliff... (*Pause...*)

The one who is my bride... (*Pause...*)

Surely she should remove my boots...? (*Pause... VISTULA goes to obey his order. But LINDSAY fixes her by the shoulder...pause...* GODANSK *is perfectly still, as if asleep...* SHARDLO *returns, alone... they look to her...*)

SHARDLO: His cries have ceased... (*Pause...*)

Or... (*She shrugs...*)

If they have not, I have ceased to hear them. And since they were addressed exclusively to me, that is all that needs concern us... (*She turns suddenly to them...*)

Oh, do admire me my (*She cannot find a word... pause...*)

Capacity to love... (*They are puzzled...*)

Things... (*Pause...*)

No, of course you can't... (*Pause...*)

You can't... (*Pause*...)

You dare not... (*She laughs, stopping at once. Without turning, she senses the reappearance of the servants in the door*...)

Keep filling...!

Keep filling the well...! (*They seem unmoved by her exhortations... they shift... a faint air of embarrassment surrounds them*... SHARDLO *turns to them*)

It must be filled... to the top... and then, paved over... (*She laughs, short*...)

Quick...! (*They do not move, but instead point to the bed where* GODANSK *lies*...)

Yes...? (*They point with more emphasis...* SHARDLO *turns to look in the direction they indicate*...)

The courier is not a servant. He does not dig or fill. Surely three of you can — (*She stops, and goes towards the bed. She looks at the body of* GODANSK, *then back to the* SERVANTS...)

Oh, you — (*She gasps in wonder. She turns to* VISTULA...)

Are they not the most —

And I think I —

I flatter myself I —

They do not want to dig another hole...! (*She bites her lip... disbelief suffuses her...* LINDSAY, *looking in horror from* SHARDLO *to the* SERVANTS, *rushes to the bed and stares at the still form of* GODANSK...)

I think —

What do you think —

I think beside the horse —

Whilst I did not sense in him any great affection for the horse, there is a certain obvious —

And to cast him in the well would I think be —

Could you bear that —

I don't think you could —

And the satchel, obviously...! (*She goes briskly to the satchel and plucks it off the floor.* LINDSAY *remains staring at the body of* GODANSK. SHARDLO *stops, the satchel hanging from its strap*...)

LINDSAY: Why not the well...? (SHARDLO *shrugs*...)

I'm not the bride but — (*The* SERVANTS *look from one of the women to another, attempting to follow the debate.*

LINDSAY *suddenly snatches the photograph from* GODANSK's *grasp where it has been clasped...*)

Not the bride but entitled to my own opinion and — (*To* VISTULA) **I'm not parting with this so do not try to make me —**
I think the well
I do
I (*She holds it out...*)
What a serious face...! (*She kisses it, deeply...*
VISTULA *suddenly marches to the body and tugs off the boots. She places the boots side by side...*)

SHARDLO: (*To the* SERVANTS) In the absence of any unanimity on the subject of the interment of the courier —

VISTULA: I don't care —

SHARDLO: My own preference for the grave of the dancing horse being almost certainly affected by a lingering sense of order which —

VISTULA: I don't care at all —

SHARDLO: With the increasing intensity of the crisis will seem positively sentimental —

VISTULA: Chuck it in the moat for all I care —

SHARDLO: You must in this instance put aside the natural instincts of a servant and allow the choice to be dictated purely by your own convenience. Can you manage that? Which of the two is nearer, the well-shaft or the horse-pit? (*The* SERVANTS *mumble...*)
Which...?

SERVANTS: The well-shaft...?

SHARDLO: There you are, then... (*They go to march to the bed.* SHARDLO *intercepts them and draws them into her arms, entwining herself about them. Their discomfort grows as she crushes them in her embrace, and they form a strange, drifting, murmuring body until at last* SHARDLO *tears loose. She staggers, and stops...*)
The odour...! The odour of them...! (*They look over their shoulders at her...*)
Labour...!
Lassitude...! (*She smells her own flesh, her palms, her wrists...*)

Same smell... (*She laughs... the* SERVANTS, *in a methodical way, go to the bed and prepare to lift the body of the messenger. They do not complete the action however, but remain holding his limbs in a fixed position... their eyes meet the eyes of*

VISTULA. LINDSAY's *gaze, lifting from the photograph, meets* SHARDLO's... *pause... they are still...*)

       We are all —

       How extraordinary —

       And I have no particular affection for unanimity —

       Seized by a single thought... (*She bites her lip...*)

A thought which arrived without an invitation but which all the same, once recognized, seems to possess an irrefutable authority... (*Pause... their eyes shift, from one to another...*)

       How hard it is to speak... (*She sobs, laughs...*)

       You think —

       I think myself —

       I should be flung into the shaft. (*She smacks her hand to her mouth. In the ensuing silence she walks a few wild paces and stops... she repeats this, stops again...*)

       He knew...

       Oh, how he knew...

       The well could not be satisfied...

       Why else was it covered...? (*She is galvanized by her own logic...*)

The courier knew many things but all the time, for all that he exerted to the full his powers of logic and experience, he succeeded only in acquiring the barest understanding of this house and its inexorable character, how could he be expected to when even we — (*Pause...*)

The well is not Roman. If it had Roman elements that merely reflects the limitless capacity for deception employed by its architect. Nor was it designed for drinking — (*She looks to the* SERVANTS...)

       Carry him...!

       Carry him if you want to...!

I am destined to die in the well and so are you...

       That is its only function... (*The* SERVANTS, *in their anxiety, let fall the limbs of the dead courier. They are panicked by her verdict and back away from the bed...* SHARDLO *is overcome by pity for them...*)

       It can't be helped...!

       Come...!

       Come...! (*She opens her arms to them... they back away...* SHARDLO *drops her arms in irritation...*)

Oh, you are so silly...! To squeal...! To fret...! When it is so obvious the courier arrived only in order to reveal the well to us... (*She is radiant. VISTULA and LINDSAY spontaneously burst into tears...*)

Oh, but it is good to know...!

And knowing... to be resolute enough to —

LINDSAY: **I am not going in the well...!**

SHARDLO: (*Complacently*) That may be how it appears to you —

LINDSAY: **I refuse...!**

SHARDLO: Yes... and yet the man you love is about to do precisely that —

LINDSAY: **I'd rather leap off the tower...!**

SHARDLO: Well, you could always try, but — (*She stops... she closes her eyes in a spasm of pain... she extends her hand to LINDSAY... who hesitates... SHARDLO rocks on her toes...*)

The way we —

Always we —

Coerce —

And are coerced —

Violence —

Pity —

Laughter —

And the weak are the worst...! (*She looks clearly at LINDSAY...*)

Take my hand —

You must forgive me for being — in this instance — Wholly correct —

LINDSAY: It's not correct —

SHARDLO: You do not wish it to be correct, but notwithstanding your preference it remains —

LINDSAY: It is not correct it is your own —

SHARDLO: Yes —

LINDSAY: Your own —

Your very own —

SHARDLO: Yes —

LINDSAY: **Inspiration —**

SHARDLO: Quite —

LINDSAY: And I — (*SHARDLO pulls LINDSAY towards her and kisses her hand...*)

SHARDLO: Yes...! Yes...! That is what it is.! And you must go — (*She turns to VISTULA*)

The pair of you —
With hats and coats and little bags —

LINDSAY: Why —

SHARDLO: Through the rockets and the firestorms you must
leap onto the running boards of flaming trains —

LINDSAY: What —

SHARDLO: In no matter what direction because —

LINDSAY: Why —

SHARDLO: **I shall certainly destroy you**. (*She looks into*
LINDSAY ...)

Hurry... (*Pause* ...)

VISTULA: She says that because
Only because
She is certain we could only fail
That we would return with our coats dragging in the dust,
apologetic and ashamed... (SHARDLO *makes no reply* ...)
That is the extent of what appeared for one fleeting moment
to be —

SHARDLO: Yes —

VISTULA: Her generosity... (SHARDLO *lowers her head* ...
pause ...)

SHARDLO: Certainly... (*She shrugs, her hand lifts, falls* ...)
Certainly, that's — (*She shrugs again* ...)
The case... with me... (*She turns to leave the room. The*
SERVANTS, *galvanized by a mutual instinct, grab her clumsily.*
She is spun round, and falls among them. LINDSAY *and*
VISTULA *are shocked into paralysis for some seconds.*
VISTULA, *recovering first, barks orders to her* ...)

VISTULA: Coats...!
Hats...!
Bags...! (LINDSAY *is beyond hearing... staring at*
the spectacle of the knot of struggling figures ...)
Coats...!
Hats...!
Bags...! (*Still she is fixed to the spot* ...)
Bags...!

Bags...! (LINDSAY *obeys the last injunction. The two*
women tear from the room... meanwhile the struggle between
SHARDLO *and the* SERVANTS, *close, suffocating, and nearly*
soundless, continues like a subdued dance... after some seconds,
the sound of aircraft is heard in the distance. This time their
approach has no effect on the SERVANTS, *who are too*
engrossed in the attempt to stifle SHARDLO *to react. As the*

*planes pass low, their guns rattle. The grotesque dance is stopped
by this new and ominous sound, echoing through the courtyards.
The group is still. Hands fall to sides. Heads hang. The sound of
the planes recedes. At last SHARDLO emerges from the group,
her clothing torn, dishevelled... she rubs her neck, comforting the
bruising... she massages her wrists... slowly, contemplatively... she seems to speak, but her ordeal obstructs articula-
tion... she swallows... she opens her lips again...)*

> I'm not dead... *(Pause...)*
> I'm not dead... *(The* SERVANTS *burst into a flood
> of weeping, wailing, inconsolable...)*
> Shh...! *(They heave, shudder...)*
> **Listen, I'm not dead...**
> I
> I for whom
> Suicide was intended
> For whom
> Rage was designed
> Am
> Shh...!
> **Not dead and they** — *(The* SERVANTS *are hushed
> by her appearance... they watch her furtively as she
> frowns in her struggle to achieve lucidity...)*
> Climb the tower... all three of you... and look...
> *(Pause...)*
> In one of the thirteen courtyards you will see the
> bodies of your mistresses... *(Pause...)*
> Together...
> Or possibly, apart... *(Pause...)*

When you have ascertained this, return to me **with the precise
location etched upon your minds...** *(They nod and
leave... SHARDLO stares in the direction of their departure.
Her loosely hanging hand is taken by the courier, otherwise
unmoving on the bed... she is perfectly still... she is suspended
between disbelief and bathos...)*

> Oh... *(Pause...)*
> Oh... *(Pause...)*
> Oh... *(He sits upright, an abrupt movement...)*

Now, listen, I — *(He draws her with a powerful movement of
his arm backwards to the mattress, holding her so firmly that in
spite of her efforts she is fixed to the spot. She concedes to his
superior power, and ceases the attempt to regain her feet. A light,
frivolous laugh comes from her. Again her legs writhe as she tries*

to sit up, but the courier's hand remains around her neck. She stops. A pause. She laughs again, longer. His expression is unchanged... she is silent...)

GODANSK: As I lay on the bed I could not divest myself of the thought that the bed, whilst inanimate, had somehow proposed itself to me as the solution to the pain of my redundancy. So perfect was my stillness as I contemplated a life of horizontal inactivity you not unreasonably concluded I had expired... (*Pause...*)

I am however, certain that whilst the entire purpose of my coming was to expose the hitherto secret existence of the well, and subsequently to fling the poet down its shaft, all this occurred solely in order to make the bed available to you... (*Pause... SHARDLO suddenly kicks violently in an attempt to sit upright, but GODANSK's firm grasp leaves her helpless. She is still...*)

I would go so far as to say that the apparently arbitrary choice of a circus horse, and even the peculiar smile on the face of the official at the ministry, could be related to the dominant imperative of your occupancy of this —

SHARDLO: **It is you that keeps me on the bed** —

GODANSK: Obviously, it's me —

SHARDLO: Let me up...!

GODANSK: Everything is me —

SHARDLO: (*Writhing*) Let me —

GODANSK: The development of the crisis, possibly even the origins of the crisis, hard as it is to decipher at this stage, belong inexorably to me —

SHARDLO: (*Calling to the servants*) *get this man off...*!

GODANSK: They've gone —

SHARDLO: **Help me...!**

GODANSK: They are running pell-mell for the horizon —

SHARDLO: Oh...!

GODANSK: Shh...

SHARDLO: Oh... (*She sobs. Her struggles subside.... At last, GODANSK removes his oppressive hand... SHARDLO does not move. He stands... he moves away from the bed... he drifts out... for a long time she is still... so long that the sky darkens. With nightfall, the sound of distant gunfire, heavy, thudding... the light of gunflashes illuminates the bed...*)